HISTORICAL DICTIONARY

The historical dictionaries present essential information on a broad range of subjects, including American and world history, art, business, cities, countries, cultures, customs, film, global conflicts, international relations, literature, music, philosophy, religion, sports, and theater. Written by experts, all contain highly informative introductory essays of the topic and detailed chronologies that, in some cases, cover vast historical time periods but still manage to heavily feature more recent events.

Brief A–Z entries describe the main people, events, politics, social issues, institutions, and policies that make the topic unique, and entries are cross-referenced for ease of browsing. Extensive bibliographies are divided into several general subject areas, providing excellent access points for students, researchers, and anyone wanting to know more. Additionally, maps, photographs, and appendixes of supplemental information aid high school and college students doing term papers or introductory research projects. In short, the historical dictionaries are the perfect starting point for anyone looking to research in these fields.

HISTORICAL DICTIONARIES OF LITERATURE AND THE ARTS

Jon Woronoff, Series Editor

Hong Kong Cinema, by Lisa Odham Stokes, 2007.

American Radio Soap Operas, by Jim Cox, 2005.

Fantasy Literature, by Brian Stableford, 2005.

Australian and New Zealand Cinema, by Albert Moran and Errol Vieth, 2006.

Lesbian Literature, by Meredith Miller, 2006.

Scandinavian Literature and Theater, by Jan Sjåvik, 2006.

British Radio, by Seán Street, 2006.

German Theater, by William Grange, 2006.

Sacred Music, by Joseph P. Swain, 2006.

Russian Theater, by Laurence Senelick, 2007.

French Cinema, by Dayna Oscherwitz and MaryEllen Higgins, 2007.

Postmodernist Literature and Theater, by Fran Mason, 2007.

Irish Cinema, by Roderick Flynn and Pat Brereton, 2007.

Australian Radio and Television, by Albert Moran and Chris Keating, 2007.

Polish Cinema, by Marek Haltof, 2007.

Old Time Radio, by Robert C. Reinehr and Jon D. Swartz, 2008.

Renaissance Art, by Lilian H. Zirpolo, 2008.

Broadway Musical, by William A. Everett and Paul R. Laird, 2008.

American Theater: Modernism, by James Fisher and Felicia Hardison Londré, 2008.

German Cinema, by Robert C. Reimer and Carol J. Reimer, 2008.

Horror Cinema, by Peter Hutchings, 2008.

Westerns in Cinema, by Paul Varner, 2008.

Chinese Theater, by Tan Ye, 2008.

Italian Cinema, by Gino Moliterno, 2008.

Architecture, by Allison Lee Palmer, 2008.

Russian and Soviet Cinema, by Peter Rollberg, 2008.

African American Theater, by Anthony D. Hill, 2009.

Postwar German Literature, by William Grange, 2009.

Modern Japanese Literature and Theater, by J. Scott Miller, 2009.

Animation and Cartoons, by Nichola Dobson, 2009.

Modern Chinese Literature, by Li-hua Ying, 2010.

Middle Eastern Cinema, by Terri Ginsberg and Chris Lippard, 2010.

Spanish Cinema, by Alberto Mira, 2010.

Film Noir, by Andrew Spicer, 2010.

French Theater, by Edward Forman, 2010.

Choral Music, by Melvin P. Unger, 2010.

Westerns in Literature, by Paul Varner, 2010.

Baroque Art and Architecture, by Lilian H. Zirpolo, 2010.

Surrealism, by Keith Aspley, 2010.

Science Fiction Cinema, by M. Keith Booker, 2010.

Latin American Literature and Theater, by Richard A. Young and Odile Cisneros, 2011.

Children's Literature, by Emer O'Sullivan, 2010.

German Literature to 1945, by William Grange, 2011.

Neoclassical Art and Architecture, by Allison Lee Palmer, 2011.

American Cinema, by M. Keith Booker, 2011.

American Theater: Contemporary, by James Fisher, 2011.

English Music: ca. 1400–1958, by Charles Edward McGuire and Steven E. Plank, 2011.

Rococo Art, by Jennifer D. Milam, 2011.

Romantic Art and Architecture, by Allison Lee Palmer, 2011.

Japanese Cinema, by Jasper Sharp, 2011.

Modern and Contemporary Classical Music, by Nicole V. Gagné, 2012.

Russian Music, by Daniel Jaffé, 2012.

Music of the Classical Period, by Bertil van Boer, 2012.

Holocaust Cinema, by Robert C. Reimer and Carol J. Reimer, 2012.

Asian American Literature and Theater, by Wenjing Xu, 2012.

Beat Movement, by Paul Varner, 2012.

Jazz, by John S. Davis, 2012.

Crime Films, by Geoff Mayer, 2013.

Scandinavian Cinema, by John Sundholm, Isak Thorsen, Lars Gustaf Andersson, Olof Hedling, Gunnar Iversen, and Birgir Thor Møller, 2013.

Chinese Cinema, by Tan Ye and Yun Zhu, 2013.

Taiwan Cinema, by Daw-Ming Lee, 2013.

Russian Literature, by Jonathan Stone, 2013.

Gothic Literature, by William Hughes, 2013.

French Literature, by John Flower, 2013.

Baroque Music, by Joseph P. Swain, 2013.

Opera, by Scott L. Balthazar, 2013.

British Cinema, by Alan Burton and Steve Chibnall, 2013.

Romantic Music, by John Michael Cooper with Randy Kinnett, 2013.

British Theatre: Early Period, by Darryll Grantley, 2013.

South American Cinema, by Peter H. Rist, 2014.

African American Television, Second Edition, by Kathleen Fearn-Banks and Anne Burford-Johnson, 2014.

Japanese Traditional Theatre, Second Edition, by Samuel L. Leiter, 2014.

Science Fiction in Literature, by M. Keith Booker, 2015.

British Radio, Second Edition , by Seán Street, 2015.

Romanticism in Literature, by Paul Varner, 2015.

American Theater: Beginnings, by James Fisher, 2016.
African American Cinema, Second Edition, by S. Torriano Berry and Venise Berry, 2015.

Historical Dictionary of
British Radio

Second Edition

Seán Street

ROWMAN & LITTLEFIELD
Lanham • Boulder • New York • Toronto • Plymouth, UK

Published by Rowman & Littlefield
4501 Forbes Boulevard, Suite 200, Lanham, Maryland 20706
http://www.rowman.com

10 Thornbury Road, Plymouth PL6 7PP, United Kingdom

British Library Cataloguing in Publication Information Available

Library of Congress Cataloging-in-Publication Data

Street, Seán.
Historical dictionary of British radio / Seán Street. -- Second edition. pages cm. -- (Historical dictionaries of literature and the arts)
Includes bibliographical references.
ISBN 978-1-4422-4922-6 (hardcover : alk. paper) -- ISBN 978-1-4422-4923-3 (ebook) 1. Radio
broadcasting--Great Britain--History--Dictionaries. I. Title.
PN1991.3.G7S77 2015
384.540941--dc23
2014047311

Printed in the United States of America

Contents

Editor's Foreword

Among national radio stations, British radio has always enjoyed a unique position, probably because of the role of the British Broadcasting Corporation—best known as the BBC or "beeb." This is partly because of its continuing production of first-class programs of all sorts, whether news, music, drama, documentaries, or sports. Even more important, in times of crisis or when people abroad cannot trust their own national radio, they tune in to the BBC, which has always proven to be reliable and still transmits worldwide. But there is more to British radio than the BBC, because the United Kingdom also has a remarkable tradition of commercial radio and public radio, ranging from the early "pirate" stations to more specialized ones of today. That being said, British radio is not without its problems, nor is the BBC, but the industry is adapting to the new technologies, taking on and adjusting to having (if not actually defeating) new competitors, and coping with tighter budgets and falling advertising revenue. This is actually one of the toughest periods for British radio, and it will be interesting to see how it transitions.

This is now the second edition of *Historical Dictionary of British Radio*, and as previously noted, it comes at a good time, since the present situation is quite different even from a decade ago. This handy guide draws a broad picture in several ways. The chronology traces the long history of British radio, from the earliest technical breakthroughs, through the landmark broadcast of Nellie Melba in 1920, to the most recent developments. The introduction sums up its role, assessing the many achievements and challenges throughout time, with the BBC clearly in charge at first and then gradually sharing the field with countless other broadcasters, all of which face an uncertain future. The dictionary offers a wealth of details, with entries on the enabling legislation, the BBC and its many rivals, key administrative and creative individuals, the more memorable programs and figures who appeared in them, and much of the technical paraphernalia. The bibliography provides sources for further reading. Along with the updated chronology and bibliography, this new edition features dozens of additional entries.

This sort of book could only have been written by someone with a particularly broad view of British radio, someone who has approached it from different angles. Seán Street has worked as a radio practitioner since 1970, including, among other things, as a board member of two radio stations and producer of his own features on BBC Radio 3 and BBC Radio 4. On the creative side, he has written several plays that have been performed. More recently, he has served as an academic, as professor of radio at the Media

School at Bournemouth University and director of the Centre for Broadcasting History Research. Moreover, he has lectured and written extensively on the topic, including the books *A Concise History of British Radio*, *The Poetry of Radio*, *The Memory of Sound*, and *Crossing the Ether*. Street has also edited the anthology *Radio Waves: Poems Celebrating the Wireless*. This is a rather exceptional foundation for updating and expanding a much-appreciated reference work on British radio.

Jon Woronoff
Series Editor

Reader's Note

To facilitate the rapid and efficient location of information and make this book as useful a reference tool as possible, extensive cross-references have been provided in the dictionary section. Within individual entries, terms that have their own entries are in **boldface type** the first time they appear. Related terms that do not appear in the text are indicated in the *See also*. *See* refers to other entries that deal with this topic.

Preface

I am particularly pleased to be writing a second edition of this book at the present time; since the first edition was published in 2006, much has changed in British radio. The medium remains strong and, as always, perhaps more than any other, continues to show itself capable of adapting to new technologies, while retaining its unique ability to speak to the individual. We are at an intriguing place in the history of broadcasting; radio—and the BBC—are approaching their centennial, and commercial radio in the United Kingdom has passed its 40th anniversary. While it is true that the industry remains in a period of rapid and dramatic change, there is continuity; the past continues to speak to—and interrogate—the present in terms of core values and standards, and as we find new ways of communicating, the capacity for the medium to connect with the individual both as a primary and secondary source is as powerful as ever.

Writing this new edition has been an exciting and personally edifying experience, but one that I would not have been able to undertake without the help and support of a number of friends and colleagues within the U.K. radio industry and among those who study radio as an academic discipline. It is a pleasure to record my thanks, in particular to Ralph Barnard, Travis Baxter, Tim Blackmore, Trevor Dann, and Tony Stoller, as well as Helen Boaden, director of BBC Radio, and Gill Carter of BBC Radio 4. Others who have helped with information, advice, and contacts include the late Barbara Bray, James Cridland, Simon Elmes, John Myers, Piers Plowright, John Theocharis, John Tydeman, and John Whitney. Colleagues at Bournemouth University and Liverpool John Moores University have offered advice and encouragement, and I extend my thanks to Hugh Chignell, Ieuan Franklin, Colin Robinson, and Julia Taylor in their respective institutions. I am also grateful to my wife Jo for her support during the writing of this book, and to my editor at Rowman & Littlefield, Jon Woronoff.

Acronyms and Abbreviations

AEF	Allied Expeditionary Forces
AIRC	Association of Independent Radio Contractors
AM	amplitude modulation
BFBS	British Forces Broadcasting Service
BFN	British Forces Network
CBA	Commonwealth Broadcasting Association
CBE	Commander of the Most Excellent Order of the British Empire
CBS	Columbia Broadcasting System
CMA	Community Media Association
COFDM	coded orthogonal frequency division multiplex
CRA	Community Radio Association
CRCA	Commercial Radio Companies Association
DAB	Digital Audio Broadcasting
DCBE	Dame Commander of the British Empire
DG	director-general
DJ	disc jockey
DMB	digital multimedia broadcasting
DRM	digital rights management
DTI	Department of Trade and Industry
EBU	European Broadcasting Union
EKCO	brand name of EK Cole, receiver manufacturer
EMAP	East Midlands Associated Press
EMI	Electrical and Musical Industries
ENSA	Entertainments National Service Association
FM	frequency modulation
GCAP	group formed by the merger of GWR and Capital Radio
GCHQ	Government Communications Headquarters
GFP	General Forces Programme

GLR	Greater London Radio
GMG	Guardian Media Group
GMT	Greenwich Mean Time
GPO	General Post Office
GTS	Greenwich Time Signal
GWR	Great Western Radio
HBA	Hospital Broadcasting Association
IBA	Independent Broadcasting Authority
IBC	International Broadcasting Company
IBU	International Broadcasting Union
IEE	Institute of Electrical Engineers
IFC	International Features Conference
ILR	independent local radio
IPA	Institute of Practitioners in Advertising
IPS	inches per second
IRDP	Independent Radio Drama Productions
IRN	Independent Radio News
ITA	Independent Television Authority
ITC	Independent Television Commission
ITMA	*It's That Man Again*
ITN	Independent Television News
ITV	Independent Television
JICRIT	Joint Industry Radio IT Futures Group
JWT	J. Walter Thompson
KCMG	Knights Commander of the Order of St. Michael and St. George
kHz	kilohertz
kW	kilowatt
LBC	London Broadcasting Company
LPE	London Press Exchange
LW	longwave
MBE	Member of the Most Excellent Order of the British Empire

MC	master of ceremonies
MHz	megahertz
MPEG	Moving Picture Experts Group Layer 3
MW	medium wave
NDO	Northern Dance Orchestra
NPR	National Public Radio
NRC	National Radio Centre
NWO	Northern Wireless Orchestra
OB	outside broadcast
OBE	Most Excellent Order of the British Empire
OFCOM	Office of Communications
PHILIMIL	brand name of the Philips-Miller recording system
PMG	postmaster-general
PSB	Public Service Broadcasting
RA	Radio Authority
RAB	Radio Advertising Bureau
RACC	Radio Advertising Clearance Centre
RAF	Royal Air Force
RAJAR	Radio Joint Audience Research
RCA	Radio Corporation of America
RDS	Radio Data System
RIG	Radio Independents Group
RPAS	Radio Production Awards
RSGB	Radio Society of Great Britain
RSL	restricted service license
SABC	South African Broadcasting Corporation
SALLIE	small-scale alternative location independents
SRA	Student Radio Association
SRH	Scottish Radio Holdings
SW	shortwave
TLRC	The Local Radio Company
TRIC	Television and Radio Industries Club

UBC	Unique Broadcasting Company
U.K.	United Kingdom
UKRD	UK Radio Developments
UPC	Universal Programmes Company
URP	Universal Radio Publicity
VHF	very high frequency
VLV	Voice of the Listener and Viewer
VOA	Voice of America
WRN	World Radio Network
WS	World Service

Chronology

1864 December: James Clerk-Maxwell delivers his paper, *The Dynamic Theory of the Electromagnetic Field*, to the Royal Society.

1877 The first electromagnetic waves are transmitted without physical means of conduction. **2 April:** The first telephone conversation takes place.

1896 2 June: A wireless telegraphy patent is taken out by Guglielmo Marconi.

1901 11 December: The first transatlantic wireless signal is sent from Cornwall, England, to Newfoundland.

1906 The triode valve is developed, providing the ability to amplify electrical currents in wireless equipment. **24 December:** An early broadcast is made by Reginald Fessenden in the United States.

1920 15 June: Dame Nellie Melba broadcasts from the Marconi Company's Chelmsford works.

1922 14 February: The first broadcasts are made from 2MT, Writtle. **11 May:** The first transmission is made from 2LO. **18 October:** The form of the British Broadcasting Company is agreed to by the British Post Office and radio manufacturers. **14 November:** Daily broadcasting starts from London station 2LO of the British Broadcasting Company Ltd. **15 November:** Birmingham Station 5IT and Manchester Station 2ZY open. **23 December:** The first regular general news bulletin is sent from London. **24 December:** Newcastle-on-Tyne Station 5NO opens.

1923 8 January: The first outside broadcast (excerpts from *The Magic Flute* from Covent Garden) takes place. **15 February:** Cardiff Station 5WA opens. **6 March:** Glasgow Station 5SC opens. **19 March:** BBC London Station moves from Marconi's Magnet House to 2, Savoy Hill. **26 March:** The first broadcast of the weather forecast takes place. **1 May:** Savoy Hill Studios opens. **28 September:** *Radio Times* is first published. **1 October:** The "Report of the Sykes Committee on Broadcasting" is published. **10 October:** Aberdeen Station 2DB opens. **17 October:** Bournemouth Station 6BM opens.

1924 5 February: The Greenwich Time Signal is inaugurated. **17 February:** The Big Ben daily time signal is introduced. **4 April:** The first broadcast to schools takes place.

1925 March: A fashion talk in English is sponsored by Selfridges, organized by Captain Leonard Plugge, and broadcast from the Eiffel Tower in Paris. **3 April:** The BBC is represented at the first General Assembly of the International Broadcasting Union at Geneva. **27 July:** Station 5XX Daventry opens, providing the 2LO service on 1,562m longwave.

1926 5 March: The "Report of the Crawford Committee on Broadcasting" is published. **4 May:** The General Strike begins. **11 November:** The agreement between the postmaster general and the British Broadcasting Company Ltd. is published, providing for the transfer of the Broadcasting Service to the British Broadcasting Corporation on 1 January 1927. **14 November:** Under a plan drawn up by the International Broadcasting Union, the number of wavelengths available to the BBC is reduced, resulting in the development of regional, as opposed to local, broadcasting. **31 December:** The license of the British Broadcasting Company Ltd. expires.

1927 The first shortwave broadcasts to Europe from Chelmsford station 5SW take place. **1 January:** The British Broadcasting Corporation is constituted by Royal Charter for a term of 10 years. John Reith becomes director-general. **22 January:** The first Association Football commentary takes place during a matchup between Arsenal and Sheffield United from Highbury. **25 March:** The first racing commentary is given at the Grand National from Aintree. **2 April:** The first commentary is given on the Varsity Boat Race. **23 April:** The first broadcast from Wembley Stadium (F.A. Cup Final, Cardiff City versus Arsenal) takes place. **14 May:** The first Cricket commentary (Essex versus New Zealand at Leyton) is given. **13 August:** The first broadcast of a BBC Promenade Concert (from Queen's Hall, London) takes place. **21 August:** Daventry 5GB Experimental opens.

1928 12 May: The first broadcast of the BBC Dance Orchestra takes place.

1929 16 January: The first issue of the *Listener* is published.

1930 9 March: The Regional Programme begins. The Brookmans Park transmitter broadcasts alternative programs for London and the Home Counties. The National Programme replaces 2LO. At the same time, Daventry 5GB starts broadcasting Midland regional programs. **22 October:** The first broadcast of the BBC Symphony Orchestra, conducted by Adrian Boult, takes place.

1931 11 October: The first International Broadcasting Company (IBC) transmission from Radio Normandy (Radio Fécamp) takes place. **29 November:** French station Poste Parisien commences English-language commercial broadcasting under the auspices of the IBC, with a record program sponsored by HMV, introduced by Rex Palmer, a former BBC staff member.

1932 15 March: Broadcasting House becomes the official London headquarters of the BBC. **15 March:** The first broadcast from Broadcasting House, London (Henry Hall, replacing Jack Payne, and the BBC Dance Orchestra) takes place. **19 December:** Empire Service from Daventry is inaugurated.

1933 15 March: Radio Luxembourg begins test transmissions. **21 August:** BBC News is read by a woman for the first time (but is discontinued shortly thereafter). **29 October:** Luxembourg begins regular Sunday programs.

1934 15 January: The Lucerne Plan, drawn up by the European Broadcasting Convention, on wavelength distribution, is implemented. **19 January:** The first edition of *Radio Pictorial* is published as a general magazine about radio. **31 August:** *Radio Pictorial* gains wider appeal when it becomes the listings journal for such continental commercial stations as Radio Normandy, Radio Luxembourg, Radio Toulouse, and Radio Lyons.

1935 6 May: King George V's Silver Jubilee celebrations take place. **16 July:** The broadcast review of the Fleet from Spithead is given.

1936 20 January: King George V dies. **28 January:** The king's funeral is broadcast. **16 March:** The "Report of the Ullswater Committee on Broadcasting" is published. **1 October:** The Listener Research Unit is formed. **1 November:** Radio Lyons starts broadcasting, with staff announcer Tony Melrose. Programs are produced in London by Vox Productions. This is the last of the major continental stations to go on air broadcasting English-language commercial radio. **2 November:** The BBC Television Service is inaugurated. **10 December:** The Royal Charter for continuance of the BBC and license and agreement between the postmaster general and the BBC is published. The announcement of the abdication of King Edward VIII is broadcast. **11 December:** A broadcast from Windsor by King Edward VIII concerning his abdication of the monarchy takes place. **12 December:** A broadcast of the Proclamation of Accession of King George VI is carried out.

1937 1 January: The new Royal Charter and License go into effect for 10 years. **12 May:** The ceremony of the coronation of King George VI and Queen Elizabeth is broadcast. **20 May:** Thomas Woodruffe broadcasts from Coronation Review of the Fleet at Spithead. **31 August:** The Tommy Farr–Joe Louis World Heavyweight Championship fight is broadcast from Yankee Stadium in New York.

1938 15 March: BBC Portuguese Service and BBC Spanish Service for Latin America begins. **30 June:** Sir John Reith resigns as the first director-general of the BBC. **31 August:** Arabic Service, the first BBC broadcast in a foreign tongue, opens.

1938 27 September: A broadcast by British prime minister Neville Chamberlain upon his return from Munich is held. BBC German Service, BBC Italian Service, and BBC French Service begins. **1 October:** F. W. Ogilvie succeeds Sir John Reith as director-general of the BBC.

1939 1 August: The first English broadcast is given to Europe. **1 September:** The BBC Home Service commences broadcasting at 8:15 p.m., in place of the National and Regional programmes. At 9:26 p.m., a supplementary service in foreign languages, for listeners in Europe, begins. The BBC Television Service closes down. **3 September:** A broadcast is given by Neville Chamberlain on the outbreak of war. **5 September:** BBC Hungarian Service starts. **7 September:** BBC Polish Service starts. **8 September:** BBC Czech Service starts. **15 September:** BBC Rumanian Service and BBC Serbo-Croat Service to Yugoslavia start. **21 September:** Radio Luxembourg closes down. **30 September:** BBC Greek Service starts. **20 November:** BBC Turkish Service starts. **31 December:** BBC Slovak Service starts.

1940 3 January: Radio International closes down. **7 January:** The BBC Forces Programme, broadcast at 6:00 p.m. nightly, opens. **18 February:** The BBC Forces Programme is extended, now broadcasting from 11:00 a.m. to 11:00 p.m. **13 October:** Princess Elizabeth and Princess Margaret broadcast from Buckingham Palace to the children of the British Empire. **15 October:** A bomb explodes at Broadcasting House in London, killing seven people. **8 December:** A landmine causes further severe damage to the Broadcasting House.

1941 17 March: BBC European Service moves to Bush House.

1942 26 January: F. W. Ogilvie resigns as BBC director-general. Sir Cecil Graves and R. W. Foot are appointed as joint directors-general. **26 July:** The first broadcast of the *Britain to America* series in the BBC North American Service, rebroadcast by NBC in the United States, takes place.

1943 13 June: The BBC Forces Programme becomes the General Overseas Service. **24 June:** Sir Cecil Graves resigns as BBC joint director-general. **1 September:** R. W. Foot is appointed sole director-general. William Haley is appointed editor in chief.

1944 31 March: R. W. Foot resigns as director-general of the BBC. William Haley is appointed director-general. **6 June:** D-Day. The Allies invade Europe. The BBC makes the first announcement at 9:32 a.m. **7 June:** The Allied Expeditionary Forces Programme commences. **23 September:** The 12th U.S. Army Group commences German-language programming aimed at retreating enemy troops as Radio 1212 from Radio Luxembourg.

1945 1 March: Adrian Boult conducts the Orchestre Nationale in the first concert to be broadcast from Paris since the liberation. **8 May:** V-E Day. Broadcasts are given by King George VI and Winston Churchill. **28 July:** The Allied Expeditionary Forces Programme is discontinued. **29 July:** The Light Programme commences. Regional broadcasting resumes. **15 August:** V-J Day. Broadcasts are given by King George VI and Clement Attlee.

1946 1 January: William Haley is knighted in the New Year Honors List. **1 July:** Radio Luxembourg resumes commercial English-language transmissions, led by Stephen Williams, who would be succeeded by Geoffrey Everitt, his assistant, with Teddy Johnson, an early postwar announcer on the station. **7 June:** The BBC Television Service resumes. **19 September:** The Third Programme starts.

1947 1 January: The third Royal Charter and License (for five years) go into effect.

1949 25 September: The Italia Prize is inaugurated.

1950 12 February: The European Broadcasting Union is formed. **15 March:** BBC radio frequencies are reorganized.

1952 6 February: The death of King George VI is broadcast. **1 July:** The Fourth Royal Charter and License (for 10 years) goes into effect. **30 September:** Sir William Haley resigns as director-general of the BBC. **1 December:** Sir Ian Jacob becomes director-general.

1953 2 June: The coronation of Queen Elizabeth II is broadcast.

1954 1 June: The cost of the combined television and radio license increases to £3.00. The radio-only license costs £1.00.

1955 2 May: The first VHF transmitter opens at Wrotham, supplying BBC radio services to London and the Southeast.

1956 3 November: Suez Crisis. Prime Minister Anthony Eden broadcasts to home and overseas audiences.

1957 1 August: The cost of the combined television and radio license increases to £4.00. The cost of the radio-only license remains at £1.00. **30 September:** Network Three starts on the Third Programme frequency, providing educational programs during the afternoon and early evening.

1958 14 April: The Radiophonic Workshop starts.

1960 1 January: Hugh Carleton-Greene becomes director-general of the BBC. **31 December:** BBC VHF transmissions cover 97 percent of the population.

1962 1 July: The fourth Royal Charter extends to July 1964. **28 August:** The BBC commences experimental stereo radio transmissions.

1964 1 January: Hugh Carleton-Greene is knighted. **28 March:** Radio Caroline commences broadcasting. **30 August:** Network Three is renamed the Third Network. The Music Programme is introduced on the Third Network's frequencies on Sunday, Sports Service on Saturday, and Study Session on the weekdays (6:30–7:30 p.m.). The Third Programme continues in the evenings.

1965 1 May: The General Overseas Service is renamed the BBC World Service. **1 August:** The cost of the combined television and Radio license increases to £5.00. The cost of the radio-only license increases to £1.5.

1967 14 August: The Marine Broadcasting (Offences) Act becomes law. All offshore "pirate" radio stations, except Radio Caroline, cease transmission. **30 September:** BBC Radio 1 opens. The other networks are renamed BBC Radio 2, BBC Radio 3, and BBC Radio 4. **8 November:** The Local Radio experiment begins with the opening of BBC Radio Leicester.

1969 10 July: *Broadcasting in the Seventies* is published.

1970 4 April: The BBC generic radio pattern is more fully developed. **19 June:** The Conservative Party wins the general election.

1971 1 February: The radio-only license is abolished. **16 June:** Lord Reith dies. **10 November:** BBC Pebble Mill, Birmingham, opens.

1972 12 July: The Sound Broadcasting Act goes into effect.

1973 12 July: The Independent Broadcasting Authority is founded. **8 October:** The first independent local radio (ILR) station, the London Broadcasting Company, begins broadcasting. **16 October:** The second ILR station, Capital Radio, begins broadcasting.

1974 28 February: The Labour Party wins the general election, halts independent local radio development, and awards more local licenses to BBC stations. **10 April:** The government announces the creation of a committee to examine the future of broadcasting (Annan).

1978 13 November: BBC Radio Wales is launched. **23 November:** The major BBC national radio frequency changes. BBC Radio Scotland commences broadcasting.

1979 27 January: Radio 2 commences 24-hour broadcasting. **4 May:** The Conservative Party wins the general elections and commits to expanding commercial radio.

1982 4 December: BBC Radio 1 and BBC Radio 2 separate in terms of content for the first time.

1988 County Sound, Guildford, becomes the first commercial station to permanently "split" frequencies (i.e., to broadcast different services on AM and FM).

1990 January: BBC Digital Audio Broadcasting runs trials from Crystal Palace. **27 August:** BBC Radio 5 begins, as the first new U.K. national radio station since 1967. BBC Radio 2 starts broadcasting on FM only, the first network to do so. **1 November:** The Broadcasting Act is published.

1991 1 January: The Radio Authority is established. (The Shadow Radio Authority was formed in 1990.) **1 May:** BBC Radio 1 commences permanent 24-hour-a-day broadcasting.

1992 RAJAR, the Radio Joint Audience Research organization, administered jointly by the BBC and commercial radio, is launched, providing industry-approved listening figures for subscribing U.K. radio services. **21 January:** BBC Radio Berkshire is launched, completing the planned BBC Local Radio network. **28 February:** BBC Radio 3 ceases AM transmission. **7 September:** Classic FM commences broadcasting on an eight-year license, the first national commercial radio station in Britain. **30 December:** Radio Luxembourg closes down.

1993 30 April: Virgin 1215 (subsequently Virgin Radio) is launched. **25 October:** Radio 1 relaunches with a new schedule.

1994 28 March: BBC Radio 5 Live launches as a replacement for the original BBC Radio 5. **1 July:** BBC Radio 1 ceases AM transmissions.

1995 14 February: Talk Radio UK (subsequently talkSPORT) begins broadcasting. **27 September:** The BBC begins the world's first Digital Audio Broadcasting transmissions from five transmitters throughout the London area.

1996 24 July: The Broadcasting Act sets out plans for the development of Digital Audio Broadcasting, including radio.

1997 The Radio Authority launches SALLIES, small-scale local licenses for smaller communities.

1998 March: The Radio Authority advertises the first national digital commercial multiplex license. **June:** Applications close for national digital commercial licenses after only one application, by Digital One. **Autumn:** Digital One is awarded the national digital license. **1 October:** Digital satellite service launches in the United Kingdom.

1999 15 November: The Digital One multiplex commences broadcasting the United Kingdom's first commercial Digital Audio Broadcasting radio service with a multiplex containing five stations: Classic FM, Virgin Radio, Talk Radio, Planet Rock, and Core. More follow in 2000.

2000 Spring: The Communications White Paper on the future of broadcasting and telecommunications is published.

2001 The Radio Authority sets up the Access Radio pilot project.

2002 2 February: BBC Radio 5 Live Sports Extra, the BBC's first digital radio-only service, is launched. **11 March:** BBC digital station 6 Music is launched at 7:00 a.m., with Phill Jupitus as the first on-air presenter. It becomes widely billed as the "first new BBC music station for 32 years." **7 May:** The government announces plans for radical changes in media and telecommunications regulation and ownership. **16 August:** 1Xtra, BBC radio's digital black music station, is launched. **15 December:** BBC7, BBC digital speech service focusing on archive comedy and drama, is launched.

2003 Renovation of Broadcasting House in London commences. Professor Anthony Everitt publishes *New Voices*, an evaluation of Radio Authority Access Radio pilot project. **July:** The Communications Bill receives royal assent. **December:** The Office of Communications takes over from the Radio Authority as general communications regulator. The Communications Act goes into effect.

2004 January: The Hutton Report, investigating the death of weapons expert Dr. David Kelly and the BBC's conduct regarding the matter, is published and leads to high-level resignations within the corporation, including the chairman, Gavyn Davies, and the director-general, Greg Dyke. **31 December:** The BBC's Pebble Mill studios close.

2005 March: The first Community Radio License is awarded to Forest of Dean Radio. **May:** Great Western Radio and Capital Radio merge to form GCap Media.

2006 Following the decision by the BBC to move a significant number of jobs to Manchester, Salford Quays is selected as the site of what will become MediaCityUK. The RadioCentre is founded after the merger of the Radio Advertising Bureau and the Commercial Radio Companies Association. **November:** BBC chairman Michael Grade resigns to join Independent Television.

2007 Global Radio is founded. **December:** BBC iPlayer goes live.

2008 October: Lesley Douglas resigns from her post as controller of BBC Radio 2 and BBC Radio 6 Music following the Russell Brand/Jonathan Ross controversy.

2009 January: Bob Shennan is appointed as controller of BBC Radio 2 and BBC Radio 6 Music.

2010 September: Mark Damazer steps down as controller of BBC Radio 4 and is succeeded by Gwyneth Williams.

2011 July: Andy Parfitt steps down as controller of BBC Radio 1. He is succeeded by Ben Cooper. **September–October:** BBC Radio 5 Live moves from London to MediaCityUK.

2012 February: John Myers publishes his review of BBC Local Radio. **12 July:** The BBC World Service relocates to Broadcasting House after 70 years at Bush House. **17 September:** George Entwistle is appointed director-general of the BBC. **October:** A television documentary examines claims of sexual abuse by radio and television presenter Jimmy Savile, leading to a substantial and rapidly growing body of witness statements and sexual abuse claims, including accusations against public bodies, among them the BBC. **10 November:** George Entwistle resigns as director-general after 54 days, following two scandals relating to reporting on the television program *Newsnight*. **14 November:** 90th anniversary of the founding of the BBC. **22 November:** Tony Hall is appointed director-general of the BBC but does not assume his post until April 2013. Tim Davie serves as the interim director-general.

2013 Sony withdraws its sponsorship of the Radio Academy Awards after 30 years. **31 March:** BBC Television Centre closes, with services moving to the newly refurbished Broadcasting House in London. **2 April:** Tony Hall becomes the 16th director-general of the BBC. **7 June:** Her Majesty Queen Elizabeth II officially opens the refurbished Broadcasting House in London. **August:** The BBC releases the *CBeebies Playtime* app for smartphones and other devices. **October:** 40th anniversary of the establishment of independent local radio. The first station of the London Broadcasting Company opens.

2014 March: Bob Shennan is appointed to the new post of director of music, tasked with the coordination of music output throughout the BBC. **April:** Dame Patricia Hodgson is appointed chairman of the Office of Communications for a three-year period. Chris Patten resigns as chair of the BBC Trust for matters of health. **August:** Rona Fairhead is appointed chair of the BBC Trust.

Introduction

The story of British radio begins long before the birth of the British Broadcasting Company (BBC) in 1922. This book tells this story through its component parts—the makers, programs, and policies that shaped the development of a system of broadcasting initially grounded in a public service ethic and subsequently struggling toward an, at times, uneasy balance of public and commercial radio.

The BBC's role in this story is, of course, considerable and unique, although seldom at any time in its history has the organization been without problems and tensions. The early pioneers, under John Reith, were young men born in Victorian Britain, and their values were instilled in the nature of broadcasting as a sacred cause, a view that created tensions as the medium became established and public needs and expectations changed. Britain, unlike many other countries in the world, did not see the arrival of legal, land-based commercial radio until late in its broadcasting history; indeed, commercial television, beginning in 1955, predated radio supported by advertising by almost 20 years. That said, as early as the 1930s, the BBC monopoly was challenged by commercial broadcasters transmitting from Europe. Indeed, much of the evolution of British radio has come about through external pressures and conflicts between public service and independent broadcasters. This is a major theme of this volume, as is the gradual relaxing of regulation, even if, for some, this process has not happened swiftly or comprehensively enough.

Since the 1930s, Britain's global radio reputation has been one of great respect and trust, not least because of the work of the BBC World Service, and this book acknowledges this important aspect of broadcasting in a number of ways, in the chronology and within the main body of the dictionary itself; however, perhaps the major theme to emerge from the book is British radio's seemingly endless capacity to survive and thrive on change. It was once predicted that television would bring about the death of the medium, but radio in the United Kingdom has adapted to new audiences and technologies, including the Internet and the downloading of programs. There seems little doubt that it will continue to evolve; the one constant is change, and within the first decades of the 21st century, U.K. radio is facing new challenges and possibilities in the continuation of that evolution. Its capacity to reinvent itself will ensure its continuing survival as a vital and exciting medium.

1

FOUNDATIONS

Radio in the United Kingdom has, from its beginnings, experienced a tension between its role as a medium of information and a purveyor of popular entertainment, two poles that have frequently manifested themselves in the roles of public service broadcasters and commercial operators. This dichotomy was initially linked to the first uses of radio as a means of utilitarian one-to-one messaging and the nature of the signals transmitted through wireless *telegraphy* rather than *telephony*, sending messages in the form of "electrical impulses and signals," as Marconi's famous first patent of 2 June 1896 had read. The modification of those impulses, the electromagnetic waves that carried the sounds and codes, came about in 1902, at the hand of Danish scientist Valdemar Poulsen. The first transmission of the human voice—effectively the first radio program—occurred four years later, the responsibility of Reginald Fessenden in the United States. It was an event made possible by the invention in 1904 of the thermionic valve, carried out by John Ambrose Fleming of University College in London.

Nonetheless, it would be some time before the technology would move into the realms of an entertainment medium. A generation of "wireless amateurs" fell upon the concept of sending and receiving signals prior to World War I, when amateur experiments were banned on both sides of the Atlantic. The war itself—the first in which wireless played a part—helped to further develop transmission equipment, and between 1914–1918, the realization came about that the medium had a more universal application than utility. In the United States, former Marconi company employee David Sarnoff, founder of the Radio Corporation of America (RCA), conceived the idea of a "Radio Music Box" in 1916, and two years later, Marconi's head of publicity, Arthur Burrows, wrote an article that was published in the *Yearbook of Wireless Telegraphy and Telephony* in which he predicts the radio as a medium for entertainment and news—as well as advertising.

The Marconi Company had established itself in the Essex town of Chelmsford in 1903, with a research station conducting transmission tests, and in 1912, it had created the world's first purpose-built factory for wireless communications equipment there. After the war, attention was directed to the future development of radio, and in December 1919, an experimental 6-kilowatt telephony transmitter was installed at the works, intended for testing reception of speech signals over long distances. Much of the future application of radio in the United Kingdom was determined by the nature of the content emanating from the Marconi station at its new station, MZX; the engineers in charge, W. T. Ditcham and H. J. Round, might have been expected to conduct their rigorous testing through formal scientific parameters and techniques. Instead, they chose to explore the medium's possibilities through the playing of records, linked with speech. Thus, the first-ever broadcast in Britain, in the modern sense, given on 15 January 1920, set the style of much that was to follow.

Gradually increasing the power of the transmissions, Ditcham and Round created a "schedule" of two 30-minute programs per day throughout January, February, and March 1920, with content that was not only exciting in the concept of the new, but pleasing and entertaining to listen to. It was as though they instinctively understood one of the precepts that was to inform all electronic media to come: The first miracle of technology is that it exists at all. Soon, however, it is its role as a platform for content that is interrogated, and it must satisfy this criterion to prove its continuing relevance. In this case, the fact that listeners identified with the content of the broadcasts and understood how it could enhance their day-to-day lives went a long way toward establishing radio's relevance and technical possibilities.

The transmissions were received over thousands of miles, and in June 1920, perceiving the immense publicity value of the interest in the experiments, Lord Northcliffe, proprietor of the *Daily Mail* newspaper, sponsored a recital of "live" music by famous Australian singer Dame Nellie Melba. Broadcasting from the Marconi Chelmsford works on 15 June, Melba delivered a 30-minute program of songs that was heard in Madrid, The Hague, Paris, Sweden, Norway, and Berlin. The event caused a sensation, and the next day the *Daily Mail* carried the story in triumphant terms: "Art and science joined hands, and the world listening in must have counted every minute of it precious."

On 30 July, the station repeated the idea, with Danish singer Lauritz Melchior broadcasting a recital of songs principally aimed at the Scandinavian audience—perhaps the first "targeted" transmission in history. Public interest was extraordinary, and it seemed as though the new medium was about to burgeon. In fact, by demonstrating that wireless/radio had a dual application, the early pioneers had created a tension that would cause a hesitation in its development.

The almost accidental utilization of radio as an entertainment medium and the enthusiastic public response to the application took both industry and regulatory authorities by surprise. There was concern that the transmissions from MZX would interfere with utility services, in particular wireless communications between aircraft and ground controls. Thus, in November 1920, the postmaster-general, the Right Honorable Albert Illingsworth, banned future Chelmsford broadcasts in an address to the House of Commons, and for a time the use of the medium was returned to message-sending for official purposes only.

But there was a growing groundswell of opinion in the form of wireless amateurs who united into large societies throughout the United Kingdom for the cause of radio listening. The British Post Office suggested the compromise of a telegraphy station, but the tide had turned in favor of telephony—a medium that could offer speech and music rather than signals and electrical impulses. In March 1921, 63 wireless societies held a conference with the goal of putting pressure on the government to provide a service supplying content of interest to members. The result was a petition at year's end, to which a new postmaster-general, the Right Honorable F. G. Kellaway, responded with an agreement that a service of speech and music should be provided by the Marconi Company once a week. A new station, with the call sign 2MT, was established in a former army hut in the village of Writtle, two miles from Chelmsford, manned by a team of nine, led by Marconi's captain, Peter Eckersley.

Building on Ditcham and Round's earlier experiments, there was an eccentrically entertaining quality to the 2MT broadcasts, which were transmitted on Tuesday evenings at 7:30 p.m. from 14 February 1922 to 17 January 1923. The content was a mixture of technical information and live and recorded music, banter and doggerel poetry delivered mostly by Eckersley himself. The lighthearted nature of the broadcasts offended some, who felt this new, sacred—almost mystical—medium should not be taken lightly, but most listeners enjoyed the informality of Eckersley's presentation, in which he scorned pomposity and instead employed an endearing casualness of style: "Well, I think we're about ready to begin now, and the first thing I've got to introduce is a record entitled. . . . Why are records always entitled, why can't they just be called something?—So here it is, a record entitled."

Soon after Writtle began broadcasting, the Post Office issued a second license to the Marconi Company, enabling it to introduce another station, which was established at the company's London premises, Marconi House on the Strand. The call sign of this second station was 2LO, and its first transmission was on 11 May 1922, under the direction of Arthur Burrows. Broadcasts from 2LO were initially on a twice weekly basis—Tuesday and Thursday evenings—with half-hour programs; however, they had a formality not present on the Writtle broadcasts; Burrows and Eckersley were two different personalities, and Burrows's view of the importance of radio stamped itself on the 2LO output, which was more sober and restrained than that of its Chelmsford counterpart. This duality was to prove a metaphor for some of the tensions and debates yet to be encountered, themes that were to characterize and polarize views as to the purpose and nature of radio in the United Kingdom, encapsulated in public service versus commercial broadcasting conflicts during the 1930s and beyond.

At the same time that these experiments were taking place in the United Kingdom, developments were quickly progressing toward scheduled radio services in the United States. In November 1920, Pittsburgh station KDKA, owned by the Westinghouse Corporation, captured public attention by broadcasting election returns in the race for the U.S. presidency between Warren

G. Harding and James M. Cox. The potential for the new medium was immediately clear; within two years, 219 stations were broadcasting, and in August 1922, the first radio advertisement was broadcast, opening a further floodgate of opportunistic entrepreneurship. Chaos threatened as the medium's growth threatened to spiral out of control, and Herbert Hoover, secretary of commerce, was quickly forced to introduce the regulation of radio.

In the United Kingdom, the government was considering its options. It was one thing for radio to proliferate in a country the size of the United States; for a similar expansion to occur on an island the size of Britain was a prospect not to be countenanced, and so, as in 1920, control was deemed necessary. In April 1922, the postmaster-general again addressed the British House of Commons with a statement that was to inform thinking in Britain relating to broadcasting for almost 40 years:

> It would be impossible to have a large number of firms broadcasting. It would result only in a sort of chaos, only in a much more aggravated form than that which arises in the United States, and which has compelled the United States, or the Department over which Mr. Hoover presides, and which is responsible for broadcasting, to do what we are now doing at the beginning, that is, to lay down very drastic regulations indeed for the control of wireless broadcasting.

COMPANY AND CORPORATION

The dilemma for the British government was based on the narrow path between allowing an unacceptable and inappropriate proliferation of radio companies on one hand and the establishment of a monopoly growing out of the Marconi Company's early lead in terms of broadcasting experimentation. A number of other companies, including Metropolitan-Vickers and Western Electric, were already, in 1922, working to establish broadcasting based in Manchester and Birmingham, respectively. Moreover, pressure was mounting on the Post Office from receiver manufacturers, who were naturally anxious that there should be a content provider to establish and develop consumer demand for the purchase of sets.

From the start, the postmaster-general sought legislation to ensure that Britain be served by a system that would be "for the benefit of the general public but not for the benefit of individuals." The solution was to license a number of regional stations run by "bona fide manufacturers of wireless apparatus" under the strict control of the Post Office itself, with only Post Office–approved sets made by the operating companies being offered for sale. In addition, the services were to be funded by a listener license fee, levied on all those capable of receiving the new service. Meetings between interested parties were held at the Institute of Electrical Engineers on the Thames Embankment in London in May 1922, and at the second of these, a name was agreed upon for the unified service provided by the various stations. This was to be the "British Broadcasting Company Ltd.," which was accordingly established with £100,000 capital in cumulative ordinary shares. Hence, British broadcasting was established through a hybrid of government control and commercialism. The studios of 2LO in Marconi House in London, were transferred to the ownership of the new company, and BBC transmissions began on a regularly scheduled daily basis on 14 November 1922. This was followed by the opening of regional stations in Birmingham, Manchester, the next day, and subsequently Newcastle, Cardiff, Glasgow, Aberdeen, and Bournemouth throughout the next 11 months, providing local programming with network potential.

Lord Gainford, a former postmaster-general, was the first chairman of the company, and the first general manager, appointed after interview, was John Reith, a 33-year-old Scot who assumed his post on 14 December 1922, becoming managing director on 14 November 1923.

From the heady days of experiment and pioneering followed a necessary period of consolidation and rationalization. Issues relating to the manufacture of sets, linked to the issuing of licenses for listeners, caused tension between the Post Office and the BBC. Licenses were only issued to those purchasing receivers carrying a BBC/PMG stamp—sets manufactured by one of the BBC constituent companies. There were, however, numerous wireless amateurs who constructed their own sets and therefore fell outside this ruling. Furthermore, the growth in interest in the new medium had resulted in a mass application for licenses, which the Post Office had considerable difficulty handling, leading to a backlog in licenses issued and a further increase in potential listeners constructing their own sets rather than waiting to purchase a licensed receiver.

The first attempt at the formalization of broadcasting in Britain came with the establishment of the Sykes Committee of 1923, which addressed the matter of licensing and began the move away from the BBC's dependence on commercial revenue gained from receiver sales. This was achieved by increasing the proportion of the license fee payable to the BBC from 50 percent to 75 percent and establishing one form of license, providing the legal right to listen to BBC programs whether the receiver was manufactured by a BBC company or another manufacturer. At the same time, the BBC's own license to broadcast was extended until 1926. In May 1923, the new company moved into its own premises, a wing of a building on the Thames Embankment owned by the Institute of Electrical Engineers; the grounds were accessed by an entrance at 2 Savoy Hill, a narrow, unprepossessing street flanking London's famous Savoy Hotel. Within a few short months, a catalog of "firsts" was achieved, including the first outside broadcast, the first play written for radio (*Danger*) by Richard Hughes, and the first broadcast symphony concert. At the same time, work was continuing throughout Britain to technically enhance the BBC's transmitter power through a series of relay stations, improving coverage nationwide.

The BBC's aim was high-minded: to inform, educate, and entertain. It fostered children's programs and encouraged listeners to savor its serendipitous approach to output with varied content that surprised the ear. At the same time, there was conflict between the new medium and established institutions; newspaper proprietors feared a loss of sales, and agreements were reached limiting the amount of news to be broadcast, stipulating that it should not be transmitted before the evening, ensuring a continuing public need for newspapers. Theater owners and impresarios also distrusted broadcasting, fearing a loss of audiences, while vaudeville entertainers disliked the sterile silence of the studio and the terrifying capacity of radio to consume material; an act that had once employed touring entertainers for years on the stage was now being disseminated to a nation in an instant.

The development of radio in the United Kingdom should be seen within the context of the growth of broadcasting within Europe; by 1925, approximately 40 services were operating on the continent, and listeners were exploring these stations with pioneering zeal. International wavelength regulation became an issue and was addressed by the formation of the International Broadcasting Union. That same year, an experiment in sponsored radio was attempted in the form of a 15-minute fashion talk supported financially by Selfridges store on London's Oxford Street. The broadcast, produced by Leonard Plugge, was transmitted from the Eiffel Tower in Paris, and although it had little impact, it was a forerunner of a commercial radio explosion that would have a considerable effect on U.K. broadcasting through the 1930s.

The 1925 Crawford Committee, which was established to explore the future of broadcasting in Britain, came to the conclusion that commercial radio, run by a series of independent companies, was not going to be the way forward in the United Kingdom and that the task should be entrusted to a single authority without ties to industry and run by "persons of judgment and independence, free from commitments." A key to defining this new organization was that the service should be "conducted by a public corporation acting as a trustee for the national interest." In July 1926, the committee's recommendations were accepted, and the British Parliament agreed that on 31 December of that year, the BBC's responsibilities should be handed to a new authority, with its power derived from a Royal Charter, reviewable and renewable on a regular basis. Thus was born the British Broadcasting Corporation.

Even before this new incarnation came to pass, the BBC was experiencing crisis and expansion in equal measure. The General Strike of 1926 brought the company into conflict with members of the public and government; the BBC was, on one hand, accused of progovernment activity, while, on the other, criticized for not handing its microphones over for government-only use. Meanwhile, John Reith and his chief engineer, Peter Eckersley, were developing new transmitters, affording the possibility of a unified national service supplemented by regional alternatives.

When the company became a corporation on 1 January 1927, the number of license holders in the United Kingdom numbered 2,178,259. With its new status, there were those who questioned the BBC's monopoly. This was exacerbated by the perception that the corporation held a paternalistic attitude toward its listeners; the first *BBC Handbook*, published in 1928, states that the BBC's working rule was to "give the public something slightly better than it now thinks it likes." A crucial factor in early BBC policy making was the strict religious upbringing of Reith, who by now had been appointed director-general of the corporation. Reith firmly believed in Lord's Day observance and insisted that Sunday programs should not demonstrate levity or what he perceived as frivolity. Indeed, at one point, BBC stations closed down for one hour at the traditional time for church services to ensure that there would be no distraction from the business of worship. This policy provided such continental-based commercial operators as Leonard Plugge with a golden opportunity to subvert the BBC's monopoly; Plugge, learning from his experiences with the 1925 Selfridges broadcast, established a business partnership with the owner of the Normandy station, Radio Fecamp. Buying airtime from the station, he then resold it to British advertisers, broadcasting a series of sponsored record programs under the title "Radio Normandy," specifically targeting the weak BBC Sunday, with its audience starved of popular entertainment.

Radio Normandy went on air in October 1931, and other entrepreneurs followed Plugge's lead, including the U.S. agency of J. Walter Thompson. In 1933, Radio Luxembourg began transmissions from a giant transmitter on the Junglinster Plateau above the city of Luxembourg. Audiences flocked to the populist output of a growing number of stations, many "sub-let," like Radio Normandy by Leonard Plugge, who formed a quickly growing organization called the International Broadcasting Company. The problem for the BBC was made more serious by the growth of relay exchanges under the collective name Rediffusion, a concept that involved sending wireless signals through telephone cables. Thousands of people—particularly in areas with poor reception—took out subscriptions to these services, which offered good reception of the two BBC services—National and Regional—plus one other. This inevitably meant that one of the commercial stations was included, thus exposing the BBC to direct competition. Ensconced in its gleaming, new art deco building, Broadcasting House, located on London's Regent Street beginning in May 1932, the BBC stood accused by many of being out of touch with the mood of the time and the needs of its listeners, particularly those of the British working class.

In 1936, with the renewal of the BBC's charter less than a year away, a committee of enquiry into the future of broadcasting chaired by Lord Ullswater examined the development of television; it also explored the issue of commercial competition, which by this time was reaching its prewar height. The Ullswater Report stated that "foreign commercial broadcasting should be discouraged by every available means," but in spite of this and the strenuous efforts of both the BBC and the Post Office, the continental stations enjoyed their most profitable years between 1936–1939. It was partly due to this pressure—and partly due to internal opinion—that the BBC somewhat grudgingly created an audience research department under J. R. Silvey; prior to this, the paternalistic attitude within the BBC had been that any form of measurement of listening figures was considered irrelevant and a distraction from the task of its somewhat prescriptive view of public service broadcasting.

The late 1930s were turbulent times for the BBC; John Reith resigned in June 1938, under government pressure, and World War II began a little more than a year later. Many felt that the onset of international conflict saved the BBC from itself. The continental competition was removed at a stroke, while the nature of the events that would take place during the following six years would underline the importance of the BBC as a public service broadcaster, enhancing its reputation immeasurably both within Britain and internationally.

WAR

The expansion of programs and reorganizing of facilities and resources within the BBC brought about by the war changed British broadcasting forever. International services were developed and the domestic networks restructured, creating a Forces Service and a Home Service. In terms of actual content, a raft of programs specifically aimed at maintaining morale was developed, including *It's That Man Again (ITMA)*, *Garrison Theatre*, *Music While You Work*, and *Workers' Playtime*. As the war progressed and the role of war correspondents became more defined, portable recording technologies were developed, and on-the-spot journalistic reporting became an accepted part of broadcast news for the first time in broadcasting history. BBC monitoring services were complemented by the BBC's own foreign-language transmissions, sometimes involving the development of new techniques. The

BBC German Service utilized short-sentence constructions to subvert Nazi jamming to considerable effect, and the value of the French-language service after the fall of France proved to be immeasurable, enabling expatriates to speak to their homeland through the important program *Les Français Parlent aux Français*. By late 1943, in addition to its English-language international service, BBC programs were being transmitted in 45 languages.

In the spring of 1944, William Haley became director-general of the BBC, and from that time onward, the construction of a postwar BBC became a priority. A new generation was now running the corporation, and there was a determination to learn from the mistakes of the past. The audiences who had been attracted by commercial radio in the 1930s had been further charmed by the influx of American and Canadian broadcasters, with their relaxed, colloquial style sharply contrasting with the traditional formality of prewar BBC presentation. Haley's vision of U.K. broadcasting included the first moves toward streamed, generic radio. In his words, "The provision of general contrast, the feeling of competition and choice in the BBC's programmes, should cause what present demand there is for commercially provided competition to subside."

The practical application of BBC philosophy took the form of a tripartite system of radio; the BBC Forces Programme would remain, with modifications, and be renamed the Light Programme; the Home Service, more traditionally "BBC," would continue to broadcast a mix of speech and light orchestral music, with regional variations, while a third channel, aimed at more "highbrow" tastes, including the arts, classical music, and drama, would be created.

These changes were swiftly implemented with the cessation of hostilities; on 29 July 1945, the Home Service began peacetime broadcasting, on the same day that the Light Programme took over. The Third Programme did not commence transmissions until September 1946. In the meantime, although the fledgling BBC Television Service, which had been inaugurated shortly before the war, resumed its transmissions from London's Alexandra Palace in June 1946, the principal investment within the British broadcasting industry remained in radio. In the financial year 1947–1948, £6,556,293 was spent on sound broadcasting, while television saw only £716,666 in terms of financial investment. In 1946, the BBC charter was renewed by the newly elected postwar Labour government under Clement Attlee, but for the first time in BBC history, the term was reduced from 10 years to five. Meanwhile, during the last year of the war, the strategically significant Radio Luxembourg had been liberated by U.S. forces and was used to transmit propaganda to retreating German troops. It was soon returned to civilian operation, heralding a resumption of continental competition, although in a reduced form; Radio Luxembourg would be the only station from Europe to challenge BBC programs after the war.

NEW WORLDS

The new structure of British radio after the war entailed the removal of Reith's beloved concept of serendipity in listening and may, in retrospect, be viewed as having been the start of a system of generic broadcasting along cultural strands that would eventually lead to the creation of such networks as BBC Radio 1, BBC Radio 2, BBC Radio 3, and BBC Radio 4 in 1967. Conversely, a focus was established for producers that enabled some highly significant programs. In 1945, the Features Department was created under Laurence Gilliam. The Third Programme generated some remarkable drama productions, including Samuel Beckett's *All That Fall*; Dylan Thomas's masterpiece *Under Milk Wood*, with Richard Burton in the role of "First Voice," was first broadcast in January 1954, produced by Douglas Cleverdon, who also fostered the work of other great poets, for instance, David Gascoyne (*Night Thoughts*) and David Jones (*In Parenthesis*); in short, the 10 years following the end of World War II can truly be claimed as a high-water mark for creative radio in the United Kingdom.

Light entertainment also entered what for some became a "golden era," with the development throughout the 1940s and 1950s of major—and sometimes long-lasting—comedy series, some of which would later transfer to television, while others, for example, the surreal *Goon Show*, exploited the concept of "pure radio." From this period came programs that have remained BBC staples to this day, including *Woman's Hour* (October 1946) and *The Archers* (January 1951). The resurgence of listening to commercial radio was not to be stemmed, however, and postwar Radio Luxembourg reestablished itself—particularly among the young—as a source of populist entertainment, modeling much of its programming on its prewar output; The League of Ovaltineys returned in 1946, with a virtually identical style and format to the one that had captivated a previous generation of children. The station also developed the idea of the record show. Thus, this potent form of music radio—relatively unfamiliar to U.K. audiences despite the work of Christopher Stone and others in the 1930s—manifested itself in Britain for the first time. Initially demonstrating this genre was Radio Luxembourg's *Top Twenty* program, which began in 1948. Starting as a program of the top twenty sheet music sales of popular songs, illustrated by records, it was an instant success, receiving thousands of letters per week, paving the way for the growth of music radio in Britain, and creating an appetite that would, in due course, challenge the BBC's relationship with its audience—particularly the young—once again.

Postwar Radio Luxembourg was a combination of the familiar and the new. Nonetheless, as the 1950s progressed, its output became increasingly dominated by music, with record shows being sponsored by companies like the Decca Group, Capitol Records, and others. Meanwhile, the BBC's programs for children—including *Children's Hour*—retained and fostered young radio audiences in more traditional ways. *Listen with Mother*, aimed at preschool children, remained in the affections of generations of youth audiences as they grew older, and the science fiction series *Journey into Space*, broadcast during the mid-1950s, attained a huge following. It was, in fact, the last evening radio drama series to defeat U.K. television in audience ratings.

Sill, as the mid-to-late 1950s spawned the rise of rock 'n' roll and the development of a true youth music, BBC radio did little to respond, and Radio Luxembourg, broadcasting to the United Kingdom in the evenings, drew increasingly large listening figures.

The BBC faced other crises; just as the General Strike of 1926 had caused tension with the British Parliament, so the Suez Crisis of 1956 pitted the corporation against Anthony Eden's government. Eden wanted the BBC to put forth an international picture of Britain as a united front with regard to the issue of the Suez Canal. The director-general, Sir Ian Jacob, resisted this, maintaining the BBC's right to impartial reporting of internal differences of opinion within the nation on the matter. Had this right been overridden by the government, the nature of the BBC would have been fundamentally changed; this crucial moment in British broadcasting left the independence of the BBC intact and maintained its international reputation—and, in particular, the World Service—during an era of increasing global mistrust and Cold War propaganda. As distinguished broadcaster Desmond Hawkins had remarked of the BBC's wartime role, "if you were traveling in Europe, you only had to mention that you were from the BBC, to be clasped by the hand and welcomed as an honored friend." This sense of trust was at stake—and ultimately preserved—at the time of the Suez Crisis.

Throughout the 1950s, the growth of television was inexorable; one of the significant moments for U.K. audiences was the coronation—in June 1953—of Queen Elizabeth II. The televising of the event had a considerable effect on television sales, but the growth of the medium as the decade progressed was general and irresistible. In 1955, commercial television came to Britain, with the BBC having its monopoly legally challenged by competition for the first time. As it would be later, the death of radio was predicted, while at the same time, the medium continued to develop and experience new innovations. The invention of the portable tape recorder, initially intended as a news tool, was seized on by such producers as Charles Parker in the BBC's Midland Region. Parker created a series of classic radio documentaries—the *Radio Ballads*—with Ewan MacColl and Peggy Seeger. These programs, broadcast throughout the late 1950s and early 1960s, redefined the nature of documentary feature making, dispensing with a narrator and utilizing actuality and the "voice of the people" in a way that would have a lasting effect on the way speech programs would be made in the future. In creative, news, and current affairs broadcasting, BBC radio remained unchallengeable; it was the youth revolution of the 1960s that instigated the next major change in British broadcasting, with cultural and technological drivers at the forefront of the new order.

REVOLUTION

During the 1960s, two linked issues influenced the development of radio in the United Kingdom. First, a growing youth market spawned by popular music, in particular from 1963, when homegrown talent, spearheaded by the Mersey Sound and the rise of the Beatles, created a demand for a media other than television that could be "owned" by this rising audience. Second, the development of the transistor enabled a new portability in receiver equipment, typified by the tiny Sony TR620 radio, which first appeared in 1960. What remained lacking, as far as the youth audience was concerned, was appropriate radio content. The Light Programme was broadcasting a small number of popular music programs, but Radio Luxembourg's evening output was still the only source of a genuine record-based music radio similar to what had been in existence in the United States for many years.

Movements had begun among certain independent radio production companies, which had made programs for Radio Luxembourg, toward the concept of a legal framework for commercial radio within the United Kingdom. These were met with a consistently negative response from the Labour government of the time, and the idea of a true competitor to go up against a BBC that had virtually retained its monopoly of radio broadcasting seemed as distant as ever. On 28 March 1964, that breakthrough came in dramatic fashion, with the first broadcast of Radio Caroline, the brainchild of a young Irish entrepreneur, Ronan O'Rahilly. The transmissions came from a ship moored in international waters, five miles off Harwich on the east coast of England. The sound was radically different from anything that had previously been heard on U.K. radio, and it spawned a host of other offshore "pirates" throughout the next three years. As with the continental stations of the 1930s, the BBC was confronted with a very real attack on its output; a deficiency in its policies had been identified, and it was once again found to be out of step with a crucial part of its audience.

Notwithstanding the growth of the offshore stations and the demonstrable popularity of their output, Harold Wilson's Labour government would not be swayed. A parliamentary act was devised to silence the stations, making it illegal for them to broadcast or be supplied from British shores. On 13 June 1967, the Marine, &c., Broadcasting (Offences) Act was created, and it went into legal effect at midnight on 14/15 August. Pirates other than Radio Caroline went off the air. Caroline has continued to broadcast sporadically in various forms, becoming an icon of the free radio spirit of the 1960s and, in many ways, mirroring the commercial pioneering of the 1930s. The movement created by the activism of the offshore stations made change inevitable; throughout the history of British radio, BBC policy has often been responsive to outside influence, as was the case in the media climate of the late 1960s. Within two weeks of the ship-based stations going off the air, many of the stations' presenters were broadcasting once more, this time as part of Radio 1, the BBC's first pop-music station, aimed exclusively at a youth market. At the same time, the BBC's director of radio, Frank Gillard, completed the process of generic streaming on BBC radio; the old Light Programme became Radio 2 and the cultural channel Radio 3, while the Home Service was renamed Radio 4.

Gillard simultaneously created BBC local radio. During the early 1960s, there had been a major development in transmitter technology, with the expansion of very high frequency—VHF (FM) to cover 97 percent of the U.K. population. The high-quality, low-power capability of VHF made it possible for the same or similar frequencies to be used by various broadcasters in different parts of the country. It is important to understand that during this time, the majority of U.K. radio listening was carried out on either medium wave (MW) or longwave (LW). VHF also carried with it the capability of stereo broadcasting and would ultimately be adopted as the standard for U.K. radio. In the meantime, VHF was the ideal carrier for Gillard's experiment in local radio, which began in November 1967, with BBC Radio Leicester. This was followed by stations in Sheffield, Liverpool, Nottingham, Brighton, Stoke-on-Trent, Leeds, and Durham. By 1970, the trial was deemed to have proven a case for local radio, and other stations began to appear, remaining part of the modern-day U.K. radio map.

By 1970, the BBC had regained its radio monopoly, apart from the continuing, although by now culturally diminished, presence of Radio Luxembourg; however, that same year, political events once again transpired to change U.K. radio industry. In 1970, a general election was held in Britain. Defying expectations, the Conservative Party, under Edward Heath, was elected to power. Unlike the Labour Party of the time, the Conservatives stood for free enterprise rather than state-supported industry and, as such, had placed the introduction of commercial or independent radio in its manifesto. A further factor in the chain of events was that the age of voting was reduced to 18, admitting a youth vote to the political system for the first time.

The plans for the legal establishment of independent, land-based commercial radio were ratified in the Sound Broadcasting Act of 1972, which coincided with the BBC's 50th anniversary. The new tier of radio broadcasting was to be administered by a new authority, the Independent Broadcasting Authority (IBA), developed out of the Independent Television Authority, created to administer Independent Television (ITV) beginning in 1955. Nearly 400 companies prepared for the application process. This was, however, to be a very different concept of commercial radio from the ideals of the offshore stations of the 1960s or the prewar continental pioneers; the early days of independent local radio (ILR) were fraught with financial hardship and political rivalry, combined with overregulation, which coalesced to threaten the very future of the new form.

INDEPENDENT RADIO

With the arrival of legally based radio supported by advertising in the United Kingdom, the caution exerted by politicians and regulators initially failed to take into account the commercial imperatives of the necessary business ethic behind the medium. It is important to understand the distinction between the words *independent radio* and *commercial radio* within the context of U.K. radio at this time. Because of a lack of forethought on the part of the politicians who had supported the idea, the new radio service took ITV as its model. ITV had been conceived as a public service, and so independent radio, rather than commercial radio, was born into a similar ethic, together with a responsibility to answer to listeners rather than shareholders in the first instance. It was also heavily regulated, with specific weekly targets for speech content, including prescribed religious programming durations and the requirement to spend a proportion of profits on the development of live music and community events.

Many unexpected and remarkable programs resulted from this overstructuring and overregulation, but in the uncertain and volatile political climate of the 1970s Britain, the first legitimate radio competition to the BBC found it hard to survive, while at the same time compromising its identity; this was not the concept of commercial radio that the earlier advocates of the form had envisaged.

The first ILR station to broadcast was, significantly, an all-speech station, the London Broadcasting Company, opening at 6:00 a.m. on 8 October 1973. It was as though the intention was to demonstrate that U.K. radio funded by advertising was a legitimate, worthy form, as far removed as possible from the stereotypical American-style music radio, the style of which had typified the approach of the offshore stations of the 1960s. The opening of the station was low key, conservative (in a nonpolitical sense), and understated. Just eight days later, on 16 October 1973, a second station began broadcasting, also in London. This was Capital Radio, primarily a popular music station; however, such was the nature of IBA regulation at the time that the station saw the need to employ a drama producer and run its own classical orchestra, the Wren Orchestra. As other stations came on air during the coming months and years, there was a sense of a diluted "voice," the IBA requirement for a balanced output often leading to a certain blandness and a curiously Reithian approach to broadcasting and the audience.

To demonstrate that ILR could produce quality programs to rival its BBC counterparts, a program-sharing scheme was established that allowed participating stations to exchange material that went beyond purely local content. This move also showed that whatever the prejudice against the stations, particularly among upper-class professionals and politicians, this was a responsible medium. The funding for this project came from a controversial tax levied by the IBA on ILR profits, which was entitled "Secondary Rental." This fund was raised by taxing a proportion of these profits (if and when they occurred) to create a pool of money that would be made available for communal use by stations in the network. Another beneficiary of this scheme was a National Broadcasting School. It was, perhaps, little wonder that the early years of the new radio form in Britain were precarious ones financially, set against a time of domestic strife, including a strike by U.K. miners and a three-day work week.

As more stations were established during the 1980s, there was a growing frustration both within the industry and in the general public. On the one hand, excessive regulation continued to threaten the existence and growth of independent radio; in February 1983, two-thirds of ILR stations currently broadcasting were losing money. Alternatively, listeners were being tempted by a new wave of pirate stations, typified by the American-style music radio of Laser 558, broadcasting from a ship off the Essex coast, with a large transmitter reaching considerable audiences with its slogan, "The music is never more than a minute away." The station, with its slick American disc jockeys and uncompromising approach to its output, made considerable inroads into the already fragile output of ILR, while also cutting into the audience for BBC Radio 1. In the meantime, national radio remained the monopoly of the BBC; in 1979, BBC Radio 2 became the first station in Britain to broadcast 24 hours a day.

A further blow to commercial radio development came with the publication of the Annan Report; although primarily concerned with the future of television, the report impacted commercial radio by clearing the way for morning television for the first time in the United Kingdom. In 1983–1984, morning radio audiences decreased by 10 percent, a particularly low point in the industry; in June 1984, the Association of Independent Radio Contractors, representing the interests of commercial radio in Britain, held a conference, from which came four crucial resolutions for action on behalf of the beleaguered medium:

1. To make public the industry's frustration at overregulation

2. To demand an early and substantial reduction in rentals
3. To press the government for new legislation on commercial radio in Britain
4. To commission an independent report on the potential for creating more stations under a lighter regulation

The conference had a major effect; within three months, many of the more petty IBA regulations had been dispensed of, and within six months, rentals had been reduced by more than a third. Within a year, an independent report, *Radio Broadcasting in the UK*, was published, demonstrating that a new "light-touch" regulation would facilitate genuine expansion in the commercial radio sector. The process that began at the 1984 conference culminated with the 1990 Broadcasting Act, which removed many of the hurdles prohibiting independent radio from being truly commercial and permitted consolidation—the purchasing of radio stations to form groups—and ultimately the creation of, the first national commercial radio stations.

DIGITAL

As a result of the 1990 Broadcasting Act, the IBA was abolished, and in its place were created two separate regulators for independent television (Independent Television Commission [ITC]) and radio (Radio Authority [RA]). The act was also pivotal in the development of commercial radio in the United Kingdom. Consolidation of company holdings was, for the first time, permitted in Britain, leading to the rise of such radio groups as Great Western Radio (GWR), the Capital Radio Group, and Emap, which consumed many stations, shaping their output to an overall group policy. At the same time, the move toward community radio began, although the reality of a "people's radio" was still a full 15 years away. Another outcome of the act was the creation of national commercial radio, and three licenses were advertised. These were won by Classic FM, which began broadcasting in September 1992; Virgin 1215 (later renamed Virgin Radio), which went on the air in April 1993; and TalkRadio UK (later talkSPORT), which commenced broadcasting in February 1995.

A classical music station as the first national commercial service was significant in elevating the sector's profile and image, and it played a key role in the following years, which were successful ones for the independent sector. The new "light-touch" authority relaxed regulation on ILR, eliminating the requirement to provide as much "meaningful speech" as had been practiced with the previous regulations and reducing some of the obstacles that stood in the way of profitability. The result was a shift away from the emphasis on programs to a focus on programming, a development of the concept of branding within radio groups—and, for some, the deterioration of program standards toward a certain predictability of sound.

Meanwhile, the BBC was changing. New structures led to an opening of its internal systems, with producer choice enabling staff producers to choose facilities outside of the corporation itself. Furthermore, program making was opened up to independent production companies, which were able to bid for program slots in all the networks in competition with staff producers and departments. In September 1995, the BBC launched digital radio, and the following year came a parliamentary act, the aim of which was to "make provision for the broadcasting in digital form of television and sound programme services and the broadcasting in that form on television or radio frequencies of other services." The concept of the digital multiplex—a technical conduit clustering a number of separate services transmitted digitally and offering the potential for a range of new stations in digital quality—came into being. The RA advertised the first commercial national multiplex in 1997; there was some caution among commercial operators, and there was only one applicant to operate the service. The license was accordingly awarded to Digital One, led by the GWR group, and the service was launched in the spring of 1999.

The technology used to enable Digital Audio Broadcasting (DAB) in Britain, in common with many other countries in Europe and Asia—although not the United States—was known as Eureka 147. The United Kingdom's DAB services initially marketed the system on the basis of improved quality, but this proved unsuccessful and the emphasis was switched to an increase in service choice. Even so, into the first years of the 21st century, a circular problem hindered the public take-up of DAB; sets were expensive, and consumers were reluctant to invest in new receiver technology for a service for which the benefits remained unclear and reception intermittent and geographically uncertain. The problem was exacerbated by a proliferation of new radio technologies and platforms, in particular the growth of Internet radio, both as live streaming and audio on demand. Satellite radio began to demonstrate a new concept in global radio, and mobile telephone manufacturers were developing 3G technologies, the first steps toward a new range of portable digital services. Technology was also at the heart of the program-making process, with digital systems being introduced beginning in the mid-1980s for the editing and storage of material.

Convergence was in the air—literally. For the first time in the history of the medium, the consumption of radio did not require an eponymous device to enable it; digital television sets carried radio output, and the industry was somewhat caught by surprise as the new century progressed, finding increasing numbers of listeners tuning in via their television receivers. These and other technological changes pointed toward another reshaping of media regulation to propel the industry forward; in June 2000, the RA published a paper for submission to the Department of Culture, Media, and Sport, as well as the Department of Trade and Industry, entitled *Radio Regulation for the 21st Century*, outlining its belief in the requirement for further deregulation. In May 2002, Tony Blair's Labour government announced the draft Communications Bill, which was aimed at dismantling existing media regulators in favor of one "super regulator" in the form of the Office of Communications (Ofcom). In May 2003, the Communications Act went into effect, and in December of the same year, the RA handed over responsibility to Ofcom for an industry that had radically changed during the 13 years of the former regulator's existence. In 1990, the U.K. commercial radio industry consisted of 80 companies; by the end of 2003, Ofcom had taken charge of the regulation of 272 local analog services, one national digital multiplex, and 45 local multiplexes carrying more than 300 commercial digital services. The Communications Act also cleared the way for further consolidation and the potential for international ownership of U.K. commercial radio services.

In June 2002, the first manufacturer to produce a sub-£100 digital receiver, Pure, launched its Evoke-1, at last heralding the development of cheaper sets, which began an increasing public take-up of the medium. Meanwhile, in the BBC sector, a range of new digital services were being launched, including BBC 7, a speech service drawing on the corporation's archive of drama and comedy radio programs. It was said that this single service, making available much-loved material from U.K. radio's past, was responsible for the surge in interest in DAB at the time of its launch in the autumn of 2002. Other BBC services available as digital-only stations included 6 Music and 1Xtra, both of which launched during 2002.

In contrast to the developments in new technologies and the potential for new commercial radio giants to inhabit the British media scene, Ofcom progressed the plans of its predecessor, the RA, to establish community radio within the United Kingdom. The concept had been a matter of discussion for some years, and the germ of "access radio," as it was called for a time, already existed in the presence of short-term licensed stations run by sectors of the community—Restricted Service Licenses. These stations, run by student, ethnic, or arts groups, usually operated under license for approximately four weeks, often coinciding with a local event or festival. Out of this came the desire to funnel back into communities a direct local voice that, for many, had been removed by the change in the ILR from its early, pre-1990 form to the branded group policy-led entity it had increasingly become in the last years of the 20th century and onward.

In June 2000, the government sanctioned the establishment of 16 stations throughout Britain as a pilot scheme. The agreed-upon definition of a community service was that of a station run as a small-scale neighborhood project, either as a community of geography or interest. The groups chosen for the pilot covered the entirety of the United Kingdom, and a commissioned evaluation of the project concluded that this third tier of British radio would ultimately prove itself to be "one of the most important cultural developments in the country for many years." In 2004, the first full-time licenses were advertised by Ofcom, to run for a span of five years, and by the summer of 2005, 20 licenses had been awarded, with a rolling program of additional awards being established the following year.

May 2005 saw the first major merger between radio groups, with the GWR and Capital groups joining forces as GCap Media. The event took place at an inauspicious time in commercial radio development, with sales remaining low and the medium struggling to compete with a content-rich BBC. There were also new trends in the way listeners consumed radio. The phenomenon of the Apple iPod and the ability to download—"podcast" radio programs— gave audiences the potential to create their own playlists of programs and music, and radios with the capability to rewind and pause enabled listeners to "spool through" commercial breaks, challenging the traditional means of funding by advertising and prompting the sector to explore new potential revenue streams.

Historically, the tensions within U.K. radio since its creation, in particular those created by the continuing evolution and redefining of public service broadcasting and the nature of competition, have created a unique medium capable of reinventing itself and adjusting to new times, technology, and challenges. Hence, by the middle of the first decade of the 21st century, British radio continued to be a thriving, vibrant medium. The refining of technology impacted the medium in many ways; revenue issues continued to present challenges and promised further changes in structure and funding. Mobility and questions relating to the interrelation of content and available platforms simultaneously pointed to the fact that radio within the United Kingdom, while broadly secure as a medium, would continue to face challenges.

Not least of these was the oft-postponed decision by the U.K. government to announce a switchover date from analog to digital radio services. In 2009, a Digital Radio Action Plan had pointed to a firm strategy and timetable, and by 2012, a date seemed imminent; indeed, pundits were even predicting it precisely, suggesting that on 16 December 2013, the communications minister, Ed Vaizey, would announce a time frame for change to begin in 2015. This was subject to the following two conditions:

1. Switchover could only begin when 50 percent of all listening was digital.
2. It would also only be viable when national DAB coverage was comparable to FM, and when local DAB radio listening reached 90 percent of the population on all roads.

When the time came for the announcement at a conference at the BBC's Broadcasting House, however, it was clear that it was still too early to set a date for the transition; there was even doubt as to whether it would happen at all. Growth had not been as extensive as expected, and there were fears among those in the commercial sector that smaller stations would suffer if the analog signal was turned off. Moreover, digital signals required boosting to create a nationwide service on par with existing transmissions. The upshot of discussions and debate within the industry and corridors of political power seemed to be that no official date should be set and that an appropriate tentative target might be a date near the end of the century's second decade. Unlike television, radio's road to a totally digital reception world was proving more complex, not least because of the sheer quantity and diversity of sets in private ownership.

A large part of the problem besetting traditional freestanding radio-set manufacturers was that, while an increasing number of people were consuming audio, the form in which it was being accessed was continually changing. The sales of sets declined, and although car manufacturers increased the percentage of digital radios in new vehicles, the development of smartphones, tablets, and other devices capable of receiving audio meant that the market for sales was fragmented between competing technologies. At the same time, the public was reluctant to turn off their traditional analog sets, which remained scattered throughout the domestic homes of Britain in considerable quantities. Also, the growth of blogging and podcasting on a personal level made for the increase of sound as a means of active expression, as well as passive entertainment. The digital world was proving to be one of almost infinite possibilities, making for an immediate future full of both challenge and opportunity, but issues other than technical would soon envelop British media, changing the public's concept and opinion of program makers and broadcasting personalities.

CHANGE, SCANDAL, AND CONTROVERSY

Partially linked to the take-up of digital services was a debate about two of the BBC's own DAB services, BBC Radio 6 Music (originally BBC 6 Music until 2011) and the BBC Asian Network. In February 2010, it became clear that discussions were in progress within the BBC regarding the possibility of closing both stations. A high-profile public campaign was inaugurated, aimed at saving BBC Radio 6 Music. Furthermore, in the event that the station survived, although the BBC Trust had noted that it needed to heighten its profile to gain more public awareness, the plan also had as its goal strengthening the station's presentation team to give it more musical credibility. BBC Radio 6 Music has since established itself more strongly within the raft of BBC audio services. In the meantime, the future of the BBC Asian Network remained less certain; with the highest per-listener budget of any radio station in the United Kingdom, it, too, had been threatened with closure in March 2010. A year later, however, this proposal was scrapped in favor of a reduction in the station's budget. It also became clear that the BBC Trust would not commit to a long-term decision regarding the station's future.

The commercial radio sector had also undergone considerable change; in 2007, Ashley Tabor founded Global Radio with the takeover of Chrysalis Radio and, a year after that, acquired the GCap Media group and its brands. These two acquisitions gave Global Radio control of a large number of commercial radio networks throughout the United Kingdom, including the Heart brand, which the group consolidated by rebranding a number of other heritage stations under the Heart logo. In 2012, Global purchased GMG Radio and, in 2013, was subject to a ruling by the Competition Commission stating that it should sell some of its stations, a decision it appealed. Notwithstanding, by 2015, Global Radio, under its parent holding company, Global Limited, remained, by far, the largest commercial radio group in Britain.

Parallel with change and reorganization, there was controversy as the 21st century progressed; both BBC and commercial radio stations came under scrutiny with regard to the rigging of on-air phone-in competitions, and in 2008, a prank phone call made by Russell Brand and Jonathan Ross on BBC Radio 2, aimed at actor Andrew Sachs, led to the departure from the network of both Brand and Ross and the resignation of the controller, Lesley Douglas. The moral responsibility of broadcasters became a major topic of investigation, and this grew to the proportions of a national scandal when, during a 2012 television program about broadcaster Jimmy Savile, who had died the previous year, it was alleged that he sexually abused children during the span of several decades. In October of that same year, the Metropolitan Police set up Operation Yewtree to investigate claims against Savile and other broadcasting personalities during a 40-year period. A further controversy erupted in November 2012, when a BBC TV current affairs program falsely leveled allegations of child abuse against prominent political figure Lord Robert Alastair McAlpine, an event that led to the resignation of the newly appointed director-general, George Entwistle, who left the corporation with a severance payout of £1.3 million after serving in the position for only a matter of weeks. Lord McAlpine died in 2014.

The BBC was also criticized for its internal staff relations, including ageism and bullying on some of its stations, as well as for excessive financial arrangements with some of its celebrity presenters. This last point, in the context of a public body largely funded by compulsory subscription in the form of the license fee, came at a difficult time for the corporation. In 2010, the television license fee, which also provides revenue to fund radio and online services, was frozen for six years at £145.50 (a cut of 16 percent) and coincided with a reduction of government financial support for the corporation. Thus, the BBC took over the financing of the World Service, the Welsh-language broadcaster S4C, and international monitoring services. With the increasing range of choice provided by satellite broadcasters, there was an ongoing debate as to whether the BBC should be funded by a license fee at all; in 2013, the *Daily Telegraph* newspaper undertook a survey that claimed to show that 70 percent of the British population favored a reduction in the license fee, with nearly 50 percent advocating its complete abolition. In January 2014, the BBC rejected a proposal from the government for a new form of subscription, by which subscribers would only pay for services they use. The corporation continued to argue that the license fee remained the most effective way of gathering funding. Nonetheless, it became increasingly clear that the future financing—and indeed existence—of the BBC in its current form would be a subject of great debate and important decision-making when both the license fee and the Royal Charter are considered for renewal in 2016 and 2017, respectively.

TOWARD THE CENTENARY

The development of technologies surrounding the consumption of audio has continued to shift the perception of radio's identity; what once was a medium in which the receiver and the content were synonymous with one another is now an increasingly interactive and personalized form of entertainment and information, feeding into daily life through a variety of mobile devices and computerized platforms. Podcasts, downloads, listen-again facilities, and such subscription-based formats as Last.FM and Spotify shape their material according to the choice of the consumer/listener, and the ability to create an online "radio station" to reflect the personal taste of the "broadcaster" means that the word *radio*—if it is relevant at all—reflects more and more the content rather than the object.

In 2012, the BBC marked its 90th anniversary with a range of programs in its various services that explored the role of radio and its changing nature; in these discussions, a recurring theme was that of the future. In 2013, U.K. commercial radio marked the 40th anniversary of its first legal and land-based broadcasts. Here, too, there was a blend of nostalgia and debate as to the years ahead. Given the rate of change since the beginning of the 21st century, it was already clear that the years leading up to the centenary of the official birth of broadcasting in Britain would continue to see major evolution in both the production and consumption of programs. Questions that had seemed straightforward a few years earlier, for instance, the switchover from analog to DAB, remained unresolved. Others appeared to be moving toward a climax. There was even discussion in some quarters as to whether the BBC would be in existence to celebrate its own centenary—at least in its current form. On the contrary, the measures being taken in the second decade of the century and the investment in new technologies and new premises promised a dynamic engagement with the unfolding era of broadcasting.

Radio—audio—is unique; it is perhaps the most personal form of electronic communication because sound is the first human sense to awaken—and some say the last to desert us. It is rooted in memory and imagination, and it creates images that live on in the mind. For this reason, our engagement with it will remain a fundamental part of our existence and experience of life, and British radio—in whatever form it takes—will continue to play its part. At the same time, the citizen broadcaster will develop more and more amidst a murmuring of voices personalizing and reflecting individual perspectives with—or without—the help of corporations and companies. When broadcasting's second century dawns, we will already have embarked on a voyage of communication that would have seemed unimaginable to the pioneers of the early 1920s. But fundamentally, the values and the emphasis on content will largely remain as they always were; a new technology may seem spectacular, but its real value is quickly identified by its relevance and the quality of the human ideas disseminated by it. The history of radio has always been one of development and questioning, and we are faced with more uncertainty in modern times than ever before. When the BBC made its first broadcasts in 1922, there was a spirit of excitement and adventure; as we have seen, everything was happening for the first time. In 2022, one hundred years after those first transmissions, the historian looking back will see greater innovation and change—both technical and cultural—than in the entire history of broadcasting. The journey of British radio continues.

A

ABRAMSKY, JENNY (1946–). After reading English at the University of East Anglia, Jenny Abramsky joined the **British Broadcasting Corporation (BBC)** in 1969, as a programs operations assistant, moving to the **BBC Radio 4** lunchtime **news** program, *The World at One*, in 1973. After editorships on *PM* and *Today*, she became editor of News and Current Affairs Radio in 1987, in charge of news and current affairs programs on the five BBC radio networks. Abramsky was founding controller of **BBC Radio 5 Live** when it launched in March 1994.

In 1995, Abramsky won the Sony Radio Academy Award for an outstanding contribution to radio, and in 1998, she was made a fellow of the Radio Academy. In January 1999, she was appointed director of BBC radio, a role that was subsequently extended under the title of director of BBC radio and music. Her responsibilities in this capacity included overseeing the five main networks and the BBC's digital stations, **BBC Radio 1Xtra, BBC Radio 6 Music, BBC Radio 7**, BBC Radio 5 Live Sports Extra, and the **BBC Asian Network**. In addition, Abramsky was responsible for the three BBC orchestras in England, the BBC Proms Television Classical Music and Radio Resources. In 2007, under her leadership, BBC radio had an audience share of 56.6 percent, reaching approximately 33.5 million listeners.

Abramsky retired from the BBC in June 2008, after serving with the corporation for 39 years, and was replaced by **Tim Davie**, who, in turn, was succeeded by **Helen Boaden** in February 2013. Abramsky was awarded the title of Commander of the Order of the British Empire in 2001, and she was elevated to the title of Dame Commander of the Order of the British Empire in 2009.

ABSOLUTE RADIO. Absolute is a national **commercial radio** station, playing popular rock **music** and broadcasting on **amplitude modulation** and **Digital Audio Broadcasting** from studios in Golden Square in London. It began as **Virgin Radio** 1215 in 1993, and was sold to the Ginger Media Group, owned by **Chris Evans**, in 1997. Subsequent owners included the Scottish Media Group and the Times Group of India, who acquired the station in 2007, and rebranded it as Absolute Radio in September 2008. In July 2013, a bid for the station was made by **Bauer Radio**, which was approved by the Office of Fair Trading in December of that year.

ACK-ACK BEER-BEER. A popular show that formed a twice-weekly variety **series** on the **BBC Forces Programme**, broadcast from July 1940 to February 1944, with no less than 324 episodes. The title derives from the Morse code words for the initials of the Antiaircraft and Balloon Barrage commands during World War II, for whom the program was intended. Among the many artists who made regular appearances were **Sandy Mac-Pherson**, **Elsie and Doris Waters**, **Vera Lynn**, **Kenneth Horne**, and **Doris Arnold**.

ACKERLEY, JOE (1896–1967). Writer and poet Joe Ackerley spent 24 years as literary editor of the ***Listener***, a post to which he was appointed in 1935. Prior to this, beginning in 1928, he had been an assistant producer in the **talks** department of the newly constituted **British Broadcasting Corporation (BBC)**. One of his most enduring friendships was with E. M. Forster, whom he had met in 1922, and it was through Forster that Ackerley acquired a wide circle of acquaintances from the world of literature. He was able to call on many of these acquaintances when recruiting speakers for talks on the BBC.

As editor of the *Listener*, he was radical, energetic, and fearless, commissioning poems and features and frequently coming into conflict with the hierarchy of the BBC, which he saw as characterized by philistines and prudes. Overtly homosexual, his charm, integrity, and insistence on the highest standards earned him the reputation of being the finest literary editor of his generation; he sustained his role for nearly a quarter of a century.

ADAMS, DOUGLAS (1952–2002). Douglas Adams was the creator of one of the great classics of radio **comedy**, the highly innovative ***The Hitchhiker's Guide to the Galaxy***. It was producer Simon Brett, after receiving a synopsis from Adams for a science fiction comedy **series**, who saw its potential and achieved a **BBC Radio 4** commission. The first program was transmitted in March 1978. Its transfer to television was not generally considered an unqualified success; however, books based on the series have continued to achieve remarkable sales, and a feature film based on the stories was issued in 2005. Adams remained fascinated by the possibilities of technology until his death in 2002, and his last radio series, *The Hitchhiker's Guide to the Future*, featured him as both writer and presenter, exploring various forms of digital communication.

ADIE, KATE (1945–). Kate Adie, familiar to both radio and television audiences in the United Kingdom as a **British Broadcasting Corporation (BBC)** war correspondent, began her career as a studio technician in **local radio**. At Radio Bristol, she worked on farming programs, joining BBC TV news in 1979. She became the BBC's chief **news** correspondent in 1989 and was known as presenter of the **BBC Radio 4** program *From Our Own Correspondent*. Among many honors, she has received the Broadcasting Press Guild Award for her outstanding contributions to broadcasting.
See also WOMEN.

AEOLIAN HALL. A famous concert hall built on Bond Street in London, in 1904. It was taken over by the **British Broadcasting Corporation (BBC)** in March 1943, after the **Variety Department's** former home, St. George's Hall, was destroyed by the Germans. From then onward, Aeolian Hall was the home of Variety programs and remained so for 30 years. At its peak in the 1960s, 20 shows a week were being recorded or broadcast live from two studios, Aeolian 1 and Aeolian 2.

ALAN, A. J. (1883–1941). A. J. Alan was a pseudonym for Captain Leslie Harrison Lambert, a London civil servant. For years before World War II, Alan enthralled listeners of the **National Programme** with his mysterious radio stories. In January 1924, his first story, *My Adventure in Jermyn Street*, was broadcast from **Savoy Hill**, and his last was transmitted in March 1940, just a year before his death. Alan's cult status was compounded by the mystery of his identity. His broadcasts were limited—only about five a year—which heightened his impact and mystique. It was only at the time of his death that his identity was revealed. In his obituary, the *Times* stated, "Broadcasting has lost one of its most popular storytellers, and one—possibly the only one—who maintained his anonymity to the end." His catchphrase was "Good Evening Everyone," which gave its title to a book of his stories published in 1928.

Beginning in July 1939, Alan also broadcast a **series** of 15-minute talks from **Radio Luxembourg** entitled "Story Telling." Outside of broadcasting, he worked in the cryptographic analysis section of the Admiralty, which subsequently became known as GCHQ and was responsible for breaking the "Enigma" code. Alan was strongly aware of the magic of the radio form, and to prevent anything from coming between him and his listeners, he pasted each page of his script onto cards to prevent paper rustle. His is a classic image of the early British broadcaster: **Stuart Hibberd** described him as a "neat figure in perfectly cut evening dress, with eye glass and a slim black brief case."
See also TALKS.

ALAN HALL ASSOCIATES. *See* FALLING TREE PRODUCTIONS.

ALLDISS, BARRY (1932–1982). Barry Alldiss was a **disc jockey** primarily associated with postwar **Radio Luxembourg**. He came to London in 1955, after working at a number of radio stations in his native Australia. Alldiss could have had a successful career as a musician and composer; he wrote more than 100 songs and was a talented pianist, working for a time as such in a Knightsbridge club after his arrival in Britain. While so occupied, he met a member of the German presentation team for the **British Broadcasting Corporation** program *Family Favourites*, who helped him make the contacts that led to his joining the staff of Radio Luxembourg a year later. For eight years, Alldiss presented the *Top Twenty* program, which, at its peak, was said to have close to 10 million listeners. In 1966, he moved to London and worked as a freelancer on such programs as *Housewives' Choice* before joining the original team of presenters on **BBC Radio 1** in 1967, presenting, among other programs, *Late Night Extra*. Alldiss returned to Radio Luxembourg in 1975, this time as general manager and presenter, positions he held until his death at the age of 50.

See also COMMERCIAL RADIO; MUSIC.

ALL THAT FALL. In 1957, **Samuel Beckett** wrote this, the first of his works for radio and his first published play written in English rather than French, for broadcast on the **British Broadcasting Corporation's Third Programme**. It was produced by **Donald McWhinnie** and featured a number of actors who have become strongly associated with his work: J. G. Devlin, Mary O'Farrell, Jack MacGowran, and Patrick Magee. The script's subtle sonic requirements led to new developments in audio production and ultimately to the formation of the **BBC Radiophonic Workshop**.

See also DRAMA.

ALLEN, CHARLES, BARON ALLEN OF KENSINGTON (1957–). Charles Allen is chairman of **Global Radio** and a nonexecutive director of Virgin Media. He was chief executive of the Granada Group from 1996–2000 and chief executive of Independent Television (ITV) from 2004–2007. In March 2012, he was appointed by Ed Miliband, leader of the British Labour Party, as chairman of the Executive Board of the party. Allen was awarded the title Commander of the Order of the British Empire in 2003; knighted in 2012; and was created a life peer in 2013, taking the title Baron Allen of Kensington.

ALLIED EXPEDITIONARY FORCES (AEF) PROGRAMME. The radio service for the AEF opened on 7 June 1944, the day after D-Day. Programs were divided jointly between Britain, Canada, and the United States. The service gave many British civilians a taste of the more relaxed style of broadcasting on the other side of the Atlantic and influenced postwar **British Broadcasting Corporation** policy, which had previously come under fire from prewar commercial interests attacking its controversial **Sunday broadcasting policy**.

Many famous American radio shows were heard on the AEF Programme, including *Amos 'n' Andy*, *The Bob Hope Show*, and regular concerts by Glenn Miller and the American Band of the AEF. The British Band of the AEF was led by George Melachrino, and among the stars who appeared on the service were Bing Crosby, Jessie Matthews, Webster Booth, and Marlene Dietrich. The service ended on 28 July 1945.

See also MADDEN, CECIL (1902–1987); WARTIME BROADCASTING.

ALLISON, GEORGE (1884–1957). George Allison was a legendary football commentator from the early days of sports **outside broadcasts**. His first broadcast was only the second ever match transmitted, the cup tie between Corinthians and Newcastle United on 29 January 1927. Born at Hurworth-on-Tees in County Durham, Allison began his career in Plymouth as a journalist, and in 1912, having secured an exclusive interview with Lord Kitchener, he joined the U.S. Hearst newspaper group, working as the European correspondent for the *American Weekly*, a post he held for more than 30 years.

Allison's 1927 debut as a **British Broadcasting Corporation** soccer commentator opened up a new career for him; his rich voice and colorful descriptive powers, together with his skill at capturing the atmosphere of major sporting occasions, quickly made him a favorite with listeners. In 1928, he was the natural choice as commentator for the FA Cup Final—the first to be broadcast. He went on to become a director of Arsenal Football Club and later resigned his directorship to become manager, leading the club to numerous successful years during the mid-1930s. Allison retired in 1947.

See also SPORTS.

AMPLITUDE MODULATION (AM). First utilized in 1906, by Reginald Fessenden, the signal is transmitted by varying the radio wave to match the sound wave variations being transmitted and converting them back into sound waves at the receiver. Medium wave and **longwave** transmissions still use AM, although with the advent of **Digital Audio Broadcasting**, it became increasingly arcane.

See also ANALOG.

ANALOG. Until the latter years of the 20th century, traditional radio systems were exclusively **amplitude modulation (AM)**, **frequency modulation (FM)**, **longwave (LW)**, and **shortwave (SW)**. These services used analog technology. The analog system consists of transmitting the actual audio signal modulated onto the radio frequency carrier. Drawbacks related to analog broadcasting include its susceptibility to unwanted interference, noise, and hiss, which undermine the audio signal. For listeners of FM, this can usually be remedied to various extents by adjusting or improving the receiver aerial or resituating the receiver itself. With the development of digital radio services in the 1990s, the British government was pressured to set a date for an analog "switch-off," thus moving the U.K. industry into a totally digital climate. The slow initial take-up of digital radio receivers has made the decision somewhat problematic, and at this time no such date has been set.
See also DIGITAL AUDIO BROADCASTING (DAB).

ANALYSIS. A **BBC Radio 4** program created by **Ian McIntyre** and **George Fischer** in 1970. It is characterized by the serious and committed tone of its engagement with **current affairs**—frequently political—and the informed nature of its narrative. It has benefited from a number of distinguished presenters, most notably, for more than 10 years, **Mary Goldring**.

ANDERSON, GERRY (1944–2014). Born in Northern Ireland, Gerry Anderson (full name Gerard Michael Anderson) began his career as a musician before moving into radio in 1985. He became a popular regional broadcaster and was particularly known for his nickname for his home city, Derry/Londonderry, which he called "Stroke City," a title that was used beginning in 1992 for a radio program broadcast on **BBC Radio 4**. As a result, BBC Radio 4 commissioned him to make a daily afternoon program on the network—*Anderson Country*—but the style and tone of the show divided audiences, and he was dropped as presenter after a year, although the program format continued until 1998. Anderson continued to make programs for BBC Radio 4, and in 1990, he received the **Sony Radio Academy Award** for best regional broadcaster.

ANDERSON, MARJORIE (1913–1999). Initially employed by the **British Broadcasting Corporation (BBC)** as an actress, Marjorie Anderson, who had trained for the stage at London's Central School of Speech and Drama, was among a number of **women** trained to become the BBC's first female presenters of record programs. For many years, she was the main presenter of *Woman's Hour* from its inception in 1946. In 1955, Anderson hosted a spin-off program, *Home for the Day*, remaining with the program until its demise in 1968. She continued on *Woman's Hour* until her retirement from broadcasting in 1972. Her style influenced many female presenters.

ANDREWS, EAMONN (1922–1987). Born in Dublin, Eamonn Andrews's first job was as an insurance clerk, a post he lost when it was learned he was broadcasting boxing commentaries on Radio Eireann. His work gradually increased on Irish radio, and in 1948, he was master of ceremonies (MC) of a stage show called *Double or Nothing* at a Dublin theater, where he was spotted by British band leader Joe Loss, who signed him—and the program—for a tour. In 1949, when **Stewart MacPherson** left the **British Broadcasting Corporation (BBC)**, Andrews applied for his job as MC of *Ignorance Is Bliss* and was hired. The rich Irish brogue immediately proved popular with U.K. audiences, and Andrews was asked to present the live weekly program *Sports Report*. He hosted the show for many years, while also working as a boxing commentator for BBC radio. By 1951, television was emerging in the United Kingdom, and Andrews was offered the role of host for the panel game *What's My Line*. Other television successes included the U.K. version of U.S. television's *This Is Your Life*, which he hosted for both the BBC and Independent Television.

In 1964, Andrews became a papal knight of St. Gregory, and in 1970, he was appointed a honorary Commander of the Most Excellent Order of the British Empire. After his death in November 1987, more than 3,000 people attended his memorial service.

See also SPORTS.

ANNAN COMMITTEE. From 1974–1977, a government committee led by Noel Gilroy Annan (Baron Annan, 1916–2000), considered the future of broadcasting in the United Kingdom and produced a 500-page report that stated the terms of operation for both radio and television during the next decade. The report, written by Annan himself, recommended the further development of local radio and suggested that broadcasters be more responsive to the public. It advocated high standards in broadcasting and insisted on the need to resist what it saw as extreme commercial pressures. There were also implications for the new and developing medium of **commercial radio**, which was to struggle to establish itself financially for years to come.

See also COMMITTEES OF ENQUIRY.

ANNOUNCERS. The earliest announcers on British radio were at 2LO, including **Arthur Burrows** and **Cecil Lewis**, who combined the task with their other roles. **Stuart Hibberd** was made chief announcer in 1928; others were **John Snagge**, **Derek McCulloch**, and **Alvar Liddell**. For a time, announcers were anonymous voices, but during World War II, the practice was introduced of announcers identifying themselves when reading the **news** to ensure that the audience was aware of the authenticity of what they were hearing. In **commercial radio**, the first staff announcer was Max Stanniforth on **Radio Normandy** in 1931. Also on this station was **Bob Danvers-Walker**, while on **Radio Luxembourg**, **Stephen Williams** was chief announcer, and Tony Melrose became "The Voice of **Radio Lyons**." As the "voice" of their respective stations, radio announcers became the first recognizable personalities in the new medium, leading to the famous song "Little Miss Bouncer Loves an Announcer," recorded by the **comedy** duo **Flotsam and Jetsam**.

ANY ANSWERS?. This program, which began airing in October 1954, was initially an opportunity for listeners to respond to the previous week's edition of *Any Questions?* Beginning in 1989, it became a "**phone-in**" and followed the second transmission of *Any Questions?*

ANY QUESTIONS?. A long-running discussion program that began as a six-week **series** in the **British Broadcasting Corporation's** West Region in October 1948 and continues to this day. It was conceived by **Frank Gillard** and dealt with controversial issues of the day, with a panel of guests debating with a live audience, who supplied the questions. Among the early panelists were **Arthur Street** and **John Arlott**. The program has evolved into a harder-edged debate, usually politically oriented. Beginning in 1954, it had an appendix in *Any Answers?*
  See also BRAIN'S TRUST, THE.

APPOINTMENT WITH FEAR. The British version of the U.S. radio **series** *Suspense*, hosted in the United Kingdom by actor **Valentine Dyall** as "The Man in Black." It ran sporadically on **British Broadcasting Corporation (BBC)** radio from 1943–1949, on the **BBC Home Service**, and was revived in 1955 on the **Light Programme**. In 1949, it was renamed *The Man in Black* but retained all other elements of its format and style. It was initially placed in the 10:30 p.m. slot, and the plays, originally created for American radio by John Dickson Carr, were produced for the BBC by **Val Gielgud** and Martyn C. Webster. In 2010, the BBC issued four surviving episodes on commercial CDs.
  See also DRAMA; MYSTERY PROGRAMS.

ARCHERS, THE. A daily radio **serial** originally billed as the "everyday story of country folk." It began its long career on Whit Monday, 1950, broadcast only in the **British Broadcasting Corporation's** Midland Region.

The writers in the first instance were Geoffrey Webb and Edward J. Mason, who were also responsible for *Dick Barton, Special Agent*. The idea for the program had been conceived in Birmingham in the late 1940s, as support for government policy to encourage the nation's farmers to grow more food. The concept was that current issues would be debated within the form of popular **drama**, and the program always carried a farming advisor. It has become a national institution, and in addition to its Monday through Friday 15-minute episodes, there is a weekend omnibus edition. Its theme tune, "Barwick Green," is also nationally famous.

The fictional home of the farming family the Archers is Ambridge, somewhere in Central England, and although this is fiction, the concerns dealt with in the serial remain very real and reflect the **current affairs** of British farming. For instance, during the foot and mouth disease epidemic in the early years of the 21st century, story lines were recorded as close to the time of transmission as possible to reflect the rapidly changing situation.

The Archers has maintained a reputation for headline gathering, most notably in 1955, on the night of the first transmission from Independent Television, when the story editors "killed" one of the program's star characters, the young Grace Archer, in a stable fire. The effect was to send the nation into "mourning" and defuse—whether intentionally or otherwise—the launch of Great Britain's first commercial television service. Another aspect of the program's continuing cult status is its ability to attract star names for cameo appearances, including members of the British Royal Family (Princess Margaret appeared in 1984, playing herself). The program has its own highly organized fan club, appropriately known as Archers Addicts.

See also SERIES; SOAP OPERAS.

"ARCHIE ANDREWS". Following the success on U.S. radio of Edgar Bergen, ventriloquist Peter Brough, in association with **Ted Kavanagh** (who chose the name) created "Archie Andrews" in 1944, for a **series** entitled *Archie Takes the Helm*. In June 1950 came the start of *Educating Archie*, which became the most popular **comedy** series on British radio. The concept of ventriloquism on radio is an odd one, but in this case it was successfully supported by off-air visual campaigns, including comic strips, and the naughty small-boy persona of Archie, by all accounts an upper-class prep school attendee dapper in a striped blazer and scarf, became readily identifiable to its 1950s audience.

ARLOTT, JOHN (1914–1991). One of the most widely known cricket commentators, John Arlott was also a published poet, and it was this quality that informed his work with the spoken word to memorable effect. His early work—as an attendant in a psychiatric hospital and later as a policeman—

was a long way from his ultimate career, although his time on the Hampshire Police Force demonstrated a keen interest in—and talent for—playing the game of cricket. Arlott's first job with the **British Broadcasting Corporation**—where he was mentored by John Betjeman—was in 1945, when he became a producer of poetry programs for the **BBC World Service's** Eastern Service. In 1946, he covered the England tour of India and produced a delighted response among listeners. It was the start of a career that would last for 34 years. He retired in 1980, appropriately after commentating on the Lords Centenary Test Match.

See also SPORTS; *TEST MATCH SPECIAL (TMS)*.

ARNOLD, DORIS (1904–1969). Although her main claim to fame is related to her being the first female **disc jockey** in U.K. radio through her work on *These You Have Loved*, Doris Arnold's association with broadcasting goes beyond this long-lasting request program. Originally a shorthand typist, she joined the **British Broadcasting Company** at its start as a secretary. As an accomplished pianist, her career was forever changed in 1930, when she stood in at short notice as an accompanist for *Children's Hour*, after which she formed a partnership with pianist Harry S. Pepper. As a duo, they made many successful and popular broadcasts. Arnold was also a respected musical arranger. She became hostess of *These You Have Loved* in 1938 and remained associated with the program for many years.

ARQIVA. A telecommunications company founded in 2005 that provides broadcast transmission facilities and infrastructure, with a network of more than 1,000 radio and television transmission sites throughout the United Kingdom and Ireland. Arqiva is the operator of the **Digital One** multiplex, a patron of the **Radio Academy**. The Arqiva Commercial Radio Awards recognize achievement within the sector in a number of categories, including presentation, programming, advertising, and marketing.

See also COMMERCIAL RADIO; RADIO ACADEMY AWARDS; SONY RADIO ACADEMY AWARDS.

ARROW, THE. A digital radio station that originally played soft rock on a London **Digital Audio Broadcasting multiplex**, as well as on Internet Radio. It was owned by **Chrysalis**. The Arrow has had a complex transmission history, being placed on and removed from a number of U.K. multiplexes. In June 2007, the station, together with **Heart**, the **London Broadcasting Company**, and **Galaxy**, was sold by Chrysalis to **Global Radio**.

See also COMMERCIAL RADIO.

ASHBRIDGE, NOEL (1889–1975). Part of the original **Marconi Company** team at **Writtle**, Noel Ashbridge served as an officer with the Royal Engineers in World War I and was one of the first wireless operators on the front line in France. He joined the Marconi Company in 1919 and worked at Writtle, constructing the 2MT transmitter and working with **Peter Eckersley** on the first broadcasts. In 1926, Ashbridge joined the **British Broadcasting Company (BBC)** and became assistant chief engineer under Eckersley. Three years later, he succeeded him as chief engineer.

In 1935, Ashbridge received a knighthood; the previous year he was made a knight of the Danish Royal Order of Dannebrog in recognition of his work establishing radio services within Europe. After spending time with the BBC team developing high-definition television in the 1930s and the subsequent wartime closure of the service, Ashbridge was appointed deputy director-general of the BBC in 1943, with special responsibility as technical advisor. In 1948, he relinquished the post to become director of technical services, in which position he played a major role in the postwar expansion of both radio and television in the United Kingdom.

In 1950, Ashbridge was the BBC's engineering representative at the Torquay conference, which established the European Broadcasting Union. He retired from the BBC in 1952, spending a further seven years as a board member of the Marconi Company.

ASKEY, ARTHUR (1900–1982). The diminutive Arthur Askey was a greatly loved comedian who, beginning in 1938, was associated with the hit radio show *Band Waggon*. With **Richard Murdoch**, Askey developed a style new to British radio of fast cross-talking nonsensical dialogue with ad-libbing, using the microphone in a focused way, which owed more to an understanding of the potential of this new medium rather than the world of the music hall, from which many of their contemporaries had come. Askey remained popular until the end of his life, when he was a regular member of the panel of the **comedy** ad-lib program *Does the Team Think?* He coined numerous catchphrases, among them "Hello Playmates" and "Before your very eyes."

ASSOCIATION OF INDEPENDENT RADIO CONTRACTORS (AIRC). A trade organization for **commercial radio** in Britain created by the first independent stations, the **London Broadcasting Company** and **Capital Radio**, in 1973. The association's purpose was to negotiate on the companies' behalf on issues relating to working practice, regulation, and marketing. It continued its work under the name **Commercial Radio Companies Association (CRCA)** from 1996–2006, when the **RadioCentre** was created by merging CRCA and the Radio Advertising Bureau under the directorship of **Andrew Harrison**. Dianne Thompson replaced **Paul Brown** upon his retirement as chair in November 2008.

AT HOME AND ABROAD. An important development in **current affairs** radio in Britain, first being transmitted in January 1954 and continuing until 1960, this program was broadcast twice weekly and featured speakers from throughout Britain and overseas who discussed issues of topical interest. It was heralded in the *Radio Times* prior to its first edition as aiming to be the "essence of current affairs broadcasting . . . [bringing] to the microphone the *right* contribution on the *right* subject at the *right* time."

AT THE LUSCOMBES. A radio **serial** that started in September 1948, in the West Region of the **BBC Home Service**. It featured the lives of a West Country village family in the fictional village of Dimstock, the location of which could be identified as being between the towns of Salisbury and Warminster. The program was broadcast on Saturday evenings in 20-minute episodes and written by Denis Constanduros and, early on, his aunt, actress **Mabel Constanduros**. Mabel was known for her characterization of Grandma Buggins in *The Buggins Family*, an early radio family serial that she also wrote. *At the Luscombes* ran for 1,000 episodes, until 1964. Denis adapted a number of story lines from the **series** as one-act plays for the stage in 1955.

See also DRAMA; SOAP OPERAS.

AUDIENCE RESEARCH. The **British Broadcasting Company/Corporation (BBC)** came relatively late to the concept of audience research, largely due to early paternalistic attitudes toward public service broadcasting. In the 1930s, this effort was led by U.S. advertising agencies, which created **commercial radio** programs for transmission from the continent to the United Kingdom; these organizations needed to demonstrate to prospective clients that radio held potential as an advertising medium and set about creating their own research units. In 1936, the BBC established its Listener Research Unit under **Robert Silvey**, who devised a number of means of exploring audience tastes and listening habits (*see also* TALLENTS, STEPHEN). Radio listening has since become increasingly dominated by ratings, which are measured and monitored quarterly by the **Radio Joint Audience Research** unit, co-owned by the BBC and the **Commercial Radio Companies Association**.

See also RADIOCENTRE.

BADDIEL, DAVID (1964–). David Baddiel is a writer, comedian, and presenter known for his work with **Rob Newman** and Frank Skinner. In 1989, Baddiel and Newman formed a successful writing partnership. They linked with **Steve Punt** and **Hugh Dennis** to create *The Mary Whitehouse Experience* on **BBC Radio 1**, a program concept that subsequently transferred to television. In 2014, Baddiel hosted a **BBC Radio 4** panel game entitled *Don't Make Me Laugh*, in which celebrities went against their instincts to try to make an audience laugh.

See also COMEDY.

BAKER, DANNY (1957–). Danny Baker is a writer and presenter who has worked for a wide range of radio and television stations. He began his career in radio on the **British Broadcasting Corporation (BBC)** station **Greater London Radio** in 1989. The following year, he joined the newly launched **BBC Radio 5**, working on various programs, notably related to sports. He became part of the presentation team of **BBC Radio 1** in October 1993 and, in 1996, combined duties on the station with some presentation on **BBC Radio 5 Live**. In 1997, Baker lost his job at the latter station when management alleged that he had incited threatening behavior relating to a soccer referee. He subsequently worked for TalkRadio in 1998 and **Virgin Radio** from 1999–2000. Baker joined BBC London 94.9 for two periods, from 2001–2002 and 2005–2012, when the program was axed as part of a policy of cutbacks at the station.

In 2007, Baker launched a series of podcasts, initially on a daily basis, under the title *The All Day Breakfast Show*. For six months, these were available for download without charge; a subsequent scheme to charge for them proved unsuccessful, and the project ended on 15 December 2007. Between 2008–2014, Baker returned for programs on BBC Radio 5 Live and, briefly, on **BBC Radio 2**, deputizing for **Jonathan Ross**, who had been suspended on disciplinary grounds. He has won a number of **Sony Radio**

Academy Awards, including Speech Radio Personality of the Year in 2011 and 2012, and the gold award for the Entertainment Show of the Year in 2013, for his Saturday morning program on BBC Radio 5 Live.

BAKER, RICHARD (1925–). Initially best known as a television news-reader, Richard Baker went on to make contributions as a radio presenter, particularly in the field of classical and light classical **music**. In 2003, he took over the long-running **BBC Radio 2** program *Your Hundred Best Tunes* following the death of the original host, **Alan Keith**. Baker retired in January 2007, when the program was axed as part of network rescheduling.

BALDWIN, PETER (?–). Peter Baldwin was deputy director of radio at the **Independent Broadcasting Authority (IBA)** under **John Thompson** until 1987, when he succeeded Thompson as director of radio. He held the post until the IBA was dissolved and was thereafter the first chief executive of the **Radio Authority** until 1995, when he was succeeded by **Tony Stoller**.
    See also COMMERCIAL RADIO; OFFICE OF COMMUNICATIONS (OFCOM).

BALLAD OF JOHN AXON, THE. In 1957, the **British Broadcasting Corporation (BBC)** commissioned **Charles Parker** and **Ewan MacColl** to make a documentary feature on the life and death of a North Country railway engine driver named John Axon. With Peggy Seeger, the two men created a new form of program, utilizing the newly acquired technology of the portable tape recorder and replacing scripted narrative with actuality and musical commentary. This was the first of what came to be known as the *Radio Ballads*, of which there were eight, broadcast between 1957–1964 on BBC radio.
    See also FEATURE.

BAND WAGGON. A highly influential program that aired from January 1938 to December 1939, effectively creating the genre of the radio "sitcom." Starring **Richard Murdoch** and **Arthur Askey**, the premise was that of the two comedians occupying a fictitious apartment on the top floor of **Broadcasting House**. Peppered with fast-moving banter and numerous catchphrases that entered the public consciousness and usage at the time, the show became extremely popular, spawning a touring stage version, a series of commercial records, and a film.
    See also COMEDY; SERIES; WARTIME BROADCASTING.

BANDWIDTH. The development of radio in the United Kingdom has frequently revolved around the availability of bandwidth, or spectrum. This is allocated to the industry regulator by the government. When the first independent local radio stations were launched in 1973, contracts issued included two frequency allocations—**amplitude modulation** (**AM**-mono) and **frequency modulation** (**FM**-stereo). Stations initially broadcast the same service on each of their frequencies. Companies subsequently used the two frequencies to broadcast alternative services.

As **commercial radio** developed, the initial bandwidth allocation was filled. By 1989, FM allocation of local frequencies was divided equally between independent radio and the **British Broadcasting Corporation**. Development of national commercial radio in the early 1990s was driven by the government-approved allocation of one national FM frequency and two national AM frequencies. Commercial radio's coverage was further enhanced in 1996, by the allocation of the bandwidth between 105 and 108 MHz. The increasing pressure to launch new services with a finite amount of bandwidth was one of the factors taken into account with the development of digital radio.

See also ANALOG.

BANNISTER, MATTHEW (1957–). Matthew Bannister has had an unusual career in radio, moving between management and presentation. He began at Radio Nottingham in 1978, before joining the news department of **Capital Radio**. Between 1988–1991, he ran **Greater London Radio**, the London station operated by the **British Broadcasting Corporation (BBC)**. As controller of **BBC Radio 1** between 1993–1998, he was responsible for taking the station through a difficult period in which the network redefined its place in the youth **music**-radio market and within the BBC. In doing so, Bannister removed many of the older presenters, some of whom had worked for the station since its inception, and introduced a "new music first" policy in the network's playlist. Other management posts included chief executive of production, director of radio, and director of marketing and communication. Bannister subsequently left management and joined the presentation team at **BBC Radio 5 Live**, staying with the station until 2005. Since then he has presented programs on **BBC Radio 2**, **BBC Radio 4**, and the **BBC World Service**. In 2011, Bannister was awarded an honorary doctorate from his alma mater, the University of Nottingham, and he is a fellow of the **Radio Academy**.

BARKER, ERIC (1912–1990). Eric Barker was a writer, actor, and comedian most associated with his 1950s series *Just Fancy*. He first began working in radio in 1933, and during the war he appeared in *Merry-Go-Round*, writing a contribution to the program featuring life in the Royal Navy (in which he served) aboard the "HMS *Waterlogged.*" His catch phrase was "Steady Barker," and the words became widely used by the public and formed the title of his autobiography. A spin-off after the war helped to launch the career of Jon Pertwee. In addition to *Just Fancy*, in which Barker starred with his wife, Pearl Hackney, who had also appeared in *Merry-Go-Round*, other radio **series** included *Passing Parade*, *Barker's Folly*, and *Law and Disorder*.

See also COMEDY.

BATCHELOR, HORACE (1899–1977). Horace Batchelor became a household name during the 1950s through his **Radio Luxembourg** program, in which he advertised his "Infra-Draw" method for winning football pools. A former insurance collector, he won his first dividend in 1948. His system became famous for a number of years, although its actual success was debatable. Based in Keynsham near Bristol, the program is mostly remembered for the **announcer's** careful spelling of the name—"K-E-Y-N-S-H-A-M."

See also COMMERCIAL RADIO.

BAUER RADIO. Bauer Radio is a U.K.-based division of the Bauer Media Group, a multinational media company based in Hamburg, Germany, and operating in 16 countries globally. In the United Kingdom, Bauer owns **Absolute Radio** and the **Magic** brand. It also operates two main groups, Bauer Place and Bauer Passion. The former consists of local services, while the latter consists of national and quasi-national **music** services mainly delivered through digital media platforms.

See also COMMERCIAL RADIO.

BAXTER, TRAVIS (1957–). Travis Baxter is U.K. content consultant and external affairs director for the German publisher/broadcaster Bauer Media. He previously worked with the **British Broadcasting Corporation** and **Emap**, among others. Baxter began his career with the **commercial radio** station Plymouth Sound in 1977. He also worked for the private equity company Advent International, where he was chairman of Radio 538 in the Netherlands, as well as for Actera Private Equity in Turkey, as an investor, board member, and advisor to the broadcast and digital media business Spectrum Medya. Baxter has been a consultant with Ariadne Capital, an investor in the Ariadne Fund. as well as with the software and data storage company Object Matrix.

See also MUSIC.

BBC. *See* BRITISH BROADCASTING COMPANY (BBC [1]); BRITISH BROADCASTING CORPORATION (BBC [2]).

BBC 6 MUSIC. *See* BBC RADIO 6 MUSIC.

BBC ARABIC. Apart from its domestic transmissions in Welsh and Gaelic, the **British Broadcasting Corporation (BBC)** only broadcast in English until 1938, when it began what was originally called the Arabic Service, broadcasting in literary Arabic. As a crucial and frequently controversial arm of what was to become the **BBC World Service**, its output was increased during the Gulf War crisis of 1991, and it continues to actively debate issues in the Middle East and North Africa, now supported by a developed online presence. Under the title BBC Arabic, it is considered one of the longest-running foreign-language news services and today exists as both a radio and television channel, the latter operating via satellite. The radio service is based at **Broadcasting House** in London, with a bureau in Cairo.

BBC ASIAN NETWORK. This radio station principally serves residents of Great Britain originating from the region of the Indian subcontinent, with production centers in Birmingham, Leicester, and London. Despite its name, the Asian Network is not aimed at members of the populace from the broader Asian continent. Although it broadcasts mainly in English, it also transmits programs in five South Asian languages.

The Asian Network originated in 1988, with experiments in ethnic broad-casting by **Radio Leicester** and BBC WM in Birmingham, and was named the Asian Network in 1996. It was relaunched nationally on 28 October 2002, via **Digital Audio Broadcasting**. It 2006, it was the recipient of a large budget increase and for a time had the highest per-listener budget of any radio station run by the **British Broadcasting Corporation (BBC)**. At the same time, with falling audiences, questions were asked relating to its viability, and in March 2010, the **BBC Trust** considered its closure, together with **BBC Radio 6 Music**. Following a strong public reaction, BBC Radio 6 Music was reprieved, although the future of the Asian Network remained in doubt. In March 2011, the BBC cut the station's budget in half, setting an audience target of 600,000 listeners per week. By the end of 2013, **Radio Joint Audience Research** was reporting that the audience had risen from less than half a million the previous year to 668,000.

BBC CHAIRMEN. Since its creation as the **British Broadcasting Company (BBC)** in 1922, the organization has had 19 chairmen who have presided over its board of governors. In 2007, oversight of the corporation shifted from the board of governors to the **BBC Trust**, at which time the title became "chairman of the BBC Trust." The role is limited to a four-year term, with the option of accepting a second term in office. **Michael Lyons** became the first permanent chairman under the new system in 2007. In chronological order, chairmen have been as follows:

Lord Gainford	1922–1927
George Clarendon	1927–1930
Rt. Hon. John Whitley	1930–1935
Viscount Bridgman	1935
R. C. Norman	1935–1939
Sir Allan Powell	1939–1946
Lord Inman	1947
Lord Simon of Wythenshawe	1947–1952
Sir Alexander Cadogan	1952–1957
Sir Arthur fforde	1957–1964
Lord Normanbrook	1964–1967
Lord Hill	1967–1973
Sir Michael Swann	1973–1980
George Howard	1980–1983
Stuart Young	1983–1986
Marmaduke Hussey	1986–1996
Christopher Bland	1996–2001
Gavyn Davies	2001–2004
Michael Grade	2004–2006
Chitra Bharucha (acting)	2006–2007
Michael Lyons	2007–2011
Chris Patten	2011–2014
Diana Coyle (acting)	2014 (April–September)
Rona Fairhead	2014–

BBC CONCERT ORCHESTRA. The orchestra was founded in 1952, and for nearly 20 years, from 1970–1989, its principal conductor was Ashley Lawrence. Light orchestral and classical **music** are its main staples, and it is the mainstay of the weekly program *Friday Night Is Music Night*, now broadcast on **BBC Radio 2**. In 1989, it performed the entire Gilbert and Sullivan Savoy Operas for the network. The BBC Concert Orchestra can also be heard on occasion on **BBC Radio 3**.

BBC DANCE ORCHESTRA. The history of this institution may be divided into three distinct eras. The first orchestra, led by Jack Payne, made its debut in March 1928, and in the four years of its existence made more than 4,000 broadcasts. In March 1932, the new orchestra made its debut under the baton of Henry Hall, celebrating the opening of the **British Broadcasting Corporation's (BBC)** new headquarters, **Broadcasting House**. One of its most enduring recordings was "The Teddy Bear's Picnic." In September 1937, the orchestra performed under the BBC name for the last time; thereafter it carried Hall's own name and toured widely. The third BBC Dance Orchestra was formed in 1939, shortly after the start of World War II, under the directorship of Billy Ternent. He remained in his post until 1944, when he resigned for health reasons and was replaced by Stanley Black, who led the orchestra for the next nine years.

See also MUSIC.

BBC DIRECTORS-GENERAL. The role of director-general of the **British Broadcasting Corporation (BBC)** dates from 1927 onward and is probably the most important, prestigious, and frequently controversial appointment in British broadcasting. The first director-general of the BBC was **John Reith**, who held the post from the creation of the BBC as a corporation in 1927 until 1938, prior to which he was general manager of the **British Broadcasting Company (BBC)**. From 1942–1943, **Cecil Graves** and **R. W. Foot** jointly served as directors-general, succeeding F. W. Ogilvie, before Foot continued individually in the role for a further year, after Graves became ill. This was the only time such an event occurred. In 2012, **George Entwistle** served the shortest term as director-general in the history of the BBC, resigning after only two months. He was temporarily replaced by **Tim Davie** until **Tony Hall, Baron Hall of Birkenhead**, took up the position on an established basis in April 2013. Incumbents in the position of director-general have been as follows (in chronological order):

John Reith	1927–1938
F. W. Ogilvie	1938–1942
Cecil Graves	1942–1943
R. W. Foot	1942–1944
William Haley	1944–1952

Sir Ian Jacob	1952–1959
Hugh Carleton Greene	1960–1969
Charles Curran	1969–1977
Ian Trethowan	1977–1982
Alastair Milne	1982–1987
Michael Checkland	1987–1992
John Birt	1992–2000
Greg Dyke	2000–2004
Mark Thompson	2004–2012
George Entwistle	September–November 2012
Tim Davie (acting)	November 2012–April 2013
Tony Hall (Baron Hall of Birkenhead)	2013–

BBC DRAMA REPERTORY COMPANY. As early as 1924, playwright George Bernard Shaw advocated the creation of a specific company, run by the **British Broadcasting Company (BBC)**, to support the specialist requirements of radio **drama**. It was not until the start of World War II, in September 1939, that such a company was founded, initially run from Evesham and subsequently, for the duration of World War II, from Manchester. Many distinguished British actors—including Marius Goring, **Valentine Dyall**, and Carleton Hobbs—have been members. Indeed, the BBC Carleton Hobbs competition continues to foster and motivate radio acting talent from Britain's drama schools. In the 1980s, the company was renamed the BBC Radio Drama Company.

See also SERIALS.

BBC FORCES PROGRAMME. A network that operated from 7 January 1940 until February 1944. It was initially created to serve the requirements of the British Armed Forces serving in France, who, it was noted, would benefit from a lighter style of programs than those available domestically on the **BBC Home Service**, which itself had developed through the merging of the **National Programme** and **Regional Programme**. This new form of programming, featuring a more relaxed mix of dance band **music** and **comedy**, became popular with civilian audiences listening in Britain and ultimately fuelled postwar changes in BBC program policy, further strengthened by the network's latter transatlantic style as the **General Forces Programme**.

Among programs that remained household names were many that were developed for specific areas of the armed forces, for example, *Ack-Ack Beer-Beer* for antiaircraft and barrage balloon stations, *Garrison Theatre* for the army, and *Sincerely Yours, Vera Lynn* and *Hi Gang!* for more general forces consumption. There were also programs designed for troops from the Commonwealth, and beginning in 1942, transatlantic material was included for American troops, including *The Jack Benny Program* and *The Bob Hope Show*, leading to concerns in some quarters about the "Americanization" of the **British Broadcasting Corporation**. In 1944, with the buildup in Europe prior to D-Day, the BBC Forces Programme was replaced by the General Forces Programme, with further cooperation from U.S. and Canadian broadcasters. After the end of the war, it morphed into the **Light Programme**.

See also BRITISH FORCES BROADCASTING SERVICE (BFBS); WARTIME BROADCASTING.

BBC HANDBOOK. The public annual report of the **British Broadcasting Corporation (BBC)** was published from 1928–1987, in book form, and is an indispensable source for historians of U.K. broadcasting. Sometimes entitled *BBC Yearbook* or *BBC Annual*, the work is not to be confused with the *Annual Report and Accounts* that have been presented to parliament each year since incorporation in 1927. The handbooks contain a wide variety of articles, statistics, and photographs depicting the life of the BBC. Most follow the same template: a review of the BBC's year, information on notable programs, and other factual information, including the names of senior staff and governors, engineering developments, audience trends, the accounts, and a copy of the BBC's **charter**.

BBC HOME SERVICE. Prior to the outbreak of World War II, **British Broadcasting Corporation (BBC)** radio services consisted of two networks, the **National Programme** and **Regional Programme**. On Friday, 1 September 1939, two days prior to the declaration of war, these were merged into one and called the Home Service. Beginning on 7 January 1940, with the creation of the **BBC Forces Programme**, the name acquired a new significance for listeners. Also at this time, many of the lighter programs were transferred to the Forces Programme to pave the way for the postwar establishment of the **Light Programme**. With the reorganization of radio services under **Frank Gillard** in September 1967, the Home Service was renamed **BBC Radio 4**.

BBC IPLAYER RADIO. The iPlayer Radio is an Internet radio service and software application developed by the **British Broadcasting Corporation (BBC)**. The original iPlayer service, which offered radio and television online, was launched in October 2005, undergoing trials until February 2006. Since then it has gone through a number of changes, including a **smartphone** application carrying BBC radio programs (iPlayer Radio). Until 2014, iPlayer Radio operated as streaming software, offering most BBC radio programs as audio streams available for as many as seven days after the program's original broadcast. Following approval by the **BBC Trust** in May 2013, work began on offering a download service for BBC radio programs; however, due to rights issues affecting certain content, **digital rights management (DRM)** limited availability. In 2014, a new iPlayer Radio download service commenced, offering most BBC radio programs as downloads with DRM.

See also IPOD; MP3; RADIOPLAYER; WEBCASTING.

BBC MONITORING SERVICE. The Monitoring Service, based at Caversham Park Reading since 1943, operates a 24-hour watch on more than 3,000 radio, television, press, Internet, and **news** agency sources, translating from as many as 100 languages. It was created on the eve of World War II as an aid for tracking foreign propaganda. Its first mission was in 1938, when at the request of the Foreign Office, it began monitoring Italian broadcasts to the Middle East, which were being used to undermine the British presence in the region.

Initially based at Evesham, the Monitoring Service produced its first full Summary of World Broadcasts in August 1939, but by the middle of the war, the importance of its work and the employment of 500 monitoring staff necessitated a move to premises at Caversham Park, an English country mansion that had formerly been a school. The Monitoring Service collaborates with its U.S. equivalent, the Foreign Broadcast Information Service in Washington, D.C. Its continuing relevance has been highlighted during numerous global conflicts and upheavals, among them the Cold War, the collapse of communism, and crises in the Persian Gulf and Balkans. Until 2010, it was funded from moneys supplied by the British government's Cabinet Office. The **British Broadcasting Corporation (BBC)** took over funding of the service using part of the **license fee** from the new BBC license fee agreement.

See also WARTIME BROADCASTING.

BBC NORTHERN DANCE ORCHESTRA. In 1951, the **British Broadcasting Corporation (BBC)** formed the Northern Variety Orchestra, and four years later, with the disbanding of the string section of the orchestra, the Northern Dance Orchestra was created. Under its first musical director, Alyn Ainsworth, the band became widely known and respected, and its appearances on such programs as *Make Way for Music* gained it an almost cult status. In the 1960s, with the changing face of popular **music**, a new image was sought, provided by Ainsworth's successor, Bernard Herrman, who rebranded the orchestra as the "NDO." In 1969, with a view to cost cutting, the BBC put forth a plan to disband the NDO. This was met with great animosity from all sides, and questions were even tabled in the House of Commons on the matter. For a time, the corporation maintained the band, but in 1974 it was reorganized as the Northern Radio Orchestra and finally disbanded in 1981.

BBC PHILHARMONIC. The orchestra, which is based in Manchester, has a long and complex history, always linked to broadcasting. In 1922, with the creation of the Manchester station 2ZY, a small orchestra of 12 players, known as the 2ZY Orchestra, was founded. Many significant works—including Edward Elgar's *Enigma Variations* and Gustav Holst's *The Planets*—received their first broadcast performances from this ensemble. In 1926, it was renamed the Northern Wireless Orchestra (NWO).

In 1930, as a result of a **British Broadcasting Corporation (BBC)** decision to establish a national symphony orchestra in the form of the **BBC Symphony Orchestra** and reduce commitment to regional orchestras, the NWO was disbanded and replaced by a small studio ensemble known as the Northern Studio Orchestra. The decision was reversed in 1933, with the creation of the BBC Northern Orchestra, which played at public concerts throughout the region during World War II. During the 1960s, the reputation of the orchestra—now as the Northern Symphony Orchestra—grew, and between 1982–1984, its playing strength was augmented to 90 and it was renamed the BBC Philharmonic.

See also MUSIC.

BBC PROMENADE CONCERTS. Sometimes known as the Henry Wood Promenade Concerts, the BBC Proms, or simply the Proms, this is an eight-week **series** of **music** concerts traditionally held throughout the British summer, mostly in the Royal Albert Hall in London. The series predates the **British Broadcasting Corporation (BBC)**, and indeed broadcasting, having been founded in 1895, when Ernest Newman created the first season in the **Queen's Hall** at Langham Place, close to the site of the current **Broadcasting House** in London. The concerts became associated with conductor Henry Wood, and in 1927, the BBC took over the administration. The link with Wood has been retained in the text on Prom merchandise, which reads, "BBC Music presents the Henry Wood Promenade Concerts."

When the Queen's Hall was destroyed by bombs during World War II, the concerts were moved to their present home, at the Royal Albert Hall in Kensington, London. Within the United Kingdom, the concerts are broadcast live on **BBC Radio 3** and online, while a number are also televised. The famous *Last Night of the Proms* is broadcast to many different countries.

BBC RADIO 1. Britain's first national pop **music** station began broadcasting on 30 September 1967, as part of the streamlining of **British Broadcasting Corporation (BBC)** radio into generic strands. The network was a necessary response to the challenge presented by **pirate radio** and employed many of the personalities who had been heard on such stations as **Radio Caroline** and **Radio London**, including **Tony Blackburn**, who, as breakfast show presenter, was the first voice to be heard on the new network.

Because of needle time restrictions, under its first controller, Robin Scott, the new station was initially something of a compromise; output was shared for a time with **BBC Radio 2**, and the networks separated only for specific programs at certain times of the day. At first heard only on medium wave (**amplitude modulation [AM]**), BBC Radio 1 opened its first **frequency modulation (FM)** frequency, broadcasting alongside its AM transmissions, in 1988. By the end of the decade, it could be heard in stereo by three-quarters of the U.K. population.

By the early 1990s, the network was experiencing a period of crisis partly caused by an upsurge in **commercial radio** success, but also by the fact that there had been little change in personnel on Radio 1 since its creation, and the radio personalities were becoming increasingly out of touch with the youth audience. **Matthew Bannister**, controller of the network, set about redefining its brand image. Many of the old order left, the audience continued to decline, and the last years of the 20th century were difficult.

By 2005, the new controller, **Andy Parfitt**, had consolidated station policy, acutely aware that one of BBC Radio 1's key issues is, and always has been, the balance between being relevant to its core youth audience in terms of music policy and its role as a public service broadcaster. This has resulted in some award-winning **documentary features**, frequently made by independent production companies, highlighting problems of drugs, AIDS, and youth violence. In the spring of 2011, the station was subject to an efficiency review conducted by **John Myers**, the object of which was to identify possible savings and consider best practice in program policy. Also in 2011, Parfitt left the station and was replaced as controller of BBC Radio 1 and **BBC Radio 1Xtra** by **Ben Cooper**, who quickly introduced major changes in staffing and program scheduling, much of which was in place by November 2012.

BBC Radio 1 initially broadcast from continuity suites in **Broadcasting House**. In 1985, the station moved its studios to Egton House, across the road from its former home, and then to **Yalding House** on nearby Great Portland Street in 1996. With the redevelopment of Broadcasting House, the station moved back into the main building in Portland Place, occupying part of the Egton Wing in 2007. This was renamed the **John Peel** Wing in 2012.

See also DISC JOCKEY (DJ).

BBC RADIO 1XTRA. This station, a sister service to BBC Radio 1, was launched on 16 August 2002, and focuses on urban music. Its audience demographic is lower than BBC Radio 1, and the output is aimed at an age group between 15 and 30 years old.

BBC RADIO 2. Created at the same time as **BBC Radio 1**, the network replaced the old **Light Programme** and brought with it many of the **features** and programs from that network. Since September 1967, the station has frequently been in the vanguard of U.K. radio broadcasting; in January 1979, it was the first **British Broadcasting Corporation (BBC)** network to broadcast a 24-hour schedule. In August 1990, it was the first to broadcast on **frequency modulation (FM)** only.

For some years, BBC Radio 2 had a somewhat staid reputation on the BBC network as being designed for an older generation. It was in January 1996, with the appointment of Controller **James Moir**, that this began to change. Moir began cleverly rebuilding the network into the most-listened-to radio station in the country, combining **music** interest for an audience disenfranchised by the reduced age of the target audience on BBC Radio 1, while retaining the loyalty of older listeners.

In May 2002, BBC Radio 2 won the Sony Gold Award for Station of the Year for the second year running, an achievement it would repeat at the 2005 event. Its hold on the U.K. radio market seemed virtually unassailable under Moir's successor, **Lesley Douglas**, who assumed control in 2004. Douglas also inherited a continuing problem for **commercial radio**, lacking resources but frequently drawing on the same audience. She resigned in 2008, amid controversy surrounding a series of obscene telephone calls made on air by comedian Russell Brand and **Jonathan Ross**, and was replaced by **Bob Shennan**.

In 2006, the station moved its studios from **Broadcasting House** to the nearby Western House. In 2011, BBC Radio 2 was subjected to an efficiency review conducted by **John Myers**. The network's listenership is predominantly adults age 35 and older, although it has recently begun to attract a younger audience through its music and presentation policy, a fact that has drawn some criticism for its program policies.

See also DISC JOCKEY (DJ).

BBC RADIO 3. In many ways, BBC Radio 3 has come to represent the **British Broadcasting Corporation (BBC)** public service ethic in its most uncompromising form. Created in this name on 30 September 1967, it grew out of former networks; the **Third Programme** had become **Network Three**, and the cultural high tone was retained for this new incarnation.

BBC Radio 3 is the greatest patron of the arts—particularly **music**—within the BBC, with a high proportion of its output given to live relays of concerts, frequently by one of the corporation's five orchestras. It also broadcasts **drama** and **features**, and its discussion programs, for instance, *Night Waves*, engage at a high level with arts, culture, and contemporary issues.

Successive controllers have explored the network's identity in various ways. During the **BBC Promenade Concerts**, it is the audio source for accessing each concert, and lately, particularly under controller Roger Wright, it has increasingly explored ethnic music and jazz as part of its output, sometimes to the chagrin of certain elements of its listenership. In 2007, Wright became director of the Proms, in addition to his other duties as controller. The other issue that has made BBC Radio 3 controversial in recent years has been the sheer cost of broadcasting live and recorded concerts involving large orchestral resources.

In 2010, the **BBC Trust** reviewed the station and recommended, among other things, that it become more accessible to new audiences and review the work of the BBC's orchestras. As a result of a capping of the **license fee** and an overall reduction in funding, a BBC paper, *Delivering Quality First*, proposed that BBC Radio 3 broadcast 25 percent fewer live or specially recorded lunchtime concerts and reduce the number of evening concerts specifically recorded or broadcast live. These changes began to be implemented in 2014.

BBC RADIO 4. Evolving out of the old **BBC Home Service** in September 1967, this was the fourth and last station of **Frank Gillard's** generic streaming policy at the time. The United Kingdom's primary speech network, broadcasting a mix of **news**, debate, **features**, **comedy**, and **drama**, it is unique both within the United Kingdom and globally. It has created such innovative work as *The Hitchhiker's Guide to the Galaxy*, alongside programs that have become much-loved institutions, including *The Archers*. Its commitment to drama is extensive, with at least one play broadcast each day of the week.

Successive controllers have become aware of the network's particular relationship with its audience; BBC Radio 4 listeners have always been vocal regarding changes to the station's output. Recent controllers **Helen Boaden** and **Mark Damazer** have been aware of this issue when developing the schedule, seeking to combine adjustments and refinements with a sensitivity to listeners' perceptions and expectations of the network.

BBC Radio 4 remains capable of innovation; it has explored the concept of interactive radio in its drama *The Dark House* and, in 2005, created the opportunity for listeners to download certain programs from its website, "podcasting" Melvin Bragg's intellectual discussion/debate *In Our Time*. The station's success has been referred to by its critics as its most problematic issue; broadcasting to a certain demographic of the United Kingdom, sometimes nicknamed "Middle England," it has historically found it difficult to attract an audience from the younger sector of the U.K. population. Since her appointment in 2010, the current controller, **Gwyneth Williams**, has widened the style of programming and increased the archival aspects of the network, with a major development being its role in *The Listening Project*.

See also CURRENT AFFAIRS; SERIALS; SERIES.

BBC RADIO 4 EXTRA. A digital station originally launched on 15 December 2002 as **BBC Radio 7**. It was rebranded under its present name in April 2011. It is a speech station broadcasting a selection of readings, **comedy**, and **drama** principally drawn from the **BBC Sound Archive**. The station's afternoon output was initially devoted to **children's programs** in two parts, *The Little Toe Radio Show* (later renamed *Cbeebies Radio*), targeting younger children, and *The Big Toe Radio Show*, with content aimed at children eight years of age and older. This policy was subsequently abandoned and a more general schedule adopted.

See also FEATURE; SERIALS; SERIES.

BBC RADIO 5. On 27 August 1990, the day **BBC Radio 2** relinquished its old medium wave (**amplitude modulation [AM]**) frequency, the **British Broadcasting Corporation** used that frequency to create a new radio station, BBC Radio 5. This was a hybrid of **news**, **sports**, and youth speech programming, including some innovative and interesting plays aimed at the teenage market. The lack of brand identity made the network problematic from the start, and audiences remained small. In March 1994, it was relaunched as **BBC Radio 5 Live**.

See also CHILDREN'S PROGRAMS; DRAMA.

BBC RADIO 5 LIVE. This **British Broadcasting Corporation (BBC)** network was born out of controversy in a number of ways. At the same time that **BBC Radio 5** was perceived to be failing, BBC radio was moving toward the idea of a rolling **news** service and had originally earmarked the **BBC Radio 4 longwave** frequency for this purpose. There was, however, considerable opposition to this from listeners in parts of the United Kingdom—and Europe—where there was not adequate **frequency modulation (FM)** reception. Thus, the failure of Radio 5 provided an opportunity to escape this impasse.

Launched on 26 March 1994, BBC Radio 5 Live created a blend of tabloid-like news coverage, magazine programs, and high-quality **sports** coverage. It also developed a strong Web-based identity and, for a time, led the way in terms of the relationship between a radio station and its Web presence.

The coming of digital radio gave listeners the opportunity to hear the station in something other than its **amplitude modulation (AM)** quality, and station chiefs used this new technology to launch an alternative service, BBC Radio 5 Live Sports Extra, an occasional service, enabling the network to cover two major sporting events simultaneously. In 2008, the BBC announced that the station would move out of London, and its broadcast home is now **MediaCityUK** in Salford, Greater Manchester.

See also CURRENT AFFAIRS.

BBC RADIO 5 LIVE SPORTS EXTRA. *See* BBC RADIO 5 LIVE.

BBC RADIO 6 MUSIC. The first **British Broadcasting Corporation (BBC)** digital **music** station, launched at 7:00 a.m. on 11 March 2002, with **Phill Jupitus's** *Breakfast Show*. The service was widely publicized as the "first new BBC music station for 32 years." When it was first proposed in October 2000, it was code-named "Network Y." It was officially known as "6 Music" from its launch until April 2011. The station controllership is shared with **BBC Radio 2**. Thus, at the time of its launch, the controller was **James Moir**.

In February 2010, there were suggestions that the station, together with the **BBC Asian Network**, should close due to lack of public awareness and low audience figures as part of a proposed cost-cutting review within the BBC. A high-level public campaign was launched to save BBC Radio 6 Music, and audience figures rose as a result. In July 2010, the **BBC Trust** rejected the proposals, and the station's success has continued to grow. With the development of **MediaCityUK** in Salford, Greater Manchester, part of 6 Music's operation was moved north from London in 2011. In April of that year, it was renamed BBC Radio 6 Music, although popularly it is still widely known as 6 Music. In 2012, BBC Radio 6 Music was named station of the year at the **Sony Radio Academy Awards**.

See also DIGITAL AUDIO BROADCASTING (DAB); DISC JOCKEY (DJ).

BBC RADIO 7. As part of the **British Broadcasting Corporation's (BBC)** development of content in **Digital Audio Broadcasting**, BBC Radio 7 was launched in December 2002. Station policy was to broadcast a range of **drama** and **comedy** from the BBC's sound archive, together with newly produced **children's programs**. In April 2011, the station was relaunched as **BBC Radio 4 Extra**.

BBC RADIO INTERNATIONAL. An international operation that syndicates radio programs by selling audio—radio and podcasts—to radio stations and other broadcasting services throughout the world. It is part of **BBC Worldwide**. Content sold thus includes **drama**; **documentaries**; and rock, popular, and classical **music** in concert form (for instance, the **BBC Promenade Concerts**).
See also BBC TRANSCRIPTION SERVICES.

BBC RADIO ORCHESTRA. The Radio Orchestra was formed in 1964, by combining the **BBC Revue Orchestra** and **BBC Variety Orchestra**. This made it a considerable musical force of 56 players, and under joint musical directors Malcolm Lockyer and Paul Fenoulhet, it created a familiar sound and was a major contributor to the **BBC Radio 2** output into the 1980s, finally being led by Iain Sutherland. It had also been conducted by Robert Farnon at its first public concert in 1971, among other occasions. In 1988, the orchestra played at a gala banquet in the presence of Prince Edward, but it was disbanded two years later as a cost-cutting measure.
See also MUSIC.

BBC RADIOPHONIC WORKSHOP. Formed in March 1958, as a response to growing requirements for sonic innovation within radio **drama**, the Radiophonic Workshop fostered some remarkable talents, including **Delia Derbyshire**, David Cain, and John Baker, among others. It also created distinctive sounds for both radio and television until its demise in 1996.
All That Fall by **Samuel Beckett**, written in 1956, for the **Third Programme**, and broadcast in 1957, epitomized the sound climate into which the workshop was born. Out of this production came others, notably *The Disagreeable Oyster* by **Giles Cooper**, which required sound to be treated as a caricatured style of an audio cartoon. The lessons learned here translated to the logical creation of the workshop in 1958.
In 1978, workshop member Paddy Kingsland was involved in possibly the most notable of its accomplishments—the creation of the sound universe for *The Hitchhiker's Guide to the Galaxy* by **Douglas Adams**. In April 1979,

the Radiophonic Workshop produced its own history for **BBC Radio 3**, *We Have Also Soundhouses*, a title borrowed from Francis Bacon's treatise *The New Atlantis*.

BBC RADIO SCOTLAND. Radio Scotland is the **British Broadcasting Corporation's** national English-language station for Scotland. The name had been used since 1974, to identify the Scottish opt-out of **BBC Radio 4**, although the station was not established as a full-time network until 1978. It is not to be confused with the offshore **pirate radio** station **Radio Scotland**.

BBC REVUE ORCHESTRA. An orchestra of 28 players, this group played for many variety programs in the 1940s and 1950s. It joined with the **BBC Variety Orchestra** in 1964 to form the **BBC Radio Orchestra**.
   See also MUSIC.

BBC SCOTTISH SYMPHONY ORCHESTRA. An orchestra founded by composer and conductor Ian Whyte in 1935, as the first full-time musical ensemble in Scotland. Growing from a small studio orchestra, one of many employed in its early years by the **British Broadcasting Corporation** throughout Britain, Whyte's vision—of a Scottish symphony orchestra that would play **music** by contemporary Scottish composers—bore fruit with the growth of the orchestra into the formidable force it had become by the time of his death in 1960. An award for young composers was established in his honor, and the group's ability to play contemporary music with a unique commitment has made it renowned among composers and audiences alike.

BBC SINGERS. A choir that dates back to 1924, when Stanford Robinson was engaged as the **British Broadcasting Corporation's** first chorus master at **Savoy Hill**. One of his first acts was to establish the Wireless Chorus, which made its debut with a broadcast performance of Rutland Boughton's *The Immortal Hour*. In 1927, an offshoot of eight performers became the Wireless Singers. When the ***Daily Service*** began in 1928, this ensemble was to be a regular part of it. In 1934, Leslie Woodgate became chorus master and held the post for more than 25 years.
   During World War II, the Singers were evacuated, first to Bristol and then to Bangor and Bedford. In 1943, they performed at the famous National Gallery concerts in London, and in 1945, the group took part in the first performance of Francis Poulenc's *Figure Humaine*. By 1950, now named the BBC Singers, they had built an international reputation through foreign tours, and when Woodgate died in 1961, to be succeeded by Peter Gellhorn, they were renamed the BBC Chorus. During the 1960s, they began a long and fruitful relationship with French composer and conductor Pierre Boulez.

John Poole was appointed chorus master in 1971, reforming and renaming the BBC Chorus with the name it has borne since—the BBC Singers. In September 2014, the choir celebrated its 90th anniversary with an evening of special programs on **BBC Radio 3**.

See also MUSIC.

BBC SOUND ARCHIVE. Founded in 1936, by **Marie Slocombe**, a resource that includes thousands of recordings, many of which date from long before the birth of radio. Most, however, are of **British Broadcasting Corporation (BBC)** broadcasts and include many of the most historic moments of contemporary history. There are also recordings of **drama** and **music**, and a number of these have been made commercially available through the BBC's own marketing arms. There is a continuing argument for more public sharing of this collection, and the BBC has been exploring ways in which it might be made more accessible. Copyright has been an inhibiting factor; on the other hand, there have been a number of occasions when the BBC itself has successfully sought help from the listening public in locating "lost" recordings from its own past.

The archive houses approximately 350,000 hours of output, and approximately 66 percent of radio output is retained, although **disc jockey**–based music shows, **local radio**, and **BBC World Service** output are less prioritized. Access to part of the archive, including material from the developing *Listening Project*, is made available to researchers through the facilities of the **British Library Sound Archive**.

BBC SYMPHONY ORCHESTRA. Founded in 1930, its first principal conductor was Sir Adrian Boult, who directed the orchestra until 1950. During World War II, the group was evacuated to Bedford. It has always retained a commitment to contemporary **music** and since its foundation has given premieres of more than 1,000 works by such composers as Béla Bartók, Benjamin Britten, Paul Hindemith, Gustav Holst, Igor Stravinsky, Dmitri Shostakovich, and Ralph Vaughan Williams. It is the resident orchestra for the BBC Henry Wood Promenade Concerts each year, making at least a dozen appearances, including the first and last nights.

BBC THEATER ORGAN. During the interwar years, coinciding with the growth of interest in theater organs in the great cinemas of the time, the **British Broadcasting Corporation (BBC)** introduced its own instrument. The first broadcast was from St. George's Hall in October 1936. The first resident organist was **Reginald Foort**, who was replaced in 1938 by **Sandy Macpherson**. The original organ was destroyed in the Blitz of 1941. Thereafter, the BBC purchased Foort's own instrument, and it began its career in

Jubilee Hall in London in 1946. There continues to be a following and enthusiasm for popular organ **music** from the BBC, as evidenced by the longevity of the weekly **BBC Radio 2** show *The Organist Entertains*, which began in 1969.

BBC TRANSCRIPTION SERVICES. The BBC Transcription Services began during the 1930s to license **British Broadcasting Corporation (BBC)** programs to overseas broadcasters, granting authority for broadcast for approximately three years for a fee. Originally called the London Transcription Service, the unit produced material on 12-inch 78-rpm discs. A complete program would usually require several such discs segued by a technical operator. In 1947, these were replaced by 16-inch discs that ran at a slower speed. The survival of a number of BBC programs from the pre–postwar era and immediate postwar era has been due to the preservation of such recordings. The BBC Transcription Services library was housed at various locations in London during its existence. The work begun by the unit still continues in the form of **BBC Radio International**, part of **BBC Worldwide**. Material is now stored at the BBC Archive Centre in Perivale. For public research, however, access is at the **British Library Sound Archive**, where approximately 20,000 programs and extracts are housed within the onsite BBC Transcription Discs collection.

BBC TRUST. The governing body of the **British Broadcasting Corporation (BBC)**, the BBC Trust is independent of BBC management and any other external body. It operates with the aim of working for the best interests of **license fee** payers within the United Kingdom. It was established under the Royal Charter of 2006 and went into effect on 1 January 2007. With a formalized executive board, it replaced the former BBC Board of Governors. Its main roles are to set the overall strategic direction and priorities of the BBC and maintain an overview of the work of the Executive Board of the BBC.

See also BBC CHAIRMEN.

BBC VARIETY ORCHESTRA. An ensemble of 28 players, this orchestra serves the same purpose—providing mostly incidental **music** for **British Broadcasting Corporation** variety shows and **series**—as the **BBC Revue Orchestra**, with which it combined in 1964, to form the **BBC Radio Orchestra**.

BBC WORLD SERVICE. From the early days of the **British Broadcasting Company (BBC)**, there was interest in creating a broadcasting service that could link the British Empire. The development of **shortwave (SW)** was a key technical element in making this connection, and although the main advances in SW came during the 1920s, the BBC was not financially in a position to undertake such a task. Given that the **license fee** provided U.K. listeners with a service, **John Reith** initially argued that the British public should not be required to fund a service beyond the domestic confines of broadcasting. This view was reversed in 1931, as in the throes of a financial crisis, the creation of such a service was deemed to be in the national interest. On 19 December 1932, the **Empire Service** was opened, and on Christmas Day, King George V spoke to the British Empire for the first time.

The service operated through five separate two-hour transmissions at different times of the day, aimed at specific areas of the world. Transmission gradually increased, and by September 1939, it was operating 18 hours a day. Programs were frequently rebroadcasts or relays of domestic shows, although beginning in 1934, there was a specific News Department. The first programs broadcast in a language other than English were those of the **BBC Arabic Service**, which began January 1938; later that same year, broadcasts in French, German, and Italian were added, countering the increasing number of propaganda broadcasts coming from Europe at the time. The United Kingdom carried out a considerable amount of overseas **wartime broadcasting**, and the BBC took over the **J. Walter Thompson** radio studios at **Bush House** in London to accommodate these transmissions.

It was between 1939–1945 that the title "Empire Service" was abolished and replaced by the General Overseas Service. With the election of a postwar Labour government, the decision was made to continue the multilanguage services that had been established, funded by the government but with content selected by the BBC. This was the basis on which the newly titled "External Services" were built and the key element that has established the global uniqueness of the service itself.

Nonetheless, the postwar years were difficult, featuring spending cuts brought about by economic depression and a serious confrontation between the Anthony Eden government and the BBC regarding the 1956 Suez Crisis, during which the BBC's determination to broadcast both sides of the argument raised, for a short time, the possibility of the BBC coming under direct government control. Other issues emerged with the development of the Cold War with the Soviet Union, and the reputation of the BBC for impartial reporting of world events at a time when propaganda continued to be rife was a major factor—coupled with the application of the **transistor** to receiver technology—in the growth of the listenership. In 1965, the General Overseas Service was renamed the World Service, and in 1988, the title was extended to include all external services of the BBC.

In 1991, the BBC World Service moved into television and today broadcasts as BBC World. In radio, the development of satellite technology has enabled **frequency modulation (FM)** relays in many areas of the world.

Added to this, in 1995, the BBC's Polish Service was the first to go online, which subsequently increased to cover all 43 languages covered by the service, in addition to English. BBC World now broadcasts 24 hours a day in English and for varying durations in its other languages. Between 2005–2011, many of its international language services were forced to close due to financial considerations. In 2012, the lease expired on Bush House, and this, together with the redevelopment of **Broadcasting House**, prompted a move in the service's radio production for the first time in many years. Until April 2014, the service was funded by grant aid through the Foreign and Commonwealth Office of the British Government. Since then, funding has been drawn from provisions taken from the United Kingdom's compulsory television **license fee** imposed on television-owning households, in common with other BBC services.

BBC WORLDWIDE. Created in 1995, from its predecessor, BBC Enterprises, BBC Worldwide Ltd. is a wholly owned commercial subsidiary of the **British Broadcasting Corporation (BBC)**. Its purpose is to sell BBC programming and related services abroad to supplement **license fee** income. Historically, the origins of this concept came from the **BBC Transcription Services** in the 1930s, which licensed BBC radio material to overseas broadcasters. In 1979, the department became BBC Enterprises. One of its key radio operations is **BBC Radio International.**

BBC WRITTEN ARCHIVE CENTRE. Housed at Caversham, Reading, the center houses thousands of files, scripts, memos, and working papers dating back to the formation of the **British Broadcasting Company (BBC)**, together with information relating to programs and broadcasting history. Academics and accredited researchers can visit the center to study these resources. It is now funded by the **license fee.**

BECKETT, SAMUEL (1906–1989). Radio was, in many ways, an ideal medium for the great Irish playwright, and Samuel Beckett created many works for the **Third Programme** and **BBC Radio 3**. Some fine examples of his poetry, prose, and plays were written specifically for the medium, including the 1957 work *All That Fall*.
See also DRAMA.

BEERLING, JOHNNY (1937–). During a long, varied, and distinguished career in British broadcasting, Johnny Beerling was often at the forefront of the industry's **music** development. Beginning as a technical operator with **British Broadcasting Corporation (BBC)** radio in 1957, he became a studio manager and then producer for the **Light Programme**. When **BBC**

Radio 1 was created, Beerling devised the first jingle package, recruited many of the presentation team, and produced the first program with **Tony Blackburn**. In 1971, he devised the first **documentaries** on the network, establishing a long tradition, and in 1973, he conceived and launched the program for which he became most remembered, *The Radio 1 Roadshow*. He became controller of BBC Radio 1 in 1985.

In 1993, Beerling left the BBC to work as a broadcasting consultant for both radio and television, and he continues to be active as a freelance producer. In 1997 and 1998, he worked with Mark Tully on **Unique Broadcasting's** *Something Understood* and produced an audio cassette, *Kenny Everett at the Beeb*, for **BBC Worldwide**. In 2001, on behalf of Unique Broadcasting Company, he acted as consultant on the acquisition of the Classic Gold digital stations.

Beerling has been chairman of the **Radio Data System** Forum, an international body that coordinates the interests of the world's broadcasters and radio manufacturers involved in data broadcasting. In May 1993, he received a **Sony Radio Academy Award** for his outstanding services to the radio industry. His autobiography, *In Search of 1's Navel*, was published in 2007, to coincide with the 40th anniversary of BBC Radio 1.

BELFRAGE, BRUCE (1900–1974). Bruce Belfrage was an actor who joined the **British Broadcasting Corporation (BBC)** in 1936, as **drama** booking manager, and who, at the outbreak of war, took up the role of radio newsreader. He became widely known due to the BBC's security policy of newsreaders identifying themselves by name. Belfrage was on air in October 1940, when a delayed action bomb exploded in **Broadcasting House**, killing seven members of the staff. He enlisted in the Royal Navy in 1942 and, after the war, entered politics, joining the Liberal Party.

See also ANNOUNCERS; NEWS; WARTIME BROADCASTING.

BENN, TONY (1925–2014). Tony Benn, a Labour Party politician, had a long and varied association with radio, beginning as a producer in the **British Broadcasting Corporation's** North American Service from 1949–1950, prior to fighting—and winning—the Bristol Southeast parliamentary seat for the Labour Party. In 1967, as postmaster general in the Harold Wilson government, he was instrumental in the creation of the **Marine, and c., Broadcasting (Offences) Act 1967**, which outlawed offshore **pirate radio** stations, of which he was an active and extremely vocal opponent. An accomplished broadcaster himself, Benn recorded his own audio diaries throughout the years. He died after a long illness, having suffered a stroke in 2012.

BENTINE, MICHAEL (1922–1996). After Royal Air Force service in World War II, comedian Michael Bentine developed his surreal sense of humor into a stage act that won him considerable success, including several seasons at the London Palladium. In 1951, he was one of the founding members of the radio show *Crazy People*, which later became **The Goon Show**. Bentine withdrew from the program after the second **series**, claiming the original concept behind it had changed. Thereafter, he resumed his solo career, initially making *The Bumblies*, a comic program that was equally appealing to children and adults. He then moved into television, creating a range of anarchic programs, including many for children, which won him a wide following. He also wrote three volumes of an autobiography, five novels, four books relating to psychic phenomena, and five children's books. Bentine was awarded the title Commander of the Most Excellent Order of the British Empire (C.B.E.) in 1995.

See also COMEDY.

BENZIE, ISA (1902–1988). Glasgow-born Isa Benzie joined the **British Broadcasting Corporation (BBC)** as a secretary in 1927. In 1933, as director of the Foreign Department, she took responsibility for a range of negotiations and cultural exchanges with overseas stations, listening to output and liaising with regard to program matters with broadcasters from throughout the world. When she married John Royston Morley, one of the BBC's first television producers, in 1937, she was forced to temporarily leave the corporation due to the Reithian rule stipulating that spouses could not both work for the BBC. She returned when the ban was lifted during World War II.

From 1943–1964, Benzie produced **talks** chiefly for the **BBC Home Service**. One of her preoccupations of this time was to find a means of expression for **women** seeking to combine motherhood with a career. In 1957, she was central to the creation of the *Today* program, which she conceived and named. With friend and contemporary **Janet Quigley**, she developed the early style of the program. Benzie was the program's first editor, although her official title was "senior producer." She retired in 1964.

BERNARD, RALPH (1953–). Prior to the merger of **Great Western Radio (GWR)** and **Capital Radio** into **GCap Media** in May 2005, Ralph Bernard was executive chairman of GWR. He trained as a journalist and, after agency and newspaper work early in his career, became one of the original newsroom staff at Radio Hallam in Sheffield in 1975. His pioneering radio **documentaries**—among the first in independent local radio—include the award-winning *Dying for a Drink*, a five-part dramatized documentary on alcoholism. Bernard joined Hereward Radio as head of **news**, moving to

Wiltshire Sound as program controller in 1982; three months after the station went on air, he became managing director and, later, chief executive. It was from here that the GWR Group began.

In 1991, Bernard formulated the proposal that eventually led to **Classic FM** winning the independent national radio license, in which GWR took an initial 17 percent interest. It later bought out the remaining 83 percent of the shares. As well as being chief executive of GWR, he became chief executive of Classic FM in 1996, in addition to his GWR responsibilities. With the creation of the new radio group—then the United Kingdom's largest **commercial radio** organization—in May 2005, Bernard became executive chairman of GCap Media. In 2008, he left the company and, in 2013, formed the independent radio and theater production company Quidem. He holds the title Commander of the Most Excellent Order of the British Empire for his services to the U.K. radio industry.

See also FEATURE; MUSIC.

BEVERIDGE COMMITTEE. *See* BEVERIDGE REPORT (CMND 8116 REPORT OF THE BROADCASTING COMMITTEE, 1949, CHAIRMAN, LORD BEVERIDGE).

BEVERIDGE REPORT (CMND 8116 REPORT OF THE BROAD-CASTING COMMITTEE, 1949, CHAIRMAN, LORD BEVERIDGE). An important report relating to the preservation of the **British Broadcasting Corporation (BBC)** monopoly in British broadcasting and the potential for commercial enterprise, presented to the British Parliament in January 1951. In many respects, it was to predict many of the changes in British media throughout the next 50 years. Beveridge reviewed the debate relating to the preservation of the broadcasting monopoly and the possibility of the introduction of commercial television. At the time, the report recommended the continuing existence of a broadcasting monopoly and was against advertising and sponsorship of programs.

A minority report by Conservative Party member of parliament Selwyn Lloyd disagreed with the findings. This report proposed the creation of a Commission for British Broadcasting to oversee the BBC as a radio broadcaster, a British Television Corporation, a number of other national commercial broadcasters for radio and television, and the provision for a potentially large number of local radio stations.

BEYOND OUR KEN. A **comedy series** that began in July 1958 and ran until 1964. It was scripted by Eric Merriman and Barry Took, and produced by Jacques Brown. The program starred **Kenneth Horne**, **Kenneth Williams**, Hugh Paddick, and Betty Marsden. In the first run, the cast also included Ron

Moody and Stanley Unwin, who left before the second run, to be replaced by Bill Pertwee. The format was later revamped with the same ensemble as *Round the Horne*.

BHARUCHA, CHITRA (1945–). Chitra Bharucha is a former vice chairman of the **BBC Trust**, the governing body of the **British Broadcasting Corporation (BBC)**. Originally from a medical background, she was appointed to various boards in the media industry between 1996–2004, including the BBC Broadcasting Council for Northern Ireland, the Independent Television Commission, and the Advertising Standards Authority, before being appointed vice chairman of the BBC Trust in October 2006, when this body replaced the BBC Board of Governors. As deputy to **Michael Grade**, she succeeded him as acting **BBC chairman** on 1 November 2006, when he resigned, holding the post until the appointment of **Michael Lyons** on 1 May 2007, when Bharucha returned to her role of vice chairman until standing down on 31 October 2010.

BIG BEN. The name given to the main bell in the clock tower of the Palace of Westminster, home of British Parliament. It has long been part of **British Broadcasting Corporation (BBC)** radio output, first broadcast in 1923, and the chimes continue to be heard "live" prior to certain broadcasts, including the 6:00 p.m. **news** on **BBC Radio 4**. For a time during the 1930s, it was also relayed from a loudspeaker behind the clock on **Broadcasting House**. It is also heard on the **BBC World Service** and, in 1932, was voted the most popular broadcast by BBC overseas listeners.

BILLY COTTON BAND SHOW. A highly popular entertainment program initially broadcast on the **Light Programme** in February 1949. It featured a blend of **comedy** songs sung by Alan Breeze, as well as more romantic fare, originally by Doreen Stephens (later replaced by Kathy Kay), linked by band leader **Billy Cotton** himself. The show ran until October 1968 and became a staple of the nation's Sunday lunchtime listening with its familiar theme "Somebody Stole My Gal." It also transferred successfully to television.
See also MUSIC; SERIES.

BINAURAL RECORDING. A highly specific method of stereo recording that seeks to replicate the conditions of actual human hearing. Usually using a model of the human head, microphones are placed where the ears would be located. It is a complex procedure and most often used in programs requiring specialist effects. From the listener's point of view, binaural stereo is best experienced using headphones rather than loudspeakers.
See also BLUMLEIN, ALAN (1903–1942).

BIRDSONG. A temporary **Digital Audio Broadcasting (DAB)** channel of continuous birdsong, originally recorded in Wiltshire in 1991. First used as a test signal on some **analog** radio stations prior to transmission, it was later heard from time to time on DAB as an interim holding signal for vacant channels within the **Digital One multiplex**. Thus, it replaced certain stations when they ceased broadcasting until the relevant channel could be occupied again. It proved surprisingly popular with listeners, at times more so than the station it replaced, and a high proportion of the audience complained when it was removed.

See also COMMERCIAL RADIO; MUSIC.

BIRT, JOHN (1944–). Subsequently Sir John Birt and Lord Birt of Liverpool, John Birt came to the **British Broadcasting Corporation (BBC)** from London Weekend Television in 1987, as deputy director-general, with special responsibility for **news** and **current affairs**. With **Michael Checkland**, he devised the concept of Producer Choice, an internal market system that offered producers the choice between using internal facilities or external suppliers. Shortly after he replaced Checkland as director-general, Birt was criticized when it became known that he had joined the BBC as a freelancer contracted to the corporation through a personal company. As a result, he became a staff member, and as director-general beginning in 1992, he oversaw the development of digital and online services and pursued further areas of restructuring, including the separation of broadcasting and commissioning.

Although his style of management was unpopular with many staff members, Birt was undoubtedly responsible for giving the BBC a secure place in the emerging digital world of broadcasting, and he gained a favorable **license fee** settlement. He resigned to become the first director-general since **John Reith** to sit in the House of Lords.

BLACKBURN, TONY (1943–). After early aspirations to become a singer, Tony Blackburn joined the **pirate radio** station **Radio Caroline** South as a **disc jockey** in July 1964. He transferred to rival pirate station **Radio London** in 1966, and after a short spell on the **Light Programme's** *Midday Spin*, he was, as breakfast show presenter, the first broadcaster on air when **BBC Radio 1** launched in September 1967. In 1980, Blackburn took over the Saturday morning children's request program *Junior Choice* prior to joining **Radio London** to present *Morning Soul* in 1984. He subsequently returned to **commercial radio**, working for such stations as **Capital Gold**, Jazz FM, **Classic Gold**, and **Smooth Radio**. In 2010, he made a number of one-off appearances on **BBC Radio 2**, which presaged a more permanent engagement when he replaced Dale Winton as host of the long-running *Pick of the Pops* program on the network.

See also MUSIC.

BLACKMORE, TIM (1944–). Beginning his radio career as a studio manager and **announcer**, Tim Blackmore was part of the team that helped launch **BBC Radio 1** in 1967. Among many programs for the network, he wrote and produced the 26-part **series** *The Story of Pop* before leaving to join **Capital Radio** in 1977. During the next six years, he served as head of **music** and then head of programs. In 1984, Blackmore was appointed as the first director of the **Radio Academy**, a position he vacated in 1989, when, with Simon Cole, he launched the **Unique Broadcasting Company**, providing independent productions for the United Kingdom's **commercial radio** sector, moving into independent production for BBC radio in 1999. That same year, the company floated on the stock market as UBC Media Group.

In 2004, Blackmore resigned from the staff of UBC Media and was appointed the group's consultant editorial director. In addition to his radio work, he wrote and produced the Brit Awards show for four years and the Ivor Novello Awards show for 21 years. Beginning in 1983, he managed the career of **Alan Freeman** until Freeman's death in 2006. Blackmore has previously been the chair of the radio industry's Sony Radio Awards Committee and was succeeded in this role by **John Myers**. In 1994, he was awarded a fellowship at the Radio Academy and, in 1999, received the award of Member of the Most Excellent Order of the British Empire for his services to independent radio production. In January 2009, Blackmore succeeded **Gillian Reynolds** as chair of the **Charles Parker Archive Trust**, a position he relinquished in October 2014, and in which he was in turn succeeded by **Mary Kalemkerian**.

BLAND, CHRISTOPHER (1938–). Sir Francis Christopher Buchan Bland, knighted in 1993, served on the boards of both the Independent Broadcasting Authority and London Weekend Television prior to becoming chairman of the **British Broadcasting Corporation** in 1996. He had disagreements with the Conservative Party regarding the appointment of a Labour Party donor, **Greg Dyke**, to the position of director-general. He resigned in 2001 to become chairman of British Telecom.

BLATTNERPHONE. During the 1920s, German Louis Blattner developed a concept pioneered by Kurt Stille for the magnetic recording of sound on metal. Blattner was, for a time, manager of the Gaiety Cinema in Manchester and used early versions of his machine as an attraction for members of the public, who could pay to hear a recording of their own voice.

In the late 1920s, The British Blattnerphone (Stille System) Company Ltd. was formed, and studios were set up in Elstree. In 1929, **British Broadcasting Corporation** engineers witnessed a demonstration of his recording method and were sufficiently impressed that they arranged for a research trial. The machine subsequently entered service at **Savoy Hill**, and the *BBC Yearbook* for 1932 (covering November 1930 to October 1931) claimed the device to be "in some ways the most important event of the year." In 1934, **Val Gielgud** and Holt Marvell used the Blattnerphone as the key plot element in their novel *Death at Broadcasting House*.

See also MARCONI-STILLE SYSTEM.

BLETCHLEY PARK. Situated in Buckinghamshire, Bletchley Park was the headquarters of the United Kingdom's Government Code and Cypher School (GC and CS) during World War II. The department was charged with decoding the secret communications of the Axis powers, and a particular success was the breaking of the Enigma and Lorenz ciphers. The site is now an educational and historical public attraction and home to the **National Radio Centre**, operated by the **Radio Society of Great Britain**.

BLUE JAM. A late-night **comedy** program created, directed, and part-presented by **Chris Morris**. Broadcast in the early hours of the morning on **BBC Radio 1** from 1979–1999, the show's mixture of **music**, synthesized voices, and surreal monologues brought it cult status and spawned CD, film, and television versions.

BLUMLEIN, ALAN (1903–1942). An electronics engineer by profession, Alan Blumlein was born in London and received a B.Sc. in electrical technology from Imperial College in London in 1923. He first worked conducting research into telephone technology and, in 1929, joined the Columbia Graphophone Company, which later became part of Electrical and Musical Industries (EMI) in 1931. At EMI, Blumlein worked to develop new recording techniques, his most notable invention being "binaural sound," which later became known as stereo. Blumlein's thinking was based on the concept that the positioning of the human ears means that sound is received with slightly differing perspectives. He incorporated this principle into an electronic system using two output speakers to reproduce the effect.

In the late 1930s, Blumlein applied some of the ideas developed from his binaural sound system into research relating to radar. On 7 June 1942, he was killed in a plane crash while experimenting with this technology. Although he was only 39 at the time of his death, he had amassed no less than 128 patents during his short career.

See also BINAURAL RECORDING.

BOADEN, HELEN (1956–). Helen Boaden is director of radio for the **British Broadcasting Corporation (BBC)**. Prior to this she was director of **news** from 2004–2013 and controller of **BBC Radio 4** from 2000–2004. She began her radio career in the United Kingdom at Radio Tees and Radio Aire before joining the BBC in 1983 as a news producer at Radio Leeds. She later became a reporter and subsequently editor of the Radio 4 **current affairs** program *File on Four*. Boaden presented *Woman's Hour* from Manchester, as well as a wide range of **features** and **documentaries**, winning a number of awards before becoming head of Business Programs in 1997 and, a year later, head of Current Affairs, the first woman to hold the post. In September 2004, she left Radio 4 to assume the role of director of BBC News.

In December 2012, Boaden temporarily stepped down from this position while the results of **Operation Yewtree**, the police investigation into allegations of sexual abuse by the late **Jimmy Savile** and others, were investigated. A second investigation launched by the BBC into possible management failings within the corporation in the handling of the Savile story led to the Pollard Report, which criticized a number of senior BBC staff, including Boaden, for the handling of the affair. Boaden resumed her duties as director of BBC News, but on 2 April 2013, she was appointed by the BBC's new director-general, **Tony Hall**, as director of radio. In this role she has overall responsibility for **BBC Radio 1**; **BBC Radio 2**; **BBC Radio 3**; **BBC Radio 4**; and the BBC digital radio stations **BBC Radio 1Xtra**, **BBC Radio 6 Music**, **BBC Radio 4 Extra**, and the **BBC Asian Network**. She also oversees the three BBC orchestras in England, the **BBC Singers**, and the **BBC Promenade Concerts**; classical **music** and performance television, factual radio, and radio **drama** production are all within her remit in the radio production department.

BOOK AT BEDTIME. A late-night **series** that began on the **Light Programme** in August 1949, growing out of an experiment in January of that year entitled *Late Night Serial*, when Arthur Bush read *The Three Hostages* by John Buchan. The concept involves dividing a book into a number of 15-minute readings, broadcast at the same time on successive evenings. By so doing, the program predicted the development of "talking books" and similar latter-day attempts at broadcast readings on such stations as **Oneword Radio** and **BBC Radio 7**. The first book to be read was Sir Arthur Conan Doyle's Sherlock Holmes story "The Speckled Band," read by Laidman Browne.

The program continues in the late evening on **BBC Radio 4**. Although the premise behind the program—that of a straight reading—has never changed, the time of transmission has, relating to the broadcasters' perceptions of British nocturnal listening habits. Originally transmitted at 11:00 p.m., it has been broadcast at 10:15 p.m. and, since 1989, 10:45 p.m.

See also TALKS.

BOOKSHELF. A **BBC Radio 4 series** in which authors were interviewed about their life and work. It ran from 1978–1993, and the first presenter was **Frank Delaney**.

BORDER RADIO HOLDINGS. A subsidiary company of Border Television, which had been formed to provide a television service for the England/Scottish border area and launched in 1961. In 1993, Border moved into radio with the launch of a station in central Scotland—Scot FM—which it ran in partnership with Grampian Television. In 1994, it launched **Century Radio**, run by **John Myers** and **John Simons** in the North East of England, with other stations following during the 1990s. Border Radio Holdings was created in 1997, to manage these developing interests. In April 2001, **Capital Radio** bought Border Radio Holdings, subsequently to become subsumed itself into **Global Radio**.

See also COMMERCIAL RADIO; INDEPENDENT LOCAL RADIO (ILR); MUSIC.

BOYLE, JAMES (1946–). James Boyle was a controversial controller of **BBC Radio 4**, succeeding **Michael Green** in 1996. Born in Scotland and coming from an academic background, he joined the **British Broadcasting Corporation (BBC)** in 1975 as further education officer in Scotland and Northern Ireland. In 1983, after a period as further education officer in Southwest England, he became manager of educational radio at **BBC Radio Scotland** in 1983 and, in 1985 was appointed head of educational broadcasting for Scotland. In 1992, Boyle became head of Radio Scotland, and under his leadership, Radio Scotland was named U.K. Radio Station of the Year at the 1994 **Sony Radio Academy Awards**.

During his time as controller of BBC Radio 4, Boyle radically reshaped the schedule and introduced a wide-ranging study of listener habits that informed production decisions and scheduling in a way not previously seen at the network. He left Radio 4 in 2000, upon his retirement from the BBC, and was succeeded by **Helen Boaden**.

BRADEN, BERNARD (1916–1993). Bernard Braden was born in Vancouver, Canada, and was a successful actor, singer, **announcer**, and writer on Canadian radio before becoming a household name in the United Kingdom. He moved to Great Britain permanently with his wife, Barbara Kelly, in 1949, Braden himself having first come to the United Kingdom on behalf of Canadian radio in 1947. From that time onward, the couple became highly popular in British radio and later television.

Among many programs in which Bernard was involved, the most important was *Breakfast with Braden*, a fast-moving **comedy** show written by **Frank Muir** and **Denis Norden** dating from 1950. Later in the year, it was moved from the **Light Programme** schedule to an evening slot, becoming *Bedtime with Braden*, and it was during this version of the program that Kelly joined the cast. Braden also appeared as an actor in many West End theater productions. He received many awards, including the BAFTA Features Personality Award, and was named the British Variety Club Light Entertainment Personality. In 1955, he was made honorary chancellor of the London School of Economics.

See also SERIES.

BRADNUM, FREDERICK (1920–2001). Frederick Bradnum was a radio dramatist, producer, and director who was prolific in both original **dramas** and adaptations, originally as a member of the North Region's drama department within the **British Broadcasting Corporation**. Between 1950–1960, he was instrumental, along with **Donald McWhinnie** and **Desmond Briscoe**, in the founding of the **BBC Radiophonic Workshop**. Notable among many works was his *Private Dreams and Public Nightmares* (1957), an early experiment blending sounds and voices that was described as a "radiophonic poem." Bradnum also directed 12 plays by Bernard Shaw for the **Third Programme** and many plays by Henrik Ibsen. From the 1970s to the 1990s, his writing and production work was mainly for **BBC Radio 4**, and his last play, *The Terraced House*, was written for that network in 1994. One of Bradnum's most significant adaptations was that of Anthony Powell's *A Dance to the Music of Time*, broadcast as a 25-part **series** from 1979–1982. The series was rebroadcast on **BBC Radio 7** in 2003.

BRAIN OF BRITAIN. The **series**, which evolved out of another program, *What Do You Know?*, began under this name in January 1967, chaired by **Franklin Engelmann**. The **quiz show** was later hosted by Robert Robinson for many years. A straightforward general knowledge quiz, each series seeks to eliminate contestants until a "Brain of Britain" is found. There is no prize, simply a title. Spin-offs have included winners from successive series competing for the title "Brain of Brains."

BRAIN'S TRUST, THE. A program that began in January 1941, on the **BBC Home Service**, under the title *Any Questions?* It should not, however, be confused with another program of the same name. It changed its name to *The Brain's Trust* in January 1942 and continued until May 1949. It also transferred to television. In its original form—that of a wide-ranging debate on issues and topics of current interest—it had a regular panel consisting of **Julian Huxley**, **Cyril Joad**, and **A. B. Campbell**. Panel members changed throughout the years, and there were guests, among them Kenneth Clark and Hannen Swaffer. The format, however, remained constant.

See also ANY QUESTIONS?; SERIES; THOMAS, HOWARD (1909–1986).

BRAND, RUSSELL (1975–). Russell Brand is an actor, comedian, writer, and broadcaster who began his radio career in 2002, on the London station **Xfm**. He lost his job on the station after reading pornographic material on the air. In April 2006, he presented *The Russell Brand Show* on **BBC Radio 6 Music**, a program that subsequently transferred to **BBC Radio 2** in November of the same year. In October 2008, Brand and **Jonathan Ross** broadcast a **series** of prank calls left on the answering machine of actor **Andrew Sachs**, with crude references to Sachs's granddaughter. The event produced considerable controversy, and both Ross and Brand were suspended by the **British Broadcasting Corporation (BBC)**. Brand resigned from his program, and the BBC was fined £150,000. He returned to radio in 2009, when he cohosted a football talk show on **talkSPORT**. In 2010, he broadcast a 20-week series of Saturday night programs on the station.

See also DOUGLAS, LESLEY (1963–).

BRAY, BARBARA (1924–2010). Barbara Bray was born in London and graduated with a first-class honors degree in English from Cambridge. After university and some lecturing in Egypt, she joined the **British Broadcasting Corporation (BBC)** as script editor of **drama** in 1953, and then worked as a writer and director within the same department. She was responsible for finding, commissioning, and bringing to realization dramatic scripts for BBC radio.

Bray, a seminal figure, was instrumental in developing and directing works by Marguerite Duras, Harold Pinter, and **Samuel Beckett**, with all of whom she continued to collaborate after first encounters. She was also active in the development and encouragement of new writers in Britain, as well as throughout Europe, Africa, India, and the West Indies. In 1960, she left the BBC and, the following year, moved to Paris, where she continued to work as a writer, translator, critic, and broadcaster. She was succeeded in her BBC post by her deputy, **Martin Esslin.**

Bray continued to write and/or direct a number of film and theater plays, as well as many pieces for radio. She also made numerous dramatic adaptations and translations. She collaborated with Harold Pinter and Joseph Losey on a film adaptation of Marcel Proust's *A La Recherche du Temps Perdu*. Bray won many international prizes for translation, including the George Scott-Moncrief Prize for translation from French, which she received four times. In 1991, she cofounded the Anglo–French Theater Company, Dear Conjunction. In 2003, she suffered a stroke, which confined her to a wheel chair, but she continued to work on a memoir of Samuel Beckett, which remained incomplete upon her death on 25 February 2010.

BRIDGEMAN, WILLIAM (1864–1935). Lord Bridgeman of Leigh, 1st Viscount, William Clive Bridgeman was a Conservative politician who joined the Board of Governors of the **British Broadcasting Corporation** in 1933. Becoming chairman in 1935, upon the death of **John Whitley**, he himself died during the year of his appointment.

BRIDSON, DOUGLAS GEOFFREY (1910–1980). D. G. Bridson began his career in 1933, as a freelance radio writer, joining the **British Broadcasting Corporation (BBC)** as a **feature** programs assistant in the North Region in 1935, at a time of considerable cultural development in social action feature-making within the department. In 1941, he moved to London to become the overseas features editor and, after the war, assistant head of Features. From 1964–1967, he was program editor for arts, sciences, and **documentaries** (sound). Bridson retired from the BBC in 1967, after more than 35 years; 800 programs had carried his name. His autobiography, *Prospero and Ariel: The Rise and Fall of Radio; A Personal Recollection*, was published in 1971.

BRISCOE, DESMOND (1925–2006). Desmond Briscoe was a cofounder and the original manager of the **BBC Radiophonic Workshop**. Working as a sound engineer and studio manager in the **drama** department of the **British Broadcasting Corporation** in the 1950s, he developed an interest in electronic and electroacoustic sound within radio production. With **Daphne Oram**, Briscoe used his technique in some of the earliest productions, including **Samuel Beckett's** *All That Fall* (January 1957), **Giles Cooper's** *The Disagreeable Oyster* (August 1957), and **Frederick Bradnum's** *Private Dreams and Public Nightmares* (October 1957).

BRITISH BROADCASTING COMPANY (BBC [1]). The full name of the BBC initially included the word *company*, not *corporation*. This grew out of the initial commercial origins of the organization. In 1922, a number of firms were involved in the development of radio; the technology to manufacture receivers had been developed with the advent of World War I, and a number of wireless amateurs were seeking a broadcasting service. There was a definite commercial imperative for manufacturers; to sell receivers, there needed to be a purpose for those receivers—a regular schedule of programs.

At the same time, the British government considered the "chaos of the ether," resulting in the nonregulation of radio practitioners in the United States, to be unacceptable in the United Kingdom, while at the same time ruling out the idea of one commercial company having a monopoly. On 4 May 1922, the **Post Office** announced to the House of Commons that "bona fide manufacturers of wireless apparatus" would be given permission to establish a number of broadcasting stations throughout Great Britain under the eye of the Post Office.

On 23 May 1922, a meeting was held at the Institute of Electrical Engineers in London, under the chairmanship of Frank Gill, the chief engineer of the Western Electric Company. Among those attending were representatives of the six companies interested in establishing a broadcasting base in Great Britain: **Marconi**, Metropolitan Vickers, the General Electric Company, the Radio Communication Company, the Western Electric Company, and the British Thomson Houston Company. This group was to guide the course of British broadcasting toward one service, and two days later, another meeting was held, at which the name "The British Broadcasting Company Ltd." was agreed upon.

The new company was established with £100,000 capital in cumulative ordinary shares. Additional financing was to be provided by the introduction of a 10-shilling **license fee** payable by all those receiving the service. The steering committee also agreed that the Post Office should be requested to approve for sale only sets made by companies constituting the BBC.

The company's first offices were in Magnet House in Kingsway, London, owned by GEC. At the same time, 2LO, the Marconi station in Marconi House on the Strand, was placed under the control of the company, which commenced regular transmissions in November 1922. Thus, the birth of regular, organized broadcasting in Britain was a curious hybrid of commercial interests and government intervention and control. The BBC achieved its initial coverage of the United Kingdom through the establishment of a **series** of local or regional stations, run by its commercial company members. These, in chronological order of first BBC broadcasts, were as follows:

2LO. This was the call sign and title of the first London station, initially run by the Marconi Company beginning on Thursday, 11 May 1922, from studios in Marconi House on the Strand. Its original name was Marconi's London Wireless Telegraphy Station. Formal programming began on 20 July 1922, and, beginning on 14 November of that year,

2LO became the London Station of the BBC, broadcasting a daily schedule. On 1 May 1923, the station moved to new premises and studios at nearby **Savoy Hill**, in a building on the banks of the River Thames, owned by the Institute of Electrical Engineers. 2LO continued broadcasting until 9 March 1930, when it was superseded by the **National Programme** and **Regional Programme** of the **British Broadcasting Corporation**.

2ZY. Metrovick began experimental broadcasts from this Manchester-based station on 16 May 1922. It became part of the BBC and, on 15 November, the day after the first daily programs from 2LO, began transmitting BBC programs. It was the first U.K. station to broadcast a program for children, *Kiddies Corner*.

5IT. This was the station operated by the BBC in Birmingham, going on the air on the same day—15 November 1922—that 2ZY began its BBC transmissions.

5NO. Opened on 24 December 1922, the BBC's Newcastle station developed an early interest in radio **drama**, and one of its associates, Gordon Lea, wrote what has been claimed to be the first book on the genre, *Radio Drama and How to Write It*, in 1926. As early as September 1923, its first drama production was a 15-minute excerpt from Shakespeare's *Romeo and Juliet* (Act III, Scene 5).

5WA. The BBC's Welsh service, 5WA, began broadcasting from Cardiff on 17 February 1923.

5SC. The Glasgow station of the BBC opened on 6 March 1923.

2BD. Opened on 10 October 1923, 2BD was the call sign of the new BBC station serving Aberdeen. It was the second Scottish station, after 5SC (Glasgow).

6BM. Opened on 17 October 1923, the BBC's Bournemouth service established an early relationship with the Bournemouth Municipal Orchestra (later the Bournemouth Symphony Orchestra) under its founder, Dan Godfrey, and weekly concerts—eventually networked—became a **feature** of its output.

2BE. The BBC established its Belfast station, 2BE, on 15 September 1924, although its official opening was on 24 October of that year. It was the last of the regional stations responsible for originating program content to be established by the company.

BRITISH BROADCASTING CORPORATION (BBC [2]). On 1 January 1927, the **British Broadcasting Company** became the British Broadcasting Corporation, licensed under Royal Charter.

See also CHARTER.

BRITISH FORCES BROADCASTING SERVICE (BFBS). In early 1944, a British Forces Experimental Service was established in Algiers, and by the end of the year, five stations were broadcasting. This was to be the foundation of the service that has become known as the British Forces Broadcasting Service, although this title was not used until the start of the 1960s.

Two days after the German surrender, on 10 May 1944, the disparate broadcasting services were unified under the name British Forces Network (BFN), using studios in Hamburg (and subsequently in Cologne). At about the same time, parallel services began operating in India, the Pacific, and the Middle East. During the next decade, this network grew to include Kenya, Malta, Cyprus, Libya, and Gibraltar. The service became familiar to domestic audiences largely through the regular weekly Sunday linkups for the **Light Programme's** *Family Favourites*, which, beginning in October 1945, enabled service men and **women** and their families to exchange messages and musical requests.

In February 1956, BFN moved to **frequency modulation (FM)** transmission, the first English-speaking network to do so. When U.K. military conscription ended, staffing of the now renamed BFBS was extended outside the armed forces, and a number of young U.K. broadcasters gained their early experience in radio broadcasting from employment with the service. A London headquarters was established, and programs reached various parts of the globe either by satellite—as the technology developed—or, in some cases, prerecorded tape.

In 1982, BFBS—previously part of the U.K. Ministry of Defence—became a branch of the Services Sound and Vision Corporation and thereafter derived income from the U.K. government and a range of commercial activities. With the cessation of the Cold War, BFBS operations in Germany were reduced considerably. The service continues globally, however, and has responded to the need of the U.K. armed forces wherever they are, including new programming initiatives in the Gulf during the first years of the 21st century. By 2005, personnel in 23 countries were receiving BFBS programs in some form.

See also WARTIME BROADCASTING.

BRITISH FORCES NETWORK (BFN). *See* BRITISH FORCES BROADCASTING SERVICE (BFBS); WARTIME BROADCASTING.

BRITISH LIBRARY SOUND ARCHIVE. A resource formerly known as the National Sound Archive, housed in London. It holds more than 1 million discs, almost 200,000 tapes, and many other sound and video recordings. The collections come from throughout the world and cover the entire range of recorded sound, including **music**, **drama**, literature, oral history, and wildlife. Copies of commercial recordings issued in the United Kingdom are kept, together with selected commercial recordings from overseas, radio broadcasts, and many privately made recordings.

The catalog includes more than 2.5 million entries and is updated daily. It also provides public access to a wide range of specialist books, magazines, and journals covering every aspect of recorded sound, including radio. Seven main subject areas are classified within the archive, each headed by its own curator: classical music, drama and literature, jazz oral history, popular music, wildlife sound, world music, and traditional music.

In 2009, the British Library recognized the importance of radio recordings as historical and cultural documents by appointing its first radio curator, Paul Wilson. In addition to thousands of off-air recordings made by the archive between 1963–2000, much more has been amassed through donations from radio stations, production companies, individual producers, performers, subject specialists, and collectors. The library's listening and viewing service provides the only public point of on-request access to the collections of the **BBC Sound Archive** and **BBC Radio International** (formerly **BBC Transcription Services**).

The scope of the material ranges from the 1920s to the present and embraces every genre, from music, drama, and the arts to **news**, **current affairs**, and experimental **community radio**. Although British broadcasting, particularly the national stations of the **British Broadcasting Corporation (BBC)**, is most strongly represented, the collection also includes regional radio, **local radio**, and independent/**commercial radio** programming, as well as a growing selection of material from overseas. The archive has linked with the BBC on a number of initiatives, including *The Listening Project*.

BRMB. BRMB was the fourth independent local radio station to be launched in Britain, going on air on 19 February 1974, and serving the Birmingham area. Contrary to belief that the name was an acronym for "Birmingham Radio, Midlands Broadcasting," it was, in fact, simply an attempt to create a brand based on the sound of American radio call signs. In addition, the title related to the nickname given to Birmingham—"Brum"—"BRM," plus "B" for the word *broadcasting*. The station was bought by **Capital Radio** in 1993 and, in due course, acquired by **Global Radio**. In 2008, because of conflicting interests in the region, Global was required to sell BRMB and a number of other stations in the West Midlands. This was accomplished in July 2009, and BRMB was bought by **Phil Riley**, former chief executive of **Chrysalis**, who had begun his radio career at the station in 1980. Riley combined this purchase and the acquisition of other stations in the area to create **Orion**

Media and rebranded BRMB as Free Radio Birmingham in March 2012. A similar rebranding simultaneously took place for other stations in the Orion Media group, namely Beacon, Mercia, and Wyvern.

See also COMMERCIAL RADIO.

BROADCASTING FROM THE BARRICADES. On 16 January 1926, a **talk** by Father Ronald Knox included simulated reports of rioting in London by the mass unemployed. Although fictional, the aim of the exercise was to draw attention to social issues that were to culminate in the general strike of May of that year. Twelve years before Orson Welles's famous *War of the Worlds* broadcast on CBS radio in the United States, the event actually convinced a number of listeners that Britain was in the throes of revolution.

See also DRAMA; FEATURE.

BROADCASTING HOUSE. "B. H.," as it is affectionately known to staff, was established as the headquarters of the **British Broadcasting Corporation (BBC)** on 15 May 1932, when the corporation moved from **Savoy Hill**. Standing in Portland Place, facing down London's Regent Street, the building was designed by Lieutenant Colonel G. Val Myer and decorated with sculptures of Prospero and Ariel by **Eric Gill**. By 1928, it had become clear that the BBC had outgrown the space available at Savoy Hill, and the search had begun for a suitable site upon which to establish new, purpose-built premises. A number of London locations were considered, the most favored being one on Park Lane; however, while this was under consideration, it became known that another site, on the corner of Portland Place and Langham Street, was about to become available at a much lower cost. The building was completed in 1931, with the BBC initially renting it, the freehold being transferred to the corporation on 16 July 1936. The structure took into account the requirements of sound broadcasting in a way that had not been possible in Savoy Hill; the studios were centrally located in a tower, separated from street noise by offices and corridors. It is a building in the art deco style, and the Latin inscription, mounted in bronze Roman lettering in the entrance hall, is indicative of the sacred cause in which early British broadcasters considered themselves to be engaged:

> To Almighty God
> The first Governors of this institution dedicated this Temple of the Arts and Muses under the first directorship of John Reith, Knight, praying for Divine help that a good sowing may have a good harvest and that everything impure and hostile to Peace may be banished from this building, and that whatsoever things are sincere and beautiful and of good report and loveable, the people, inclining its ear to these things with a contentment of mind, may follow in the path of virtue and wisdom.

The building was badly damaged in World War II, although broadcasting continued uninterrupted. Since its creation, the term *Broadcasting House* has been adopted as generic for all main U.K. regional BBC premises. In the first years of the 21st century, there was a large-scale redevelopment on the eastern side of the building, greatly extending the facilities to meet the requirements of the digital age of broadcasting, as part of the BBC's consolidation of its London operations, bringing many services formerly housed in Television Centre and **Bush House** onto one site. This involved the demolition of postwar extensions and creation of a new wing, which was completed in 2005, and named the **John Peel** Wing in 2012, after the late presenter. The official name of the refurbished building remains Broadcasting House; however, the BBC now uses the phrase "new Broadcasting House" in publicity referring to the extension, while titling the original building "old Broadcasting House."

BROADCASTING HOUSE. Not to be confused with the building from which it originates, *Broadcasting House* is a **news** and **current affairs** program on **BBC Radio 4**, first presented by **Eddie Mair** and broadcast beginning in1998. It airs between 9:00 a.m. and 10:00 a.m. on Sunday mornings, and unlike a number of other current affairs programs on the network, it is noted for having a somewhat less serious tone. Since Mair's departure in 2003, it has had a number of presenters, including **Fi Glover**, **Matthew Bannister**, and Paddy O'Connell.

BROADCASTING IN THE SEVENTIES. A **British Broadcasting Corporation** paper of 1969 that created considerable controversy. In terms of radio, the practical result was to strengthen the identities of the main networks established in 1967, further developing the generic form of "branded" broadcasting, which would increasingly dominate U.K. radio in the latter part of the 20th century and into the 21st.
See also COMMITTEES OF ENQUIRY.

***BROADCASTING POLICY* (CMND 6852. GOVERNMENT WHITE PAPER, JULY 1946).** The first postwar government white paper dealing with broadcasting. In addition to announcing that the **British Broadcasting Corporation's charter** would be renewed without extensive review and that a new structure of consumer licensing would be introduced, combining radio and television for a £2 per annum cost, the newly installed Labour government's policy review proposed a new cultural radio station, to be known as the **Third Programme**. Another innovation as a result of this paper was the instigation of a daily radio review of proceedings in the British Parliament.
See also COMMITTEES OF ENQUIRY.

BROOK, NORMAN (1902–1967). Norman Craven Brook, Lord Norman-brook of Chelsea, was given a peerage in 1963, and became **BBC chairman** the following year. He took the role seriously, and his relationship with incumbent director-general **Hugh Greene** was amicable. Brook died in office, and his place was briefly taken on a temporary basis by Robert—later Sir Robert—Lusty.

BROOKMANS PARK TRANSMITTING STATION. Situated in Greater London, between Potters Bar and Hatfield in Hertfordshire, the Brookmans Park Transmitting Station, completed in October 1929, played a key part in the development of British broadcasting. It was the first purpose-built twin transmitter station in the world capable of broadcasting two radio programs simultaneously; it also played an important role in the initial development of television. The commissioning of the station was one of the first acts of the newly formed **British Broadcasting Corporation (BBC)**, signaling the development of the BBC's regional broadcasting scheme, conceived in 1924, by its chief engineer, **Peter Eckersley**. Brookmans Park was the first transmitter in this scheme, serving London and the Home Counties.

See also BRITISH BROADCASTING COMPANY (BBC [1]); DA-VENTRY.

BROUGH, PETER (1916–1999). *See* "ARCHIE ANDREWS"; COMEDY; *EDUCATING ARCHIE*; SERIES.

BROWN, PAUL (1945–). Paul Brown was chief executive of the **Commercial Radio Companies Association (CRCA)**. From 1970–1984, he worked in Forces radio and U.K. **commercial radio**. In 1984, he joined the Independent Broadcasting Authority as head of radio programming. He was deputy chief executive of the Radio Authority from 1990–1995, chairman of the U.K. Digital Radio Forum from 1999–2001, and president of the Association of European Radios from 1998–2000. Brown was a fellow and is a former chairman of the U.K. Radio Academy, as well as a board member of **Radio Joint Audience Research**. He was made a Commander of the Most Excellent Order of the British Empire for his services to the radio industry in 2003. He saw the CRCA transformed into the **RadioCentre** in 2006 and was succeeded upon his retirement in December 2008 by Dianne Thompson, who has combined this role with the duties of chief executive officer of the National Lottery Operator in Camelot.

See also HARRISON, ANDREW (1964–).

BUCKERIDGE, ANTHONY (1912–2004). Creator of one of the most affectionately remembered children's **series** of the late 1940s and 1950s, Anthony Buckeridge was a prep school master who wrote stories in his spare time. He created a schoolboy character named Jennings and, in 1948, submitted a script based on the story to *Children's Hour* producer **David Davis**. The result was a series of radio productions under the title *Jennings at School*. The series was so successful that Buckeridge gave up teaching in 1950, to concentrate on writing books based on the radio characters. By 1977, 23 books had been published and, despite the period nature and extreme "Englishness" of the scenario, translated into 12 languages, proving particularly popular in Norway, where the characters of the fictional Linbury Court School were dramatized afresh.

Buckeridge wrote more than 100 radio plays for adults, as well as children, but it is for *Jennings* that he will be remembered. In the 1980s, after a period when the stories went out of fashion, they were revived in book form, and Buckeridge wrote two new *Jennings* stories in 1994. By that time, however, there was little in the way of children's radio that could provide an audio platform for dramatizations of the stories. They were nonetheless issued as audio cassettes.

See also CHILDREN'S PROGRAMS.

BUGGINS FAMILY, THE. Created by **Mabel Constanduros**, this **series** of radio sketches, which later grew into larger playlets, created the first radio "family" and continued through intermittent appearances from 1925–1948 in various guises and on numerous programs on both the **British Broadcasting Company/Corporation** and **Radio Normandy**. Constanduros herself played the main character Grandma Buggins, who became an extremely popular feature of the program, particularly during the war years.

See also COMEDY; DRAMA; SERIALS.

BURKISS WAY, THE. Written by Andrew Marshall and David Renwick, *The Burkiss Way* was a **comedy series** broadcast on **BBC Radio 4** between 1976–1980, featuring a number of successful performers, including **Chris Emmett**. The concept was that of fictional correspondence courses run by one Professor Emil Burkiss, and the show was highly popular for its surreal comedy style. After running for 47 episodes during the course of six series, it was repeated in later years on **BBC Radio 4 Extra**.

BURROWS, ARTHUR (1882–1947). Arthur Burrows was the first program director of the **British Broadcasting Company (BBC)** and a major figure in radio's pioneering days. He began his career as a journalist and specialized in wireless telegraphy. In 1920, he was working for the **Marconi**

Company in **Chelmsford** and organized the highly important **"Melba" broadcast**, by Dame Nellie Melba, from the factory. Burrows was program organizer for 2LO in 1922, as well as chief **announcer**, and he continued these duties when the BBC took over the station in November of that year. He was also the first newsreader in British radio, coeditor of the *Radio Times*, and author of an early book on radio entitled *The Story of Broadcasting* (1924). In 1925, Burrows left the BBC to assume the post of the first secretary-general of the Union Internationale de Radiophonie based in Geneva.

BUSH HOUSE. Contrary to some opinions, the Bush House was not named for the well-known radio and television manufacturers, but for Irving T. Bush, an American businessman and head of an Anglo–American trading organization who financed the creation of the original building. Designed by Harvey Corbett, Bush House was built in 1923, with extensions added between 1928–1935.

During the 1930s, the imposing building in London's Aldwych, looking up Kingsway, was occupied by the Radio Division of the **J. Walter Thompson Organization**. Near the end of the decade, the division built state-of-the-art studios designed to record programs for transmission on **Radio Luxembourg** and other continent-based **commercial radio** stations. Technology included variable studio wall textures to change acoustics and the high-quality **Philips-Miller recording** machines.

In 1941, the Foreign Language Broadcasting Service of the **British Broadcasting Corporation (BBC)** relocated to Bush House from **Broadcasting House** after the latter was damaged by bombs, thus inheriting the J. Walter Thompson facilities. Throughout the years, the BBC's External Services occupied the building, and for many it will always be associated with the **BBC World Service**; however, the corporation never owned Bush House, which has been the property, sequentially, of the Church of Wales, the **Post Office**, and a Japanese business organization. Nevertheless, the BBC continued to broadcast from the premises in more than 30 languages worldwide until its lease expired in 2012. Services were subsequently moved to the redeveloped Broadcasting House.

C

CADOGAN, ALEXANDER (1884–1968). The Right Honorable Sir Alexander George Montagu Cadogan was chairman of the **British Broadcasting Corporation (BBC)** from 1952–1957, appointed the same year that **Ian Jacob** became director-general. The relationship between the two men was a good one, due in part to Cadogan's tactful interpretation of his regulatory powers. As both director of the Suez Canal Company and friend of Tory prime minister Anthony Eden, he was in a potentially difficult position at the time of the Suez Canal Crisis, when he successfully defended the BBC's impartial reporting of the crisis in the face of government pressure.

CAMPBELL, ARCHIBALD (1881–1966). A. B. Campbell came to broadcasting in August 1935, when he gave a **talk** entitled *The Last Voyage of the Otranto*, an eyewitness account of the loss of the warship upon which he had been serving in World War I. The success of the talk led to others, including *Men Talking* and later *The World Goes By*. He proved himself to be a natural, fluent, off-the-cuff speaker, someone for whom radio broadcasting was instinctive—a born storyteller.

Campbell became nationally famous as a member of the original team—with **Julian Huxley** and **Cyril Joad**—of *The Brains Trust* in 1940. Campbell had a key role in forming a bridge between his intellectual fellow panelists and listeners. His blend of style and common sense gave him an air of being the listeners' friend, and he became extremely popular. Campbell made more than 200 appearances on *The Brains Trust* between 1941–1946, and he also worked as an advisor to troops preparing for the Normandy landings.

After the war, he continued to give radio talks based on his maritime experiences, including *The Old Sea Chest*, a **series** for **Children's Hour**, and *Commander Campbell Talking* for **Woman's Hour**. Campbell made a series for the newly formed Independent Television in 1956, and he made his final radio appearance—on the *Today* program—in February 1959. He wrote a number of books, including memoirs, one of which, *When I Was in Patagonia* (1953), took its title from a phrase with which he had become associated during his time on *The Brains Trust*.

CAPITAL GOLD. A network of **commercial radio** "oldies" stations run by **GCap Media**. It merged with the **Classic Gold Network** in 2007 to form **Gold**. The resulting group of stations is now owned by **Global Radio**.

CAPITAL RADIO. Britain's oldest commercial **music** station began operations on 16 October 1973 (eight days after the first commercial station, **London Broadcasting Company**, commenced broadcasting). Originally housed in Euston Tower in London, it is now established in the city center's Leicester Square. The station has been involved with many metropolitan initiatives throughout the years, including the Capital Radio Music Festival. When the 1990 Broadcasting Act eased the regulations governing consolidation of ownership, Capital was at the heart of an expanding empire of radio stations nationwide. Between 1993–2005, the Capital Radio group expanded its operations from two to 52 analog and digital stations, with a total of nearly 8 million listeners. In May 2005, the group merged with the other major U.K. radio group, **Great Western Radio**, to form **GCap Media**. In 2008, **Global Radio** officially took control of GCap Media and its brands for the sum of £375 million. Subsequent to this, in January 2011, Capital London became part of a nine-station Capital Radio network operated by Global Radio.

See also COMMERCIAL RADIO.

CARPENTER, HUMPHREY (1946–2005). Humphrey Carpenter was a prolific writer of biographies, including those of J. R. R. Tolkien, W. H. Auden, Ezra Pound, and Benjamin Britten. In addition, he wrote the definitive history of the **Third Programme** and **BBC Radio 3**, *The Envy of the World* (1996). It was an appropriate subject for him; he became a notable presenter on the network, presenting, among other programs, the nightly arts and cultural magazine *Night Waves* and a wide range of other musical programs, to which he brought an infectious enthusiasm and thorough research. Carpenter began his radio career as a trainee in 1968, and joined Radio Oxford when it was established in 1970. He was diagnosed with Parkinson's disease in his later years but continued to work with his usual ambition. He died suddenly on 4 January 2005, shortly after returning from a New Year's trip to France with his wife Mari.

See also DOCUMENTARY; FEATURE; TALKS.

"CAT'S WHISKER". The popular term for a piece of early, rather crude radio technology that consisted of a length—usually of about two inches—of thin wire positioned on a piece of suitable material, for instance, a crystal of gallenium arsenide, that rectified and thus "detected" **amplitude modulation (AM)** broadcasts. The device was patented by German scientist Ferdinand

Braun in 1899 and, because of its cheapness and convenience, was used in preference to **John Ambrose Fleming's valve** during the initial years of wireless receiver development.

See also CRYSTAL SET.

CBEEBIES RADIO. CBeebies is the brand name used by the **British Broadcasting Corporation (BBC)** for its multimedia programming that provides young children with education and entertainment. It was launched in February 2002, on television, and has since developed a wide variety of programs online, increasingly using new mobile technology. With the launch of the digital radio station **BBC Radio 7**, a range of programs for children were broadcast during the afternoons, becoming branded as *CBeebies Radio.* When the station itself was relaunched as **BBC Radio 4 Extra** in 2011, this policy ceased. A number of audio programs use the CBeebies website, as well as **BBC iPlayer Radio**.

See also CHILDREN'S PROGRAMS; SMARTPHONE; WEBCASTING.

CELADOR RADIO BROADCASTING. Celador is a media company founded in 1983, with interests in radio and television production and ownership. Its portfolio of 18 radio stations includes the Breeze network and the **Jack FM** stations.

See also COMMERCIAL RADIO.

CELLO AND THE NIGHTINGALE. In 1924, a series of extraordinary **outside broadcasts** began that, at an early stage of radio history, demonstrated, more than anything else, the power of the sound medium for a mass audience. Celebrated cellist Beatrice Harrison (1892–1965) had discovered that while playing her instrument in the garden of her house, Foyle Riding, in Surrey, a nightingale in the woods nearby would sing to her playing. She contacted **John Reith**, suggesting that the **British Broadcasting Company** broadcast the phenomenon, and, on 19 May 1924, more than 1 million listeners tuned in at midnight to hear her play a duet with the bird. The nightingale concerts continued each May for 12 years, and thousands of people came to Foyle Riding in May to witness the phenomenon. Harrison used the image of the bird on her publicity material and concert dresses.

A commercial recording was issued, and the "duet" became world famous. After the event, while Harrison was engaged in recording Edward Elgar's *Cello Concerto* at HMV's Abbey Road, London studios, she met King George V, who was on a tour of the building. Upon being introduced to her, he said, "Nightingales, nightingales! You have done what I have not yet been able to do. You have encircled the Empire."

CELLULOSE-NITRATE DISC. *See* DISC RECORDING.

CENTURY RADIO. The brand name for a group of **commercial radio** stations in the north of England developed beginning in 1994 by **John Myers**, managing director, and **John Simons**, program director. The original owner was **Border Radio Holdings**, but in 2000, the **Capital Radio** group acquired the brand. In 2005, **GCap Media** bought the stations, but Myers and Simons, now with the **Guardian Media Group (GMG)**, reassumed control in 2006, developing them alongside the **Real Radio** brand. On 31 March 2009, Century Radio was itself renamed Real Radio to conform to the broader network branding. In 2012, **Global Radio** bought GMG and, in February 2014, rebranded the Real Radio stations as **Heart**.

CHARLES PARKER ARCHIVE TRUST. Housed in Birmingham Central Library, the Charles Parker Archive is devoted to the preservation and study of the work of radio producer **Charles Parker** and contains an extensive collection of tapes, papers, books, and memorabilia that belonged to him. The Charles Parker Archive Trust exists to administer the collection and promote interest in and study of Parker's work, including the annual **Charles Parker Day** conference. The trust has had three chairmen: **Gillian Reynolds**, **Tim Blackmore**, and **Mary Kalemkerian**.
    See also FEATURE.

CHARLES PARKER DAY. An annual conference held in April, close to the birthday of distinguished radio producer **Charles Parker**. It was founded by Seán Street, professor of radio at Bournemouth University, to celebrate not only Parker and his work (notably the *Radio Ballads*), but the genre of the radio **feature** itself—its past, present, and future. The first Charles Parker Day was held in 2004, in Bournemouth (his birthplace), on his birthday, 5 April, and included the launch of the first Charles Parker Prize for Student Radio Features. The conference is characterized by its mobility; it is held in a different location each year. Since 2010, it has been directed by Andy Cartwright of the University of Sunderland, and the event is supported by the **Charles Parker Archive Trust**.

CHARTER. The **British Broadcasting Corporation (BBC)** is constitutionally established by a Royal Charter, usually reviewed for renewal every 10 years, although the period is variable. Attached to this is an accompanying agreement whereby the corporation's editorial independence is recognized and its public obligations are stated. The creation of a British Broadcasting Corporation in 1927, under charter, to replace the previously commercially founded **British Broadcasting Company**, has been at the center of British broadcasting for many years. The first charter, which ran for 10 years, beginning on 1 January 1927, was very much the product of **John Reith's** wish to place the organization above political machinations and commercial interest; it was Reith who pressed for a charter to be granted to the BBC under Royal Seal. A key element of the charter renewal process and, in later years, an increasingly contentious issue in its own right, has been that of the funding of the BBC through a public requirement to purchase a receiving license. The frequently permissive nature of successive charters has also often proved controversial, particularly among commercial broadcasters and some politicians. The current BBC charter was granted in 2006, running for 10 years. Intensive discussions relating to the future of the BBC when this charter is due for renewal in December 2016 were expected to commence in June 2015, following the general election in the United Kingdom. Details of charters from 1927 to 2006 are as follows:

1927: The first charter went into effect on 1 January 1927, and led to the creation of the British Broadcasting Corporation. It was granted after parliamentary consideration of the **Crawford Committee** report (1925), which recognized the need for an independent responsible body to further develop radio in the national interest along the lines already established by the British Broadcasting Company. This established the long-term policy of a Board of Governors responsible for the day-to-day control of the BBC, although parliament would have "ultimate control." The charter was awarded for a span of 10 years.

1937: The second charter was granted after parliament considered the findings of the **Ullswater Committee** of 1935. It was granted for a further 10 years and permitted the BBC to further develop overseas broadcasting, which had begun to be transmitted to various parts of the British Empire in 1932, "for the benefits of [its] dominions beyond the seas and territories under [its] protection." The charter also followed up the findings of the Selsdon Television Committee of 1934, which had been endorsed by Ullswater, permitting the BBC to develop a television service, which accordingly began transmission on 2 November 1936, from Alexandra Palace.

1947: The third BBC charter was initially only granted until 1951, although it was ultimately extended until June 1952. Following World War II and the BBC's extension of its **Empire Service** to encompass an overseas service of many languages and destinations, the document authorized the BBC to provide broadcasting services that could be received "in other countries and places" outside the British Commonwealth.

1952: The fourth charter took into account the report of the Beveridge Committee, known as the **Beveridge Report**, of 1949, as well as various government white papers, notably that of May 1952, issued by the Winston Churchill administration, in which the government stated that it had "come to the conclusion that the expanding field of television provision should be made to permit some element of competition"; therefore, the license received by the BBC from the postmaster general was, for the first time, a nonexclusive one. The charter provided for the establishment of National Broadcasting Councils for Scotland and Wales, with powers for radio, and was extended to July 1964.

1961: The fifth charter was, for the first time in BBC history, granted for the duration of 12 years. It had been preceded by the report of the Pilkington Committee of 1960 and authorized the BBC to borrow up to £10 million for temporary banking accommodation and up to £20 million for capital expenditure subject to the approval of the postmaster general. Second, the National Broadcasting Councils for Scotland and Wales were granted the power to make decisions relating to local/regional content similar to those already in place regarding radio. In 1969, a Supplemental Royal Charter was granted to take into account the transfer of powers, formerly exercised by the postmaster general in relation to broadcasting, to the minister of posts and telecommunications. In 1973, the government announced its intention to extend the duration of the charter to July 1981.

1981: The charter of 1981 took into account the findings of the **Annan Committee** in the context of a developing climate of commercial competition, both in radio and television. The charter was granted for 15 years, expiring on 31 December 1996.

1996: The 1996 charter coincided with the start of one of the most significant times in U.K.—and global—media development. Running for 10 years, ending at the end of 2006, its life included the development of digital media and publication of the 2003 Communications Act, highlighting greater convergence and enabling the creation of the **Office of Communications**. In 2003, the process of charter review commenced and was concluded at the end of 2006, at which time a new BBC charter, granted for a further 10 years, went into effect.

See also COMMITTEES OF ENQUIRY.

CHECKLAND, MICHAEL (1936–). Sir Michael Checkland joined the Finance Department of the **British Broadcasting Corporation (BBC)** in 1964, with a background as a chartered accountant. He subsequently held the posts of director of Television Resources and chairman of BBC Enterprises prior to his appointment as director-general in 1987, following the resignation of **Alastair Milne**. Checkland described his objectives as introducing efficiency measures, diverting money to specific programs, and accommodating new independent production quotas. He was committed to a more economical BBC and was robust in his defense of its independence. Like his predecessor in the post, Checkland was publicly critical of Chairman **Marmaduke Hussey**. He resigned and was replaced in 1992, by his deputy, **John Birt**, 21 months before the end of his contract.

CHELMSFORD. A town in Essex, 30 miles northeast of London, credited in U.K. broadcasting history as being the "birthplace of radio." In 1896, **Guglielmo Marconi** came to the town with the hopes of starting a business. He found premises in 1898 and, the following year, opened the world's first wireless factory in a former silk mill in Hall Street, employing about 50 workers. The building is now occupied by Essex and Suffolk Water. A plaque proclaims the following: "In this building was established in 1899 the first radio factory in the world, by the Wireless Telegraph and Signal Co. Ltd., later known as Marconi's Wireless Telegraph Co. Ltd."

Business expanded rapidly, and in 1912, the company moved into a purpose-built factory in New Street. This was the first purpose-built factory for radio communications, built in 17 weeks. In 1920, from the New Street works came the first officially publicized sound entertainment broadcasts in the United Kingdom, one of them featuring prima donna Dame Nellie Melba (*see* "MELBA" BROADCAST, THE). Two years later, the first regular wireless programs, also operated by the Marconi Company, were transmitted from the nearby village of **Writtle**. The original New Street building was extended in the 1930s.

Evidence of the presence of the **Marconi Company** can be found throughout Chelmsford; from 1968–1994, the company produced radar components at their Writtle Road factory. The old building remains and has been converted into apartments as part of a wider housing development on the former factory site, while in Waterhouse Lane, Marconi Applied Technologies continues to design and manufacture optical components for space, medical, industry, and radar markets.

CHESTER, CHARLIE (1914–1996). Charlie Chester was widely known as a comedian in Britain beginning in the 1930s, having made his radio debut in 1937. He came to further prominence through appearances on such programs as *Stand Easy* and ***Workers' Playtime***. In 1969, he was given a daily radio show on **BBC Radio 2**, which later moved to early Sunday evenings, becoming *Sunday Soapbox*. The program's premise was a mix of records and social help; Chester and the program offered help and assistance to the poor and disadvantaged, helping to recycle items for the benefit of those in need, both nationally and internationally. He continued on the program virtually until his death in June 1996.

See also COMEDY; MUSIC; SERIES.

CHILDREN'S CHOICE. A Saturday morning **Light Programme** record request show that started on 25 December 1952, and was created as a youth version of the long-running weekday program *Housewives' Choice*. Present-ers included Donald Pears and "Uncle Mac" (**Derek McCulloch**), who was also with the show during its second incarnation as *Children's Favourites*.

See also CHILDREN'S PROGRAMS.

CHILDREN'S FAVOURITES. The new name for *Children's Choice* be-ginning in January 1954. It ran in its original form—starting at 9:05 a.m. on Saturday mornings—and was initially presented by **Derek McCulloch**. It featured a mixture of novelty records and some light classics. As the children who had first tuned in grew into teenagers, so the 1960s boom influenced the **music** choice, and "old school" presenters like "Uncle Mac" gave way to **disc jockeys**, while the music became more pop orientated. In 1965, a second edition was introduced on Sunday mornings, but by this time it was already something of an anomaly. When the **Light Programme** was succeeded by **BBC Radio 1** in 1967, the program ended and was replaced by *Junior Choice*. By dropping the word *children* from the title, the new network was able to foster the growing teen market.

See also CHILDREN'S PROGRAMS.

CHILDREN'S HOUR. An iconic program that began airing in December 1922, and ended on Good Friday, 27 March 1967. The first *BBC Handbook* includes a suggestion regarding the origin of its title; in an article devoted to the program, the writer quotes poet Henry Wadsworth Longfellow, stating, "Between the dark and the daylight, When the night is beginning to lower, Comes a pause in the day's occupations, that is known as the Children's Hour."

A number of distinguished and devoted staff broadcasters were associated with the show throughout the years, including **Derek McCulloch** ("Uncle Mac") and **David Davis**, who was in charge of the program at the end of its life. It was a blend of stories, quizzes, **music**, natural history **features**, seri-als, and plays. Among the most famous and popular were *Toytown*, *Jen-nings at School*, and *Norman and Henry Bones*. The controversial decision to take the program off the air was made by **Frank Gillard** when he was director of sound broadcasting, provoking a heartbroken Davis to end the final edition with a reading of Oscar Wilde's *The Selfish Giant*, a tale of a bully who prevents children from playing in his garden. Despite its title, the program was, for most of its existence, aside from the editions that aired between 1937–1939, less than an hour in duration.

See also CHILDREN'S PROGRAMS.

CHILDREN'S PROGRAMS. Radio programs for children were among the earliest priorities for the medium. In May 1922, the **Marconi Company** announced that its broadcasting plans would include bedtime stories for children, and the tradition of broadcasters assuming the persona of radio "uncles and aunts" was created. With the formation of the **British Broadcasting Company (BBC)**, the tradition was first maintained with *For the Children* and subsequently *Children's Hour*. During the 1930s, children's programs were broadcast on **Radio Normandy** and **Radio Luxembourg**, including the *Ovaltineys' Concert Party*, which was revived on the station in the 1940s and 1950s.

During World War II, a series entitled *Children Calling Home* was broadcast, linking evacuated children from as far away as Canada and the United States with relatives in Britain, running from September 1941 to May 1944. Record request programs aimed at a young audience included *Children's Choice*, first broadcast in 1952, and renamed *Children's Favourites* in 1954, on the **Light Programme**, running until 1967.

Broadcasting to children became an increasing challenge for radio with changing technologies and listening habits. In 1964, amidst great controversy, **Frank Gillard**, director of sound broadcasting for the **British Broadcasting Corporation (BBC)**, announced plans to take *Children's Hour* off the air, acknowledging that the program's time slot, between 5:00 p.m. and 6:00 p.m., was unable to compete with television. By this time the rise of **music** radio, reflecting the popular music revolution of the 1960s, had altered tastes and expectations, with such stations as Radio Luxembourg, **Radio Caroline**, and other **pirate radio** stations assuming increasing importance in youth culture.

Attempts have been made by a number of independent companies to revive radio broadcasting for children, and when the digital radio station **BBC Radio 7** was created in 2002, segments of the schedule included *The Little Toe Show* (later renamed *CBeebies Radio*) for young children and *The Big Toe Show* for an older age group. With the introduction of **smartphone** applications and **MP3** players, radio's traditional relationship with the young continued to diminish during the first decades of the 21st century.

See also JUNIOR CHOICE.

CHILTON, CHARLES (1918–2013). Charles Chilton is best known as writer and producer of *Journey into Space*, the cult science fiction **series** that captivated British radio audiences in the 1950s. He joined the **British Broadcasting Corporation (BBC)** as a messenger boy in 1932, at the age of 14, and worked his way up to the position of producer, being involved in, among other things, the first American broadcasts of **Alastair Cooke**. A passionate lover of jazz **music**, Chilton presented programs on the genre for the Variety Department, including *Swing Time* and *Radio Rhythm Club*. During the war, he joined the Royal Air Force and was sent to what was then called Ceylon (Sri Lanka) to run the forces radio station there with **David Jacobs**.

Returning to the BBC, Chilton created many notable programs, both **documentaries** and popular **dramas**, most notably *Riders of the Range* and *Blood on the Prairie*. He was also responsible for *The Long, Long Trail* in 1961, a program that juxtaposed Edwardian music hall songs with accounts of the carnage of World War 1. In 1963, it was developed for the stage by **Joan Littlewood** at the Theatre Royal in Stratford East under the title *Oh What a Lovely War*, which, in turn, became the basis for a highly successful film. Chilton remained on the staff of the BBC until his retirement in 1979 but continued to write thereafter and, in 1981, created a 90-minute sequel to *Journey into Space*. He also conceived of another series reworked under the title *Space Force* in 1984. In 2008, a further sequel was broadcast on **BBC Radio 4** called *Frozen in Time*. Chilton's autobiography is entitled *Auntie's Charlie*. He was awarded the title Member of the Most Excellent Order of the British Empire in 1976.

See also FEATURE; MYSTERY PROGRAMS.

CHOICE. Choice was a **commercial radio** station based in Brixton, London, that opened in March 1990, covering South London. It was Britain's first 24-hour black **music** station, and in 1995, it opened a second operation in Birmingham. This license was sold to **Chrysalis** in 1999 and rebranded as **Galaxy**. In the meantime, the London interest expanded, and a second station opened in North London in 2000. **Capital Radio** gained control of the station in February 2004, moving it to the group's Leicester Square headquarters. In 2005, Capital merged with **Great Western Radio** to form **GCap Media**. GCap Media was subsequently taken over by **Global Radio**, by then the owner of the Galaxy network of stations, and Choice was branded as part of this for the purposes of advertising; however, when Global rebranded the Galaxy stations as Capital FM in 2010, Choice was given renewed autonomy. In October 2013, Choice was rebranded as Capital Xtra.

CHRYSALIS. Chrysalis was founded in 1967, by Chris Wright and Terry Ellis, who set up the Ellis Wright Agency, an agency for **music** management. From this grew a record label, Chrysalis (a combination of Wright's first name and Ellis's last). In 1993, the radio division was established with the first station, 100.7 Heart FM, launched in Birmingham in September 1994, followed by the London station, Heart 106.2, a year later. Then came the creation of the Galaxy brand of stations in Bristol (since sold), Manchester, Yorkshire, and Birmingham. In September 2002, the group acquired the London **talk** station **London Broadcasting Company**, making Chrysalis one of the largest players in the U.K. **commercial radio** industry. In 2007, Chrysalis was sold to **Global Radio** for £170 million.

CLAPHAM AND DWYER. Charlie Clapham and Billy Dwyer are notable in British radio history as the first major **comedy** double act to have had their reputations created by radio. In 1926, just one year after their formation as an amateur duo, they made their first radio appearance, and after two years they were being featured on variety stages throughout Britain, beginning in 1928, with an appearance at Shepherd's Bush Empire. Some of their routines were controversial in the somewhat censorious climate of the 1930s **British Broadcasting Corporation (BBC)**; for one routine, deemed to be in bad taste, they were banned from the BBC for several months, and the corporation even broadcast a public apology in its evening **news** bulletin. Clapham and Dwyer's career as a double act ended in 1943, with the sudden death of Dwyer.

See also ANNOUNCERS; MUSIC.

CLARENDON, GEORGE (1877–1955). George Herbert Hyde Villiers, the Sixth Earl of Clarendon, was the first chairman of the **British Broadcasting Corporation (BBC)**, as opposed to the **British Broadcasting Company**, taking over the position vacated by Lord Gainford in 1927. There was tension between Clarendon and **John Reith** regarding their respective spheres of authority relative to one another. Clarendon left the BBC in 1930, to become governor-general of South Africa.

CLARKE, NICK (1948–2006). Nick Clarke was a presenter and journalist primarily known for his work on **BBC Radio 4**. He joined the **British Broadcasting Corporation (BBC)** in 1973, as northern industrial correspondent. After work in television, his first major radio job was on *The World This Weekend*. From 1994 until his death, Clarke presented *The World at One*. He also presented a number of other Radio 4 programs, including *Round Britain Quiz*. He won the Broadcasting Press Guild award for broadcaster of the year in 2001. Among his literary works is a biography of **Alistair Cooke**.

In 2005, Clarke was diagnosed with cancer, documenting his experiences with the disease—including the amputation of one of his legs—for an audio diary that was broadcast on Radio 4 in June 2006. He returned to hosting *The World at One* in August 2006, with his last appearance coming on 12 September. He died on 23 November 2006. His memory is honored by the Nick Clarke Award, inaugurated by the BBC in 2007, to recognize the best broadcast interview of the year.

See also CURRENT AFFAIRS; DOCUMENTARY; NEWS.

CLASSIC FM. In September 1992, Classic FM became Britain's first national **commercial radio** station. The 1990 Broadcasting Act had provided opportunities for three national channels, but the successful bid for the license ultimately won by Classic FM initially went to another consortium, Showtime, with a format of **music** from West End shows. The company behind Showtime was unable to raise the required capital, and the license went to the second in line, Classic FM.

Initial reaction to an all-classical commercial station was mixed, but after nearly five months on air, the station was boasting 4.3 million listeners a week, almost double its expectations at launch, making it the fourth largest in the country. Classic FM is now owned by **Global Radio** and has broadcast from Global's studios in Leicester Square, London, since March 2006. The station has a long association of sponsorship with the Royal Liverpool Philharmonic Orchestra.

CLASSIC GOLD NETWORK. A network of radio stations that played "oldies"-style music on both **analog** and **Digital Audio Broadcasting** platforms. Most of the stations initially used the medium wave frequencies of existing local **commercial radio** stations. Starting with Mercia Sound in Coventry, which was bought by **Great Western Radio**, the stations were sold to the **Unique Broadcasting Company** in 2000 and 2002, and then to **GCap Media** in 2007, which merged the stations with its **Capital Gold** network and rebranded them as **Gold**. The resulting network is now owned by **Global Radio**.

CLEVERDON, DOUGLAS (1903–1987). Douglas Cleverdon was one of the most imaginative and creative radio producers of his era. Joining the **British Broadcasting Corporation** in 1939, he held the post of war correspondent for a short period; however, it was from the 1940s to the 1960s that his most lasting work was carried out. Cleverdon was particularly skilled at developing radio work with poets, producing, among others, David Jones's *In Parenthesis* (1946) and David Gascoyne's great **radio poem** *Night Thoughts* (1955). Nonetheless, he is best known for his collaboration with Dylan Thomas on *Under Milk Wood* (1954). It was Cleverdon who commissioned the work and guided and cajoled the unreliable Thomas for seven years and beyond, even after the poet's death, when he saw the work through to transmission with Richard Burton as "First Voice."

See also DRAMA; FEATURE.

CLITHEROE KID, THE. A popular situation **comedy** starring a diminutive Lancashire comedian named Jimmy Clitheroe (1922–1973), who played a mischievous school boy in a **series** that ran from 1958–1972—16 series for a total of 280 episodes—and was regularly listened to by more than 10 million people.

COATES, ERIC (1903–1957). Eric Coates was a composer of light orchestral **music** who created melodies that can still be heard on modern-day **British Broadcasting Corporation** programs. His *By a Sleepy Lagoon* is the theme tune for the long-running celebrity record show *Desert Island Discs*. The *Knightsbridge March*, from his *London Suite*, achieved huge popularity when it was selected as the theme for the weekly **series** *In Town Tonight*, and the introductory music to *Music While You Work* was Coates's *Calling All Workers*.

COCK, GERALD (1887–1973). Although Gerald Cock was most associated with the birth of high-definition television in the United Kingdom, he began his broadcasting career in radio. Joining the **British Broadcasting Company (BBC)** in 1925, he was responsible for widening and enhancing the range and quality of programs and events covered by BBC microphones. One of the most significant broadcasts organized by Cock was that of King George V. In February 1935, Cock was appointed the first director of television for the BBC, a post he held until transmissions ceased at the outbreak of war, when he became the BBC's North American representative. He retired in 1945, for health reasons.

See also CURRENT AFFAIRS; ROYAL BROADCASTS.

COLE, ERIC KIRKHAM (1901–1966). Eric Cole was a radio engineer who, in 1922, set up his own business manufacturing radio sets, taking advantage of the demand following the establishment of the **British Broadcasting Company** that same year. In October 1926, in partnership with fellow businessmen in his native Essex, he established a private company, using his own name to form what was to become a famous acronym in U.K. radio manufacturing: Ekco.

In 1930, Ekco began manufacturing radios using a new material called Bakelite, enabling the more adventurous design of cabinets than had been possible with conventional wood. Some of the Ekco designs from the early 1930s became classics, and by 1934, Cole's company had increased its turnover to more than 1 million pounds a year.

Cole set high standards and, as a result, Ekco sets gained a reputation for reliability. During World War II, the company worked on a number of projects for the government, including radio sets for bombers. After the war, Ekco took over Dynatron (1955) and Ferranti (1957), and moved into television manufacturing. In 1960, the company merged with Pye to form British Electronic Industries, with Cole as vice chairman. He retired in 1961, following a management disagreement.

COLES, RICHARD (1962–). Richard Coles is a priest, musician, and broadcaster, as well as a former member of the successful band the Communards. He has presented *Nightwaves* on **BBC Radio 3** and, in March 2011, succeeded **Fi Glover** as regular host of the **BBC Radio 4** program *Saturday Live*.

COLLINS, NORMAN (1907–1982). Norman Collins was creator and first controller of the **Light Programme** and instigator of numerous programs during the extraordinary period of innovation between the birth of the network in 1945 and his transfer to television, where he became controller in 1947. Always a pioneer, Collins later moved to the newly formed commercial television sector, where he was vice chairman of Associated Television from 1955–1977.

See also COMEDY; MUSIC.

COMEDY. Radio and comedy have been linked since the earliest days of the medium; however, during this time period, many comedians viewed the new medium with suspicion for two main reasons. First, entertainers schooled in the music hall tradition were used to audience feedback in the form of laughter and applause; the silence of the studio was initially unnerving and called for a different kind of timing. Second, radio was—and is—a voracious consumer of material; an act that might have toured the music halls for years was heard by millions in one performance.

Early comedians broadcasting on 2LO included Bill Beer and **Norman Long**, who became known for his "Song at the Piano" beginning on 28 November 1922. Many consider **John Henry** to be the first "pure radio" comedian. Henry was first heard on 31 May 1923, and he developed a specific microphone technique that would influence many later comedians, from **Tommy Handley** to **Tony Hancock**. The introduction of studio audiences solved the issue of timing and response, and many writing teams developed partnerships with comedians and comic actors to create sitcoms and sketch shows using a framework that included stock characters who appeared briefly each week, playing on the audience's sense of familiarity. Among the most successful of these were **Frank Muir** and **Denis Norden** with *Take It From Here*, **Ray Galton** and Alan Simpson with *Hancock's Half Hour*, and **Barry Took** and **Marty Feldman** with *Round the Horne*. Perhaps the most quintessential radio comedy series was the surreal *Goon Show*, written by **Spike Milligan**. In these examples, the "pictorial" nature of radio—its ability to create images in the mind—became a staple part of the humor, perhaps none more so that *Educating Archie*, which involved a ventriloquist's dummy as the central character.

Oxbridge humor and satire established itself in the schedules during the 1960s through such programs as *I'm Sorry I'll Read That Again* and the influence of a new breed of program controller, namely **David Hatch**. The blend of stand-up, sitcoms, panel games, and **quiz shows** has continued into the 21st century, with radio continuing to develop new writing and such performing talents as **David Baddiel**, **Steve Punt**, **Hugh Dennis**, and **Chris Morris**.

See also BEYOND OUR KEN; CLITHEROE KID, THE; NAVY LARK, THE.

COMMERCIAL RADIO. Although commercial—"independent"—radio officially began in the United Kingdom on 8 October 1973, its history considerably predates that year. Sponsored broadcasts from stations on the continent were part of the early radio scene even before the birth of the **British Broadcasting** Company. On 15 June 1920, opera singer Dame Nellie Melba broadcast from the **Marconi** works at **Chelmsford**, a recital sponsored by the *Daily Mail*, owned by Lord Northcliffe, a fervent supporter of commercial radio. There were many other experiments, notable among which was a 1925 fashion **talk** sponsored by **Selfridges** and transmitted from the Eiffel Tower. The broadcast lasted 15 minutes and received little attention at the time. It was, however, a precursor of more extensive activity, and its producer, **Leonard Plugge**, went on to found the **International Broadcasting Company (IBC)**, establishing **Radio Normandy** on 11 October 1931, and broadcasting populist material from the French port of Fécamp.

The IBC's programming interests grew throughout the 1930s, and by the middle of the decade, English-language broadcasts were extensively attacking the BBC monopoly and reaching large U.K. audiences, who felt dissatisfied and disenfranchised by the BBC's strict Sabbatarian **Sunday broadcast-**

ing policy introduced by **John Reith**. Among European stations involved in the broadcasts were **Radio Toulouse**, Poste Parisien, **Radio Côte D'Azur**, Radio San Sebastian, Radio Ljubljana, Radio Lyons, Radio Valencia, Radio Madrid, Radio Athlone, and Radio Aranjuez. In addition, and significantly, on 3 December 1933, transmissions began from **Radio Luxembourg**, using a giant transmitter on a pirated wavelength in contravention of international broadcasting law.

Throughout the later years of the 1930s, a highly successful commercial industry broadcast increasingly sophisticated popular programs, including **soap operas** and **quiz shows**, recorded in well-equipped studios in London by major advertising agencies, the largest of which was the American **J. Walter Thompson Organization**, occupying premises in London's **Bush House**. World War II ended these operations, and after the war, only Radio Luxembourg returned and resumed highly successful evening broadcasts that provided alternative listening during the 1940s, 1950s, and early 1960s.

Further commercial attacks on public service broadcasting began in March 1964, with a station broadcasting from a ship in the North Sea. **Radio Caroline**, owned by Irish entrepreneur Ronan O'Rahilly, was the first of many marine-based stations that flourished for three years, as the **British Broadcasting Corporation** once again found itself out of tune with popular youth culture. "Free Radio" became a political issue, as it had been in the 1930s, with Harold Wilson's Labour government establishing a determined campaign to outlaw the stations. Labour Party postmaster generals Edward Short and, subsequently, **Tony Benn** were instrumental in removing most of the stations from the airwaves under the new Marine Broadcasting (Offences) Act, which became law in August 1967. Commercial pirates continued spasmodically even after this; Radio Caroline has continued in a number of forms, gaining iconic status. In the 1980s, the U.S.-run **Laser 558** proved popular until it was removed under the same legislation.

Meanwhile, pressure had been mounting for the establishment of legally constituted land-based commercial radio, and in 1972, the Conservative government under Edward Heath passed the law that permitted the **London Broadcasting Company (LBC)** to be the first station in Britain to be legally supported by advertising. The station went on the air on 8 October 1973 and was followed shortly thereafter by **Capital Radio**. The early days of independent local radio (ILR), as it was known, were difficult ones. Overregulated by the **Independent Broadcasting Authority (IBA)**, stations initially found it difficult to succeed financially, although growth in advertising revenue created a somewhat healthier climate during the 1980s. The 1981 Broadcasting Act developed the system laid down in 1972, without changing the original public service ethic upon which ILR had been based. Control remained tight; the 1981 act limited the concept of program sponsorship, although the IBA sanctioned the first sponsored program in *The Network Chart Show*. Notwithstanding, station owners lobbied for more relaxed regulation.

The Broadcasting Act, published on 1 November 1990, abolished the IBA and established the **Radio Authority (RA)** as the body for specific regulation of commercial radio. The RA also permitted stations to concentrate more on developing successful business plans, rather than being forced to adhere to the unrealistic public service model of programming under which they had been forced to operate previously. As a further consequence, the RA permitted consolidation—the ability of companies to buy other stations and form groups—thus establishing the pattern of ownership that would lead U.K. commercial radio into the 21st century.

Commercial sound broadcasting continued to develop throughout the late 1990s; on 7 September 1992, the first national station opened in the form of **Classic FM**. In March 1998, the RA advertised the first national digital commercial **multiplex** license, and in the spring of 2000, **Digital One** began transmissions. In December 2003, the newly implemented Communications Act disbanded the RA, putting in its place the **Office of Communications (Ofcom)**, a regulatory body the role of which was seen as encompassing the increasingly diverse platforms available to broadcasters. The possibility of overseas ownership of U.K. interests became a real issue, with most British commercial radio stations already in the hands of a relatively small group of companies. This trend of consolidation continued with the foundation in 2007 of **Global Radio**, which, following the acquisition of **Chrysalis**, **GCap Media**, and others, became the largest commercial radio group in the country.

See also COMMERCIAL RADIO COMPANIES ASSOCIATION (CRCA); GREAT WESTERN RADIO (GWR); MUSIC; PIRATE RADIO; RADIOCENTRE; RADIOPLAYER.

COMMERCIAL RADIO COMPANIES ASSOCIATION (CRCA). The CRCA was the voluntary and nonprofit trade group for **commercial radio** companies in the United Kingdom. It was formed as the Association of Independent Radio Contractors by the first radio companies when independent radio began in 1973. The association always enjoyed the overwhelming support of the radio industry—all but a handful of stations were in membership—and it was an influential force in British broadcasting throughout its existence. In addition to promoting the importance of commercial radio, CRCA played an active role in campaigning for conditions that facilitated the future success of the industry. It was funded by the subscriptions of its member radio companies, which shared the cost in proportion to their shares of the industry's broadcasting revenue.

CRCA represented the interests of U.K. commercial radio to the British government, British Parliament, the **Office of Communications**, the European Commission, the European Parliament, and other organizations concerned with radio and broadcasting. Beginning in 1984, the association was especially active in this area, having provided significant input into the 1987 green paper "Radio: Choices and Opportunities," as well as the 1990 Broadcasting Act (which substantially deregulated independent radio), the 1996 Broadcasting Act, the Communications Act of 2003, and the 1996 and 2006 **British Broadcasting Corporation (BBC) charter** reviews. CRCA lobbied to ensure that commercial radio's views were taken into account during the passage of the 2003 Communications Act; key concessions were made in content-regulation and ownership rules, which led to consolidation in the U.K. commercial radio industry.

With the BBC, CRCA owned **Radio Joint Audience Research**, the company that oversees radio audience measurement in Great Britain. It administered the Radio Advertising Clearance Centre—the U.K. commercial radio industry's advertising clearance body—and jointly owned the Joint Industry Commercial Radio IT Futures Group with the Institute of Practitioners in Advertising. On 1 July 2006, the association merged with the Radio Advertising Bureau to form the **RadioCentre**, which continues its role and responsibilities.

COMMITTEES OF ENQUIRY. Significant committees of enquiry in the development of U.K. broadcasting have included the **Sykes Committee**, **Crawford Committee**, Selsdon Television Committee, **Ullswater Committee**, Hankey Television Committee, Beveridge Committee, Pilkington Committee, **Annan Committee**, Hunt Committee, Peacock Committee, and Davies Committee.

Sykes Committee. The Sykes Committee was appointed on 24 April 1923. The "Broadcasting Committee Report" was released on 25 August 1923. It discussed **British Broadcasting Company (BBC)** funding by license and the company's monopoly on broadcasting. The committee recommended funding for the **license fee**, no advertising, and the transfer of broadcasting from private to public. The company continued its monopoly and funding by license, eventually becoming a public corporation.

Crawford Committee. The Crawford Committee was appointed on 20 July 1925. The "Report of the Crawford Committee on Broadcasting" was released on 5 March 1926. It discussed broadcasting organization and its effect on audiences and recommended that broadcasting be run by a public service corporation with no direct parliamentary control and license fee funding for 10 years. The **British Broadcasting Corporation** was established by Royal Charter.

Selsdon Television Committee. The Selsdon Television Committee was appointed on 14 May 1934. The "Report of the Television Committee" was released on 14 January 1935, and discussed television broadcasting in the United Kingdom, as well as whether the Baird or **Marconi** systems should be adopted. Recommendations included that television broadcasting should be established within the public sector and that a London station should be set up using both systems until one proved better. The BBC commenced broadcasting from Alexandra, and the Marconi system was eventually adopted.

Ullswater Committee. The Ullswater Committee was appointed on 17 April 1935. The "Report of the Ullswater Committee on Broadcasting" was released on 16 March 1936. It discussed broadcasting, including overseas broadcasting, funding, and the nature of programming. The report called for regional broadcasting to be decentralized and expanded, the government to assume control during national emergencies, the BBC to have the freedom to report antigovernment views, no funding from advertising, an increase in the license fee, the impartiality of news programs, an increase in schools broadcasting, and an increase in the number of BBC governors by two. The BBC and its programs were further expanded.

Hankey Television Committee. The Hankey Television Committee was appointed in September 1943. Its report, released on 29 December 1944, discussed postwar television services and recommended a BBC monopoly of television services, television in the regions, high-definition television on 405 lines, television receiver standards, more coordinated research and development, and financial independence for television. Outcomes included the postwar BBC television service, which remained monopoly until 1956, and the expansion of BBC research and development.

Beveridge Committee. The Beveridge Committee was appointed on 21 June 1949. It released its "Report of the Broadcasting Committee, 1949" on 15 December 1950, discussing the BBC monopoly and funding. The report called for the BBC to continue as sole broadcaster; **charter** renewal and license fee funding, but under review; regional devolution; broadcasting of minority views; more political broadcasting; and trade union recognition.

Minority Report. In the Minority Report, Selwyn Lloyd recommended the end of the broadcasting monopoly. When the Conservative Party won the 1950 general election, Lloyd's recommendations were consolidated into a white paper, ultimately leading to the establishment of Independent Television (ITV).

Pilkington Committee. The Pilkington Committee was appointed on 13 July 1960. It released its "Report of the Committee on Broadcasting" on 1 June 1962. Discussed was the organization of the broadcasting industry and programs. Recommendations included the following: renewal of the BBC charter and license fee funding, extended radio hours, adult education broadcasting, a second BBC television channel, color television on 625 lines, local broadcasting, and better commercial television regulation. The Open University, BBC **local radio**, BBC 2, and the color television license were created.

Annan Committee. The Annan Committee was appointed on 10 April 1974. It released its "Report of the Committee on the Future of Broadcasting" on 24 February 1977. Discussed were the broadcasting industry as a whole, including the development of new technologies and their funding; the role and funding of the BBC and **Independent Broadcasting Authority**; and program standards. The report called for BBC funding by license fee, a fourth independent television channel, the long-term restructuring and diversification of broadcasting, the establishment of the Broadcasting Complaints Commission, the privatization of BBC local radio, BBC independence from direct political control, and an increase in independent production. The license fee was increased and Channel 4 created (1980).

Hunt Committee. The Hunt Committee was appointed on 6 April 1982. Its "Report of the Enquiry into Cable Expansion and Broadcasting Policy" was released on 28 September 1982, discussing the organization and future of cable broadcasting. The report called for a cable regulatory authority, the creation of programs by cable providers, and BBC and ITV programs to be carried free of charge. Cable broadcasting, which was eventually overtaken by satellite broadcasting, was expanded.

Peacock Committee. The Peacock Committee was appointed on 27 March 1985. Its "Report of the Committee on Financing the BBC" was released on 29 May 1986. Discussed were BBC funding (whether via taxation, sponsorship, advertising, or license fee), efficiency, and cable and satellite broadcasting. The report called for the license fee to continue, **BBC Radio 1** and **BBC Radio 2** to be privatized, additional broadcasting hours, independent production quotas, ITV companies franchise auctions, and the removal of cable and satellite broadcasting restrictions. The charter and license were renewed, staff cuts were made within the BBC and the BBC was made more efficient, nighttime broadcasting began, the independent production sector expanded, ITV was deregulated, and satellite broadcasting commenced.

Davies Committee (Independent Review Panel). The Davies Committee was appointed on 14 October 1998. Its report, "The Future Funding of the BBC," was released on 28 July 1999. It discussed funding of the BBC until charter review in 2005–2006. The report called for the license fee to be frozen after 2001, the license fee to be the sole income for domestic services, new money from efficiency savings, digital services to be funded by a license fee supplement, and the sale of part of **BBC Worldwide** and BBC Resources. Digital license fee plans were dropped because of government opposition, and funding was instead incorporated into the main license fee.

COMMONWEALTH BROADCASTING ASSOCIATION (CBA). The CBA is a body representing public service broadcasters from throughout the British Commonwealth. It is funded by subscriptions from 102 members and affiliates in 53 countries. The association was founded on 15 February 1945, at a conference held in the council chamber of **Broadcasting House** in London, bringing together representatives of organizations that had cooperated to broadcast reports during World War II. The stated aim of the CBA is "promoting best practices in public service broadcasting and fostering freedom of expression." It holds a biennial conference and supports its members through training, bursaries, and consultancies.

See also BBC WORLD SERVICE; MIALL, LEONARD (1914–2005).

COMMUNICORP. Communicorp is an Irish media organization formed in 1989. The owner of radio stations in eight countries throughout Europe, in February 2014, the company announced that it would be acquiring eight U.K. stations from **Global Radio**, sold by requirement of the U.K. Competition Commission following Global's purchase of the **Guardian Media Group** in 2012. Communicorp operates three stations in the **Smooth Radio** brand under franchise.

See also COMMERCIAL RADIO.

COMMUNITY RADIO. The U.K. community radio movement grew out of a number of initiatives during the early 1980s, culminating in the establishment of the Community Radio Association (CRA) in 1983. This organization evolved as a broad coalition of campaigners, academics, unlicensed stations, workshops, and community activists. From the beginning, the aim was to establish a third sector of U.K. radio alongside the **British Broadcasting Company (BBC)** and commercial interests.

The CRA gained early recognition in 1985, when the U.K. government, acknowledging the demand for community radio, agreed to a limited experiment; however, the experiment was cancelled after the government concluded that no satisfactory regulatory structure existed whereby community radio could operate. In 1987, a green paper, *Radio: Choices and Opportunities*, was published. It proposed a rapid expansion in local and community radio services. Legislation reached the statute books with the Broadcasting Act 1990. The newly formed **Radio Authority (RA)** then recognized the CRA as the representative body for community radio in Great Britain and confirmed that the new legislation would provide scope for the development of community radio.

Following a resolution passed at the 1997 Community Media Conference, it was decided that the name of the association should be changed to reflect the growth of diversity of community expression through various media, including television and the Internet. The movement is now known as the Community Media Association (CMA).

As the United Kingdom moved toward a third tier of radio provision in the form of community radio, a number of experiments took place involving incremental stations (1989–1990) set up by the IBA, specializing in specific forms of output frequently relating to ethnic groups and SALLIEs (small-scale alternative location independents). For a time, the regulator toyed with the title of "Access" radio for the new services, before the word *community* was reinstated.

In the fall of 2002, the RA was replaced by a new "super regulator" in the form of the **Office of Communications (Ofcom)**. One of the first acts of Ofcom was to sanction the development of community radio, and experimental stations were accordingly established throughout Britain. The success prompted the regulator to invite license applications for five-year franchises for community stations, advertised in the winter of 2004–2005. A total of 292 applications were received. The first to be successful was **Forest of Dean Radio** in Gloucestershire, one of the initial experimental stations, which was awarded its license in March 2005. The station ceased full-time broadcasting on 31 December 2009. By November 2010, 228 stations had been licensed in two rounds (the second coming in 2007). Of these, 181 were broadcasting at the time, with a number either returning their licenses or failing to reach the broadcasting stage.

See also COMMERCIAL RADIO; STOLLER, TONY (1947–).

CONCERT HALL (BROADCASTING HOUSE). *See also* RADIO THEATRE (BROADCASTING HOUSE).

CONSTANDUROS, MABEL (1880–1957). Coming quite late to the world of entertainment, Mabel Constanduros trained as an actress at the Central School in London, where she discovered an ability for writing and creating cockney character sketches. She joined the **British Broadcasting Company** Repertory Company in February 1925, and made her first broadcast in March of that year. Constanduros is best remembered for her creation of *The Buggins Family*. She initially played all the characters but ultimately became known for her portrayal of Grandma Buggins. She was also instrumental in the creation of *The Robinson Family*, with her nephew, Denis Constanduros. Her work was significant in establishing and developing a "voice" for British radio **comedy**. Constanduros also wrote more than 100 plays for the stage, her most successful being *Acacia Avenue* (1943).

See also DRAMA; SERIALS; SERIES; WOMEN.

CONTINUITY. The term given to presentation between radio and television programs. In British radio, the main users of continuity **announcers** are **BBC Radio 4** and the **BBC World Service**. On BBC Radio 4, announcers also have other duties, for example, **news** presentation and the reading of the shipping forecast.

CONVERSATIONS ON A TRAIN. An important **series** created in 1931, by **Hilda Matheson**. The concept behind the program was a number of simulated chance encounters on train journeys, made up of content that would be entertaining and/or topical. The programs initially used the work of such literary figures as E. M. Forster, Dorothy L. Sayers, and Aldous Huxley, supported by relevant train sound effects. The formula was not a success, and actors were used instead, in cooperation with the Drama and Features Department of the **British Broadcasting Corporation**. This transformed the series, which became extremely popular, running from 1932–1938 and drawing considerable audiences.

COOKE, ALASTAIR (1908–2004). Alastair Cooke's most famous contribution to radio broadcasting was his long-running *Letter from America*, a weekly 15-minute **talk** broadcast on the **BBC Home Service**. It was later aired on **BBC Radio 4** beginning in 1946 until within weeks of Cooke's death in 2004. Cooke was born in Manchester, England, but became a U.S. citizen in 1941. He had worked in radio in the United States, serving as NBC's London correspondent from 1935–1937. He continued working for the network until 1938 and, from 1939–1940, took over the role of film and theater critic for New York station WQXR.

In 1938, Cooke made his first full **series** of radio programs for the **British Broadcasting Corporation (BBC)** entitled *I Hear America Singing*, a set of talks illustrated with a range of actuality material gathered on location throughout the United States. The material was destroyed by German bombs during World War II.

One of Cooke's greatest influences was American critic H. L. Mencken (1880–1956); in his weekly *Letters* on BBC radio, he delighted listeners with his cool appraisal of U.S. events and political developments, always delivered in elegantly crafted scripts. Beyond these weekly programs, Cooke continued to make various major contributions to BBC Radio, including a return to his interests in American music in a series made with producer Alan Owen between 1974–1987 and broadcast on BBC Radio 4 and **BBC Radio 2**.

See also CURRENT AFFAIRS; DOCUMENTARY; FEATURE.

COOPER, BEN (?–). Ben Cooper took over as controller of **BBC Radio 1** and **BBC Radio 1Xtra** in October 2011, following the departure of the former incumbent, **Andy Parfitt**, in July of that year. Earlier in his career Cooper had worked at **Radio London**, BBC Hereford and Worcester, and Three Counties Radio before joining BBC Radio 1 as a producer. After a brief spell at **Capital Radio** as an executive producer, he rejoined BBC Radio 1 as head of mainstream, rising to the position of head of programs, a post he held from 2006–2009, when he was appointed deputy controller for the station. He became acting controller in July 2011, when Parfitt made the decision to leave, being appointed controller on a permanent basis on 28 October 2011.

See also MUSIC.

COOPER, GILES (1918–1966). Giles Cooper was a major influence on the development of radio **drama**, particularly in his use of sound effects as part of the aural narrative. Such plays as *Under the Loofah Tree* and *The Disagreeable Oyster* were instrumental in the creation of the **BBC Radiophonic Workshop** in the late 1950s. Of more than 60 dramas, produced on the **Light Programme**, **BBC Home Service**, and **Third Programme** in the 1950s and 1960s, his first to be broadcast was *Thieves Rush In*, which was produced for the Home Service in 1950. Cooper's disturbing *Unman, Wittering, and Zigo*, produced on the Third Programme in 1958, was later produced as a film starring David Hemmings. Cooper was also a masterly adapter, and his creations in this area included radio dramatizations of *Lord of the Flies* and *The Day of the Triffids*, as well as the works of Charles Dickens and Rudyard Kipling. He died in 1966, after falling from a train on his way to his home in Midhurst, Sussex. In 1978, his work was commemorated by the foundation of the annual **Giles Cooper Awards** for radio drama.

COSTA, SAM (1910–1981). Sam Costa began his radio career as a dance band singer with the **Jack Jackson** Band in 1935. In 1939, he changed his emphasis from **music** to **comedy** when he joined the cast of *It's That Man Again*. After the war, a third career in radio opened up when he became presenter of the **Light Programme** show *Record Rendezvous*. With the advent of **BBC Radio 2**, Costa hosted a number of programs, including *Sam on Sunday*, *Melodies for You*, and *Glamorous Nights*. His adopted signature tune was "Sam's Song." Costa was also a vocalist on the ***Billy Cotton Band Show***.

COTTON, BILLY (1899–1969). Billy Cotton was a cockney bandleader who hosted the ***Billy Cotton Band Show*** on the **Light Programme** and (for the program's last year) **BBC Radio 2** from 1949–1968. A former racing driver, he was famous for his trademark opening of the program, "Wakey-Wakey!" followed by his theme tune, "Somebody Stole My Gal." Vocalists on the program included Al Bowlly, Alan Breeze, **Sam Costa**, Kathy Kaye, and Doreen Stephens.

See also COMEDY; MUSIC.

COUNT ARTHUR STRONG'S RADIO SHOW!. Broadcast on **BBC Radio 4**, this **comedy series** was written by Steve Delaney, featuring "Count Arthur Strong," a fictional former variety performer. The program has had many radio series and a television version, and it has also toured as a stage production. In 2009, it won gold for best comedy show at the **Sony Radio Academy Awards**. It has been produced live in numerous theater locations by Komedia Productions and also by **Mark Radcliffe** for **Smooth Operations**.

COUNTY SOUND. This independent local radio station, serving Surrey, is noteworthy in that it was the first in the United Kingdom to divide its **amplitude modulation (AM)** and **frequency modulation (FM)** transmissions to provide separate services on a full-time basis. Prior to this, beginning in 1986, Hull-based **Viking Radio** had divided its FM and AM services on Saturdays only to provide an alternative for Rugby fans in its area. In June 1988, County Sound launched a completely separate **Gold** service on AM, alongside and independent of its FM service, which it renamed Premier. In 1990, it also launched a localized FM service, Delta Radio, for Haslemere. County Sound was also one of the pioneers in the use of computerized radio programming in Britain.

See also COMMERCIAL RADIO.

CRAWFORD COMMITTEE (CMND. 2599). This important government committee was set up by the postmaster general in 1925, under the chairmanship of the Earl of Crawford and Bacarres, to explore the future of the **British Broadcasting Company (BBC)** beyond its initial form. Through its deliberations, it moved the company from the status approved by the 1923 **Sykes Committee** toward the established **British Broadcasting Corporation** in 1927, thus formalizing the model of public service broadcasting that the BBC would thereafter represent. Crawford was also interested in the social effects of broadcasting; there were concerns from some quarters that wireless listening would encourage a cultural passivity, while at the same time undermining the financial security of such public entertainments as concerts and theater.

The committee's conclusions led to the creation of the British Broadcasting Corporation (the committee's recommendation that it should be the British Broadcasting *Commission* was one of the few to be rejected) under **charter** and replacement of the nine main regional broadcasting stations throughout Britain by two main services—the **Regional Programme** and **National Programme**. It also recommended no direct parliamentary control, **license fee** funding for 10 years, and the development of educational programs. The license fee—set at 10 shillings and under the authority of the postmaster general—was to continue and be collected by the **Post Office**.

See also COMMITTEES OF ENQUIRY.

CRAZY PEOPLE. See GOON SHOW, THE.

CRIDLAND, JAMES (1971–). James Cridland is the managing director of **media.info**, formerly known as Media UK, a Web resource that supplies current **news** and information relating to the U.K. media industry. Cridland has been described as a "radio futurologist" and is a writer and consultant, as well as an authority on technical and platform strategy in developing radio. He began his career as a technical operator on Pennine FM's Classic Gold service in 1989, moving into presentation on a number of **commercial radio** stations during the early 1990s, before going to work for **Emap** as a trainer of producers and presenters. From 2001–2005, Cridland was head of strategic development of new media, and from 2005–2007, he served as director of digital media at **Virgin Radio**, before joining the **British Broadcasting Corporation (BBC)** in July 2007, as head of future media and technology, audio, and music, moving to the role of executive product manager of A/V products in March 2009. He left the BBC later that year to found **RadioDNS**, a technology that brings together broadcast radio and the Internet. Cridland has also been a consultant for **Radioplayer**, as well as a trustee of the **Radio Academy**.

CROOK, TIM (1959–). Tim Crook is an author, teacher, and producer. He worked as a presenter and reporter for the **London Broadcasting Company** and, in the field of radio **drama**, formed **Independent Radio Drama Productions** in 1987. As a writer and producer, he has created work for U.K. independent radio, National Public Radio in the United States, and **British Broadcasting Corporation** radio. He has also written numerous books on radio, including radio drama and radio journalism. Crook is a senior lecturer in communications at Goldsmiths College at University of London, where his research interests include media law and ethics, the practice and history of radio drama, and propaganda in radio.

CRYSTAL SET. The term given to the earliest and simplest radio receivers. The key part of the technology was a diode detector made from the junction of a fine wire (*see* "CAT'S WHISKER") touching a mineral crystal, hence the name. A "plug-in" electrical source was not required. Thus, the device became popular among young hobbyists after the introduction of the **valve**, or tube.

See also FLEMING, JOHN AMBROSE (1849–1945).

CURRAN, CHARLES (1921–1980). Sir Charles John Curran was the first person from a nonpublic school background to be appointed as director-general of the **British Broadcasting Corporation (BBC)**. Having served in the Indian Army, he first worked for the BBC in the Talks Department but resigned after a dispute. He rejoined the corporation in 1951, in the Monitoring Department, subsequently holding the posts of secretary and director of External Broadcasting. As director-general, Curran was more popular with the Board of Governors than the staff, who criticized his decision-making abilities. During his time, he was also president of the European Broadcasting Union for three terms. He died of a heart attack in 1980.

CURRENT AFFAIRS. The origins of current affairs radio in the United Kingdom lie in the "Topical Talks" of the late 1920s and 1930s. Most **talks** were educational, but some dealt with political, economic, and social issues that today might be termed *current affairs*. One of the main topical issues concerned unemployment; however, this type of talk was less concerned with explaining the causes or examining the effects of unemployment than trying to create social cohesion.

It was the perceived ignorance of modern affairs generally demonstrated by the British soldier before World War II that led to one of the earliest known uses of the term. An attempted remedy for this ignorance was provided in the form of provision of a **series** of "current affairs" classes in European geopolitics.

Within the **British Broadcasting Corporation (BBC)** itself, the term appears in the staff lists for 1958, where "Current Affairs Talks Department" is mentioned. There are many examples of current affairs radio programs, almost all of them on the BBC. They can be broadly divided into "magazine" and single-subject documentary strands. Of the former, the most important is the *Today* program, while of the latter, *Analysis* is the most significant. In the early days of **Independent Radio News**, the weekly program *Decision Makers* offered the **commercial radio** network a form of current affairs in a half-hour format.

See also NEWS.

CUTFORTH, RENÉ (1909–1984). As with others of his generation of **news** correspondents, René Cutforth was a reporter whose love of words and the observance of detail marked him as a highly distinctive voice in radio. He broadcast reports from the Korean War and subsequently worked as a free-lancer, specializing in travel programs and capitalizing on his clear eye and ear.

D

DAILY MAIL. This national newspaper can claim to have had a longer association with the development of radio than any other newspaper in Britain. In 1920, it was the *Daily Mail* that sponsored the **Marconi Company's** famous broadcast of Dame Nellie Melba from **Chelmsford**, later declaring the event a success in the following terms: "Art and Science joined hands, and the world listening in must have counted every minute of it precious."

DAILY SERVICE. This 15-minute act of worship, now broadcast at 9:45 a.m. on **BBC Radio 4 longwave**, began in 1928. It is one of the world's longest-running radio programs, with a formula that has remained virtually unchanged since it's inception, as the direct result of one listener, a Mrs. Kathleen Cordeux, who maintained a determined campaign of pressure on **John Reith** and wrote in a 1926 edition of the *Radio Times*, putting forth the idea of a daily service containing a "little sacred music, hymns, a brief reading or address to comfort the sick and suffering and the lonely."
    See also RELIGIOUS PROGRAMS.

DAMAZER, MARK (1955–). Mark Damazer was controller of **BBC Radio 4** from October 2004, when he succeeded **Helen Boaden** in the post, until April 2010, when he left the **British Broadcasting Corporation (BBC)** to become master of St. Peter's College in Oxford. Prior to his role at BBC Radio 4, he had been deputy director of **news** at the BBC since April 2001. He was previously assistant chief executive of the News Division beginning in December 1999, with responsibility for the quality and standards of news programs for the BBC networks.
    Educated at Cambridge, where he attained a double-starred first in history, Damazer joined the **BBC World Service** in 1981, as a **current affairs** producer. He then spent two years with Independent Television as a producer with TV-a.m., returning to BBC TV in 1984, where he helped launch the *Six O'Clock News*. He became output editor of *Newsnight* in January 1986, followed by deputy editor of the *Nine O'Clock News* in 1988, becoming editor of the program in 1990.

In 1996, Damazer became head of weekly programs, news, and current affairs; the department was restructured and renamed Current Affairs in 1997, and he then had responsibilities in both radio and television, overseeing radio policy affecting such programs as *File on Four*, *From Our Own Correspondent*, and *Law in Action* . He also is a fellow of the **Radio Academy**. Upon leaving his post as controller of BBC Radio 4, Damazer was replaced by **Gwyneth Williams**.

DAN DARE. In July 1951, **Radio Luxembourg** broadcast the first episode in what was to become a remarkably popular **series** of science fiction programs featuring *The Adventures of Dan Dare, Pilot of the Future*. Dan Dare was a character that originated in the children's comic *The Eagle*, as well as the radio version, which was sponsored by Horlicks, was announced by **Bob Danvers-Walker**, and starred Noel Johnson as Dan. The identity of Johnson was kept secret due to the fact that he also starred in *Dick Barton, Special Agent*, the eponymous **British Broadcasting Corporation** series, of which the final episode had aired (prior to a 1970s revival) in March 1951, a little more than three months before the Dan Dare programs started. Radio Luxembourg broadcast the last episode in the series on 25 May 1956; however, in April 1990, to mark the 40th anniversary of the first publication of the *Eagle*, **BBC Radio 4** created a new stereo version of the first of the Dan Dare **serials** in four episodes.

DANGER. Also called *A Comedy of Danger*, this play is arguably the first such work specifically written for radio as a medium, although a children's play by Phyllis M. Twigg entitled *The Truth about Father Christmas* (broadcast on 24 December 1922) has also been suggested as the first. The author, Richard Hughes, was invited by the **British Broadcasting Company** to write the work in January 1924, and it was created in one weekend. Made during an era when film was still silent, Hughes's introductory remarks to the published edition of the play are significant, describing how the brief was to "write a play for effect by sound only, in the same way that film plays are written for effect by sight only." Hence, this was the first "listening play." Nigel Playfair was the producer, and the play was broadcast from **Savoy Hill** on 15 January 1924. The action was set in a coal mine. Mary says, "Hello! What's happened?" Jack responds, "The lights have gone out!" It was suggested to the audience that they listen in darkness; thus, Hughes and Playfair had identified early in its development the unique imaginative interaction between broadcaster and audience, something that would continue to inform radio ever after.
    See also DRAMA.

DANIELS, BEBE (1901–1971). Bebe Daniels was an American movie actress, first as a child star in silent film, and later, during the 1930s, in a **series** of major Hollywood successes. In 1930, she married **Ben Lyon**, and in 1935, the couple moved to London, where they became major celebrities and personalities, starring in the wartime comedy *Hi Gang!* for which Daniels wrote most of the material. After the war, Lyon and Daniels starred in a new radio show called *Life with the Lyons*, a **comedy** version of their own life, featuring their real-life son and daughter, Richard and Barbara. During the 1960s, Daniels suffered a series of strokes and was cared for by her husband until her death in 1971.

See also WARTIME BROADCASTING.

DANN, TREVOR (1951–). Trevor Dann's career in radio has included work as a **local radio** reporter and producer (Radio Nottingham, 1974–1979), a **BBC Radio 1** producer (1979–1983), and managing editor of the **British Broadcasting Corporation's (BBC)** London radio station **Greater London Radio** (1988–1993). From 1996–2000, he was head of BBC Music Entertainment, responsible for the BBC's in-house pop **music** production, including BBC Radio 1, **BBC Radio 2**, and **BBC World Service** pop output and international distribution. Dann was managing director of popular music for **Emap** (2000–2002) and, from 2006–2010, chief executive of the **Radio Academy**. His production company, TDC, has made programs for BBC Radio 2 and **BBC Radio 4**. His work has won recognition at the **Radio Academy Awards**, and in 2014, he received gold and silver at the New York Radio Awards. Dann is also visiting professor at Lincoln University and Nottingham Trent University.

DANVERS-WALKER, BOB (1906–1990). Before World War II, Bob Danvers-Walker was a well-known presenter on **commercial radio**, broadcasting from continental Europe, most notably on **Radio Normandy** and other stations owned by the **International Broadcasting Company (IBC)**. Although born in England, he was brought up in Tasmania and began broadcasting in Australia. He joined the IBC in 1932 and remained with the company 1939, during which time he helped established a number of the stations in the group with English-language content. When the war ended the enterprise, Danvers-Walker became the voice of Pathé newsreels.

See also DISC JOCKEY (DJ); MUSIC.

DAVENTRY. The name "Daventry" is one of the most significant in British broadcasting history. Within two years of the **British Broadcasting Company (BBC)** commencing broadcasting, a network of nine main medium wave (MW) transmitters, augmented by 11 **relay stations**, each with its own studio, had been established throughout the United Kingdom. Due to the qualities of MW transmissions, however, it was not possible to adequately serve all stations with a common program from London. The BBC therefore set up plans to create a giant **longwave (LW)** transmitter that would be capable of such coverage. The requirement was for a site in Central England, and after investigation, Borough Hill, on the outskirts of Daventry in Northamptonshire, was chosen.

The station, using the call sign 5XX on a frequency of 187.5 kHz, was opened with considerable pomp by the postmaster general on 27 July 1925. A poem was even commissioned from poet Alfred Noyes and read during the opening ceremony. An extract demonstrates the almost mystical aspirations of early broadcasting:

> You shall hear their lightest tone
> Stealing through your walls of stone;
>
> Till your loneliest valleys hear
> The far cathedral's whispered prayer,
>
> And thoughts that speed the world's desire
> Strike to your heart beside your fire;
>
> And the mind of half the world
> Is in each little house unfurled.

With an output power of 25 kW, Daventry was the most powerful transmitter in the world and the first to use LWs. Reception reports soon confirmed that the range of the station was 300 kilometers for **valve** receivers and that 85 percent of the U.K. population could receive transmissions from the station.

In March 1992, after 67 years, the Daventry transmitter was closed down because of a reduction in the BBC's total transmission requirements. The site is now a broadcasting maintenance depot.

See also BROOKMANS PARK TRANSMITTING STATION.

DAVIE, TIM (1967–). Tim Davie joined the **British Broadcasting Corporation (BBC)** in 2005, as director of marketing, communications, and audiences, after a career in marketing. In 2008, he replaced **Jenny Abramsky** as director of audio and **music**, with overall responsibility for the BBC's national radio networks and the corporation's music output in all media. In November 2012, Davie became acting director-general of the BBC, following the resignation of **George Entwistle**. He remained in the post until the new incumbent, **Tony Hall**, took up the position in April 2013, at which point Davie became head of **BBC Worldwide**.

DAVIES, GAVYN (1950–). Gavyn Davies, who became chairman of the **British Broadcasting Corporation (BBC)** in 2001, has a background as an economist, and he chaired a 1999 enquiry into BBC funding. He joined the Board of Governors as vice chairman in 2001, and took over the chairmanship during that same year, upon the departure of **Christopher Bland**. He resigned after the circulation of the 2004 Hutton Report, which investigated the death of government weapons expert Dr. David Kelly.

DAVIS, DAVID (1908–1996). Born in Bishop's Stortford, David Davis was a producer and presenter of **British Broadcasting Corporation (BBC) children's programs**. He joined the staff of *Children's Hour* as a pianist in 1935, remaining with the show until its demise in 1964. From Queen's College in Oxford, Davis's career prior to the BBC included four years as a schoolmaster beginning in 1931. During the war, he served in the Royal Naval Volunteer Reserve (1942–1946), after which he returned to the BBC. He became head of *Children's Hour* in 1953 and, from 1961–1964, rose to head of children's programs. When *Children's Hour* ended as part of the program policy of **Frank Gillard**, it is said that it left Davis a broken man. It was his decision to end the final edition with a symbolic reading of Oscar Wilde's *The Selfish Giant*. Davies then moved to the BBC Radio Drama Department as a producer until his retirement in 1970. He fostered many talents and program ideas, among the most successful being *Jennings at School* by **Anthony Buckeridge**.
   See also DRAMA; SERIALS; SERIES.

DEARMAN, GLYN (1937–1998). Glyn Dearman was originally a child actor who appeared in two film adaptations of Charles Dickens's *Nicholas Nickleby* and *A Christmas Carol*. He also played the part of Jennings for a time in **Anthony Buckeridge's** school **series** for radio, *Jennings at School*. He later became a respected radio producer and made **drama** and **features** of the highest quality. Dearman produced **Andrew Sachs's** wordless play *The Revenge* (1978) and the *Earthsearch* series by James Follett, along with a significant amount of other distinguished work. At the lighter end of production, he worked on the popular **serials** *Mrs. Dale's Diary* and *Waggoners' Walk*. Dearman died in an accident in 1998.
   See also CHILDREN'S PROGRAMS; SOAP OPERAS.

DEATH AT BROADCASTING HOUSE. A thriller novel published in 1934, under the authorship of **Val Gielgud** (head of productions at the **British Broadcasting Corporation** since 1929 and brother of famous actor John Gielgud) and "Holt Marvell," the pseudonym of **Eric Maschwitz**, at the time editor of *Radio Times*. It is unique in that it shows the action driven by radio production within **Broadcasting House** itself. Filmed in November 1934, on location within Broadcasting House, the story revolves around the murder of an actor perpetrated during the recording of a play and "captured" on a new piece of recording technology—the **Blattnerphone**.

See also DRAMA.

DECISION MAKERS. This weekly half-hour **documentary** program was produced by the Parliamentary Unit of **Independent Radio News (IRN)** and funded by the **Independent Broadcasting Authority (IBA)**. Dealing with major **current affairs** issues of the day, it started in 1976, and was distributed by IRN to the **commercial radio** network for 10 years. *Decision Makers* was taken off the air in 1986, when IBA funding was withdrawn at a time when commercial radio stations were becoming increasingly reluctant to broadcast 30-minute speech programs.

See also NEWS.

DEE, SIMON (1935–). Simon Dee was the first voice on **Radio Caroline**, the **pirate radio** station run by Ronan O'Rahilly from a ship in the North Sea beginning on Easter Sunday 1964. Absorbed by the **British Broadcasting Corporation** in 1966, even before the creation of **BBC Radio 1**, he presented such programs as *Housewives' Choice*. Dee also worked for **Radio Luxembourg** and, in a mixed broadcasting career, became, for a time, a considerable television personality, hosting his own chat show, *Dee Time,* on Saturday evenings.

See also COMMERCIAL RADIO; DISC JOCKEY (DJ); MUSIC.

DE MANIO, JACK (1914–1988). Jack de Manio was an idiosyncratic and eccentric broadcaster who presented the **BBC Radio 4** program *Today* from 1958–1971. He had joined the **British Broadcasting Corporation** in 1946, as an **announcer**, but it was on *Today* that he gained his reputation, largely, and ironically, due to his notorious inability to give listeners the correct time. Until 1970, he was the only presenter of the program; it became a two-person presentation show when he was joined by John Timpson. De Manio left the following year and began a new Radio 4 afternoon series known as *Jack de Manio Precisely*, which lasted until 1978, after which his radio career effectively ended.

See also NEWS.

DELANEY, FRANK (1942–). Known for his work as a novelist, journalist, and broadcaster, Frank Delaney began his radio career in 1970, as a newsreader for the Irish radio and television network RTE. He subsequently became a **news** reporter for the **British Broadcasting Corporation** in Dublin.

After five years in this role, he moved to London, working in arts and cultural broadcasting. In 1978, he was founding presenter of the **BBC Radio 4** literary program *Bookshelf.* In 1992, Delaney was the first presenter of *Word of Mouth*, produced by **Simon Elmes**. He lives in Connecticut in the United States.

DELL, ALAN (1924–1995). Alan Dell was a sophisticated and knowledgeable presenter of **music** programs, with a long-running association with the **Light Programme** and **BBC Radio 2** that lasted from the 1950s until shortly before his death. Born in Cape Town, South Africa, he joined the record library staff of the South Africa Broadcasting Corporation in 1943, and was one of the first presenters on Springbok Radio when it started in 1950. He then went to the United States and the United Kingdom to study radio production and acoustics, and settled in England in 1953. In addition to his work for the **British Broadcasting Corporation**, Dell made programs for **Radio Luxembourg**. His style was relaxed and intimate, and the music played on his programs was usually that of such big band, swing, and middle-of-theroad artists as Frank Sinatra. He presented *Sounds Easy* on BBC Radio 2 until his death from cancer in 1995.

See also DISC JOCKEY (DJ).

DENNIS, HUGH (1962–). Hugh Dennis is a comedian and writer known for his partnership with **Steve Punt**. Their radio work developed from *The Mary Whitehouse Experience*, which was first broadcast in 1990, on **BBC Radio 1**, and subsequently transferred to television. Other radio work with Punt included *It's Been a Bad Week* for **BBC Radio 2** and *The Now Show* for **BBC Radio 4**.

See also COMEDY.

DEPARTMENT OF TRADE AND INDUSTRY (DTI). The British government's DTI has historically been a major influence on the development of radio in the United Kingdom. It has been responsible for the allocation of frequencies, notably for amateur, marine, and mobile services, and has policed **pirate radio** throughout the years. DTI has actively supported the development of radio technology in the United Kingdom and, through its Global Watch industry missions, funded comparative research trips exploring the possible future of radio in such countries as the United States, Korea, and Singapore. After the 2005 general election, DTI was renamed the Department for Productivity, Energy, and Industry, only to revert to its old name within a week.

See also COMMITTEES OF ENQUIRY.

DERBYSHIRE, DELIA (1937–2001). This gifted and innovative composer joined the **British Broadcasting Corporation (BBC)** as a trainee studio manager in 1962, but was soon seconded to the **BBC Radiophonic Workshop,** based at studios in Maida Vale, London, to create sound effects and theme **music** for BBC **drama.** Working in both radio and television, Derbyshire's best-known work was her realization of Ron Grainer's music, which became the theme tune of the popular television **series** *Dr. Who.* She created many other themes and sounds for BBC media and worked outside of the corporation with many leading contemporary composers, including Karlheinz Stockhausen and Peter Maxwell Davies. Derbyshire left the BBC in 1973, disillusioned by what she saw as an increasing artistic conservatism. She continued to innovate for the rest of her life, and shortly after her death, she was celebrated in a **BBC Radio 4** play entitled *Blue Veils and Golden Sands*, written by Martin Wade and titled after one of her own compositions.
See also WOMEN.

DERBYSHIRE, VICTORIA (1968–). Victoria Derbyshire is a broadcaster and journalist who presented **news** and **current affairs** programs on **BBC Radio 5 Live**. After reading English at Liverpool University, she studied radio and television journalism at what was then known as Preston Polytechnic (now the University of Central Lancashire). Prior to joining BBC Radio 5 Live in 1998, Derbyshire worked in **local radio**. The BBC Radio 5 Live breakfast show, of which she was copresenter, won a gold **Sony Radio Academy Award** in 1998 and 2002. After taking maternity leave, she moved to the morning news program in August 2004. This program also won a gold Sony Radio Academy Award for best news and current affairs program in 2011. The following year she received the award for best speech broadcaster of the year, winning it again at the 2014 **Radio Academy Awards**. Derbyshire left BBC Radio 5 Live in September of that year to move into television.
See also WOMEN.

DESERT ISLAND DISCS. Devised by **Roy Plomley** in 1942, and probably the best known of all U.K. radio record shows, the format of this program continues to be the same as when it was conceived. Each week, a guest celebrity is invited to choose eight records he or she would want to take with them if they were to be marooned on a desert island. They are also permitted to take one luxury item and one book, other than the Bible and Shakespeare. The guest is interviewed about his or her life as they explain their choices.

Individuals from every walk of life have appeared on the program throughout the years. Plomley himself summed up the essence of the show's continuing appeal in his 1975 book *Desert Island Discs*, writing, "I believe *Desert*

Island Discs adds a dimension to a listener's mental picture of a well-known person, giving the same insight he would receive from visiting the celebrity's home and seeing the books, pictures, and furniture with which he surrounds himself." Since Plomley's death in 1985, the program has been presented by Sue Lawley and then Kirsty Young.

See also MUSIC.

DICK BARTON, SPECIAL AGENT. Dick Barton was a dashing former commando hero of postwar British radio, the eponymous central character initially played by Noel Johnson. First broadcast on the **Light Programme** in October 1946, it was the first daily radio **serial** broadcast by the **British Broadcasting Corporation (BBC)**. Famous for its theme tune, "The Devil's Gallop," the program quickly gained an enormous audience; originally aimed at adults, it also appealed to young listeners, and the BBC adjusted the content accordingly, making Barton (the hero) a teetotaler. At its peak, the show was required listening for approximately 15 million listeners each evening. It ran for 711 episodes, with the final episode being broadcast in March 1951. It was revived for a short **series** in 1972, for the BBC's jubilee, with Johnson reprising his original part.

See also DRAMA; SOAP OPERAS.

DIGITAL AUDIO BROADCASTING (DAB). The **British Broadcasting Corporation (BBC)** initially pioneered DAB in the United Kingdom and was the first broadcaster in the country to build a transmission network, commencing in 1995. In 1998, the first commercial digital radio license was awarded to **Digital One**. By 2003, Digital One was covering 85 percent of the United Kingdom.

DAB has been enthusiastically developed by both the commercial and public service sectors by way of the Eureka 147 system, which uses MPEG and COFDM (Coded Orthogonal Frequency Division Multiplex) technology, which converts the content from an **analog** signal into a digital (binary) code. The result is a greatly reduced possibility of transmission interference. With DAB, there is virtually no possibility of hiss and fade, as with previous methods of transmission.

The other principal quality of DAB is its ability to transmit radio signals in clusters, known in the United Kingdom as **multiplexes**. This technology permits broadcasters to transmit more radio stations within the same comparable amount of radio spectrum compared to **frequency modulation (FM)**, providing listeners with a wide range of digital-only stations. For example, **GCap Media** created such stations as Core and Planet Rock, which are aimed at specialist or niche audiences, while BBC radio launched five digital-only stations in 2002, including **BBC Radio 1Xtra** and **BBC Radio 7**.

DAB receivers have the capability of accessing data, and small screen displays scroll text with program or auxiliary information. The initial public take-up of digital radio in the United Kingdom was slow; receivers were priced too high to attract potential listeners, and there was a blurred focus as to the benefits of the new service. Since the turn of the century, however, manufacturers have marketed increasingly cheaper, more stylish receivers, and growth has been more rapid, although not sufficient enough to warrant an expected switchover from **analog** radio services.

DIGITAL ONE. A pioneer of digital broadcasting in U.K. **commercial radio**, Digital One was the sole applicant for the 1998 U.K. National Multiplex license and was thus awarded the license by the **Radio Authority**. It started broadcasting in November 1999, on a renewable 12-year term. Founder stations on the **multiplex** were **Classic FM**, **Virgin Radio**, **talkSPORT**, Core, Life, **Oneword Radio**, **Planet Rock**, and Primetime Radio. Of these, Core, Life, Oneword Radio, and Primetime subsequently closed down. As of 2014, owned by **Arqiva**, the multiplex covered 90 percent of the United Kingdom, with 14 stations. These include **Absolute Radio**, Absolute Radio 80s, Absolute Radio 90s, the **British Forces Broadcasting Service**, **Classic FM**, the **London Broadcasting Company**, Planet Rock, Premier Christian Radio, **Smooth Radio**, Capital Xtra, **Kiss FM**, **talkSPORT**, Team Rock, and UCB UK.

DIGITAL RIGHTS MANAGEMENT (DRM). A term that refers to technology used to control the use of digital content after sale or broadcast. It is used by hardware manufacturers, publishers, and copyright holders, and has had a number of variations as platforms and devices have evolved throughout the years. First-generation DRM sought to control the copying of material. A second-generation version has been introduced, with the intention of controlling, executing, viewing, copying, printing, or altering works or specific devices. The term is sometimes referred to as copy protection, copy prevention, and copy control, and it remains controversial in some areas.

DILLON, FRANCIS (1899–1982). Known to his colleagues as "Jack," Francis Dillon saw active service in World War I, after which he spent time with a number of fighting units, including, it was said, the White Army in Russia and the Black and Tans in Ireland. In contrast, he subsequently found work as a tax inspector in Manchester, and he retained the job until 1936, when he began writing for the burgeoning **British Broadcasting Corporation (BBC)** North Region radio Features Department under **E. A. Harding**.

In 1938, Dillon moved to Bristol to assume the post of West Regional features producer before moving to London in 1941, to work in the Features and Drama Department. It was there that he met **Louis MacNeice**, and the two men became close friends and working colleagues. In MacNeice's autobiographical poem *Autumn Sequel*, Dillon is represented by the character "Devlin." In 1942, Dillon started the radio **series** *Country Magazine*, on which he worked with **Desmond Hawkins**. The program was a response to a request from the government's Ministry of Agriculture, which felt that such a concept would raise morale at a time when travel restrictions brought about by war meant that public access to the countryside was limited. The program ran for 12 years.

In 1949, Dillon won a **Prix Italia** award in the first year of the competition's existence for one of a **series** of fairy tale adaptations he undertook at the time, *The Old and True Story of Rumpelstiltskin*. He retired from the BBC in 1959, but continued to work as a freelance writer and producer from his Sussex home. He died of pneumonia on 9 December 1982—his 83rd birthday.

See also FEATURE.

DIMBLEBY, RICHARD (1913–1965). Richard Dimbleby was best known to television audiences for his presentation of the **British Broadcasting Corporation (BBC) news** and **current affairs** program *Panorama*. He was, however, first and foremost a radio correspondent of the highest order, and in 1936, he virtually created the role of radio reporter, insisting that the BBC needed the voice of an on-location observer to bring news events alive. As the BBC's first war correspondent, he had the unique ability to portray a scene in words so graphic that listeners felt that they were present with him at some of the most extreme locations of the conflict. Famous among these were his recorded commentaries of an Allied bombing raid on Germany, in which the audience could hear the gunfire of German antiaircraft batteries exploding around him, and his memorable account of the liberation of Belsen. The first reporter to enter the camp, he completed his recorded report and then, so he later confessed, became physically sick.

After the war, Dimbleby moved into radio light entertainment, presenting *Down Your Way* for five years and serving as a panel member of the *Twenty Questions* program for 18 years. In 1990, he received the unique posthumous honor for a broadcaster of having a memorial dedicated to him in Westminster Abbey, where, in 1953, he had commentated on the coronation of Queen Elizabeth II.

DISC JOCKEY (DJ). An American term that went into usage in the United Kingdom as a result of U.S. broadcasts to Europe during the war. Prior to this, the **British Broadcasting Corporation (BBC)** and **commercial radio** had employed personalities as "presenters of Gramophone Record Recitals." There is some variance of opinion as to the first U.K. representative of the role. **Peter Eckersley** introduced occasional records from **Writtle** in the earliest **Marconi Company** experiments in 1920.

The first regularly scheduled weekly program broadcast by the BBC began in March 1924, presented by Compton MacKenzie, editor of *Gramophone Magazine*; however, Mackenzie's son-in-law, **Christopher Stone**, was the first "professional" DJ in the United Kingdom, broadcasting beginning in 1927, on the BBC, followed by on **commercial radio**, from the continent. Other key presenters from this time period included **Radio Luxembourg's Stephen Williams**. The first **woman** DJ in the United Kingdom was **Doris Arnold**, who presented *These You Have Loved* on the BBC **National Programme** beginning in 1938 and into the mid-1960s.

After World War II, the concept of the personality DJ developed, most notably on such BBC programs as *Housewives' Choice*. Specialist **music** DJs emerged, as well as wholly original talents like **Jack Jackson**, who, beginning in 1948, redefined the role with his interaction between music and speech in programs the likes of *Record Roundabout*. Postwar Radio Luxembourg continued to develop new household names, particularly familiar to the popular music-seeking young, including Teddy Johnson, **Peter Murray**, and **Barry Alldiss**.

Such North Sea **pirate radio** stations as **Radio Caroline** and **Radio London** took up the mantle in the 1960s, and presenters like **Simon Dee** and **Tony Blackburn** brought a new informality and U.S.-style pace and dynamism to music broadcasting. This would be the foundation of the late flowering of music radio in Britain.

Toward the end of the 20th century, the role of the DJ on local stations was frequently diminished by automation and format-based programming in which personality broadcasting gave way to formulaic and functional-link-based presentation. The term gained more currency in live club performances, with many popular DJs complementing their radio programs on youth stations and networks with live performances in clubs, using discs as instruments with techniques like "scratching," something that the new technology of computer-based music selector devices in radio studios could not replicate.

Two distinct types of broadcasters emerged, one as artist in their own right, interacting through the music to dancers in clubs, while on air the term was being replaced more and more by the word *presenter*, which demonstrated wider knowledge and skills in production and interviewing beyond the music itself. This change became necessary for broadcasters to maintain the relevance of music radio in a climate of downloads and the creation of personal playlists on **MP3** players.

The popularization of classical music by **Classic FM** has brought DJ-style presentation to a form of music radio that had previously been typified by the more formal style of **BBC Radio 3**, and this relaxed approach to such programming has, to a certain extent, crossed over into the policy of the latter network. More broadly, the role of the DJ/radio presenter is now that of a companion with the ability to inform on a range of popular cultural issues. This has been notable on such stations as **BBC Radio 1** and **BBC Radio 1Xtra** through the work of presenters like **Trevor Nelson**, personalities with the ability to become role models for distinct sections of the listening community. Female disc jockeys have included **Annie Nightingale** and **Jo Whiley**.

DISC RECORDING. Discs were, for many years, the favored means of reproduction for radio, and in 1930, **Cecil Watts** created a system of economical, efficient recording using an aluminum-based cellulose nitrate lacquer-coated disc that enabled playback directly after recording. The advantage of the Watts system was that while the coating was soft enough to enable the recording stylus to cut, it was durable enough to withstand repeated playbacks of as many as 20 times. The system was widely used through the 1930s and beyond.

DOCUMENTARY. The development of documentary program making in Britain is almost as old as the medium itself. For many years, however, the form of radio documentary was dictated by the limitations of technology. Scripted **talks** and discussions were frequent examples of factual programs broadcast by the **British Broadcasting Company/Corporation (BBC)**, and this persisted into the 1930s. The introduction of recording and, in particular, mobile recording created more creative possibilities, and the development of such **features** units as those in Manchester, run by **E. A. Harding**, before the war and London, under **Laurence Gilliam**, postwar gave producers the opportunity to interrogate the factual genre in varied ways.

As radio freed itself from restrictions imposed by early agreements formed between the BBC and the newspaper associations, programs became more journalistic and investigative. Postwar, the radio documentary has been an increasingly significant form, with important and sometimes difficult topics explored by experienced journalists and producers in the field of **news** and **current affairs**. Beginning in 1973, with the coming of U.K.-based **commercial radio**, a new generation of documentary makers were given the opportunity to add documentary voices, and some powerful work resulted from outside the BBC. The documentary form has been flexible, and the use of **drama** documentary to explore the implication of facts beyond the explicit statement has, on occasion, been used to considerable effect.

Many distinguished program makers from the field of news have been associated with the documentary genre, among them **René Cutforth**, **Richard Dimbleby**, and Feargal Keane. Programs as diverse as *File on Four* from BBC radio and, in the 1970s and 1980s, *Decision Makers* from **Independent Radio News** and *Face the Facts* contrasted with the more impressionistic work of producers like **Charles Parker**, who sought to explore the realm of documentary through location and direct contact with his subjects in such **series** as the *Radio Ballads*.

DOES THE TEAM THINK?. One of British radio's longest-running **comedy quiz shows**, the program was a parody of the **British Broadcasting Corporation's** *The Brain's Trust* and *Any Questions?*, with four comedians, including **Jimmy Edwards**, who devised the program, ad-libbing answers to listeners' questions. It ran from 1958–1976.

See also SERIES.

DONOVAN, PAUL (1949–). Paul Donovan has been a radio columnist for the *Sunday Times* since 1988, in addition to much other distinguished writing on radio matters, including *All Our Todays* (1997), marking 40 years of **BBC Radio 4's** *Today* program. He has, on several occasions, been a judge for the **Sony Radio Academy Awards**, and until 2005, was convener of the Broadcasting Press Guild radio awards.

DOUBLE YOUR MONEY. A popular **quiz show** that ultimately became a major attraction on newly formed Independent Television in 1955, running until 1968. *Double Your Money* was originally a radio program for **Radio Luxembourg**. Broadcast on the station beginning in October 1954, it was sponsored by Lucozade and devised by **Hughie Green**, who also acted as the show's master of ceremonies.

DOUGLAS, LESLEY (1963–). Lesley Douglas was appointed controller of **BBC Radio 2** and **BBC Radio 6 Music** in October 2003. She assumed the post in January 2004, succeeding **James Moir**. Douglas began her career as a production assistant and, in 1986, joined the Promotions Department. In 1988, she became a producer in the Music Department, returning to Promotions in 1990, as a producer, before being promoted to editor of BBC Radio 2 Presentation and Planning in 1993. In May 1997, Douglas became managing editor of BBC Radio 2 and, in 2000, was appointed head of programs.

In 2004, she was awarded the top prize at the UK **music** industry's Woman of the Year Awards. Douglas resigned from her position on 28 October 2008, following controversy relating to inappropriate on-air phone calls relating to a relative of actor **Andrew Sachs** made by presenters **Russell Brand** and **Jonathan Ross** during Brand's BBC Radio 2 program. Brand resigned from the **British Broadcasting Corporation (BBC)**, and Ross was suspended from his program. It was later revealed that Douglas had not listened to the offending part of the program (which was recorded) prior to transmission. Following a meeting with **BBC director-general Mark Thompson**, Douglas tendered her resignation and was succeeded by **Bob Shennan**. After leaving the BBC, she became a trustee of the Sage Centre in Gateshead, and in 2008, she assumed a new post as director of programming and business development at the British subsidiary of the Universal Music Group.

DOWN YOUR WAY. A program that was part travelogue, part record request show, *Down Your Way* ran in its original form from 1946–1987. Successive presenters were **Stewart MacPherson**, **Richard Dimbleby**, **Franklin Engelmann**, and **Brian Johnston**. Always broadcast at the same time on the **BBC Home Service/BBC Radio 4**—late afternoon on Sundays—the format never varied, consisting of a radio visit to a village or town, interviews with local characters and personalities, and the invitation to these participants to choose a piece of **music**.

DR. FU MANCHU. A **series** began on **Radio Luxembourg** on 6 December 1936, adapted from the novel by Sax Rohmer and sponsored by Milk of Magnesia. The program ran for 62 episodes, ending with "The House of Hashish" on 6 February 1938.

DRAMA. Radio drama has been a feature of British radio since the earliest days of the medium. The first broadcast drama in the United Kingdom is said to have been scenes from three Shakespeare plays, broadcast in February 1923, and the first play specifically written for the sound medium has been claimed to be *Danger* by **Richard Hughes**, broadcast by 2LO on 15 January 1924. The first novel dramatization was of Charles Kingsley's *Westward Ho!* in April 1925. The first book on the subject, *Radio Drama and How to Write It*, was written in 1926, by Gordon Lea, who worked in Newcastle and had made some drama productions for the local station, 5NO.

It soon became clear to producers that radio had the potential to create drama in a completely new image; experiments were conducted in which casts for radio plays were anonymous, with details of the actors being neither broadcast nor published. This was resisted and opposed by the actors' union, but the principle—of retaining realism and maintaining illusion in a "blind" audience by maintaining an "antipersonality" policy—was an interesting and radical one. By the early 1930s, the work of such producers as **Val Gielgud**, **Lance Sieveking**, and Tyrone Guthrie had made the art of radio drama a specific genre, and the era saw a rise in use of poetic drama, including works by T. S. Eliot, for example, *Murder in the Cathedral* and *The Waste Land*, which was produced by **D. G. Bridson** in 1938.

The 1930s also witnessed the concept of multistudio productions, sometimes live plays being produced by various regions in a complex, layered sound picture. Documentary drama and feature drama sometimes used this technique, which was costly and tied up resources to a considerable degree. Many playwrights have been drawn to the medium, and some, for instance, **Giles Cooper** and **Samuel Beckett**, have understood and exploited the uniqueness of storytelling in pure sound, taking the concept to an extraordinarily sophisticated level.

In the early days of **commercial radio**, a number of companies, including **Capital Radio** (Anthony Cornish), **Radio Clyde** (Hamish Wilson), the **London Broadcasting Company** (**Tim Crook**), 2CR (Seán Street), Swansea Sound, and Downtown Radio in Northern Ireland, were active in drama production. After passage of the 1990 Broadcasting Act, with its relaxation of regulations relating to speech content, such work became rarer, and by 2006, drama was virtually nonexistent in the commercial sector.

At the same time, there was a growth in drama productions made by independent production companies for **British Broadcasting Corporation (BBC)** radio. **BBC Radio 4** remains the biggest commissioner of new drama in Britain, with a daily afternoon play Monday through Friday and at least one play in its schedule each day of the week. **BBC Radio 3** broadcasts substantial dramas, including classics, cutting-edge new drama, and experimental work.

Drama **serials** have ranged from the first, ***Dick Barton, Special Agent***, first heard in 1946, and ***The Archers***, to BBC Radio 4's *Classic Serial*, broadcast on Sunday afternoons. At the outbreak of World War II, 1930s commercial radio had already begun to develop "**soap opera**" popular drama based on the U.S. radio model and produced by agencies, with such productions as ***Young Widow Jones***, *Stella Dallas*, and ***Dr. Fu Manchu***. Postwar, **Radio Luxembourg** serialized *Dan Dare*, *Pilot of the Future* during the 1950s, while roughly parallel in chronological terms, BBC radio captured the imagination of a generation with the science fiction serial ***Journey into Space***.

See also FEATURE; INDEPENDENT RADIO DRAMA PRODUCTIONS (IRDP); SERIES.

DROITWICH. The **British Broadcasting Corporation (BBC)** transmitter in the Worcestershire town of Droitwich was opened on 6 September 1934, and took over the transmission of the **National Programme** from **Daventry** on 7 October, at a power of 150 kW, broadcasting on the 1,500 meters, **longwave (LW)** frequency. The mast height was 700 feet, and the transmitter equipment was installed by the **Marconi Company**.

During World War II, the site was used by the BBC for overseas broadcasts and subsequently as a blocking device to disorientate enemy aircraft. At this time it also expanded to house the transmitter for the **BBC Forces Programme** and a high-power medium wave (MW) transmitter. In a major overhaul in 1960, the 1934 transmitters were replaced with more powerful units, increasing LW capability to 500 kW. By 2006, the site was still active, transmitting **BBC Radio 4** on LW and **BBC Radio 5 Live**, **talkSPORT**, and **Virgin Radio** on MW.

See also BROOKMANS PARK TRANSMITTING STATION.

DUNHILL, DAVID (1917–2005). David Dunhill was a well-known **British Broadcasting Corporation (BBC)** "voice" who joined the corporation at the end of World War II, as a staff **announcer** and newsreader for the **Light Programme**. His voice was also associated with the **comedy series** *Take It from Here* during the 1950s. When BBC **local radio** was created, he worked as a voice and presentation coach, remembered with affection by a new generation of radio broadcasters.

DUNN, JOHN (1934–2004). John Dunn, a much-loved presenter, began his radio career as a studio manager with the **British Broadcasting Corporation's (BBC)** External Services in 1956. In 1958, he became an **announcer** and news reader in the General Overseas Service, before moving into domestic radio in 1959. Among **Light Programme** shows, he was most associated with *Friday Night Is Music Night*, *Housewives' Choice*, and *Roundabout*. At the launch of **BBC Radio 2** in September 1967, Dunn hosted the breakfast show, a role in which he continued until 1973, when he moved to the early evening slot, remaining a highly popular host until 1998, the year of his retirement. In 1983, Dunn was voted the Variety Club's Radio Personality of the Year and gained a **Sony Radio Academy Award** in 1998, for the best drive time **music** show. In 2003, he was inducted into the Sony Radio Academy's Hall of Fame, almost exactly a year prior to his death from cancer.

DYALL, VALENTINE (1908–1985). Valentine Dyall was an actor known for playing dark and sinister characters in radio plays of mystery and the imagination. He was most associated in the memories of U.K. listeners as "The Man in Black" in the program *The Man in Black* and narrator of

Appointment with Fear, a **drama series** that aired during the 1940s and was revived under the eponymous character's name in 1949 and 1955. Also during the 1950s, Dyall made a number of appearances on *The Goon Show*, parodying this persona, on one occasion playing "the man in grey, due to very cheap dry cleaners." Later in his radio career, he played Gargravarr in *The Hitchhiker's Guide to the Galaxy*.

See also MYSTERY PROGRAMS.

DYKE, GREG (1947–). Greg Dyke was director-general of the **British Broadcasting Corporation (BBC)** from 2000–2004, when he was forced to resign after circulation of the Hutton Report, which investigated the death of government weapons expert Dr. David Kelly. The report severely criticized the editorial decision of the BBC to broadcast a report during the **BBC Radio 4** program *Today* about the government's decision to go to war in Iraq. The event overshadowed a period in the BBC during which Dyke, coming from a commercial television background, had emphasized directing money into programs and making savings in nonprogram-making departments. In so doing, he became closer to program makers and was largely popular with BBC staff.

E

EAQ MADRID. Working under the subtitle "Radio Aranjuez," this **short-wave** station carried half an hour of English-language programming each night, produced by the **International Broadcasting Company (IBC)** from 1932 until July 1936, when the Spanish Civil War made U.K. transmissions untenable. Although it was never fully developed by the company, this policy—known as "keeping a station warm"—was one adopted by the IBC elsewhere in Europe. The idea here, as far as **Leonard Plugge** and his company were concerned, seems to have been to undermine the **British Broadcasting Corporation's (BBC)** newly formed **Empire Service** (December 1932). The IBC added the name "IBC Empire Service" to its EAQ transmissions, continuing to do so in spite of BBC insistence that it should not use the title. Although it ended in 1936, the IBC retained intentions of reopening EAQ as a transmission site, which never occurred.

See also COMMERCIAL RADIO; RADIO NORMANDY.

EBDON, JOHN (1923–2005). John Ebdon was director of the London Planetarium but became well known for more than 25 years for programs on the **BBC Home Service** and **BBC Radio 4**, which explored, in an idiosyncratic style, the **British Broadcasting Corporation's (BBC)** sound archives. In this capacity, Ebdon made more than 1,000 programs, after BBC producer Denys Geuroult had heard him giving a presentation at the planetarium. His was a dry, educated wit that affectionately exposed the foibles of the English, with an unerring eye and ear, and sharp sense of the ludicrous. Upon Ebdon's death, Geuroult commented on him, saying he was the "most professional broadcaster I have known in 32 years, and, sadly, one of the last of the band of literary broadcasters."

ECKERSLEY, PETER PENDLETON (1892–1963). Peter Eckersley was a dynamic, controversial, and charismatic visionary and a true pioneer of radio: an engineer who also understood the entertainment potential of the medium. He directed and took part in experimental transmissions from the **Marconi Company's** site in the village of **Writtle** in Essex. These began on

14 February 1922, and Eckersley was subsequently appointed by **John Reith** as the first chief engineer for the **British Broadcasting Company** in 1923. He was dismissed in 1929, after being cited in divorce proceedings, and thereafter became involved in the development of **commercial radio**, in particular the radio relay system.

Eckersley's controversial career was complicated by his association with Sir Oswald Mosley, founder of the British Union of Fascists, as well as the involvement of his wife and stepson in a 1945 trial, in which they were charged with "conspiring to assist the enemy" through the medium of propaganda. In his 1942 book *The Power behind the Microphone*, Eckersley set out his thinking relating to the future of radio broadcasting, predicting the coming of both digital sound and cable transmission.

EDMONDS, NOEL (1948–). Noel Edmonds first worked in radio for **Radio Luxembourg** in 1968, before joining **BBC Radio 1** in 1969, taking over the Saturday morning show from **Kenny Everett** and becoming the network's youngest presenter. From 1970–1974, he switched to Sunday mornings, introducing the formula of prank telephone calls that was to characterize much of his subsequent career both in radio and television. In 1974, Edmonds inherited the breakfast slot from **Tony Blackburn** and remained host in this capacity until 1978, by which time he had a burgeoning career in television. In 1989, he became a founding director (with **Tim Blackmore** and Simon Cole) of the independent production company **Unique**. Edmonds cashed in his stake in the company in August 2005, for £1.35 million.

See also DISC JOCKEY (DJ); MUSIC.

EDUCATING ARCHIE. The idea of a ventriloquist act on radio—although apparently anomalous—has a number of precedents, not least *The Edgar Bergen and Charlie McCarthy Show* on the U.S. network NBC, which began in the 1930s, and the U.K. ventriloquist Saveen. In Britain, the most famous partnership in radio was that of Peter Brough and his dummy, **Archie Andrews** (a name invented by **Ted Kavanagh**, one of the brains behind the show). First broadcast in June 1950, and running for 10 **series** on the **Light Programme** throughout the decade, the show was significant in its fostering of new talent, including Julie Andrews, Max Bygraves, **Tony Hancock**, Hattie Jacques, and Beryl Reid. The story lines revolved around the adventures of a naughty schoolboy named Archie and his girlfriend Monica (Beryl Reid). The first seven series were written by Eric Sykes, whose inventive scripts contributed much to the success of the program.

See also COMEDY.

EDWARDS, JIMMY (1920–1988). Jimmy Edwards came into broadcasting shortly after the war. In 1948, he joined Dick Bentley and **Joy Nichols** in the successful **comedy series** *Take It from Here*. He was also a regular member of the spoof panel game *Does the Team Think?* Famous for his large handlebar mustache, he carried the nickname "Professor." Edwards also had a successful career in television and was a musician, frequently using his playing of the trombone as a part of his comedy act.

EKCO. A famous receiver manufacturer founded in 1922, by **Eric Kirkham Cole**. During the 1930s and 1940s, Ekco created a series of sets that became highly collectable largely due to their unique circular design, made possible, in part, by the use of Bakelite in their manufacture.

ELECTROPHONE. An important early precursor of "wireless," the electrophone was invented by Frenchman Clement Ader in 1881, and first introduced in France the same year as the "Theatrephone." The principle was that of relaying audio entertainments through telephone lines. Thus, Ader demonstrated live performances from the Paris Opera to audiences at the Paris Electrical Exhibition that year. The system became popular in Europe and the United States, and was introduced to Great Britain in the early 1890s by the National Telephone Company, licensed by the **Post Office** under the name "Electrophone," with its central exchange in Gerrard Street, London. Queen Victoria became an early adopter of the system, having it installed at Windsor Castle.

A subscription service, it offered customers a choice of theater performance and other events, including church services, via headphones. "Receivers" were installed in domestic homes and public places, where the electrophone offered a "pay-per-listen" service. There were two levels of subscription: A £5 charge enabled listeners to connect to a preselected service, while for £10, subscribers could choose their own selection. During World War I, the electrophone was installed in some hospitals for the entertainment of convalescent troops. Church services were relayed on Sundays.

The system survived for some years after the introduction of wireless radio services, offering choice and "live" quality relays at a time when the fledgling wireless service was overcoming early transmission and reception issues. The last electrophone relay service reputedly ended as late as 1938—in Bournemouth—when the final subscriber died.

ELMES, SIMON (1950–). Simon Elmes is creative director of **documentaries** and **features** for radio at the **British Broadcasting Corporation (BBC)**, based at **Broadcasting House** in London. He joined the corporation in August 1974, as a studio manager and, after a period in television and schools radio, became a full-time feature producer in domestic radio's archive features unit. Early commissions included the story of Cornish tin miners (*Men of the Granite*, 1980), the experiences of servicemen who witnessed the 1950s Pacific A-bomb tests (*Witness!*, 1985), and the experience of spending 24-hours in a motorway service (*Stop-Off*, 1990). His numerous documentaries about dialect, as heard through the stories of ordinary people, *Talk of the Town, Talk of the Country*, effectively combines Elmes's love of language with the heartfelt narratives of tough, ordinary living. In a similar vein, he produced and subsequently edited **Word of Mouth**, **BBC Radio 4's** magazine program about spoken English, and he also developed, with Melvyn Bragg, four **series** of *The Routes of English*. In 1990, Elmes devised *Friday Lives* (later *Tuesday Lives*), a series of live, hour-long programs telling themed stories about ordinary lives in short form. The program earned him a gold **Sony Radio Academy Award** in 1992, while *The Routes of English* won a **Voice of the Listener and Viewer** award. In 2005, he created BBC Radio 4's long-running feature strand *Lives in a Landscape*.

Since 1985, Elmes has been involved in production training and creative development throughout the BBC, and he has also written extensively on language (*The Routes of English*, 2000; *Talking for Britain*, 2005) and radio's history (*And Now on Radio 4*, 2007; *Hello Again*, 2012). He is the recipient of the BBC's Gold Award for services to radio.

ELRICK, GEORGE (1903–1999). George Elrick was a Scottish musician known as a drummer in dance bands during the 1930s and 1940s. Examples include those run by Bert Ambrose and **Henry Hall**. In 1946, he began an association with *Housewives' Choice* on the **Light Programme**, which lasted until 1967. He became one of the program's most popular presenters, being voted "DJ of the Year" seven times by the British press.

EMAP. Formed as a newspaper and magazine company in 1947, Emap has expanded into all areas of media, including radio. In 1990, the company acquired the London dance station **Kiss FM** and, the following year, bought Radio City in Liverpool. Other acquisitions followed, with a strong North Country bias when making purchases. In 1998, Emap bought London station Melody FM, renaming it Magic 105.4. This began the development of the Magic brand—nine stations aimed at the 35-year-old to 44-year-old age group and complementing the group's Big City brand (eight stations), targeting the 15-year-old to 34-year-old age group. Emap also moved into digital radio, operating 13 **multiplexes** throughout the United Kingdom. In April 2005, the group's burgeoning radio aspirations were demonstrated by the creation of a new division, Emap Radio, and Emap acquired **Scottish Radio Holdings** in June 2005.

See also COMMERCIAL RADIO.

EMMETT, CHRIS (1938–). Chris Emmett is a highly experienced and successful radio **comedy** actor who has worked on many popular programs, including the 1970s **BBC Radio 4** series *The Burkiss Way* and the long-running *Week Ending*. He is also noted for a number of collaborations with **Roy Hudd**, including the **BBC Radio 2 series** *The News Huddlines*, in which he appeared beginning at its launch in 1975 until its final program on Christmas day 2001. Furthermore, Emmett worked with Hudd on several other programs, most notably *Huddwinks*, *Crowned Hudds*, and *The Newly Discovered Casebook of Sherlock Holmes*.

"EMPEROR ROSKO" (1942–). Born Michael Pasternak, the son of film producer Joe Pasternak, this iconic **disc jockey (DJ)** joined **Radio Caroline** in 1966, where his brash American style gained him great popularity. Educated in Paris, Switzerland, and California, "Rosko" was equally at home broadcasting in French, and after leaving Caroline, he worked on the French services of Radio Monte-Carlo and **Radio Luxembourg**, where he operated using the pseudonym "Le Président Rosko."

His style was strongly influenced by American DJs Emperor Hudson and Wolfman Jack. In 1967, Rosko was a member of the original team at **BBC Radio 1**, although, due to his continental commitments, his programs were initially prerecorded. Beginning in 1968, by which time he had become a resident of the United Kingdom, his shows went "live," and he stayed with Radio 1, broadcasting on various shows until September 1976, when he returned to the United States to be near his ailing father. Rosko returned to the network in 1982, for a further four years, taking part in the 25th anniversary celebrations in 1992. He then worked for **Virgin Radio** before returning to the United States to work in California, continuing to be heard by U.K. audiences on the **Classic Gold Network**. In more recent years, he has been broadcasting the syndicated program *The LA Connection* from his home in California, which can be heard on a number of European stations. He has also been heard on the Internet radio station Big L International.

See also COMMERCIAL RADIO; PIRATE RADIO.

EMPIRE SERVICE. Launched by the **British Broadcasting Corporation (BBC)** in December 1932, this service was the beginning of the BBC's international aspirations as a broadcaster. Studios were initially at **Broadcasting House**, later moving to **Bush House** and transmitted from **Daventry**. The service initially broadcasted in five time zones, targeting Canada, West

Africa, South Africa, India, and Australasia. It later became known as the General Overseas Service, External Services, and ultimately the **BBC World Service**.

ENGELMANN, FRANKLIN (1908–1972). Franklin Engelmann was a popular broadcaster on British radio for more than 30 years, and his warm tones were associated with many programs, including *What Do You Know?* and the program that replaced it, *Brain of Britain*. Engelmann was the original host of *Pick of the Pops*, but he is most remembered for his role as presenter of two long-running programs, *Down Your Way*, which he hosted from 1955–1972, and *Gardeners' Question Time*. Having chaired the latter program from 1961–1972, he died during the week in which the 1,000th edition aired. His nickname was "Jingle."

ENNALS, MAURICE (1919–2002). Maurice Ennals was the first manager of a **British Broadcasting Corporation (BBC) local radio** station, **Radio Leicester**, which opened in 1967. Prior to this he had worked on the introduction of local radio and was jointly responsible for deciding where many of the stations were to be sited. In 1970, he was responsible for the launch of BBC Radio Solent, part of the second tier of stations to roll out after the success of the initial experiment. He remained as manager of Radio Solent until his retirement in 1976, after which he lived in Dorset, acting as a talent scout for local football teams.

ENTWISTLE, GEORGE (1962–). George Entwistle succeeded **Mark Thompson** as director-general of the **British Broadcasting Corporation (BBC)** on 17 September 2012. Coming from a career in magazine journalism, he joined the BBC in 1989, as a producer of principally factual and political programs, becoming director of BBC Vision prior to his appointment as director-general. Following controversy relating to a report on the television program *Newsnight* that falsely implicated Lord McAlpine, a former senior Conservative politician, in a child abuse scandal, Entwistle resigned on 10 November 2012. It was the second serious editorial scandal to hit the program within weeks, following reports of an investigation into sex abuse by the late presenter **Jimmy Savile**. Entwistle's resignation after just 54 days in the post made him the shortest-serving director-general in the history of the BBC. He was succeeded on an interim basis by **Tim Davie** and, ultimately, by **Tony Hall**, who took over the job as a permanent appointment in April 2013.

See also OPERATION YEWTREE.

EPILOGUE, THE. A program that was part of **John Reith's Sunday broadcasting policy**, heard at the close of transmissions on Sunday evenings beginning in 1926. In its original format, it was a Bible reading, although this was later added to by hymns and psalms, broadcast on the **BBC Home Service** and latter **BBC Radio 4**. The final broadcast was in 1980.

See also RELIGIOUS PROGRAMS.

ESSLIN, MARTIN (1918–2002). Of Hungarian origin, born and educated in Vienna, Martin Esslin was a theater scholar and radio producer who came to London because of the Anschluss and joined the **British Broadcasting Corporation**, becoming a producer and scriptwriter. He worked for the European Service from 1941–1955, eventually becoming head of the European production department. Esslin translated many pieces of European theater into English, which led to a number of significant **drama** productions. In 1961, he became assistant head of radio drama, becoming department head in 1963, a post he retained until 1977, when he began spending more time in the United States. He was selected to the Most Excellent Order of the British Empire in 1972. Esslin's book *The Theatre of the Absurd* (1962) defined a movement and created a term that remains extant.

EUREKA 147. A system developed by a consortium of 12 partners widely adopted in 1994 as an international standard for the transmission of **Digital Audio Broadcasting**. A large proportion of the world's broadcasters have implemented the system. Exceptions are the United States, which has embraced both satellite digital radio and high-definition radio—In Band, On Channel (IBOC)—and Japan, where cable is the chosen method of new radio format delivery. Other countries, including South Korea, have used Eureka 147 as the delivery system for the development of Terrestrial Digital Multimedia Broadcasting(T-DMB) in mobile devices.

EVANS, CHRIS (1966–). Born in Lancashire, Chris Evans's first job in radio was for Manchester's Piccadilly Radio. He soon moved to the **British Broadcasting Corporation's (BBC)** London station, Greater London Radio. In 1992, Evans gained national prominence as host of the television show *The Big Breakfast*, and he built on his newfound celebrity by establishing his own production company, Ginger Productions, responsible for his Channel 4 **quiz show** *Don't Forget Your Toothbrush*. The program format was sold worldwide, and much of Evans's media empire was built on the money from the show.

In 1994, Evans left *The Big Breakfast* and, the following year, signed on with **BBC Radio 1** to present the breakfast show at a time when the network was moving—under the controllership of **Matthew Bannister**—toward a new image and definition of itself after a period of decline and stagnation. Between his arrival at the station and October 1996, he had increased the breakfast show audience from 1 million to 7 million listeners; however, his time at Radio 1 was not without controversy, and Evans was frequently censured for his remarks and inappropriate jokes. In January 1997, he was sacked after his demands to work a four-day week were refused by Bannister.

Evans moved to **Virgin Radio**, where he worked as a presenter, but in 1997, his Ginger Media Group bought the station for £85 million. Less than three years later, the station was once again sold, this time for £225 million. Evans continued to broadcast for the station, but he was let go in 2001, after failing to appear for his program for five consecutive days. In 2005, after multiple unsuccessful television ventures, he made a number of guest appearances on BBC programs, including a charity broadcast to raise money for victims of the Asian tsunami and an **outside broadcast** from the London *Live 8* concert held in Hyde Park. Also in the summer of 2005, he signed a contract to present programs on **BBC Radio 2**. After a stint on the station's *Drivetime* show, he took over hosting duties of the BBC Radio 2 *Breakfast Show* from **Terry Wogan** in January 2010. Evans was named Music Radio Personality of the Year at the 2006 **Sony Radio Academy Awards**.

See also DISC JOCKEY (DJ); MUSIC.

EVERETT, KENNY (1944–1995). Kenny Everett was a **disc jockey**/presenter who developed a style of radio that used the medium's technical resources in a creative and innovative way, unlike much of the pop **music** programming of the 1960s and 1970s. He first came to the attention of the British public on the **pirate radio** station **Radio London** and joined the **BBC Radio 1** team when the station was created in 1967. He was sacked by the **British Broadcasting Corporation (BBC)** in 1970, after making a joke in which he suggested that the transport minister's wife had passed her driving test because of a bribe. Everett returned to the BBC in 1981, but he was again the subject of controversy two years later, after making a remark about Margaret Thatcher. He also worked for **Capital Radio**. Everett died of AIDS in 1995.

F

FAIRHEAD, RONA (1961–). Rona Fairhead was appointed chair of the **BBC Trust** in August 2014, succeeding **Chris Patten**, who resigned in May due to ill health, and the interim chair, Diane Coyle. Fairhead was the first woman to hold the post on a permanent basis. Prior to this, she had worked in a number of industry and business positions, including for the Financial Times Group, where she was chief executive from 2006 until her appointment with the BBC Trust.

See also BBC CHAIRMEN.

FALLING TREE PRODUCTIONS. Originally created by **Alan Hall** in 1998, as Alan Hall Associates, the company became Falling Tree Productions in 2004. It has won numerous international awards; in 2012, Falling Tree received accolades in all three categories of the **Prix Europa**, and in the same year, the company won gold and silver awards in the **documentary feature** and **drama** categories respectively at the **Sony Radio Academy Awards**.

See also INDEPENDENT PRODUCTION.

FAMILY FAVOURITES. A highly popular record request program that began airing in 1945, on the **Light Programme**, and ran until 1984. The format was that of a two-way linkup between the **British Broadcasting Corporation** and the British Forces Network in Germany. Created by Maurice Gorham, the program had two famous presenters, **Jean Metcalfe** in London and Cliff Michelmore in Hamburg, who subsequently married. Beginning in January 1960, the program became known as *Two-Way Family Favourites*. On certain occasions, the brief was widened to include other British forces throughout Europe, including those in Cyprus and Malta. Broadcast on Sundays at lunchtime, it was a focus for many during the immediate postwar years, linking servicemen and servicewomen abroad with their families at home. Its theme tune was "With a Song in My Heart."

See also MUSIC.

FARMING PROGRAMS. British radio has maintained specialist programs for farmers since 1929, although, in many cases, research has shown that the programs are also listened to by an audience beyond the farming community. In 1937, a new program, *Farming Today*, was launched, presented by Anthony Hurd of the *Times*, father of future Conservative Party home secretary Douglas Hurd. The program was initially broadcast weekly, but since 1960, it has become a daily part of the output, first of the **BBC Home Service** and subsequently of **BBC Radio 4**. It is broadcast Monday through Saturday, early in the morning, while on Sunday agricultural interests are catered to by *On Your Farm*. Most **British Broadcasting Corporation** farming programs have originated from Birmingham, and it was here, in 1948, that the well-known and perennially popular **serial *The Archers*** began and from where it continues to be produced.

FEATURE. The radio feature has a rich history in U.K. broadcasting. Developed early as a hybrid of **documentary** and **drama**, its growth in the 1930s was particularly enhanced by the development of mobile recording technologies. The sense that the radio feature could explore facts from a dramatized or stylized stance gave program makers the freedom to create material that had considerable emotional impact and could also express the implicit opinion of the producers themselves. The work of **E. A. Harding**, **D. G. Bridson**, **Olive Shapley**, and others in Manchester during this time was exceptionally powerful in examining issues of poverty, unemployment, and inner city and industrial strife.

The use of poetry as a strand in features continues to be a strong narrative device, as does the use of **music** and adapted or created material that makes use of actors, blended with journalistic techniques like interviews. The postwar radio Features Department of the **British Broadcasting Corporation (BBC)**, run by **Laurence Gilliam**, was extremely fruitful and creative in the development of the genre, and from this time comes the work of such major producers as **Douglas Cleverdon** and **Louis MacNeice**. Dylan Thomas's great verse drama *Under Milk Wood* originated from this department. From the BBC regions, as before the war, work of great importance originated, including the programs of **Charles Parker** in Birmingham.

The works of **Simon Elmes**, Peter Everett, **Alan Hall**, **Piers Plowright**, **John Theocharis**, and Matt Thompson have continued the tradition, and a younger generation of program makers, many working for **independent production** companies, is using digital technology to reach new, younger audiences on networks the likes of **BBC Radio 1** and **BBC Radio 1Xtra**. The duration of the radio feature has proved to be infinitely flexible, ranging from large-scale 90-minute programs to short form. The heart of the feature has always been the desire and ability to tell stories in imaginative ways.

FELDMAN, MARTY (1934–1982). Marty Feldman was a writer and performer known for a number of television **series**; however, it was in a writing partnership for radio with **Barry Took** that his **comedy** credentials were formed. This relationship lasted for twenty years, from 1954–1974, and is most notable for the creation of *Round the Horne*, which aired from 1964–1967. (A final series, in 1968, was penned by other hands.)

FELTZ, VANESSA (1962–). Vanessa Feltz is a television and radio broadcaster who has presented programs for **BBC Radio 2** and BBC London 94.9. In 2009, she was named Speech Radio Personality of the Year at the **Sony Radio Academy Awards**.
See also CURRENT AFFAIRS; WOMEN.

FERRARI, NICK (1960–). Journalist and radio presenter Nick Ferrari is widely known for his work with the **London Broadcasting Company (LBC)**, where he fronts an award-winning discussion show based on **news** and current political issues, and involving listener participation through text, e-mail, and **phone-in**.
See also CURRENT AFFAIRS.

FESTIVAL OF NINE LESSONS AND CAROLS. An annual radio Christmas institution first broadcast from King's College in Cambridge on Christmas Eve 1928 and has continued ever since. It is also now broadcast on television.
See also RELIGIOUS PROGRAMS.

FFORDE, ARTHUR (1900–1985). Sir Arthur Frederic Brownlow fforde held the post of chairman of the **British Broadcasting Corporation** from 1957–1964. An unobtrusive incumbent, he suffered from intermittent periods of ill health, during which his vice chairman, Sir James Duff (1898–1970), deputized for him.

FILE ON FOUR. A weekly **current affairs** program created in 1977, by **Michael Green**, in Manchester, for **BBC Radio 4**. It has included on its reporting team a future controller of the network, **Helen Boaden**. *File on Four* is an investigative **series** that specializes in firsthand reporting on topical issues, either of international or domestic concern.

FISCHER, GEORGE (?–?). George Fischer was a key figure in the development of the **BBC Radio 4 current affairs** program *Analysis*. He joined the **British Broadcasting Corporation** in 1963, as a program assistant in External Services, and moved to network radio in 1967, where he met **Ian**

McIntyre, with whom he worked as a producer. He was the first producer of *Analysis*, producing 45 editions of the program from 1970–1974, most of them with McIntyre as presenter. From 1972–1987, Fischer served as editor of Documentaries and Talks for Radio and then head of that department. He remained a close ally of McIntyre, and together they continued to espouse Reithian broadcasting values into the 1980s.

FIVE TO TEN. A short **religious program** broadcast on weekday mornings from 1950–1970, on the **BBC Home Service** and **BBC Radio 4**. Its subtitle was "A Story, a Hymn, and a Prayer."

"FLEET'S LIT UP". In 1937, Lieutenant Commander Thomas Woodruffe was scheduled to broadcast a commentary on the coronation review of the fleet at Spithead. Unfortunately, Woodruffe was onboard his old ship, HMS *Nelson*, and had enjoyed considerable boardroom hospitality prior to the broadcast and was demonstrably drunk by the time of the broadcast. After several minutes, he was faded off the air, but the incident was far-reaching, leading to the introduction of continuity **announcers** whose role was not only to link programs, but monitor output. Woodruffe's commentary caused such a sensation—"The Fleet's lit up. . . . It's lit up by fairy lights. . . . It's like fairyland . . . the ships are lit up . . . even the destroyers are lit up"—that the incident produced a West End stage musical called *The Fleet's Lit Up*.

FLEMING, JOHN AMBROSE (1849–1945). John Fleming was an English engineer born in Lancaster but brought up in North London. He made numerous contributions to electronics and wireless telegraphy and, in 1899, started working with the **Marconi Company**. Fleming was responsible for designing the transmitter that facilitated the first transatlantic message, but he is best known as inventor of the thermionic **valve**, or Fleming Valve, which was patented in 1905, and was highly significant in the development of radio technology. Fleming became a consultant to the Edison Electric Light Company and was a popular tutor at University College in London. He was knighted in 1929, for his valuable and wide-ranging contributions to electrical and electronic engineering.

FLETCHER, CYRIL (1913–2005). Cyril Fletcher was a well-known comedian and raconteur, famous for his rich voice and comic verse, which he coined "Odd Odes." This aspect of his work became popular in 1938, when he recited "Dreamin' of Thee," a Cockney caricature of "The Lovesick Tommy's Dream of Home" by Edgar Wallace. Others followed, and Fletcher's success with **comedy** voices made him a natural favorite on radio. He made his first **series**, *Thanking Yew*, in 1940, and frequently worked with his wife, actress and singer Betty Astell, most notably in the 1952 comedy series *Fletcher's Fare*. He also worked in television and was one of the first comedians to work in the medium in the United Kingdom, from the **British Broadcasting Corporation** studios in Alexandra Palace in 1936.

FLOTSAM AND JETSAM. A comedy duo formed by B. C. Hilliam (Flotsam) (1890–1968) and Malcolm McEachern (Jetsam) (1883–1945). They made their broadcasting debut in 1926, and their contrasting high and low voices made them immensely popular for nearly 20 years, with a **series** of successful radio programs, including *Round the World with Flotsam and Jetsam*, *Our Hour*, and *Signs of the Times*. Many of their songs took radio as their theme, for example, "Weather Reports," "Big Ben Calling," and, most famously, "Little Betty Bouncer Loves an Announcer Down at the BBC."
See also COMEDY.

FOORT, REGINALD (1893–1980). Reginald Foort was the first resident organist to be appointed by the **British Broadcasting Company/Corporation (BBC)**, holding the post until 1938, when he became a freelance performer. Such was the public feeling at the time of his resignation that the BBC received some 10,000 letters from listeners, and Foort personally replied to each one. In 1926, at the height of his radio success, his recording of Albert Ketelby's *In a Monastery Garden* sold 3,250,000 copies. He continued to broadcast, amassing more than 2,000 programs by 1951, when he immigrated to the United States, making his home in Florida. Foort returned to the United Kingdom for a tour, at the age of 78, and his familiar style of mixing "popular classics and light melodies" renewed memories for the many listeners who nostalgically recalled his time at the BBC.
See also MUSIC.

FOOT, R. W. (1889–1973). Robert William Foot, Most Excellent Order of the British Empire, was joint director-general of the **British Broadcasting Corporation (BBC)** with **Cecil Graves** from 1942–1943, and sole director-general until 1944, after Graves retired in 1943. He had been a solicitor and became general manager of the Gas, Light, and Coke Company. He had originally been commissioned to investigate inefficiencies and overspending within the BBC under the director-generalship of **F. W. Ogilvie** and was appointed joint director-general upon Ogilvie's departure. Essentially an administrator after Graves retired, Foot worked with **William Haley**, who managed programming as editor in chief until succeeding Foot as director-general in 1944. During his time with the BBC, Foot decentralized management and improved relations with the British government.

FOREST OF DEAN RADIO. Following the experiment into the viability and desirability of a U.K. **community radio** sector, the government media regulator, the **Office of Communications**, granted the first five-year license to Forest of Dean Radio in Gloucestershire in March 2005. The station ceased full-time broadcasting on December 31, 2009.

See also COMMERCIAL RADIO.

FRANCIS, RICHARD (1934–1992). Sir Richard Francis was director of **British Broadcasting Corporation** radio from 1982–1986. He conceived of the idea of forming the **Radio Academy** to provide a radio equivalent of film and television's British Academy of Film and Television Arts. Francis subsequently became director-general of the British Council.

FRANKAU, RONALD (1894–1951). Ronald Frankau was a highly popular comedian and reciter of monologues, and a personal favorite of **John Reith**. This is surprising, given the nature of much of Frankau's material, which was frequently risqué. He first broadcast in 1925, in a relay of his concert party, *Cabaret Kittens*. He appeared in films and wrote several books. In 1932 alone, Frankau sold more than 100,000 records of his comic routines and songs. His regular accompanist was Monte Crick, who went on to become one of four actors to play the character Dan Archer in the **serial** *The Archers*. He became a close friend of **Tommy Handley**, and they worked together numerous times, most notably as the **comedy** duo Mr. Murgatroyd and Mr. Winterbottom.

FREE RADIO BIRMINGHAM. *See* BRMB.

FREEMAN, ALAN (1927–2006). Beginning his radio career as an **announcer** for the Melbourne station 7LA in 1952, Alan Freeman spent two years at **Radio Luxembourg** before joining the **Light Programme** in 1960. He was one of the presenters for *Housewives' Choice* and, in 1962, took over the program with which he would mostly be associated, *Pick of the Pops*. In 1972, Freeman became a regular presenter on **BBC Radio 1** and, the following year, presented the first *Radio 1 Roadshow*. For 10 years, from 1979–1989, he worked for **Capital Radio**, before rejoining the **British Broadcasting Corporation** to present *Pick of the Pops* in a new format until his retirement.

Freeman was widely known by the nickname "Fluff." Although associated with popular **music**, he had a great love for and knowledge of classical music, in particular opera, and he would often punctuate his programs with jingles drawn from these sources. In his later years, Freeman suffered from severe arthritis and asthma, and lived at Brinsworth House, a retirement home for performers in Twickenham, run by the Entertainment Artistes' Benevolent Fund. It was here that he died on 27 November 2006, at the age of 79.

See also DISC JOCKEY (DJ).

FREQUENCY MODULATION (FM). Previously known as very high frequency (VHF), FM relates to wavelengths within the 87.5 to 108 MHz range. British radio progressively moved away from the use of medium wave transmission in the 1970s, 1980s, and early 1990s, toward the exclusive use of FM for its domestic services, a status quo that would remain until the introduction of **Digital Audio Broadcasting** at the end of the century. Due to the slow roll out of digital services and receivers, it is likely to remain the main source of radio listening for some years.

See also ANALOG.

FRIDAY NIGHT IS MUSIC NIGHT. One of British radio's longest-running **music** programs, having started on the **Light Programme** in 1953, as a showcase for the newly formed **BBC Concert Orchestra**, *Friday Night Is Music Night* continues to air on **BBC Radio 2**. A key figure in the formulation of its policy was conductor, arranger, and composer Sidney Torch, who created a format of light music reflecting everything from popular classics to show tunes. The program usually features a guest singer or singers, and it is recorded in front of a large audience. The show was originally broadcast from the Camden Theatre, and subsequently from the Golders Green Hippodrome, although it has also toured the country extensively.

FROM OUR OWN CORRESPONDENT. A program consisting of short **talks** from **news** correspondents from throughout the world, broadcast on **BBC Radio 4** and the **BBC World Service**. Now introduced by distinguished broadcast journalist **Kate Adie**, the theme is usually topical and either relates to the main news or is based on other issues within the correspondent's geographical sphere of work. It has produced some of the finest reflective **current affairs** writing to be heard on British radio. **John Tusa** once likened the program to "postcards from the world," adding, "like real postcards, they come at unexpected times from unlikely places, telling improbable adventures." The program first began airing in October 1946, as a 15-minute **series** on **BBC Radio 3**, and remained on the network throughout the 1940s. It was first heard on BBC Radio 4 in its now-familiar half-hour version beginning in September 1955.

FRONT LINE FAMILY. A daily radio **serial** that aired on the General Overseas Service (formerly the **Empire Service** and later the **BBC World Service**) starting on 21 April 1941. The intention was to provide listeners outside the United Kingdom with a sense of home front life in London during the war. The program was written by Alan Melville, and on 30 July 1946, it was transferred to the **Light Programme** and rebranded as *The Robinson Family*.

See also DRAMA; SOAP OPERAS; WARTIME BROADCASTING.

G

GALAXY. Galaxy was a radio network that began with the launch of Galaxy Radio in Bristol in 1990. Subsequent stations opened in Birmingham, Manchester, Yorkshire, Scotland, the northeast and south coasts of England. **Chrysalis** owned the network, but it was purchased by **Global Radio** in 2007, and rebranded in February 2011, to form a new identity as the Capital FM network.

See also COMMERCIAL RADIO.

GALTON, RAY (1930–), AND SIMPSON, ALAN (1929–). Linked through their prolific joint careers, Ray Galton and Alan Simpson are considered to be among the finest of U.K. **comedy** writing partnerships, and the innovation of their situation comedy writing—both for radio and television—has helped define the genre. Galton and Simpson met as teenagers in 1948, while convalescing from tuberculosis in a sanatorium. They started writing material for hospital radio and submitted material to the **British Broadcasting Corporation (BBC)**, attracting the attention of comedian Derek Roy, who commissioned them as writers for his radio program *Happy-Go-Lucky*. Mentored by the show's producer, **Dennis Main Wilson**, they progressed to work on *Calling All Forces*, where they first wrote for **Tony Hancock** in 1952, and *Star Bill*, again with Hancock in 1953–1954.

It was during this time that they approached Main Wilson with the concept of a half-hour program featuring Hancock, but using only one story line per episode rather than sketches. The result was ***Hancock's Half Hour***, which ran from 1954–1959 on radio and successfully transferred to television. They also wrote extensively for **Bernard Braden** and, increasingly moving into television, created *Steptoe and Son* in 1962. Galton and Simpson were awarded lifetime achievement awards by the Writers' Guild in 1997, and they were each given Most Excellent Order of the British Empire honors in 2000.

GAME SHOWS. *See* QUIZ SHOWS.

GARDENERS' QUESTION TIME. A program in a long tradition of broadcast information and advice services for U.K. horticulturalists that began under the title of *How Does Your Garden Grow?* in 1947, capitalizing on a newly developed enthusiasm for gardening arising from the government's wartime "Dig for Victory" campaign. The name change came in 1951. The format was that of an audience, often comprising members of a local horticultural society, posing questions and problems to a resident team of experts. When the show began, this team comprised Fred Loads and Bill Sowerbutts, who were joined by Alan Gemmell in 1950. The team was so close that when Loads died in 1981, Gemmell retired the following year and Sowerbutts a year later. Since then there have been various teams and chairmen, and the location-based format in front of a live audience continues, with the **series** being produced in Manchester, where it originated. In one change to the format, the introduction of every third program is now studio-based, during which time listeners can submit questions by post.

GARRISON THEATRE. A Saturday evening wartime **comedy series** that began in August 1940, and attained high popularity ratings, making a star of its central figure, **Jack Warner**. It was devised by Charles Shadwell and produced by Harry S. Pepper. The program re-created the atmosphere and mood of troop shows from the previous war and was usually broadcast in front of a boisterous invited audience from Clifton Parish Hall in Bristol. A stage version of the show was also broadcast and toured until 1942, although the original program ended in 1941.
See also WARTIME BROADCASTING.

GARTHWAITE, NINA (1981–). Having begun her career in television **documentary**, Nina Garthwaite subsequently moved into the field of radio and audio. In 2010, she founded *In the Dark*, with the aim of bringing to radio some of the wider cultural support that she experienced working in the film and television industry. *In the Dark* replicates the culture of cinemagoing and film screenings through communal "listening events" aimed at public audiences.
See also FEATURE.

GCAP MEDIA. With the merging of **Great Western Radio (GWR)** and **Capital Radio** in May 2005, the newly formed GCap Media became the United Kingdom's largest **commercial radio** company, with one national and 54 local **analog** stations and 100 digital radio stations. In addition, the company could boast an interest in 28 digital radio **multiplexes** and a controlling shareholding in the United Kingdom's only national commercial digital radio multiplex, **Digital One**.

The geographical spread of ownership was also enhanced by the merger, giving the group ownership or interest in local and regional analog stations in South East England, South West England, the Midlands, East Anglia, Northern England, Wales, and Scotland. **Ralph Bernard** of GWR became the group's first executive chairman, with Capital Radio's **David Mansfield** serving as chief executive; however, Mansfield resigned within six months of the merger. In June 2008, **Global Radio** completed a takeover of the company for £375 million, and use of the name GCap Media was discontinued in November of that same year.

GENERAL FORCES PROGRAMME. A station that ran from February 1944 to December 1946. It grew out of the **BBC Forces Programme**, established in 1940, and the **General Overseas Service**, created in 1943, to provide programming of appeal to the British Armed Forces. During preparations for D-Day, it became clear that a wider range of output was needed to cater to the more international nature of the listenership, including troops from the United States. At the request of General Dwight D. Eisenhower, the **British Broadcasting Corporation (BBC)** created the General Forces Programme, which was transmitted on **shortwave** frequencies previously allocated to the **Empire Service** (*see also* BBC WORLD SERVICE). The network combined BBC programs with material supplied by U.S. stations and the Canadian Broadcasting Corporation. It was also heard on **longwave** and listened to by domestic civilian audiences in Britain, who gained a taste for the more informal style of transatlantic programs, available in the United Kingdom for the first time. On 29 July 1945, the General Forces Programme was transformed into the **Light Programme**.

See also BRITISH FORCES BROADCASTING SERVICE (BFBS); WARTIME BROADCASTING.

GENERAL OVERSEAS SERVICE. The origins of the General Overseas Service began in November 1942, when a service was launched to serve British troops in North Africa and the Middle East. It was expanded and renamed as the Overseas Service, and then the General Overseas Service in 1943. Prior to D-Day in 1944, it was further re-branded as the **General Forces Programme**.

GENERAL STRIKE. Beginning on 4 May 1926, the General Strike was a major event in British broadcasting and the first time that the **British Broadcasting Company (BBC)** faced a crisis in its relationship with the government. As the country came to a standstill and newspapers ceased publication, radio became the only source of information. **John Reith**, who later referred to the time as "those exciting but very difficult days of the General Strike," had the task of trying to keep the BBC free from the influence of right-wing politicians and was criticized by left-wing activists for progovernment policy in BBC broadcasts. Winston Churchill demanded that the BBC be commandeered to become the voice of government; this did not happen, although, at times, some critics felt it had come close to this.

Reith's own assessment, recorded for the 1961 program *Scrapbook*, summed up both the problem and the opportunity of the strike for the BBC, which was in its last year prior to becoming a corporation. It was a tremendous opportunity to demonstrate what broadcasting could do. Hitherto the BBC had not been permitted to give the news before 7:00 p.m.; new arrangements had been made for bulletins at 10:00 a.m., 1:30 p.m., 4:00 p.m., 7:00 p.m., and 9.30 p.m. The major issue was whether the BBC would become part of government, broadcasting only what was passed along by some government representative, or whether BBC independence was to be preserved, the BBC being trusted to broadcast information it deemed as being in the best interests of the country.

GERALDO (1904–1974). Born Gerald Bright, this popular dance band leader was heard on the radio throughout the 1930s and during World War II. His **music** was always that of the "easy listening" variety, and many of his broadcasts came from such major hotels as the Savoy in London. His radio shows featured a number of lead singers throughout the years, most notably in the late 1930s, with appearances by crooner Al Bowlly. After the war, Geraldo organized bands for P&O transatlantic liners.

See also WARTIME BROADCASTING.

GIBBONS, CARROLL (1903–1954). Born in the United States, Carroll Gibbons came to the United Kingdom in 1924, playing at the Savoy hotel as a pianist. The resident band at the time was the Savoy Orpheans, of which he became leader in 1927. Capitalizing on the close proximity of the hotel to **British Broadcasting Company (BBC)** headquarters in **Savoy Hill**, literally next door, the band made frequent appearances in the early days of radio.

The band disbanded in 1928, and Gibbons joined HMV as director of light **music**. He briefly returned to the United States to work in film and was back in Britain by 1931, when he reformed the Orpheans, leading the band until the end of his life. Beginning in December 1933, Gibbons elevated the band's popularity through its numerous appearances on **commercial radio**, in particular on **Radio Luxembourg**, where it attracted keen sponsorship from major advertisers, while maintaining a BBC presence. He also appeared solo in such **series** as *Carroll Calls the Tune*. His signature tune was "On the Air."

GIELGUD, VAL (1900–1981). The elder brother of actor Sir John Gielgud, Val Gielgud was the founding father of British radio **drama**, a department he led within the **British Broadcasting Corporation** from 1929–1963. Among his most significant productions was *The Man Born to Be King*. He also pioneered international work in *World Theatre* and was a prolific writer in his own right. Gielgud collaborated with Holt Marvell (the pen name of **Eric Maschwitz**) on the crime novel *Death at Broadcasting House*, which was filmed in Broadcasting House and in which he himself played a central role. He famously rejected **Samuel Beckett's** *Waiting for Godot* for broadcast in 1953. Gielgud produced a number of highly popular **series** during the 1940s and 1950s, including the suspense drama *Appointment with Fear*.

GILES COOPER AWARD. Founded in 1978, in honor of radio playwright **Giles Cooper**, who died in 1966, this annual award for plays broadcast on **British Broadcasting Corporation (BBC)** networks, with the exception of the **BBC World Service**, has, throughout the years, marked the work of many famous writers, some of whom, at the time of winning their award, were new names in the medium. In the first year of the awards, recipients included Richard Harris, Don Haworth, and Fay Weldon. Among the winners in subsequent years have been Harold Pinter, Peter Barnes, John Arden, Wally K. Daly, Peter Tinniswood, and Anthony Minghella.
  See also DRAMA.

GILL, ERIC (1882–1940). The carvings of Prospero and Ariel on the façade of **Broadcasting House** in London are among the best-known work of Eric Gill, artist, stone carver, and writer. The adoption of Shakespeare's Ariel, the invisible spirit of the air, from *The Tempest* was an appropriate metaphor for the new science of broadcasting. In addition to the figures of Ariel and his master, which adorn the main entrance, others develop further metaphors for sound broadcasting, showing "Ariel between wisdom and gaiety," "Ariel listening to music," and "Ariel piping to children." Inside the main reception area, Gill created a carving entitled "Sower," a man broadcasting seed. Beneath it is the inscription, "Deus incrementum dat" ("God giveth the increase," from Corinthians, Chapter 3, verse 7). Gill's work on Broadcasting House was not universally liked; the carving *Prospero and Ariel*, in particular, caused controversy, as one critic claimed it to be "objectionable to public morals and decency."

Gill was born in Brighton, the son of a nonconformist minister. While he was apprenticed to a London firm of architects as a young man, he became fascinated by the art of calligraphy. Absorbed by the Arts and Crafts movement and its philosophies, he set up three self-sufficient religious communities, where he worked with other artists as a sculptor, wood-engraver, and type designer. (His most famous typeface is Gill Sans, which was used by a number of corporate institutions—including the BBC—for their logos.)

GILLARD, FRANK (1908–1998). Born in Exford, Somerset, Frank Gillard was a distinguished broadcaster and war correspondent who proved himself to be as forceful and effective a manager of broadcasting as he was a presenter. For nine years, he worked as a school teacher, before becoming a freelance broadcaster beginning in 1936. He joined the staff of the **British Broadcasting Corporation (BBC)** in 1941 and, using new portable recording technology equipment made available to war correspondents for the first time, broadcast reports of the Normandy landings and broke the **news** of the linkup between U.S. and Soviet forces at the River Elbe in 1945.

After the war, as head of programs for the BBC West Region in Bristol, Gillard conceived the highly successful program *Any Questions?* Later, as director of sound broadcasting in 1964, he was the subject of much controversy following his decision to take the much-loved *Children's Hour* off the air. Moving to the post of managing director of BBC radio, he oversaw the creation of **BBC Radio 1**, **BBC Radio 2**, **BBC Radio 3**, and **BBC Radio 4** in 1967, and was the driving force behind the establishment of BBC **local radio** that same year. Gillard was awarded the Most Excellent Order of the British Empire in 1946, followed by the title Commander of the Most Excellent Order of the British Empire in 1961.

See also WARTIME BROADCASTING.

GILLIAM, LAURENCE (1907–1964). Laurence Gilliam first worked in the U.K. recording industry, for the Gramophone Company, before freelancing as a journalist, actor, and producer until 1932, when he joined the staff of *Radio Times*. The following year, he moved to the Drama Department, where his particular interest was in creating programs characterized by their sound pictures. Typical of this was *'Opping 'Oliday*, a sound picture of hop picking in Kent, which he produced in 1934, using the newly created mobile recording van, then being developed by the **British Broadcasting Corporation (BBC)** for location work.

In 1933, Gilliam began his lifelong association with the production of worldwide Christmas Day programs, which traditionally aired prior to the annual message from the monarch on Christmas afternoon. These programs were technically complex and helped develop radio's potential in the United Kingdom. In 1936, **drama** and **features** divided, with Gilliam having responsibility for the latter, and during the war, his work in this field reached new heights, culminating in his editorship of *War Report*.

Postwar, his work encouraged writers and poets to enrich the radio feature and inspired great loyalty amongst his colleagues, generating some of the most memorable radio of all time, including the work of **Francis Dillon**, **Nesta Pain**, **Wynford Vaughan-Thomas**, and **Douglas Cleverdon**. It is true to say that the development of the radio feature owed more to Gilliam than any other single person. During his last years, the BBC begin to dismantle his department, which was disbanded in 1965, a few months after his death.

See also DOCUMENTARY.

GILLIGAN, ANDREW (1968–). As defense and diplomatic correspondent for the **BBC Radio 4** *Today* program, Andrew Gilligan was the journalist at the center of the 2003 controversy regarding the reporting of Iraqi weapons capability, a major factor in the U.K. government's prosecution of the Iraq War. The case led to the Hutton Report, which resulted in a number of high-level resignations within the **British Broadcasting Corporation**, and ultimately Gilligan's own, in January 2004.

See also CURRENT AFFAIRS; NEWS.

GIVING VICTIMS A VOICE. The name given to a report published in January 2013, on allegations against broadcaster **Jimmy Savile** of sexual abuse. The report formed part of **Operation Yewtree** and was produced by the Metropolitan Police and the National Society for the Prevention of Cruelty to Children. Between 1955–2009, the report stated, there were 450 alleged victims, of whom 328 were minors at the time, with victims aged between 8 and 47 years, with the largest number being between the ages of 13 and 16. Some of the alleged offences had been perpetrated on **British Broadcasting Corporation** premises.

GLENDENNING, RAYMOND (1907–1974). Raymond Glendenning was a **sports** commentator known for the extreme speed of his description of live events. He started his working life as a chartered accountant but joined the **British Broadcasting Corporation (BBC)** in 1932, as an organizer on *Children's Hour*, based in Cardiff. He left the staff in 1945 and, from then onward, worked as a full-time freelance sports commentator, equally at ease describing the action in football, boxing, racing, tennis, show jumping, greyhound racing, and other athletics. He was the voice of sports on BBC radio for many years until his retirement in 1963.

GLOBAL POSITIONING SYSTEM (GPS). Satellite navigation technology that provides location and other information to anywhere with a direct line of sight to the relevant satellites. First developed as early as 1973, it became fully operational in 1995, and has since been adopted for a variety of purposes. Since the development of technical capabilities in **smartphones** and wireless, its usage in creating audio experiences linked to location, for example, **Hackney Hear**, has been actively explored by sound artists and digital program makers.

GLOBAL RADIO. Global Radio was founded by **Ashley Tabor** in 2007, at which time Global purchased **Chrysalis** and took control of the radio brands **Heart**, **Galaxy**, the **London Broadcasting Company**, and the **Arrow**. A year later, in October 2008, Global took control of **GCap Media** and its brands, and the GCap Media name was dropped. Stations under the Global banner then included **Classic FM**, **Xfm**, and **Gold**, amongst others. Heritage **local radio** stations in areas not already served by Heart were gradually rebranded and incorporated into a larger Heart Network, which covers most of Southern England and parts of North Wales. The remaining stations were ultimately merged with the Galaxy network and **Capital Radio**, London into the Capital network.

In June 2012, Global acquired the **Guardian Media Group** in a deal that became subject to a regulatory review. In May 2013, the Competition Commission ruled that Global was required to sell seven stations in the network. Global Radio is the largest **commercial radio** company in the country and Tabor continues as its president, with **Charles Allen** as group chairman and **Richard Park** as group executive director and director of broadcasting. By 2014, Global owned 40 percent of the U.K. commercial radio market, and its various stations had a total weekly audience of 19.5 million listeners.

See also MUSIC.

GLOVER, FI (1970–). Fi Glover is a writer and broadcaster who has presented on **BBC Radio 4**, **BBC Radio 5 Live**, **BBC Radio 2**, **BBC Radio 1**, and **Greater London Radio (GLR)**. She joined the **British Broadcasting Corporation (BBC)** trainee scheme in 1993, and worked for a number of radio stations throughout the United Kingdom before presenting the breakfast program on GLR. In 1996, she joined Radio 5 Live, where, for a number of years, she hosted a number of key programs. In 2005, Glover presented *Broadcasting House* on Radio 4, before being involved as presenter with the team that launched *Saturday Live* on the same station in 2006. She has been the voice of the BBC's *The Listening Project* on Radio 4 and was part of the major project *Generations Apart*, a **series** of programs that spanned three years, beginning in 2011, that tracked the lives of people from two different generations—the 1940s and 1990s—reporting on how their experiences were shaped by the times in which they were born. Glover is on the board of **Sound Women** and has won a number of **Radio Academy Awards** for her work.

GOLD. The term *Gold* is often used in radio to denote **music** from past eras with strong nostalgia value. More specifically, in the United Kingdom, it is the name of a network of "oldies" radio stations formed in 2007, by the merger of two existing groups, **Capital Gold** and the **Classic Gold Network**. Gold traditionally directed its output at the mature listener 50 years of age and older; however, as policy changed, a younger audience of listeners in their 30s was targeted, with music from more contemporary artists of approximately the past 15 years. The Gold network is owned by **Global Radio**.

See also COMMERCIAL RADIO.

GOLDRING, MARY (?–). A journalist with an ability to pinpoint issues and detail, Mary Goldring was business editor of the *Economist* and a key member of the presentation team for the **BBC Radio 4** program *Analysis*. She won many awards for her work, including the Broadcasting Press Guild Award for an "outstanding personal contribution to radio." She received the award of Most Excellent Order of the British Empire in 1994.

See also CURRENT AFFAIRS.

GOON SHOW, THE. Growing out of the 1951 program *Crazy People*, a groundbreaking **comedy** show that first aired on 22 January 1952, and featured **Spike Milligan**, **Peter Sellers**, **Harry Secombe**, and **Michael Bentine**, although Bentine left after the first **series**. Also integral were musicians Max Geldray and the Ray Ellington Quartet. The style—a blend of army and surreal—was anarchic and hugely influential in the development of postwar broadcast comedy. Mostly written by Milligan, for whom the strain of writing material during the course of 10 series and eight years resulted in several breakdowns, the program was broadcast on the **BBC Home Service** from 1952–1960, with a revival edition, *The Last Goon Show of All* (1972), being produced as part of the 50th anniversary celebrations of the **British Broadcasting Corporation**. Among the program's greatest admirers was HRH, the Prince of Wales.

GORDON, JAMES ALEXANDER (1936–2014). James Alexander Gordon was a Scottish-born radio **announcer** and newsreader who became famous for reading the classified football results each Saturday on **BBC Radio 5 Live**. Having suffered from polio as a child, he worked in **music** publishing until 1972, when he joined the **British Broadcasting Corporation (BBC)**, working mostly for **BBC Radio 2**. In 1974, he began reading the football results on Radio 2, later continuing on Radio 5 Live. Following surgery to remove his larynx due to cancer, Gordon retired in July 2013. Nicknamed "JAG," his style and intonation made him a highly recognizable and much-loved broadcaster.

See also SPORTS.

GORDON-WALKER, PATRICK (1907–1980). A leading academic before World War II, Patrick Gordon-Walker became increasingly interested in politics, eventually becoming a Labour Party member of parliament, and finally, as Lord Gordon-Walker, a member of the European Parliament in 1975–1976. During the war, he became closely involved with the European Service of the **British Broadcasting Corporation (BBC)**, and after a number of freelance talks, he joined the staff at **Bush House**. When U.S. forces reached Luxembourg in 1944 and took control of **Radio Luxembourg** from the retreating German army, Gordon-Walker was among the BBC staff seconded to the station; from there, he traveled with Allied troops into Germany, reporting as he went, including powerful broadcasts from the Belsen concentration camp. After the war, he became a member of parliament for Smethwick and thereafter devoted himself to politics.

See also WARTIME BROADCASTING.

GOSLING, RAY (1940–2013). Having begun his broadcasting career as a researcher for **Charles Parker**, Ray Gosling went on to become one of the most unique program makers in British radio, with a personal style that was both reflective and perceptive. He made several **series** for both radio and television, exploring the specifics of living. Gosling's commentaries were often characterized by the style and stance of an outsider, written with a poet's eye and objectivity, and delivered in his own idiosyncratic style of speech.

During the 1990s, work became scarce, and he spent much of his time nursing his partner through the final stages of pancreatic cancer. A longtime alcoholic, Gosling was declared bankrupt in 2000. He was an early gay rights activist and, in 2010, courted controversy by making a false claim during a television program that he had killed a lover in an act of euthanasia. Gosling died on 19 November 2013, at the age of 73, at the Queen's Medical Center in Nottingham. His personal archive of tapes, scripts, press cuttings, and films gathered during a span of more than 40 years were obtained by Nottingham Trent University in 2005, and the collection is now preserved in the School of Arts and Humanities.

See also DOCUMENTARY; FEATURE.

GRADE, MICHAEL (1943–). Michael Ian Grade, Commander of the Most Excellent Order of the British Empire, became chairman of the **British Broadcasting Corporation (BBC)** in May 2004, after the resignation of **Gavyn Davies** as a result of the Hutton Report, which investigated the death of government weapons expert Dr. David Kelly. Grade had previously had ambitions to become BBC chair in 2001, but Davies had been appointed in his stead. Having begun in print journalism, he worked in his family's theatrical business and subsequently moved into television. Among numerous management roles, he was controller of **BBC Radio 1** and chief executive of Channel 4 Television. In November 2006, upon his appointment to a position at rival Independent Television (ITV), Grade and the BBC announced his resignation from the chairmanship of the Board of Governors, or the **BBC Trust**, as it had become. He became executive chairman of ITV in January 2007.

GRAND HOTEL. A long-running program of light orchestral **music** first transmitted from the Palm Court of the Grand Hotel in Eastbourne on 28 July 1925, under the leadership of well-known violinist Albert Sandler. It was hugely popular leading up to the outbreak of World War II. In 1943, the show was revived from the Concert Hall of **Broadcasting House**, still with Sandler and the Palm Court Theatre Orchestra, and with potted palms specially imported to create the appropriate ambience. The first program in its revived form featured popular tenor Frank Titterton. (There was always a guest singer who performed with the small musical forces, usually comprising a piano trio, occasionally augmented with extra musicians and instruments, including a Mustel organ and celeste.) *Grand Hotel* continued for many years after the war, and its theme tune of "Roses from the South," by Johann Strauss II, became a familiar part of Sunday evening listening.

GRAVES, CECIL (1892–1957). After the departure of **F. W. Ogilvie** as director-general of the **British Broadcasting Corporation (BBC)** in 1942, Cecil Graves took on the role jointly with **R. W. Foot** for one year, taking on responsibilities for programming, while Foot took administrative control. Graves had joined the BBC in 1926, from a military background. He was the first director of the **Empire Service** and deputized for both **John Reith** and Ogilvie. Indeed, Graves was Reith's preferred choice for a successor; however, Graves had been plagued by ill health and retired from the BBC in 1943.

GREAT WESTERN RADIO (GWR). In 1985, the independent local radio station Wiltshire Radio merged with Radio West in Bristol, which was relaunched as Great Western Radio (GWR), although the acronym was, from the start, more identifiable than the full name and has remained so. GWR acquired Plymouth Sound in 1987, Radio 2-Ten in Reading, and Two Counties Radio (2CR, Bournemouth) in 1989. This was the foundation of the GWR Group, which, prior to the merger with **Capital Radio** in May 2005 to form **GCap Media**, would become the largest pure radio group in the United Kingdom. In 1991, under the leadership of **Ralph Bernard**, the GWR Group took an initial 17 percent share of the first national **commercial radio** station in Britain, **Classic FM**. It bought the remaining 83 percent of the shares in 1996, for £71.5 million.

The **local radio** operations of the GWR Group continued to grow, with the Chiltern Radio Group, the Mid-Anglian Radio group, East Anglian Radio, the Orchard Media Group, and the Marcher group of stations joining GWR, giving the group control of 32 local licenses, in addition to Classic FM. In May 2005, the group merged with the **Capital Radio** Group to form **GCap Media**. In 2007, this was, in turn, purchased by **Global Radio**.

GREATER LONDON RADIO (GLR). GLR was the name given to a **British Broadcasting Corporation (BBC)** station that served London from 1988–2000. The BBC's **local radio** policy when applied to London has long been fraught with difficulties, not least because of name confusion relating to the **pirate radio** station **Radio London**. The BBC's local London service initially adopted the same name but subsequently instigated a number of experiments with different identities in providing a radio service to Londoners. The most notable of these was GLR, which, while it brought with it some controversy, spawned a number of significant presenters who went on to become mainstream voices on many U.K. radio and television networks, notably under the early development of the station's first managing editor, **Matthew Bannister**, and program organizer **Trevor Dann**. Among these were **Chris Evans** and **Fi Glover**. The station was relaunched in 2000, as BBC London Live 94.9, being rebranded yet again in 2001, as BBC LDN, in an attempt to bring together regional radio, television, and online services under one tri-media brand. Further attempts at establishing identity led to its present name, BBC London 94.9. It has continued in its tradition of developing significant radio talent, including **Danny Baker**, Jon Gaunt, and **Vanessa Feltz**.

GREEN, HUGHIE (1920–1997). Hughie Green was born in London but moved to Canada, becoming a Canadian citizen. Returning to Britain at the age of 13, he gained a reputation as a gifted impersonator and came to public notice after an appearance on *In Town Tonight* in 1933. By the time he was 15, he had become the highest-paid child star in Britain. Green worked extensively on **commercial radio**, including **Radio Luxembourg**, appearing on such programs as *Horlicks Picture House* before World War II. After the war, he devised and presented ***Opportunity Knocks*** for Radio Luxembourg. The show was later transferred to television. Green was involved in an unsuccessful legal battle with the **British Broadcasting Corporation** for alleged blacklisting.

See also QUIZ SHOWS.

GREEN, MICHAEL (1941–). Michael Green became controller of **BBC Radio 4** in 1986. and was largely popular with staff for his work, although his decision to move ***Woman's Hour*** from its afternoon slot to a morning slot in the network schedule provoked considerable controversy. Among his many achievements was the establishment of ***File on Four***. Green began his broadcasting career with Swiss Radio International, before joining **British Broadcasting Corporation local radio** when it began in 1967. He went on to a distinguished career in radio journalism, including work as a producer on the *Analysis* program. He retired in 1996, and was succeeded as controller of Radio 4 by **James Boyle**.

GREENE, HUGH CARLETON (1910–1987). Sir Hugh Carleton Greene, Most Excellent Order of the British Empire, Knights Commander of the Order of St. Michael and St. George, brother of novelist Graham Greene, was **British Broadcasting Corporation (BBC)** director-general from 1960–1969, succeeding Sir **Ian Jacob**. After joining the corporation to lead the BBC German Service in 1940, he took on successive roles of director of **news** and **current affairs** and director of administration. Greene was heavily involved in modernizing the BBC and encouraged new program ideas and program making, including, for radio, ***I'm Sorry I'll Read That Again*** and a range of satirical material. He was admired for his leadership, and his evidence to the Pilkington Committee helped in the renewal of the BBC's **charter**. Greene resigned due to marital problems but subsequently served for two years on the BBC Board of Governors, where he robustly defended the corporation's editorial independence. After his retirement, he oversaw operations at Greene King Brewery, the family business.

GREENING, KEVIN (1962–2007). Kevin Greening was a presenter who worked on a number of national radio stations after an early career in **local radio** and as a studio manager at the **BBC World Service**. In 1993, he joined the newly launched **Virgin Radio**, before moving to **BBC Radio 1** in 1994. Subsequent work included periods on Jazz FM, **Heart**, and **Xfm**. From 2005–2007 he was a popular voice on **Smooth Radio**. He regularly commentated on the **Sony Radio Academy Awards** via the academy's live website online feed. In 2001, Greening was awarded a **Radio Academy** fellowship.

He was a great supporter of the **Student Radio Association (SRA)**; after his death in December 2007, from a heart attack, the SRA introduced the Kevin Greening Award for unique on-air creativity.

See also DISC JOCKEY (DJ); MUSIC.

GREENWICH TIME SIGNAL. On 5 February 1924, at 5:30 p.m., the **British Broadcasting Company (BBC)** first broadcast the Greenwich Time Signal. The event was preceded by an introductory **talk** by astronomer royal Frank Dyson. The idea for the time signal—affectionately referred to ever after as the "Pips"—came from **John Reith**, after a radio talk by horologist Frank Hope-Jones at the introduction of British Summer Time in 1923. It was Hope-Jones who devised the system, based on two clocks built by E. Dent and Company in 1874, with Dyson.

Electrical contacts attached to the pendulum of the clocks at the Greenwich Observatory sent pulses to the BBC's headquarters at **Broadcasting House**, where an oscillatory **valve** circuit converted the signal to the tones. The clocks operated until 1949, when more up-to-date technology was implemented. The system was the first of its kind in the world and was the model for time signals on all other broadcasting services.

Today the BBC keeps its own time using two atomic clocks in Broadcasting House, kept in step by signals received from the Global Positioning Satellite system and information received from the Rugby radio transmitter facility operated by BT Aeronautical and Maritime, under contract to the National Physical Laboratory. Since 1972, time signals have been based on atomic time due to the fact that Greenwich Mean Time (GMT) drifts as the speed of the Earth's rotation changes, thus causing discrepancies.

Differences between atomic time and GMT are compensated for by occasional extra seconds that are added to the signal. This is the reason for the last "Pip" being slightly longer; if a seventh tone has to be added to compensate, an elongated last tone is required to demonstrate the true end of the signal.

GREGG, HUBERT (1916–2004). Although Hubert Gregg was, for a short time, an **announcer** on the **Empire Service** in 1936, it was his radio programs, linked to his long and illustrious theater career—and the memories engendered by it—that made his **BBC Radio 2 series** *Thanks for the Memory* such a long-running success. Beginning in 1972, it was still a staple part of the **British Broadcasting Corporation's** output, and it remained so upon his death in March 2004, with its blend of popular songs from the past and personal anecdotes. Gregg was an actor, singer, director, writer, and composer, in addition to his role as a broadcaster; he was the author of probably the most famous song ever written about London, "Maybe It's Because I'm a Londoner."

See also MUSIC.

GRENFELL, JOYCE (1910–1979). Joyce Grenfell was a much-loved, multitalented broadcaster with a special skill for monologues that characterized and often gently satirized the English middle class and certain colonial attitudes. She was the first radio critic of the *Observer* newspaper, and after the war, she created, with **Stephen Potter**, the *How To. . .* **series** for the fledgling **Third Progamme**. The series ran from 1943–1962.

GRISEWOOD, FREDDY (1888–1972). Freddie Grisewood was chairman of *Any Questions?* beginning in 1948, when the program began, until his retirement due to ill health in 1968. He had joined the **British Broadcasting Corporation** in 1929, as an **announcer**, and was assistant chief announcer under **Stuart Hibberd**. Grisewood's voice became a well-known part of the program schedule from that time onward. He appeared in many radio shows, including *Children's Hour*, *In Town Tonight*, and the long-running *Scrapbook* series from 1933. He was a cousin of **Harman Grisewood**.

GRISEWOOD, HARMAN (1906–1997). Harman Grisewood began his career as an actor and a radio **announcer** during the 1930s. In 1941, he moved from presentation to organization and became assistant controller to the European Service of the **British Broadcasting Corporation (BBC)**, based at **Bush House** in London. After the war, he briefly worked in **talks** but resigned in 1947, although he was almost immediately offered a post in the planning department of the newly formed **Third Programme**, of which he became controller from 1948–1952. While there, he launched the long-running *Record Review* program, which later became *CD Review*.

From 1952–1955, Grisewood was director of the spoken word and finally chief assistant to the director-general of the BBC from 1955–1964. During the Suez Crisis, he did much to maintain the BBC's political independence while facing considerable government pressure. He was awarded the title Commander of the Most Excellent Order of the British Empire in 1960 and retired from the BBC in 1964, briefly joining the *Times* under **William Haley**, with whom he had worked at the corporation. He was a cousin of **Freddy Grisewood**.

GUARDIAN MEDIA GROUP (GMG). A mass media company that owns a number of operations, among them the newspapers the *Guardian* and the *Observer*. The group is owned by Scott Trust Limited. Until June 2012, its interests included GMG Radio, which was acquired by **Global Radio** at that time.

See also COMMERCIAL RADIO.

H

HACKNEY HEAR. Hackney Hear, created by producer **Francesca Panetta** in 2012, uses the concept of location-based audio triggered through the **Global Positioning System (GPS)** satellite technology to enable a personal sound experience centered on Place. Using **smartphones** as receivers and an application tethered to locations throughout and surrounding the urban area of London Fields in the U.K. capital, it offers a way of exploration in sound, using memories and stories from local writers, musicians, and residents, and activated at various points as the listener moves throughout the area. At the 2012 **Prix Europa** awards, Hackney Hear won the prize for innovation, and the idea has subsequently been developed in other locations and with differing variations.

HALEY, WILLIAM (1901–1987). Sir William John Haley, Knights Commander of the Order of St. Michael and St. George , a native of Jersey, was a journalist and one-time editor of the *Manchester Evening News*. He joined the **British Broadcasting Corporation (BBC)** in 1943 and became director-general in 1944. A widely respected figure, he was admired by **John Reith** and largely instrumental in the establishment of the BBC's role after World War II, with the establishment of the tripartite structure of the **BBC Home Service**, **Light Programme**, and **Third Programme**. After leaving the BBC in 1952, Haley became editor of the *Times* and, prior to his retirement, *Encyclopaedia Britannica*.

HALL, ALAN (1963–). Alan Hall began his production career in 1990, as a staff producer for the **British Broadcasting Corporation (BBC)**. In April 1998, he left the Corporation to work as an independent producer and formed Alan Hall Associates, a production company creating **documentary feature** programs for the BBC networks, as well as for international broadcasters, including Ireland's Newstalk, the Canadian Broadcasting Corporation, and the Australian Broadcasting Corporation. In 2004, the company changed its name to **Falling Tree Productions**. Hall and his company have won numerous awards for productions, including the **Prix Italia** and **Prix Europa**, as well as honors at the Third Coast Festival and the **Sony Radio Academy Awards**. Hall also works as a writer, teacher, and speaker, promoting the art of storytelling in sound.

HALL, HENRY (1898–1989). Henry Hall was probably the most famous dance band leader in British radio. He first broadcast in August 1924, with the Gleneagles Hotel Band from Glasgow. He came to the attention of **John Reith** and, in 1932, succeeded **Jack Payne** as leader of the **BBC Dance Orchestra**. Five years later, Hall went freelance, but his programs remained a staple part of BBC radio's schedule. His presentation style was somewhat hesitant and diffident, but this only endeared him to audiences all the more. His regular greeting was, "Hello everyone, this *is* Henry Hall speaking," and it may be said that his program *Henry Hall's Guest Night* was the first British radio "chat show." Throughout his career, Hall was in charge of no less than 32 dance bands. His most famous commercial recording was "The Teddy Bears' Picnic."
See also MUSIC.

HALL, TONY, BARON HALL OF BIRKENHEAD (1951–). In April 2013, Tony Hall took over the role of director-general of the **British Broadcasting Corporation (BBC)**, succeeding the interim director-general, **Tim Davie**, and the former incumbent, **George Entwistle**, who had resigned in November 2012. Prior to this he had been chief executive of the Royal Opera House in Covent Garden. Hall joined the BBC in 1973, and worked as a producer on various **news** and **current affairs** radio programs, including *Today*, *The World at One*, *The World Tonight*, and *PM*. He moved into television and, in 1990, became director of BBC News and Current Affairs Television, subsequently being appointed director of news in radio and television in 1993. In 1999, Hall was an unsuccessful candidate for the role of director-general. He was officially appointed to the post on 22 November 2012 but did not take up his position until 2 April 2013.

HANCOCK, TONY (1924–1968). Tony Hancock was a troubled genius whose comic persona of "Anthony Aloysius St. John Hancock" was the basis for *Hancock's Half Hour*, which has been hailed as one of the greatest radio **comedy series** of all time. He made his radio debut in 1941, on a light entertainment program called *A La Carte*, but gained more recognition from his time on *Educating Archie* from 1951–1953. His partnerships with writers **Ray Galton** and Alan Simpson, and producer **Dennis Main Wilson**, were first formed on the radio comedy show *Happy Go Lucky*, and they served as the potent roots of his success. By all accounts, Hancock was a difficult man to work with, and his career dwindled toward the end of his life. He died by his own hand.

HANCOCK'S HALF HOUR. A show that ran from November 1954 to December 1959, transferring to television in 1956. The central character was **Tony Hancock** himself, or rather a version of himself, and he was joined in various **series** by a number of other characters, played by Sid James, Bill Kerr, Hattie Jacques, and **Kenneth Williams**. The programs were a blend of well-drawn, well-played characters and skillful plot lines that revolved around Hancock's fictional home at "23, Railway Cuttings, East Cheam." At its best, the writing of **Ray Galton** and Alan Simpson elevated the situation **comedy** genre to a series of unique short television plays in some ways akin to the work of **Samuel Beckett**.

HANDLEY, TOMMY (1896–1949). Tommy Handley was a greatly loved comedian who became an institution of his generation. Coming from a **music** hall background, his career was boosted by his first radio appearance in 1924; however, it is for his work on *It's That Man Again* that he is best remembered, and his fast-moving delivery, together with producer **Ted Kavanagh's** concept of a show chock full of running gags and oddball characters, was perfectly suited to the war years and changed radio **comedy** forever. When Handley died in 1949, from a brain hemorrhage, there was unprecedented national mourning; the director-general of the **British Broadcasting Corporation**, **William Haley**, broadcast a tribute, and a memorial service was held in St. Paul's Cathedral. Handley's funeral was attended by 10,000 mourners.

See also SERIES; WARTIME BROADCASTING.

HAPPIDROME, THE. A **comedy series** set in an imaginary variety theater and broadcast from the Grand Theatre in Llandudno, *The Happidrome* ran for a number of series from 1941–1947, with a "special" final show that aired on 14 November 1947, marking the Silver Jubilee of the **British Broadcasting Corporation**. A live transmission on Sunday evenings, it was performed in front of an audience of war workers and fronted by a regular trio of characters played by residents Harry Korris, Cecil Frederick, and Robbie Vincent. An impressive range of guests from throughout the world of variety also made appearances. The program's popularity was enormous; the first series, initially intended to run for six episodes, was extended several times and finally lasted for 53 editions. Stage and film spin-offs came out of the format, and a number of records relating to the show were made.

See also WARTIME BROADCASTING.

HARDCASTLE, WILLIAM (1918–1975). William Hardcastle was a distinguished print journalist for many years prior to the start of his radio career, working both in Great Britain and the United States and rising to the role of editor of the *Daily Mail*. He lost this job in 1963, only to find a new life in radio beginning in 1965, when the new **BBC Home Service** lunchtime **news** program *The World at One* was launched. Hardcastle quickly adapted to the medium and became the recognizable voice of the program, reveling in the speed and immediacy of radio. He brought a new edge to British radio journalism, born from his experience in the United States, and his uncompromising interviewing style—particularly of politicians—would be of lasting influence. His excessive, self-imposed workload led to his premature death following a stroke in November 1975. He had presented *The World at One* just a few days before his passing.

See also CURRENT AFFAIRS.

HARDING, EDWARD ARCHIBALD (1903–1953). E. A. ("Archie") Harding joined the **British Broadcasting Corporation (BBC)** London station in 1927, as an **announcer**, and quickly became a member of a group of producers working in the Drama Department, experimenting with new formats. From this period of innovation came the concept of narratives conveying aura pictures using sound words and **music**. It was the birth of the radio **feature**, a form that would preoccupy Harding for the rest of his life.

In 1931, he produced *Crisis in Spain*, the first British example of radio reportage, and the following year, he made the first Christmas Day program linking speakers from various Commonwealth countries. It ended with a message from King George V. Harding was subsequently asked to make a similar program linking European countries. *New Year over Europe*, broadcast on New Year's Eve 1932, created a storm of controversy due to Harding's political approach, when a statement in the program about Polish armaments led to an official protest from the Polish ambassador and a debate in the British Parliament. Harding was consequently removed to the BBC's headquarters in Manchester.

Harding embraced this three-year period of "exile," and during that time, he established a thriving left-wing Features Department, surrounding himself with new, talented writers committed to making radio a medium for the voice of ordinary people. He recruited **D. G. Bridson**, encouraged **Francis Dillon**, and nurtured the talent of **Wilfred Pickles**, among many others.

In 1936, Harding returned to London to work in the BBC's Staff Training Department, initially as chief instructor and subsequently as director. After World War II, in 1948, he became deputy director of the Drama Department under **Val Gielgud**. Harding recruited **Louis MacNeice** to the BBC and is represented as "Harrap" in MacNeice's *Autumn Sequel*.

See also DOCUMENTARY.

HARDING, GILBERT (1907–1960). Gilbert Harding was a major figure in 1950s radio and the first chairman of *Twenty Questions*. He also hosted *Round Britain Quiz* and, for a time, *The Brain's Trust*. His first work for the **British Broadcasting Corporation** had come shortly before World War II, when, as a skilled linguist, he worked for the **BBC Monitoring Service**. Harding had an extremely complex personality, and his persona was irascible and oftentimes downright rude. He was fired from *Twenty Questions* after an infamous incident during which he presented the program while drunk.

See also QUIZ SHOWS; SERIES.

HARDING, MIKE (1944–). Mike Harding is a folk singer and writer who, as a stand-up comedian, has appeared on numerous radio and television programs, as well as the **BBC Radio 2** Folk Awards. From 1997–2012, he hosted *The Mike Harding Show*, a weekly program of folk **music** broadcast on the network. His last program on the network aired on 26 December 2012, ending due to schedule changes on Radio 2, and folk music audiences were subsequently catered to by **Mark Radcliffe's** *Folk Show*. In 2013, Harding launched his own weekly Internet radio program of folk music.

HARRISON, ANDREW (1964–). Andrew Harrison was founding chief executive of **RadioCentre**, the U.K. industry trade body formed from the merger of the **Commercial Radio Companies Association (CRCA)** and the Radio Advertising Bureau (RAB). He held the post for the first seven years of the organization's existence, from 2006–2013. Prior to radio, Harrison was a leading advertising client at Procter and Gamble, Coca-Cola, and Nestle. During his tenure at RadioCentre, he also held a number of industry roles, including chairman of RAB from 2008–2010, and he was founding chairman of **Radioplayer**, the joint industry online platform between the **British Broadcasting Corporation** and **commercial radio** from 2010–2013. Harrison is also a fellow of the **Radio Academy** and was a board member of **Radio Joint Audience Research** and Digital Radio UK. After leaving RadioCentre, he returned to the brands and marketing sector with the global marketing services group Wire and Plastic Products. Harrison was succeeded in his post at RadioCentre by **Siobhan Kenny**.

HATCH, DAVID (1939–2007). David Hatch moved from being a member of the anarchic radio **comedy** show *I'm Sorry I'll Read That Again*, which ran for nine years beginning in 1964, to controller of two radio networks. As a member of the Cambridge Footlights, he worked with future stars the likes of John Cleese. He joined the **British Broadcasting Corporation (BBC)** in 1964, as a producer. In 1980, Hatch became controller of **BBC Radio 2** and, the following year, controller of **BBC Radio 4**. In 1987, he was appointed managing director of BBC Network Radio. He created the original **BBC Radio 5** in 1990 and left the BBC in 1996, to become chairman of the National Consumer Council and subsequently the Parole Board for England and Wales, for which service he was knighted in 2003. Hatch was often heard on BBC radio chairing panel games, including *Wireless Wise* from 1999–2003. He was also chairman of the Services Sound and Vision Corporation and a fellow of the **Radio Academy**. He died in 2007.

HAVE A GO. A traveling **quiz show** that was one of the most popular U.K. radio shows of all time, running for 21 years with the same format. At the center of the program was **Wilfred Pickles** and his wife Mabel; they traveled Britain with their production team, interviewing and questioning members of communities in front of audiences from those communities. *Have a Go* was a celebration of everyday people. The show's main strength was the telling of stories. Beginning in the Northern Region in March 1946, it ran until January 1967, always from a different location, and at its peak it attracted as many as 20 million listeners.

See also COMEDY; SERIES.

HAWKINS, DESMOND (1908–1999). Desmond Hawkins initially worked for the **British Broadcasting Corporation (BBC)** as a freelance writer and producer. He worked with Francis Dillon on *Country Magazine* and was on the staff from 1945–1970, primarily in **features**. It was in this capacity that he worked at the receiving end of many of the great contributions from BBC correspondents in the last year of the war on the nightly program *War Report*. Hawkins went on to become head of West Region programs and finally regional controller for the South and West of England, based at Bristol. During this part of his career, he developed wildlife programs and founded the Natural History Unit.

Hawkins was a passionate advocate of the English countryside, literature, and ecology; he was also an expert on the work of novelist and poet Thomas Hardy and became widely known for his radio dramatizations of some of Hardy's finest novels. After his retirement, Hawkins continued to work as a freelance writer and broadcaster until his death at the age of 90.

See also DOCUMENTARY; DRAMA; WARTIME BROADCASTING.

HAYES, BRIAN (1937–). Born in Perth, Australia, Brian Hayes worked in radio in his native country for a number of years, before coming to the United Kingdom to work for **Capital Radio** in 1973. Between 1976–1990, he was the controversial host of the **London Broadcasting Company's** morning

phone-in program, inspiring many imitations throughout the country. He has worked for **BBC Radio 5 Live** and **BBC Radio 2**, and won many awards for his work, including a number of **Sony Radio Academy Awards**.

See also COMMERCIAL RADIO.

HEART. Heart is the name given to a network of stations owned by **Global Radio** that broadcasts localized material during certain times of day and shared content during others. The first Heart station launched in September 1994, in Birmingham, broadcasting soft, adult-oriented rock and pop **music**. In 1995, **Chrysalis** launched a sister Heart station in London, followed by a third opening in the East Midlands when **GCap Media** sold **Century Radio** to Chrysalis in 2005. Chrysalis was subsequently bought by Global Radio in 2007. Between June and September 2010, Global began a policy of closing some of the heritage stations within its ownership and merging content and transmission areas to create a smaller network of local and regional stations. The brand name Heart was applied to these stations, which, with the application of mainly generic content, effectively created one service covering Britain, delivered via local sources. In February 2014, Global announced that it would rebrand **Real Radio** stations in its ownership as Heart.

See also COMMERCIAL RADIO.

HEMSLEY, HARRY (1877–1951). Harry Hemsley was a child impersonator who became famous for his imaginary "family" of children, Elsie, Winnie, Johnny, and baby Horace—collectively known as the Fortune Family—in the 1930s **Radio Luxembourg** program *Ovaltiney's Concert Party*. He was the son of scenic artist W. T. Hemsley, born in Swindon, Wiltshire. His father's intention was to develop his son in his footsteps, as an artist, but Hemsley took to the stage at a young age and appeared in a number of productions as a child and young adult, including the ill-fated production of Sir Arthur Sullivan's opera *Ivanhoe*. Work as a bass-baritone in a number of concert parties followed, and in 1901, he joined *The Follies*. It was while working with this troupe that Hemsley developed his child mimicry, and by 1905, he had perfected his act to the degree that he became nationally known amongst juvenile audiences, appearing regularly at St. George's Hall in London and on national tours.

Hemsley also developed his inherited artistic talent as a cartoonist and used the skill in a **series** of spin-off books based on his characters. He first broadcast in 1927, and was a part of the hugely successful *Ovaltineys* radio project beginning at its inception in December 1934. After the war, his radio series included *Old Hearty* (1947) and *Hemsley's Hotel* (1949). He also appeared on television toward the end of his career.

See also CHILDREN'S PROGRAMS; COMMERCIAL RADIO.

HENLEY, DARREN (1973–). Darren Henley is managing director of **Classic FM**. After working at Invicta FM and the **London Broadcasting Company**, he joined Classic FM as a full-time staff member in 1994, assuming a number of journalistic roles before being appointed station manager in 2004, followed by managing director in 2006. Henley has written a number of books on **music**, including the authorized history of the Royal Liverpool Philharmonic Orchestra. He has also been actively involved with music education in the United Kingdom, authoring an independent review of cultural education in England for the government's Department of Education, as well as the Department for Culture, Media, and Sport, in 2011. He is also director of Government Liaison for **Global Radio**, Classic FM's parent company.

Henley has received numerous awards for his work in radio and music education, including Commercial Radio Programmer of the Year at the 2009 **Arqiva** Awards and a fellowship of the **Radio Academy** in 2011. He was a recipient of the Charles Groves Prize for his "outstanding contribution to British music" in 2013, and in the Queen's New Year Honors List for the same year, Henley received the Most Excellent Order of the British Empire for his contributions to music.

See also COMMERCIAL RADIO.

HENRY HALL'S GUEST NIGHT. A program that evolved almost accidentally. **Henry Hall** had been in charge of his own program for two years, when, in 1934, on the evening of the Oxford/Cambridge boat race, a number of guests joined him in the studio, including Lupino Lane, **Elsie and Doris Waters**, and **Anona Winn**. The resulting informality of unscripted conversation relating to social and show business gossip struck a chord with listeners and staff alike, and when Hall invited his guests to return the following week, the "chat show" was effectively born. The program ran throughout World War II and finally ended in the late 1950s, by which time it had been broadcast 972 times and had included some of the greatest variety performers in the world, including Noel Coward, Laurel and Hardy, and Bob Hope. Hall had two theme tunes: To start the show the band played "It's Just the Time for Dancing," while Hall's closing signature was "Here's to the Next Time."

See also MUSIC.

HENRY, JOHN (?–?). John Henry was the first comedian to be "made" by radio, adapting his delivery—in a lugubrious Yorkshire dialect—to the microphone in a way that previous comic broadcasters—more tuned to the technique of the stage and the **music** hall—had failed to do. Regarding his first broadcast, on 31 May 1923, the *Radio Times* wrote, "John Henry will try to entertain you." Referring to the second broadcast, which was set to air half an hour later, the *Times* said, "John Henry will try again." In May 1925,

Henry expanded his act to become "John Henry and Blossom," introducing the concept of the hen-pecked husband and nagging wife, creating the first example of domestic **comedy** in British radio. He made a number of commercial records, including *John Henry's Wireless Elephant* (1923) and *A Curtain Lecture* (1925—with "Blossom"). He also appeared in a comic strip cartoon in the *Daily Sketch* newspaper. Henry was the forerunner of a number of great radio comedians, among them **Tommy Handley, Gillie Potter, Arthur Askey, Frankie Howerd**, and **Tony Hancock**.

HENRY, STUART (1942–1995). Having trained first as an actor, Stuart Henry came to radio in 1965, at the height of the **pirate radio** boom, working as a **disc jockey** for **Radio Scotland** and broadcasting from a converted lightship off the Scottish coast. Because of his severe seasickness, he was permitted to record his programs on land, enabling him to develop personal appearances at Scottish dance halls. He was among the first intake of **BBC Radio 1** presenters in 1967, and became best known for his Saturday show; his unique style, which was quiet, with a gentle Scottish brogue, was in direct contrast to the louder mid-Atlantic style of some of his contemporaries. In 1974, Henry moved to **Radio Luxembourg**, settling in the country with his wife, Ollie; however, he soon began showing the first symptoms of multiple sclerosis (MS), including a slurring of his speech, which ultimately made it impossible for him to continue broadcasting. He spent his last years campaigning for MS research and cowrote the book *Pirate Radio: Then and Now*. Henry died at his Luxembourg home in November 1995.

See also COMMERCIAL RADIO; MUSIC.

HIBBERD, STUART (1893–1983). After a military career, Stuart Hibberd, a well-known **announcer**, joined the **British Broadcasting Company (BBC)** on its second anniversary, 13 November 1924, becoming chief announcer four years later. He was at the microphone for many historic events, including the **General Strike**, when he broadcast bulletins that sometimes lasted as long as an hour. He announced the news of the death of Adolf Hitler and, nine years earlier, had created his most memorable phrase when reporting the impending death of King George V in 1936: "The King's life is drawing peacefully to its close." Hibberd was also remembered for his closing announcement: "Goodnight everybody . . . goodnight." When asked, he explained that the pause was to permit listeners to respond. Another of his well-known phrases, "This—is London," became the title of his autobiography. He retired from the BBC in 1951, but continued to broadcast on certain programs for a time.

HI GANG!. A **British Broadcasting Corporation comedy** and variety series that ran from 1940–1949. It featured **Ben Lyon**; Lyon's wife, **Bebe Daniels**; and **Vic Oliver**. The show often featured appearances by such well-known American stars as Judy Garland, Cary Grant, Hedy Lamarr, and Tyrone Power. A postwar series, *Hi Gang 1949*, ran from February until August of that year and incorporated a number of notable British personalities, among them **Vera Lynn** and **Christopher Stone**. More than 100 shows were aired during the nine years of the program's existence. There was also a commercial movie spin-off.

See also WARTIME BROADCASTING.

HILL, CHARLES (1904–1989). Charles Hill, Lord Hill of Luton, was a medical doctor known to listeners between 1942–1950 as the "Radio Doctor." He became a member of parliament for Luton and held a number of posts in both the House of Commons and House of Lords, including that of postmaster general at the time of the Suez Crisis, when he came into conflict with the **British Broadcasting Corporation (BBC)** regarding the corporation's policy of broadcasting the event. Later, as chairman of the Independent Television Authority, Hill was, at times, openly hostile toward the BBC. Thus, his appointment as **BBC chairman** in 1967 came as a shock to many, and a number of members of the Board of Governors resigned in protest. As chairman, Hill was encouraged by Prime Minister Harold Wilson to take an active role in making editorial decisions. This frequently brought him into conflict with Hugh Greene, director-general. Hill retired in 1972.

HILL, TREVOR (1925–). Born in Southampton, Trevor Hill joined the **British Broadcasting Corporation (BBC)** in 1942, as a sound effects assistant on *It's That Man Again*. From that point onward, he worked as a writer, producer, and director, and, with his wife, author Margaret Potter, was heavily involved in the production of *Children's Hour*. During his career, Hill worked in **drama** and **features**, as well as producing such programs as *Round Britain Quiz* and *Transatlantic Quiz*. His final staff post in the BBC was assistant head of BBC Network Radio, from which he retired in 1983; however, he remained an active freelance broadcaster and, in 1998 and 2001, made two feature **series**, broadcast by the **British Forces Broadcasting Service**, in which listeners in England and Germany were taken back to the days of **wartime broadcasting** in both countries. In 2005, Hill published a memoir, *Over the Airwaves*.

See also CHILDREN'S PROGRAMS; COMEDY; QUIZ SHOWS.

HITCHHIKER'S GUIDE TO THE GALAXY, THE. A unique **comedy drama series** created from the writing of **Douglas Adams**. The series gained a cult following on **BBC Radio 4** beginning with the first series in 1978. It was later transferred to television, formed the basis for a series of novels, and became a feature film. Radio, however, remained its true home, and in its early years, the program fused skillful writing with technical sound innovation (created by Paddy Kingsland of the **BBC Radiophonic Workshop**) in a way that pushed back the boundaries of radio comedy. The parodying of everyday "little English" values and petty bureaucracy, set within a cosmic context, was central to the show's continuing success. It was revived in 2004 and 2005, in its original radio form.

HOFFNUNG, GERARD (1925–1959). Gerard Hoffnung, a German-born eccentric, raconteur, artist, writer, and musician, came to the attention of producer **Ian Messiter** in 1951. Messiter enlisted him as a member of the team for his new series, *One Minute, Please* (which later became *Just a Minute*). Although he was only 34 when he died of a brain hemorrhage, Hoffnung looked and sounded much older, and this quality, together with his original wit, made him a unique radio personality. His most famous creation was *The Bricklayer's Story*, supposedly based on a genuine letter to a builder's trade press journal, which the **British Broadcasting Corporation** recorded in 1958, during a presentation by Hoffnung to the Oxford Union. It was later commercially issued on records and cassettes.
See also COMEDY.

HORLICKS PICTURE HOUSE. A major weekly variety **series** that began airing on **Radio Luxembourg** in April 1937, and ran for more than 200 editions. A one-hour program, it attracted some of the greatest stars of its time and was prerecorded at the Scala Theatre in London. Film star Jessie Matthews was featured in its first transmission, Maurice Chevalier in the second, and Richard Tauber in the third. The producer was Stanley Maxted.
See also COMMERCIAL RADIO.

HORNE, KENNETH (1907–1969). A Cambridge University graduate, Kenneth Horne began working in the retail trade, selling safety glass, but gained his first major radio opportunity in the service **series** *Ack-Ack Beer-Beer*. He then linked with **Richard Murdoch** on the long-running **comedy** series *Much-Binding-in-the-Marsh*. Horne returned to his work in senior business management after the war until suffering a severe stroke. After recovering, he devoted himself to radio comedy. Following the dismissal of **Gilbert Harding** from *Twenty Questions*, Horne assumed the role of chairman. His respectable, avuncular style was exploited to its greatest effect in the two comedy programs for which he is most remembered, *Beyond Our Ken* and *Round the Horne*.

See also QUIZ SHOWS; WARTIME BROADCASTING.

HOSPITAL BROADCASTING ASSOCIATION (HBA). Established in 1992, the HBA represents approximately 230 volunteer-run hospital broadcasting groups throughout the United Kingdom. The aim of these stations is to provide contact and entertainment for patients in hospitals, hospices, and nursing homes. HBA's patron is Alan Dedicoat, head of presentation at **BBC Radio 2**. The association offers advice and guidance, as well as training events and the National Hospital Radio Awards, presented at its annual national conference, which is held during the spring of each year.

HOUSEWIVES' CHOICE. A record request program that began airing in 1946, on the **Light Programme**, and ran until shortly before the launch of **BBC Radio 1** and **BBC Radio 2** in 1967. It was created by the Light Programme's first controller, **Norman Collins**. In its heyday, the 1950s, it was immensely popular in its morning transmission slot of 9:10 a.m. and, within two months of its first broadcast, was receiving 4,000 requests a week. The show caught the attention of postwar Britain with its theme tune "In Party Mood," and its range of presenters, each of whom took charge of the program for two weeks at a time, included **Eamonn Andrews**, **Sam Costa**, **George Elrick**, and **Gilbert Harding**.

See also MUSIC.

HOWARD, GEORGE (1920–1984). Lord Howard of Henderskelfe was a long-serving governor of the **British Broadcasting Corporation (BBC)** who was appointed chairman in 1980. Nicknamed "Gorgeous George" because of his habit of dressing in caftans, he owned Castle Howard and also chaired the County Landowners' Association. He was a strong defender of the BBC's public service status and its impartiality, particularly during the Falklands War. Lord Howard's relationship with his director-general, **Ian Trethowan**, was supportive, and his wide-ranging knowledge on subjects spanning from the arts to engineering was valuable at a time when content and technology were becoming key issues in the modern media. He retired in 1983, due to ill health.

HOWE, PAMELA (1929–2004). Pamela Howe joined the **British Broadcasting Corporation (BBC)** as a secretary at the age of 18, working in the Features Department with such writers and producers as **Laurence Gilliam**, **Francis Dillon**, **René Cutforth**, and **Louis MacNeice**. This background, coupled with her own love of literature, colored her later work, and after her arrival in the BBC West Region, at Bristol, in the late 1960s, Howe concentrated on producing a range of programs reflecting this, including *A Good Read* and her recordings of Martin Jarvis's readings of Richmal Crompton's *Just William* stories. While working as producer of a regional edition of *Woman's Hour*, Howe was sent the manuscript of Winifred Foley's memoir of the Forest of Dean, which she recorded with June Barrie as the reader, provoking huge interest in the story, which would eventually be published as *A Child in the Forest*, leading to a best-selling trilogy.

See also DOCUMENTARY; DRAMA; WOMEN.

HOWERD, FRANKIE (1917–1992). After an undistinguished prewar career, Frankie Howerd, a much-loved comedian, found his niche during World War II, as a concert party entertainer. Shortly after the war, due, in part, to the foresight of **Jack Payne**, he made his first radio appearance on *Variety Bandbox* in December 1946. He became an immediate success with radio audiences, although because of manipulation of contracts by Payne and his agency, Howerd did not receive appropriate financial gain from his work for many years. From radio he moved into films, becoming a major television star, and after a period of professional failure in the late 1950s and early 1960s, his career was revived, and by the end of his life he had become something of an institution for U.K. audiences, young and old.

See also COMEDY.

HUBBLE, MARGARET (1914–2006). Margaret Hubble was a radio broadcaster best known as a presenter of *Woman's Hour* during the 1950s. She was born in Kent, the youngest of five children of a farmer. After attending a boarding school in Sussex, she joined the **commercial radio** department at the advertising agency Erwin, Wasey and Company in 1938. Two years later, she gained her first job at the **British Broadcasting Corporation (BBC)**, as a secretary, moving into presentation shortly thereafter. Hubble became an overseas presentation assistant in 1941, and then chief **announcer** for the BBC African Service in 1942, presenting *Forces Favourites*, a request program in which members of the armed forces abroad and their families at home could request their favorite **music**. During this time she mentored **Jean Metcalfe** in her first broadcast.

Hubble was the first woman announcer to broadcast on the **Allied Expeditionary Forces Programme**, the successor to the **General Forces Programme**, and she was one of the first announcers on the **Light Programme** in 1945. In that year she married, and left the BBC, returning in 1948 after her husband's death. She occasionally presented *Family Favourites* between 1945–1952. Hubble became a presenter on *Woman's Hour* with **Marjorie**

Anderson and Jean Metcalfe. After her second marriage, in 1950, she turned to broadcasting on a freelance basis, working on *Children's Hour* and rejoining *Woman's Hour*. Beginning in 1969, she also presented for the **British Forces Broadcasting Service**.

See also WARTIME BROADCASTING; WOMEN.

HUDD, ROY (1936–). Roy Hudd is a comedian and actor who began his radio career in 1959, on the much-loved program *Workers' Playtime*. He has made numerous radio appearances, including as Max Quordlepleen on *The Hitchhiker's Guide to the Galaxy*; however, he is best known for his central role in the second longest-running radio **comedy series** in British broadcasting history, *The News Huddlines*, which ran from 1975–2001.

See also DRAMA.

HUGHES, DAVID (1831–1900). David Edward Hughes was a British-born inventor who grew up and was educated in the United States. He is best known as inventor of the carbon microphone, which he created in 1878. Hughes discovered that a loose contact within a circuit containing a battery and a telephone receiver created the potential for sounds in the receiver, which could match the vibrations on the diaphragm of a telephone or transmitter. His device was crucial to the development of the telephone but also played a part in microphone development for broadcasting during the 1920s.

Hughes also researched the theory of magnetism and, in 1857, received a U.S. patent for a telegraph printer. He brought this printer to the United Kingdom when he returned to live and work there in 1857, after some years teaching and studying the science of sound at St. Joseph's College in Bardstown, Kentucky. Using his research, he created what, in essence, was the world's first transmitter at his home in Langham Street, London, just a few yards from where **Broadcasting House** now stands.

HUGHES, RICHARD (1900–1976). Richard Hughes's association with U.K. radio was brief but important. While at Oriel College in Oxford, immediately after World War I, he began to write—and publish—poetry and plays. In 1924, commissioned by the **British Broadcasting Company**, he wrote *Danger*, in response to a request for a piece of **drama** that could only succeed in a purely sound medium. Produced by Nigel Playfair, it was broadcast from the London station on 15 January of that year. Thereafter, Hughes abandoned drama and, in a varied career, wrote novels, screenplays, and histories, and worked in academia. His 1929 novel *A High Wind in Jamaica* brought him international celebrity.

HUMPHRYS, JOHN (1943–). John Humphrys joined the *Today* program on **BBC Radio 4** in January 1987, and remained as a presenter thereafter, becoming known for his powerful and stringent interrogation of interviewees, particularly politicians. He has become one of the most respected journalists at the **British Broadcasting Corporation (BBC)**. He joined the BBC as a reporter based in Liverpool in 1966 and, a year later, became the corporation's northern industrial correspondent. Humphrys moved to London in 1970, and at the age of 28, he became the BBC's youngest-ever television correspondent and first full-time television correspondent to the United States. Other television posts followed, including that of **news** presentation to camera. Since 1987, however, he has chiefly been associated with BBC Radio 4 output; in addition to *Today,* he has presented *On the Ropes* for the network, in which well-known personalities recall difficult times in their lives and careers.

See also CURRENT AFFAIRS.

HUSSEY, MARMADUKE (1923–2006). Lord Hussey of North Bradley, Marmaduke Hussey, was the only chairman of the **British Broadcasting Company/Corporation (BBC)** to sit for two full terms, making him the longest-serving chairman in the history of the BBC. Coming from a background in print journalism, he admitted upon his appointment in 1986 that he knew nothing about broadcasting. He went on to preside over the dismissal from the director-generalship of **Alastair Milne** and resignation of **Michael Checkland**. He later came into conflict with **John Birt** when he disapproved of the latter's style of management. Lord Hussey left the post in 1996.

HUXLEY, JULIAN (1887–1975). The older brother of novelist Aldous Huxley, Julian Huxley was a zoologist and philosopher who became nationally famous through his radio **talks** and, in particular, his role on the successful wartime radio discussion program *The Brain's Trust*. A major figure of his time in the philosophy of science, one of his great contributions was serving as the popularizer of his subject to a mass audience. Huxley was notably significant as the mentor of German sound recordist **Ludwig Koch**, whom he championed upon his arrival in Britain in 1936.

I

IANNUCCI, ARMANDO (1963–). Armando Iannucci has worked as a radio producer, television director, writer, and presenter in the field of satirical **comedy**. His radio work has included the programs *Armando Iannucci* and *Charm Offensive*, as well as **On the Hour**, which was made for **BBC Radio 4** and later transferred to television as *The Day Today*. The program was notable for Iannucci's creative partnership with **Chris Morris**, a collaborative relationship that spawned other radio successes, including **Blue Jam** and *The Chris Morris Music Show*, for **BBC Radio 1**. He has worked extensively in television and is also a novelist.

See also SERIES.

I'M SORRY I HAVEN'T A CLUE. Subtitled "The Antidote to Panel Games," *I'm Sorry I Haven't a Clue*, devised by Graeme Garden, grew out of the **comedy** show **I'm Sorry I'll Read That Again**, with the original panel members—Garden, Bill Oddie, Jo Kendall, and Tim Brooke-Taylor—coming from the latter program. Kendall and Oddie were later replaced by Barry Cryer and Willie Rushton. After Rushton's death, the program continued, with a variety of guests joining the regulars. Hosted by **Humphrey Lyttelton**, the program was first broadcast on 11 April 1972, and it has been heard on both **BBC Radio 2** and **BBC Radio 4**. Its appeal is largely based on wordplay and punning, and the popularity of the program has increased during its span of more than 30 years. One of its most enduring components is a parody of board games "Mornington Crescent," the humor of which is in its impenetrably complex rules. Originally recorded in front of an invited audience in a number of London venues, for instance, the Playhouse and Westminster theatres, as well as the Paris Studios on Lower Regent Street, the program has more recently been taken on the road, touring regional venues.

Following the death of Lyttelton in 2008, the show was temporally shelved. Production once again commenced in June 2009, with three hosts—Stephen Fry, Jack Dee, and Rob Brydon—being used in rotation. Dee has subsequently continued in the role on a permanent basis. The chairman's script has been written by Iain Pattinson since 1992.

See also QUIZ SHOWS; SERIES.

I'M SORRY I'LL READ THAT AGAIN. A **comedy** show broadcast on **BBC Radio 2** from 1964–1968 that epitomized a sea-change in British humor following the boom in satire in the early part of the decade, in particular with *Beyond the Fringe.* The majority of radio comedy had previously grown out of the music hall tradition and wartime conventions. Largely originating from an Oxbridge review background, notably the Cambridge Footlights **drama** club, the main cast members of *I'm Sorry I'll Read That Again* purveyed a themeless, anarchic silliness in their quick-fire presentation that captured the mood of the time and even turned their satire on the **British Broadcasting Corporation.** The program helped launch many successful media careers, among them those of John Cleese, Tim Brooke-Taylor, Jo Kendall, Graeme Garden, Bill Oddie, and future **BBC Radio 2** and **BBC Radio 4** controller **David Hatch.**

IMPERIAL WIRELESS COMMITTEE (1920). During World War I, it became clear that wireless was an important form of strategic communication. Prior to this, the usefulness of the telegraph had been recognized in business and government (*see also* TELEGRAPHY ACTS). After the war, it became increasingly evident that there was an immediate priority to extend the new medium of wireless for use in business, government, and journalism. It was also certain that there was a potential in home entertainment, but this relied on the spread of receiver ownership. In May 1920, Sir Henry Norman was appointed chairman of a committee to examine the possibilities of the creation of an imperial wireless network. Among its findings, the Imperial Wireless Committee stated "that an Imperial wireless scheme . . . would afford reliable, expeditious, and economical communication for commercial, social, and press purposes throughout the Empire." Thus, it might be seen that the concept of an **Empire Service**, later to become the **BBC World Service**, was present in legislative thinking even prior to the establishment of a domestic broadcasting service.

See also COMMITTEES OF ENQUIRY.

INDEPENDENT BROADCASTING AUTHORITY (IBA). When legalized **commercial radio** began in Britain in 1973, regulatory responsibility was placed in the hands of the IBA, a body developed from the Independent

Television Authority. In 1990, it was dissolved, and a radio-specific regulator, the **Radio Authority**, was established in its place. IBA had two directors of radio: **John Thompson** from 1973–1987 and **Peter Baldwin** from 1987–1990. Baldwin vacated the position when he became chief executive of the new authority. IBA was criticized by many commercial operators for what was seen as the overstringency of its regulatory powers, which at first threatened to stifle the development of the new sector. At the same time, this same regulatory rigor produced much imaginative programming in independent local radio in its first 17 years.

See also COMMITTEES OF ENQUIRY; OFFICE OF COMMUNICATIONS (OFCOM).

INDEPENDENT LOCAL RADIO (ILR). *See* COMMERCIAL RADIO.

INDEPENDENT PRODUCTION. In 1994, **British Broadcasting Corporation (BBC)** radio initiated a commitment to commission a minimum level of 10 percent of nonnews programs from the independent production sector. Certain networks, for example, **BBC Radio 4**, controlled this by establishing an approved supplier list to ensure that only companies with appropriate skills and a known track record of production could offer program ideas at commissioning rounds. The policy of having in-house and independent program makers provide content for BBC networks is one that had previously been introduced in television. Since its inception, the amount of independently produced content on BBC radio has grown throughout all the networks.

See also RADIO INDEPENDENTS GROUP (RIG).

INDEPENDENT RADIO DRAMA PRODUCTIONS (IRDP). IRDP, a nonprofit company formed with the intention of promoting radio **drama** to expand opportunities for writers coming to the medium for the first time, was founded in 1987. Run by Tim Crook, Richard Shannon, and Marja Giejgo, the company ran festivals and competitions, resulting in the production and broadcast of writers who otherwise would not have had the chance to hear their work on the air. IRDP's work was frequently heard in the United States via the National Public Radio (NPR) network, and NPR commissioned a number of original productions, including *The Sherlock Holmes Stories*.

IRDP had a theater subsidiary, On-Air Theatre Company, which mounted a number of stage productions in and around London during the 1990s, as well as a U.S. sister organization, the Anglo-American Radio Drama Company, run by Charles Potter, with Crook and Shannon as vice presidents. Like IRDP, this company has achieved a number of prestigious commissions from

NPR, and it continues to develop productions. IRDP supplied a season of drama to **Oneword Radio** in 2003, but it subsequently ceased trading in the United Kingdom. It uses the Internet to disseminate its work globally.

See also COMMERCIAL RADIO; INDEPENDENT PRODUCTION; INDEPENDENT RADIO NEWS (IRN); RADIO INDEPENDENTS GROUP (RIG).

INDEPENDENT RADIO NEWS (IRN). IRN began broadcasting on 8 October 1973, the day that **commercial radio** was officially launched in the United Kingdom. The first bulletins came from basement studios in Gough Square, just off Fleet Street in London, at that time the center of the British national newspaper industry, and IRN's first client was the **London Broadcasting Company**. IRN's role, then as now, was to provide a 24-hour service of national and international **news** to the U.K. commercial radio network. It was initially funded by cash payments from the stations receiving the service, and material was distributed by landline and teleprinter.

The method of funding changed in 1987, when *Newslink* was introduced. This was a system whereby advertising airtime replaced cash payments from stations, making the service free to companies receiving it. By the early 1990s, the *Newslink* scheme was so successful that IRN was able to pay its client stations an annual loyalty bonus. Other innovative developments that have contributed to IRN becoming one of the world's most successful radio news providers have been the introduction of computer technology (in 1985, the switching of distribution from landline to satellite) and the implementation of Internet distribution (2001).

By 2005, the number of stations using the IRN service in the United Kingdom had risen to almost 300, with a total audience of 26 million listeners. Until 2009, IRN's main news supplier was Independent Television News (ITN), but beginning in March that year the source switched to **Sky News Radio**. The long-term managing director of IRN, beginning in 1989, was **John Perkins**, who retired in 2009, and was succeeded by Tim Molloy. In 2012, the contract with Sky was renewed, with subsequent extensions to March 2016, with options to continue beyond that date. The majority shareholder in IRN is **Global Radio**, the other two being **Bauer Radio** and ITN.

See also INDEPENDENT RADIO DRAMA PRODUCTIONS (IRDP).

INMAN, PHILIP (1892–1979). Philip Albert Inman, Lord Inman of Knaresborough, held the post of chairman of the **British Broadcasting Corporation** for just four months in 1947. Involved with both the medical profession and the church, he was also a member of the Labour Party and resigned shortly after his appointment to take up the post of Lord Privy Seal in the Labour government of Clement Attlee.

INTERNATIONAL BROADCASTING COMPANY (IBC). The purpose of the IBC, established by **Leonard Plugge** in March 1930, was to sell and broadcast sponsored programming to the United Kingdom from transmission sites on the continent, breaking the **British Broadcasting Corporation's** monopoly. This began with **Radio Normandy** in 1931, and the company applied its principles of buying airtime to resell to clients on other stations, including Radio Paris, Radio Rome, **Radio Toulouse**, Radio Ljubljana, and **Radio Côte d'Azur**. IBC initially set up its headquarters at 11 Hallam Street in London, adjacent to the site of **Broadcasting House**, at this time still under construction, but as the company gained in financial strength, it moved to larger premises in Portland Place. Program information was carried by only one national newspaper, the *Sunday Referee*, due to a boycott of **commercial radio** stations by the British newspaper industry. This was countered by the establishment of an IBC program sheet in 1933, and subsequently by the establishment of the more sophisticated *Radio Pictorial* from August 1934 until the outbreak of World War II.

During its existence, the IBC instigated a series of initiatives to develop listenership and create a sense of itself as a truly international organization. Among these was the IBC Club, advertised in June 1933, in the *Sunday Referee* and—according to its own publicity—attracting a nationwide membership. Other uses of the IBC brand included the "IBC Empire Transmission" from Spain, **shortwave** transmissions sponsored by Philco All-Wave Radios (*see* EAQ MADRID) and the "IBC Yankee Network," a series of transcription programs from WNAC, Boston, and WEAN, Providence. These ran from December 1934 to September 1935.

After World War II, despite strenuous but unsuccessful efforts to reestablish its flagship station, Radio Normandy, IBC was unable to operate as it had previously, but it remained in existence as a production house in one form or another into the 1970s.

IN THE DARK. A volunteer-based organization that focuses on communal listening events, bringing together an eclectic mix of work drawn from a combination of national radio, sound archives, podcasts, audio art, and field recordings, usually curated around a theme. The concept was created in 2010, by **Nina Garthwaite** in London, with the aim of attracting fresh audiences to audio and providing a new platform for creative sound works. In the Dark sessions have subsequently taken place in Bristol and Manchester, as well as in various cities in Belgium, the Netherlands, Germany, and Australia. In the Dark also commissions original audio for the purpose of communal listening through the Sound Bank, a commissioning body set up to offer practitioners the chance to experiment with their craft. Many of the pieces produced by this process have been broadcast on national and public radio stations throughout the world. In 2014, In the Dark created an award for audio, presented at the Sheffield Doc/Fest.

See also DOCUMENTARY; FEATURE.

IN TOUCH. A weekly **BBC Radio 4** program for the visually impaired that began airing in 1961, and was believed to be the world's only national radio **series** for the blind. The show's presenters have been blind themselves, from its first, David Scott Blackhall, to **Peter White**, who also became disability affairs correspondent for the **British Broadcasting Corporation**.

The aim of the program is to bring **news**, issues, and **current affairs** topics relating to the blind to as wide an audience as possible. One of the program's great strengths has long been the fact that there is a strong interactive spirit between the production team and the audience, from whom many of the issues that make up the content arise.

IN TOWN TODAY. A program broadcast on Saturdays at lunchtime on the **British Broadcasting Corporation's Light Programme** that attempted to preserve the formula that had sustained *In Town Tonight* since 1933, in the face of changing listener habits brought about by the coming of television. The first edition, which aired on 24 September 1960, came exactly one week after its predecessor's final broadcast. A blend of interviews with current personalities and celebrities presented by Nan Winton, Michael Smee, and Tony Bilbow, it ran for more than five years, ending in December 1965.

IN TOWN TONIGHT. *In Town Tonight* was a significant development in popular U.K. radio entertainment and broke new ground in its reflection of the "working-class" voice, juxtaposed with "star" names of the day. The first edition was broadcast on 18 November 1933, and featured, among many others, Bette Davis. The last program was broadcast on 17 September 1960. One of the key features was its use of **outside broadcasting** as an integral part of its content. It was a key part of U.K. Saturday evening radio entertainment for 30 years, with its iconic opening announcement, "Once again we stop the mighty roar of London's traffic," and its signature tune, "The Knightsbridge March" by Eric Coates.

IPOD. The computer company Apple launched the iPod **MP3** player in 2002. The device quickly became a style icon for the young, at the same time becoming a key part of the download revolution that began to change the **music** industry significantly. The capability to download songs cheaply, create playlists (effectively the listener's own schedules), and gain control of music consumption forced new thinking among music stations on a global level. In a short period of time, executives perceived that programming had the potential to move from a "push" culture (output determined by radio stations and sent to a largely passive audience) to a "pull" one, whereby listeners select what they want to listen to and, with the aid of such devices as the iPod, can choose to listen when and where they want to.

IT'S THAT MAN AGAIN (ITMA). *ITMA* was the most popular and well-known radio **comedy** program of the World War II years—and, some would argue, of all time. Created by **Ted Kavanagh** and starring **Tommy Handley**, it took its title from a *Daily Express* headline on Adolf Hitler. It ran for 310 episodes, through many **series**, from July 1939 to January 1949, and captured the heart of the nation with its blend of quick-fire humor and zany characters who became familiar through their regular appearances.

See also WARTIME BROADCASTING.

J

J. WALTER THOMPSON ORGANIZATION. A major U.S. advertising agency that played a crucial role in the development of prewar **commercial radio** in Great Britain. Having learned from its experience in the United States, it set up the first purpose-built radio studio for commercial radio in Britain. The Ariel Studio, in **Bush House**, was highly sophisticated and used the **Philips-Miller recording system** for film. At its peak, in 1938, the unit was run by a staff of 40, producing 44 programs a week to be shipped to continental stations, including **Radio Luxembourg** and **Radio Normandy**, for transmission back to the United Kingdom.

JACK FM. A brand licensed by Sparknet Communications to radio markets in Canada, the United Kingdom, the United States and Russia. Stations under the Jack FM brand mostly play a mix of **music** from the 1960s to the 1990s. In Britain, Jack FM stations are licensed to OXIS Media. U.K. stations are in Bristol (December 2009), Hampshire (formerly the Coast, July 2011), Swindon (formerly More Radio, May 2012), Oxford (August 2013), and Reading (formerly Reading 107, March 2014). In addition, a Jack FM station serving Hertfordshire was launched in May 2010, but it was rebranded as Bob FM in March 2014.
See also COMMERCIAL RADIO.

JACKSON, JACK (1907–1978). Originally a band leader in the 1930s, Jack Jackson's career as a radio presenter began with a **series** on **Radio Luxembourg** sponsored by Oxydol that first aired in January 1939, introducing a new style of dance **music** combined with zany humor. After the war, Jackson turned more to radio record shows, including his highly successful *Record Roundabout*. Produced in his own studio, it was this program that developed his new style of intercutting comedy recordings to make a dialogue between the records; it was highly innovative and predicted the later developments of such presenters as Adrian Juste and **Kenny Everett**. On Radio Luxembourg, after the war, he presented a series of Decca-sponsored music shows. In the late 1960s, Jackson was heard in a highly popular Saturday lunchtime slot on **BBC Radio 1**. It might be said that Jackson was, for some years, the only exponent in Britain of a U.S.-style music presentation.

See also COMMERCIAL RADIO; DISC JOCKEY (DJ).

JACOB, IAN (1899–1993). Sir Ian Jacob, who was director-general of the **British Broadcasting Corporation (BBC)** from 1952–1959, succeeding **William Haley**, came from an army background, having served as military assistant secretary to the British War Cabinet. In 1946, he was invited by the BBC to run its European Service, from which his responsibility extended to management of the General Overseas Service. After a period out of the corporation, during which time he worked for the Ministry of Defence in 1951, he returned as director-general in 1952, with an emphasis on corporate planning rather than direct involvement with programs. He was a popular figure within the BBC.

JACOBS, DAVID (1926–2013). David Jacobs's varied career included work as a **disc jockey (DJ)**, actor, and **quiz show** host. After serving in the Royal Navy from 1944–1947 (during which time he made his first broadcast, in *Navy Mixture*), he joined Radio Seac in Ceylon in 1945, as chief **announcer**, becoming assistant station director prior to his departure for the **British Broadcasting Corporation (BBC)** General Overseas Service in 1947, where he worked as a newsreader before going freelance. He narrated *Journey into Space* and contributed a number of small parts to the **series**. It was, however, as a **music** presenter that he left his most enduring mark, hosting numerous programs, including *Housewives' Choice* and *Pick of the Pops*. Jacobs also recorded programs for transmission on **Radio Luxembourg**.

More recently, Jacobs presented *The David Jacobs Collection* on **BBC Radio 2**, a program he presented until 4 August, 2013, less than a month before his death. He had announced his retirement on 22 July 2013, citing ill health (he had been suffering from Parkinson's disease and liver cancer). During his long career, he was voted "Top DJ" six times, and other radio honors included BBC Radio Personality of the Year (1975) and the Special Sony Award for an Outstanding Contribution to Radio (1984). Jacobs also established himself as a major television personality. He was awarded the title Commander of the Most Excellent Order of the British Empire in 1996 and inducted into the **Radio Academy** Hall of Fame in 2004.

JAMES-MOORE, JONATHAN (1946–2005). Jonathan James-Moore was a **British Broadcasting Corporation (BBC)** radio producer and executive. He was born in Worcestershire and educated at Bromsgrove School and

Emmanuel College in Cambridge. After spending some years in theater management, he joined the BBC in 1978, as a producer in a department that was then known as Light Entertainment, Radio. He became script editor in 1987 and, in 1989, head of the department. In this role, James-Moore enabled a number of classic **comedy series**, including *The Wordsmiths of Gorsemere* for **BBC Radio 4** and *Huddwinks* for **BBC Radio 2**. The latter, starring **Roy Hudd**, won a Gold award during the 1987 **Sony Radio Academy Awards**. James-Moore left the BBC in 1999 but continued to produce programs alongside other interests, including involvement with the Liverpool Institute of Performing Arts. He died of cancer in November 2005.

JENNINGS AT SCHOOL. A **series** of plays that came from the pen of former prep school teacher **Anthony Buckeridge** at the suggestion of *Children's Hour* producer **David Davis**. Jennings was a young boy in the fictitious "Linbury Court" school, and he and his friend Darbishire and their teachers, Mr. Wilkins and Mr. Carter, became household names to British children in the late 1940s and the 1950s. The first program in the first series was broadcast in October 1948. The series proved so popular that beginning in September 1954, the plays were broadcast in adult schedules, in addition to on *Children's Hour*. Today the few extant recordings and their situations might seem anachronistic given the stories' clearly "upper-class" origins, but in their time they were hugely successful and remain the object of some affectionate memories amongst the older generation. Among the actors to play the part of Jennings was **Glyn Dearman**, later a distinguished **British Broadcasting Corporation** radio producer.

See also CHILDREN'S PROGRAMS; SERIALS.

JOAD, CYRIL (1891–1953). Philosopher Cyril (C. E. M.) Joad, a scholar of Plato and Aristotle, and one-time head of philosophy at Birkbeck College at the University of London, came to popular public attention as a member of the team of thinkers on *The Brain's Trust* in 1941. With **Julian Huxley** and **A. B. Campbell**, he became a household name, with a distinctive high-pitched voice and habitual proviso, presaging everything he said with, "It all depends what you mean by . . . ," which became a national catchphrase. Joad's fame from the program catapulted him to celebrity status, and he began opening bazaars, giving after-dinner speeches, and even advertising tea. His good reputation carried him until April 1948, when he was convicted of boarding a train from Waterloo without a ticket. He was fined £2.00, but the event reached the press, and he was withdrawn from *The Brain's Trust* by the **British Broadcasting Corporation**.

JOHNSTON, BRIAN (1912–1994). Brian Johnston joined the **British Broadcasting Corporation (BBC)** in 1946, as a member of the radio **outside broadcast** team. From 1948–1952, he had his own outside broadcast **feature**, *Let's Go Somewhere*, within the magazine program *In Town Tonight*. He became the BBC's first cricket correspondent in 1963, initially working in television. In 1970, Johnston switched to radio as part of the *Test Match Special* presentation team, where he became notable for his gaffes, rather school-boy interplay with the other presenters, and propensity to "break up" on the air. From 1972–1987, he also presented *Down Your Way* on **BBC Radio 4** and was a familiar voice throughout the years on many outside broadcast commentaries, including the coronation of Queen Elizabeth II and the wedding of Prince Charles and Lady Diana Spencer in 1981. Johnston retired in 1993 and died the following year.

See also SPORTS.

JONES, PETER (1920–2000). Best known to radio audiences for his roles on *The Hitchhiker's Guide to the Galaxy* and *Just a Minute*, Peter Jones joined the theater upon leaving school at the age of 16. During the early years of his career, he established himself as a comedian and writer, costarring with Richard Attenborough in 1952, in his own play, *Sweet Madness*. That same year, he created a successful radio partnership with Peter Ustinov in the **series** *In All Directions*, a groundbreaking program in its time, using an improvised format at a time when many programs were still strictly scripted. In the 1960s, Jones became famous to millions of television viewers for his role as the put-upon factory manager in the sitcom *The Rag Trade*; he subsequently further developed the somewhat confused persona of this character and conformed it to his own style, carrying it into his most enduring work, that of an avuncular but permanently bewildered member of the team of *Just a Minute.* As the "Voice of the Book" in the cult series *The Hitchhiker's Guide to the Galaxy*, Jones reached new audiences and generations. He worked almost to the end of his life and died after a short illness in April 2000.

See also COMEDY; DRAMA; QUIZ SHOWS.

JOURNALS. The first broadcasting journals were aimed at the enthusiastic market of amateurs who wished to construct their own **crystal sets**, through which they could "listen-in" to radio experiments on headphones. As curiosity grew, technical journals proliferated, and during the early 1920s, a large number of weekly papers circulated with the words *wireless* or *radio* in the titles. This phenomenon reached a peak by the autumn of 1924, when the *Wireless Constructor* alone had a circulation of 250,000 copies. Some of those involved in the experiments, for example, **Arthur Burrows**, who was working for the **Marconi Company**, collaborated with such technical radio magazines as *Amateur Wireless*, *Popular Wireless Weekly*, and the *Broadcaster*.

As wireless sets became more complicated, some of the tinkering quality that had made radios so attractive to some individuals was lost. The market could not sustain the large number of broadcasting titles, many of which had disappeared by 1927. Home construction no longer required extensive technological knowledge and could be achieved by buying and assembling a kit; in some cases, a screwdriver was even supplied with the component parts. According to the advertisement, the 1928 *Melody Maker* could be assembled by those with "something less than the average amount of dexterity." Moreover, greater attention was being paid to the nature of the material being transmitted. The **British Broadcasting Company (BBC)** initially depended on the national and local press to advertise its programs, but following a brief boycott, the idea was conceived for the BBC to publish its own journal, and the first installment of *Radio Times*, published by George Newnes Ltd., rolled off the press on 28 September 1923.

In keeping with its heritage from the technical magazines, the *Times* featured articles explaining wireless technology and educational items, in addition to program information. It also carried regular columns, including a weekly letter from the company's general manager, **John Reith**, and articles, with photographs, of the broadcasters and artists manning the microphones. Meanwhile, another aspect of radio interest was spreading throughout the population—that of "distant listening." With careful tuning and patient listening for the stations' identifying call signals, the programs being broadcast by foreign radio stations could be picked up. It became a competitive activity, with enthusiasts vying for the honors of who could pick up the most distant signal. In 1925, the BBC launched its *Radio Supplement*, later renamed *World Radio*, which listed the program details of foreign radio stations; it, too, included articles for the more technically minded reader.

A third BBC publication, the *Listener*, was launched in January 1929. The original idea had been to add gravitas to the spoken word by printing some of the more erudite broadcast talks. The journal soon established its reputation for the high quality of its articles and reviews. In contrast to this "highbrow" publication, *Radio Pictorial* began circulation in 2 January 1934. This journal, published by the **International Broadcasting Company (IBC)**, was specifically pitched as a populist magazine. The IBC had established the journal in response to a government ban on newspapers printing the listings of continental **commercial radio** stations under pressure from the BBC, which was trying to protect its monopoly from the competition of entrepreneurs buying airtime from European radio stations and selling it to advertisers.

This competition was defeated by the advent of World War II, which eventually forced the closure of the European stations and put the BBC back on the center of the broadcasting map.

After the end of the war, and with the rise of television, radio-specific journals ceased publication, with *Radio Times* remaining the sole journal to carry full domestic radio programs listings alongside an increasingly dominant television section. The **BBC World Service shortwave** program listings were carried by a journal called *London Calling*, which had originally been named the *Empire Programme Pamphlet* and then *BBC Empire Broadcasting*, renamed in mid-1939 to reflect the call sign of the station, "This is London calling." After the war it became *BBC Worldwide* and finally *BBC on Air*. The last edition was published in 2004.

JOURNEY INTO SPACE. Written by **Charles Chilton**, the first **series** of the **Light Programme's** highly successful science fiction **serial** opened on 21 September 1953, with Captain Jet Morgan, played by Andrew Faulds, leading his crew into an adventure originally intended to last for no more than eight episodes. The program's grip on the public imagination was so great that it went through a number of series, finally ending in 1958, by which time it had been translated into 17 languages and broadcast globally. Other characters were "Doc" Matthews (Guy Kingsley-Poynter), "Mitch" Mitchell (Don Sharpe, later David Williams), and Lemmy Barnett (David Kossoff, later Alfie Bass). Other parts were played by **David Jacobs**. *Journey into Space* is notable in the history of radio in that it was the last evening program of its era to attract an audience larger than the one watching television at the time.

See also DRAMA; MYSTERY PROGRAMS.

JOYCE, WILLIAM "LORD HAW-HAW" (1906–1946). It is a strange fact of British broadcasting that one of the most remembered and listened-to personalities of the mid-20th century was also one of the most hated and feared of all enemy propagandists of World War II. Born in New York, of Irish descent, but with a forged British passport (his undoing, since because of this he was convicted and executed after the war as a traitor), William Joyce joined Oswald Moseley's Blackshirts in the 1930s and formed his own National Socialist League before moving to Germany in 1938. His thin, nasal tones, the sneering quality of his voice, and his trademark call of "Germany calling, Germany calling" transfixed British audiences, who tuned in to the broadcasts in vast numbers (at one point 27 percent of population), as if hypnotized, to hear his uncanny predictions and inside knowledge of what was happening in the country—and where the next strike would fall. It was said that 6 million listeners tuned in nightly to hear him.

Joyce's nickname, "Lord Haw-Haw," was coined by Jonah Barrington, a journalist working for the *Daily Express*, although Barrington's original target for the name was another broadcaster. By mid-1940, even German radio was introducing Joyce using the name. Broadcasting from Hamburg, his transmissions were relayed via **Radio Luxembourg** while the station was in German hands. Joyce's last broadcast, on 30 April 1945, was slurred by drink. He was hanged for high treason at Wandsworth Prison in London.

JUNIOR CHOICE. When **BBC Radio 1** went on the air on Saturday, 30 September 1967, one of its first programs was *Junior Choice*, the successor to the **Light Programme's** *Children's Favourites*. Broadcasting on Saturday and Sunday mornings, the first presenter was Leslie Crowther, who was succeeded by Ed Stewart in 1968. A record request show, the program took into account the changing youth **music** trends that had created Radio 1. It differed from its predecessor in that music was chosen by the program producer for its overall mix rather than being governed by program policy—as previously—based on demand and volume of request for specific items. By the time Stewart was succeeded by **Tony Blackburn** in 1979, the show had attained a remarkable audience of—at its height—16 million listeners. In the early 1980s, with changing audience trends and the growth of independent local radio, the program was taken off the air.

See also CHILDREN'S CHOICE; CHILDREN'S PROGRAMS.

JUPITUS, PHILL (1962–). Phill Jupitus is a comedian, television and radio presenter, and performance poet. His radio work has included hosting the breakfast program on **BBC Radio 6 Music** and serving as a panelist on the **BBC Radio 4 quiz show** *I'm Sorry I Haven't a Clue*. In 1995, he began hosting a program on **Greater London Radio** and continued in the role until 2000. When BBC Radio 6 Music was launched on 11 March 2002, Jupitus presented the breakfast show, and continued to do so until 30 March 2007. It was an experience that inspired his book, *Good Morning Nantwich: Adventures in Breakfast Radio*, published in 2010.

See also COMEDY; DISC JOCKEY (DJ).

JUST A MINUTE. Devised by **Ian Messiter** as a successor to the program *One Minute, Please*, *Just a Minute* revolves around the idea of being able to talk about a set subject, without hesitation or deviation, for one minute. The four panelists are permitted to challenge one another and, if successful, acquire the remaining time on the clock. Panelists have included Clement Freud, Derek Nimmo, **Peter Jones**, Paul Merton, Wendy Richard, and **Kenneth Williams**. When the program began in 1967, producer **David Hatch** originally invited **Jimmy Edwards** to take the role of chair. Edwards was unavailable, and the chairmanship was offered to Nicholas Parsons, who has since served in the position.

See also QUIZ SHOWS.

JUST FANCY. A gentle **comedy series** written and performed by **Eric Barker**, with coordinating performances by Deryck Guyler, Kenneth Connor, and Pearl Hackney. A sketch show largely based on Barker's gift for human observation, it ran from 1951–1962; almost contemporaneous with the more famous *The Goon Show*. *Just Fancy* was, in its own way, equally popular in its time, with similar listening figures, and the show was quietly revolutionary in its development of radio comedy, notably via the absence of a studio audience.

JUST WILLIAM. A phenomenon of British children's radio postwar, Richmal Crompton's own adaptations of her original stories were first heard in October 1945, and captured the hearts of a generation. William Brown was the central character, a naughty but loveable boy whose antics and misdemeanors attracted large audiences of children and parents. The stories had come from a magazine called *Happy Mag*, the earliest dating from 1919. The radio dramatizations continued until 1952, and included such actors as Charles Hawtrey, Anthea Askey (daughter of **Arthur Askey**), Andrew Ray (son of **Ted Ray**), and Patricia Hayes.

Beginning in 1986, a new generation discovered "William" through a **series** of highly popular readings on **BBC Radio 4** by actor Martin Jarvis. They continued until 1990, when the last series was simultaneously released as an audio book by the **British Broadcasting Corporation**, with unprecedented success in terms of commercial sales of the spoken word. Crompton (1890–1969) was a classics mistress at a girls' school in Kent, but when she was struck by polio, she devoted herself to writing full time, producing more than 400 *Just William* stories.

See also CHILDREN'S PROGRAMS.

K

KALEIDOSCOPE. A daily arts magazine program that began airing in 1973. Conceived by **BBC Radio 4** controller **Tony Whitby**, the original premise was to provide a spectrum for both arts and sciences, but this proved a failure, and science devolved to a new strand entitled *Science Now*. Prior to its removal from the air in 1997, by the controller, **James Boyle**, the show remained an arts-only strand, moving through a series of formats and incarnations. The last of these used a series of presenters, identified by a particular day and specialty, with a "live" afternoon transmission and an evening edited repeat. There was also the addition of a weekly *Kaleidoscope Feature*, a half-hour **feature** program on a specific topic.

KALEIDOSCOPE 1. A large radio experiment broadcast by the **British Broadcasting Corporation** in 1929. Produced "live" in eight studios by **Lance Sieveking** and featuring more than 100 performers, it was described by *Radio Times* as a "play too purely radio to be printed for reading." It represented the life of man from the cradle to the grave.

KALEMKERIAN, MARY (?–). Mary Kalemkerian launched **BBC Radio 7** as controller and subsequently oversaw the rebranding of the network as **BBC Radio 4 Extra**. Her first role at the **British Broadcasting Corporation** was with **BBC Radio Scotland**, and she subsequently moved into Schools Radio as a producer. When **BBC Radio 5** was launched, Kalemkerian became the network's chief producer of youth magazine programs. In 1993, she took up a post as commissioning editor for **BBC Worldwide**. Following her retirement, her role as controller of BBC Radio 4 Extra was undertaken by an integrated management team from the network and **BBC Radio 4**. In October 2014, Kalemkerian became chair of the **Charles Parker Archive Trust**, succeeding **Tim Blackmore** in the post.

KAVANAGH, TED (1892–1958). New Zealand-born Ted Kavanagh was a significant figure in the development of radio **comedy**, understanding, as few had done before him, the nature of the medium in relation to comic writing.

He began working with **Tommy Handley** in the 1920s, but it was for their collaboration on the **series *It's That Man Again (ITMA)***, considered by many to have been the most popular radio comedy show ever broadcast, that both men are principally remembered. The combination of Kavanagh's writing and Handley's comic timing made *ITMA* one of the great radio memories for a generation of listeners.

KEILLOR, GARRISON (1942–). Garrison Keillor began his broadcasting career on Minnesota Public Radio in 1968, as a presenter on a morning classical **music** program. It was in 1974 that he developed his most famous show, the live *A Prairie Home Companion*, and out of his warm, quiet, melancholic humor came a series of books, for example, *Lake Wobegon Days* and *Leaving Home*, that introduced him to British audiences through readings on **BBC Radio 4** beginning in 1986. Thus, it was radio that launched his career as an author in Britain, and Keillor's BBC Radio 4 readings were subsequently issued commercially by the **British Broadcasting Corporation (BBC)**. When the BBC launched its digital speech station, **BBC Radio 7**, in the fall of 2002, British audiences were also able to listen, for the first time, to *A Prairie Home Companion*. The program continues to be heard on the station, which has been renamed **BBC Radio 4 Extra**.

KEITH, ALAN (1908–2003). Born Alec Kossoff in 1908, he changed his name to Alan Keith in the 1920s, while studying at the Royal Academy of Dramatic Art. He was the brother of actor David Kossoff and uncle of rock guitarist Paul Kossoff. Keith's radio career began in 1935, as a variety show master of ceremonies and an interviewer on *In Town Tonight*. He was always most associated with the program of his own devising, *Your Hundred Best Tunes*, which he presented from 1959 until his death. Keith had announced that the program scheduled to be broadcast on 30 March 2003 would be his last. He died between recording and transmission, at the age of 94. By way of a tribute, **BBC Radio 2** broadcast the program as planned.
See also MUSIC.

KENNY, SIOBHAN (?–). Siobhan Kenny took over as chief executive of the **RadioCentre** in 2013, succeeding **Andrew Harrison** in the post. She had previously worked for HarperCollins UK and been director of strategy and communications at the Department of Culture, Media, and Sport. From 1994–1999, Kenny worked in the press office of Number 10 Downing Street for prime ministers John Major and Tony Blair.
See also BROWN, PAUL (1945–); COMMERCIAL RADIO; COMMERCIAL RADIO COMPANIES ASSOCIATION (CRCA).

KERSHAW, ANDY (1959–). Andy Kershaw is known for his love and fostering of world **music**. A broadcaster on **BBC Radio 1** and subsequently **BBC Radio 3**, his music shows champion work that would seldom gain a hearing elsewhere. Kershaw is most notable, however, for his active interest in the cultures from which the music springs, and he has made **documentary features** that examine, for example, issues and problems in West Africa. Significant among these was a three-part series he made in 1989, in Mali, for **BBC Radio 4**. Other acclaimed features included *Ghosts of Electricity*, first broadcast by BBC Radio 1 in 1999, telling the story of the infamous Bob Dylan "electric" concert at Manchester Free Trade Hall in May 1966. A period of ill health beginning in July 2007 forced Kershaw to be absent from the airwaves for a time, but he returned to BBC Radio 3 in 2011, with a program called *Music Planet*. In 2008, he received a three-month prison sentence in the Isle of Man for breaching a restraining order issued to prevent him from contacting his former partner. In July 2011, Kershaw published his autobiography, *No Off Switch*.

KISS FM. A purveyor of dance **music** that started its life as an unlicensed **pirate radio** station and, from its beginnings in 1985 to 1988, became something of a cult. Founded by London club **disc jockey** Gordon McNamee and entrepreneur George Eracleous, Kiss FM finally closed down as a pirate in 1988, only to successfully apply for one of the new incremental licenses being offered by the **Independent Broadcasting Authority**. Supported by **Virgin Radio** and **Emap**, it continued its policy of broadcasting club-based music, but this time legally. Now owned by **Bauer Radio**, the station is available as Kiss UK, far beyond its original London base, throughout Britain, via the **Digital One multiplex**.
See also COMMERCIAL RADIO.

KOCH, LUDWIG (1881–1974). Born in Frankfurt am Main, Germany, Ludwig Koch was one of the most significant figures in the sound recording of the natural world. Before World War I, he was a developing musical talent and had obtained success as a concert singer. With the outbreak of war in 1914, he worked in German military intelligence and remained with the German government until 1925, when he resumed his musical career; beginning in 1928, he worked for the German subsidary of Electrical and Musical Industries.

As a child, Koch had been given an Edison phonograph recorder and some cylinders, which he had used to record the sounds of family pets. In his new post, he returned to this enthusiasm, using state-of-the-art equipment to make wildlife recordings. He developed the idea of "sound books," the inclusion of sound recordings within conventional illustrated books on animals. With the coming of the Nazi regime, Koch, a Jew, traveled to Britain, where, in 1936, ornithologists encouraged him to participate in a sound book on British birds. By the end of 1936, *Songs of Wild Birds* had been published, followed by two other sound books.

One of Koch's mentors in the United Kingdom was **Julian Huxley**, who suggested, early in World War II, that Koch offer his services to the **British Broadcasting Corporation (BBC)**. By the end of the war, his voice had become a familiar part of radio programming, and beginning in 1946, he became an integral part of the growth of natural history programs from the BBC's west regional center in Bristol.

In 1948, the BBC purchased Koch's private collection of animal recordings, at which time he joined the staff and continued to record on location and broadcast in his distinctive manner, retaining a strong German accent that became instantly recognizable to British listeners during the 1940s and 1950s. His collection is now housed at the **British Library Sound Archive**. Koch is rightly credited for bringing the true sounds of the countryside to radio, which had hitherto been limited by studio-bound discussions on the subject. He was awarded the title Member of the Most Excellent Order of the British Empire in 1960.

L

LASER 558. This popular **pirate radio** station operated for a few years off the Essex coast from the motor vessel *Communicator*. The station was American owned and staffed by U.S. **disc jockeys**. It went off the air in November 1985, after severe storms and **Department of Trade and Industry**–based blockades. During its short life, it highlighted the fact that the bland **Independent Broadcasting Authority** version of independent local radio had failed to replace the excitement in **music** radio provided by the 1960s pirates. Another station that began operations at about the time Laser came off the air, **Kiss FM**, ultimately provided a groundswell of pressure from popular listener support and gained legal status.

See also COMMERCIAL RADIO.

LAUGH AND GROW FIT. Hailed as the first daily on-air keep-fit program on radio, *Laugh and Grow Fit* was broadcast on **Radio Normandy** from 1937–1938. Devised and presented by comedian Joe Murgatroyd, accompanied at the piano by his wife, "Poppet," the 15-minute programs went out—usually live—at 7:45 a.m. on weekday mornings and consisted of a **series** of jokes and exercises set to **music**.

See also COMMERCIAL RADIO.

LEAGUE OF OVALTINEYS. The radio club linked to the *Ovaltiney's Concert Party*, which began on **Radio Luxembourg** in February 1935. Children joining the club received a badge, rulebook, and details of the Ovaltiney's code, which enabled them to interpret "secret" messages on the program each week.

See also CHILDREN'S PROGRAMS; COMMERCIAL RADIO.

LEONARD, JOHN (1949–). John Leonard is managing director of **Smooth Operations**, part of the **7digital** group. He began his career at BBC Radio Sheffield, working largely on folk **music** programs. In 1982, he joined the **British Broadcasting Corporation's (BBC)** network production center in Manchester, where he became head of music in the North of England for

BBC Radio 1 and **BBC Radio 2**. In 1995, Leonard left the BBC to run the Smooth Operations **independent production** company with Nick Barraclough, developing a number of successful **series** for BBC radio, including the award-winning *New Radio Ballads* in 2006. When, in 2007, Smooth Operations was purchased by **Unique Broadcasting Company**, Leonard remained on as managing director and is head of production for the group of companies. With the merger in 2014 of UBC with the digital music company 7digital, he took on the role of leading the production teams in the development of digital radio services to be streamed throughout the world. Leonard has won seven gold **Sony Radio Academy Awards** and numerous silver and bronze awards for his productions. He became a fellow of the **Radio Academy** in 2007.

LETTER FROM AMERICA. A weekly 15-minute **talk** broadcast to **British Broadcasting Corporation (BBC)** listeners from 1946 until the death in 2003 of **Alastair Cooke**, the broadcaster with whom it was inextricably associated. Originally called *American Letter*, the program was a reflection of **current affairs** in the United States, interpreted from a personal standpoint by Cooke. The elegance of his style of prose and the intimate presentation gave the show a quality that ensured its longevity for approximately 3,000 editions, heard in 52 countries worldwide. Many of the broadcasts have, by their very nature, become historical documents, responding as they do to some of the most significant moments in U.S. and world history, but with the eye of an interested observer and chronicler. Cooke's *Letter* gave those living outside the United States a view of issues and events beyond the journalistic angle of the news reporter, including John F. Kennedy's assassination, Watergate, the Clinton impeachment hearings, and the attack on the World Trade Center. Since his death, a selection has appeared in book form.

LEVIS, CARROLL (1910–1968). Associated with prewar **British Broadcasting Corporation (BBC)** and **Radio Luxembourg** amateur talent shows, Carroll Levis had achieved a successful radio career in his native Canada prior to his arrival in Great Britain in 1935. He toured the country, auditioning hopeful entertainers and choosing the best of the best to appear on his program, *Carroll Levis Discoveries.* After the war, he continued with the broadcasts, but a mental breakdown resulted in his temporary return to Canada in 1947.

In 1950, Levis had resumed his touring talent shows, but with an unsuccessful lawsuit brought by **Hughie Green** against Levis and the BBC regarding an alleged conspiracy to keep Green's own talent show, ***Opportunity Knocks***, off the air, Levis' career began to decline. He had moved into television by this time but did not broadcast after November 1959. Despite numerous attempts at relaunching his career, he died financially impoverished in obscurity in London.

LEWIS, CECIL (1898–1997). In a long and remarkable life, Cecil Lewis made his mark in many areas of entertainment, including work in Hollywood as a scriptwriter, where he won an Oscar for his screenplay *Pygmalion*. It is, however, as one of the founding fathers of the **British Broadcasting Company (BBC)** that he is widely remembered in Great Britain. After winning the Military Cross for his work as a pilot in World War I, he joined the staff of engineering firm Metropolitan Vickers. In the early 1920s, this company became one of a consortium seeking to launch broadcasting in Britain. Thus, Lewis became the partner of **John Reith** in the foundation of the BBC, as program manager.

Lewis mounted the first plays to be heard on radio and produced the early broadcasts of *Children's Hour*, in which he appeared as "Uncle Caractacus." He spent only four years with the BBC, resigning in 1926, because his artistic nature baulked at the growing bureaucracy within the organization. He wrote one of the first books on the subject of radio, *Broadcasting from Within*, published in 1924.

After working as a flight instructor in World War II, he came under the influence of the ideas of Russian mystic George Gurdjieff and set up a farming community in South Africa to preserve the philosopher's ideas. Thereafter, he worked as a radio producer for the United Nations and briefly for Associated Rediffusion at the time of the launch of **commercial television** in the United Kingdom. Beginning in 1956, he became involved as organizer of the *Daily Mail's* Ideal Home Exhibition.

Lewis spent the last years of an extraordinary life on the island of Corfu and continued to write books and plays. He married three times and died in London in January 1997, two months short of his 99th birthday.

LICENSE FEE. Since its inception, the license fee has been the mainstay of **British Broadcasting Company/Corporation (BBC)** finance. The system was introduced on 1 November 1922, set at a price of 10 shillings. The fee remained unchanged until 1946, when it was doubled to one pound. With the advent of television, the license was combined for both media, again rising in 1965, to 25 shillings. In 1971, a television-only license was introduced, and from that time onward radio in the United Kingdom has been license free for consumers. Apart from its value as revenue, the compulsory license fee offered a useful measurement of the potential total audience for radio, particularly prior to the introduction of a systematic listener research unit in 1936.

As pressure has increased on the BBC to make financial cutbacks and instigate more efficient ways of operating, the license fee has become a major issue in terms of funding. A number of other BBC services and operations previously funded from other directions have become reliant on it as a source of income. For instance, until 1 April 2014, the **BBC World Service** was funded by grant aid by the British government; however, since that date, the costs of the service have been met by the license fee. In the financial year 2013–2014, total license fee income was £3.7261 billion. The cost per household was £145.50 for the year in question, and compulsory payment became increasingly controversial with the proliferation of non-BBC channels and thus a decreased share of the audience.

See also CHARTER; COMMITTEES OF ENQUIRY.

LIDDELL, ALVAR (1908–1981). Coming from a Swedish background, Aver Liddell was a **British Broadcasting Corporation (BBC) announcer** who was considered the on-air epitome of "received" pronunciation. Beginning his career as a singer, he joined the BBC in 1932. Liddell was present at the microphone to announce or introduce some of the most significant moments in U.K.—and world—history, for instance, the abdication of King Edward VIII and Neville Chamberlain's broadcast of 3 September 1939, informing the nation that war had been declared. Liddell retired in 1969.

LIFE WITH THE LYONS. A highly successful family situation **comedy** show first broadcast on the **Light Programme** in November 1950, starring American husband and wife **Ben Lyon** and **Bebe Daniels** (billed as "Hollywood's happiest married couple") and their real-life offspring, Richard and Barbara. The quick-fire George Burns and Gracie Allen–style show was written by Daniels and revolved around fictional situations in the rearing of their children. The program ran for 10 series and produced two film spin-offs (1953 and 1954) and a book of recipes by Molly Weir, who played the family's housekeeper, Aggie MacDonald. The program ended its last run in May 1961. Three television versions aired between 1955–1961.

LIGHT PROGRAMME. With the coming of World War II and creation of the **BBC Forces Programme**, the **British Broadcasting Corporation (BBC)** had taken a major step toward streaming of radio output, with the transfer of "light" entertainment into one predominant network, with other material being carried by the **BBC Home Service.** After the war, the latter service continued, and the Forces Programme, which, with its successor, the **Allied Expeditionary Force Programme**, had proved hugely popular with domestic listeners, was transformed into the new Light Programme. The change came on 29 July 1945, with a broadcast of **music** from the **BBC Theatre Organ**, played by **Sandy Macpherson**. On 30 September1967, the Light Programme became **BBC Radio 2**.

LISTEN WITH MOTHER. A much-loved program for children five years of age and younger that began airing in January 1950. A 15-minute mix of stories, songs, and nursery rhymes set to **music** by Ann Driver, it was originally—and for many years—broadcast at 1:45 p.m., prior to *Woman's Hour*. Its presenters were Daphne Oxenford and Julia Lang, although for the last seven years of the show's life they were replaced by Nerys Hughes and Tony Aitken. For several generations of small children, its theme tune—the Berceuse from Gabriel Fauré's *Dolly Suite*—and traditional opening words—"Are you sitting comfortably? Then I'll begin . . ."—became iconic, and there was a national outcry when, in September 1982, the program was taken off the air, having already been transferred to a less-effective morning slot, resulting in fewer listeners.

See also CHILDREN'S PROGRAMS.

LISTENER, THE. The second weekly **journal** established by the **British Broadcasting Corporation (BBC)**, after *Radio Times* was launched in January 1929, the *Listener* was published with the aim of "capturing the fugitive word in print." Initially a medium for transcriptions of broadcast **talks**, it expanded to become a respected journal containing reviews and general **features**. One of its original acknowledged objectives was to "promote the BBC's work in adult education, by linking up the interests of the occasional listener with those of the serious, regular student." During its publication, the journal had numerous distinguished editors, including Richard Lambert (1929–1939), Anthony Howard (1979–1981), and Alan Coren (1987–1989). From a circulation peak of 150,000 in the early 1950s, its popularity gradually declined until 1990, when it was selling a mere 17,000 copies a week. With losses amounting to £1 million a year by this time, the BBC decided to cease production of the periodical, and the last issue appeared in January 1991.

Reporting its 10th anniversary celebration in January 1939, the *BBC Handbook* for 1940 quoted one critic as saying that it would be "invaluable to the historian as a guide to the multiple and changing interests and tastes of the age." This view remains an accurate assessment of the journal's legacy.

LISTENING IN **(1).** Although never broadcast, a noteworthy stage show in that it was the first show of its kind based on the new medium of radio. Billed as a "Musical Burlesque in Fifteen Radio Calls," *Listening In* opened in London in July 1922, with Will Hay as "Professor Broadcaster."

"LISTENING IN" (2). "Listening In" was the common phrase used to denote the act of experiencing radio programs in the first years of the new medium. **John Reith** disliked the phrase, as it implied some form of eavesdropping, and in his early book *Broadcast over Britain* (1924), Reith goes out of his way to denounce this "objectionable habit," writing, "This is a relic of the days when he actually did listen in to messages not primarily intended for him; now he is the one addressed, and he accordingly listens. Only the unlicensed listen-in."

LISTENING PROJECT, THE. The *Listening Project* is both a **series** of programs and a major partnership between **BBC Radio 4**, BBC **local radio**, and the **British Library Sound Archive**, based on recordings of conversations between family members and friends from throughout the United Kingdom. These are broadcast on local radio, and a digest is transmitted on programs on Radio 4, presented by **Fi Glover**. The *Listening Project* is an ongoing concept, started in 2012 and inspired by *StoryCorps*, a U.S. initiative set up by American radio producer David Isay. Once broadcast, material is stored at the British Library Sound Archive as a repository of oral history for future generations.

LITTLEWOOD, JOAN (1914–2002). Although best known as a theater director through her work in developing the left- wing Theatre Workshop at Stratford in East London, Joan Littlewood had early connections with radio in Manchester. It was as a student at the Royal Academy of Dramatic Art in 1934, that she was seen by **E. A. Harding** of the **British Broadcasting Corporation (BBC)**. Harding was taken with her voice and talent. When he moved to Manchester, Littlewood was encouraged to join him and so began her involvement with radio, working with, among others, **D. G. Bridson**. Notable among projects she developed with Bridson were the radio **features** *Cotton People* and *Coal*, created in 1938. Littlewood would later acknowledge the formative nature of her experiences during this time. It was while in Manchester that she met Jimmie Miller, later known as **Ewan MacColl**, to whom she was married for a time.

See also DOCUMENTARY.

LOCAL RADIO. U.K. radio has always been firmly rooted in localness and regionality. The first **British Broadcasting Company (BBC)** stations, created between 1922–1924, were essentially local, born out of the limitations of transmitter power at the time. The concept of the establishment of a network of BBC local radio stations, which began in 1967, with the creation of **Radio Leicester**, began as an experiment initiated by the director of BBC radio, **Frank Gillard**. Gillard had conceived of the idea after a visit to the United

States in the 1950s but determined that the BBC model would chiefly be based on speech and community. Stations were initially closely involved with local authorities, who partly funded the experiment during its early days.

Throughout the years, BBC local radio has been at the forefront of a number of funding crises, and threats of closure have occasionally arisen. By 2005, however, the network of 40 stations, grouped in 11 regions, was in a powerful position, and audiences were loyal, largely from a 55-plus demographic. In addition, the number of ethnic inner city stations reflected the growing multicultural nature of the United Kingdom. BBC local radio increasingly sought to play a proactive role in communities, in many cases working toward a policy of interactivity with audiences, working within and with those communities rather than limiting their involvement to that of the traditional broadcaster–listener relationship.

In October 1973, independent local radio began with the establishment of the **London Broadcasting Company** and **Capital Radio**, and for nearly 20 years **commercial radio** in Britain developed on a purely local basis, initially with a strong community base founded on a public service ethic (hence the early insistence on the use of the term *independent radio* rather than *commercial radio*). As the digital revolution of the late 1990s and early 21st century gained momentum, local **multiplexes** developed alongside their national equivalents, providing opportunities for new digital-only local stations. Concurrent with this came the movement toward another tier of local broadcasting in the form of **community radio**, which developed out of a limited experiment, with the first full licenses being granted in the spring and early summer of 2005.

LOCAL RADIO COMPANY, THE (TLRC). In May 2004, TLRC was formed to purchase the complete share capital of Radio Investments, a long-time investor in U.K. **commercial radio**. Radio Investments had been a shareholder in **Capital Radio** in 1973. Since that time, the company had specialized in the development of local stations, and the new company, based in High Wycombe, assumed control of 26 radio stations, covering a wide geographical spread of Britain, from Falkirk in Scotland to the Isle of Wight. In 2005, a 27th station was added to the company's roster in the form of Durham FM. In 2009, TLRC was acquired through a majority share by **UK Radio Developments**.

LODGE, OLIVER (1851–1940). Eminent English physicist Sir Oliver Lodge was born in Penkull, Staffordshire, and studied at the Royal College of Science and University College in London, becoming professor of physics at Liverpool University in 1881. In 1900, he was appointed first principal of

Birmingham University and knighted in 1902. Especially distinguished for his work with electricity, Lodge was a pioneer of wireless telegraphy. In 1894, he demonstrated wireless telegraphy spanning more than 50 yards to the British Association. He established the importance of tuning to wireless communications and patented a circuit for this purpose in 1897. Unfortunately, Lodge dismissed the possibilities and did not pursue his research in the area. Nevertheless, he received the Albert Medal for his work from the Royal Society of Arts in 1919. Lodge was a frequent and popular broadcaster of **talks** and became interested in psychical research and communication with the spirit world, seeking to combine science and religion. Among his writings on the subject of wireless are *Signaling across Space without Wires* (1897) and *Talks about Wireless* (1925).

LONDON BROADCASTING COMPANY (LBC). First heard on 8 October 1973, LBC was the United Kingdom's first legal land-based **commercial radio** station. The station initially weathered troubled times both in terms of finance and listenership, and throughout its subsequent existence, it has been the subject of a number of takeovers, reinventions, and franchise renewals. Closely connected in its initial incarnation with **Independent Radio News**, in the early 21st century, LBC was bought by **Chrysalis**, which heavily invested in high-profile presenters in its relaunch of the station. Apart from the continuity of its name, LBC remains what it was when commercial radio began in Britain, committed to—and licensed to provide—an all-speech program format.

In February 2007, **Global Radio** purchased the radio interests of Chrysalis Radio, including LBC, and in December 2008, the station's studios were moved to Global's headquarters in Leicester Square in London. In February 2014, LBC began broadcasting nationally on **Digital Audio Broadcasting**, adjusting its on-air slogan from "London's Biggest Conversation'" to "Leading Britain's Conversation." The station has a sister station, LBC News 1152, which broadcasts a rolling **news** service and weather and travel information to London on medium wave and the local digital **multiplex**.

LONG MARCH OF EVERYMAN, THE. An epic **series** of 26 programs, each lasting 45 minutes, broadcast beginning on November 1971, on **BBC Radio 4**, during a span of six months, as the most ambitious social history project ever mounted by **British Broadcasting Company/Corporation (BBC)** radio. Produced by **Michael Mason**, *The Long March of Everyman* featured a vast cast of historians, and there was a major sonic contribution by the **BBC Radiophonic Workshop**. The managing director of BBC Radio, **Ian Trethowan**, was an advocate of the series, describing it as a "demonstra-

tion of faith that radio continues to be as effective in imaginative broadcasting as it is on all sides acknowledged to be in the fields of music and of **news**."
See also FEATURE.

LONG, LONG TRAIL, THE. A radio **feature** by **Charles Chilton** broadcast in 1961, on the **BBC Home Service**. The program told the story of World War I through songs sung by soldiers and was created out of Chilton's personal desire to learn more about his father, whom he never met and who was killed in March 1918. *The Long, Long Trail* formed the basis of the stage and film musical *Oh What a Lovely War*, in association with **Joan Littlewood** and the Theatre Royal in Stratford East, London.

LONG, NORMAN (1893–1951). Norman Long was a musical comedian whose act revolved around semisung monologues to his own piano accompaniment. Having first been heard on the opening evening of transmissions from both **Marconi House** and **Savoy Hill**, he could claim to be the first comic whose reputation was principally created by the medium of radio. He also took part in the first Royal Command Performance to be broadcast (1927). Long later appeared on commercial stations, including **Radio Luxembourg**, and many of his routines used radio as their subject. These included "London and Daventry Calling" (1926); "Luxembourg Calling" (1935); and his satire on **British Broadcasting Corporation** censorship, "We Can't Let You Broadcast That" (1933). He retired after World War II and ran a hotel in Salcombe, Devon, until his death.

LONGWAVE (LW). An archaic term still used to describe the section of the radio spectrum used in broadcasting near the 1,500 meters wavelength. Like medium wave (MW), its transmitters use **amplitude modulation (AM)**. LWs advantage over MW is that its ground wave is capable of greater distance than the higher frequencies employed in MW transmissions. It has also been of value in the past due to its capacity for being receivable on the most rudimentary of radio sets.
See also ANALOG.

LORD HAW-HAW. *See also* JOYCE, WILLIAM "LORD HAW-HAW" (1906–1946).

LORD OF THE RINGS. An ambitious and highly successful adaptation of the J. R. R. Tolkien epic created by Brian Sibley and Michael Bakewell, and first broadcast in 1981, on **BBC Radio 4**. In its original form, it was broadcast in 26 episodes, later repeated twice—in 1982 and 2002—in 13 hour-long episodes. The **British Broadcasting Corporation** also issued the broadcast commercially. The production featured many major personalities from the theater, including Ian Holm, Michael Hordern, and Robert Stephens.

See also DRAMA; SERIES.

LUSTIG, ROBIN (1948–). Robin Lustig is a journalist, presenter, and radio broadcaster. He presents programs on the **BBC World Service** and **BBC Radio 4**, most notably *The World Tonight*. Lustig joined the **British Broadcasting Corporation (BBC)** in 1989 and, on 31 August 1997, presented a special **news** program covering the death of Diana, Princess of Wales. From 1998–2006, he presented the global **phone-in** program *Talking Point* (later renamed *Have Your Say*), which was transmitted simultaneously on the World Service, BBC World TV, and online. He later concentrated on *The World Tonight* and *Newshour*, although he continued to present special BBC programs on important occasions. On 13 December 2012, Lustig presented his final *The World Tonight* and, on 18 December, his final *Newshour*.

See also CURRENT AFFAIRS.

LUX RADIO THEATRE. First heard by U.K. audiences on **Radio Luxembourg** in 1938, *Lux Radio Theatre* was broadcast on Sundays to large audiences. London theater producer C. B. Cochran took over the show, and it became a vehicle for some of the major stars of the time, among them Flanagan and Allen, Beatrice Lillie, Jessie Matthews, and Elsie Randolph.

See also COMMERCIAL RADIO; DRAMA; SERIES.

LYNN, VERA (1917–). Vera Lynn made her first broadcast in 1935, with the Joe Loss Orchestra, but her career was made by her role in radio during World War II. Working with producer Howard Thomas, she hosted the radio **series** *Sincerely Yours* in November 1941, in which she read dedications and messages for those in the armed forces from loved ones at home. Combined with such songs as "We'll Meet Again" and "The White Cliffs of Dover," the series established Lynn as a major star and earned her the popular title of the "Forces' Sweetheart." After the war, she continued in radio and television, including a 1951 series for **Radio Luxembourg** called *Vera Lynn Sings*.

Lynn was the first British artist to reach the top of the U.S. charts with the song "Auf Wiedersehen Sweetheart." She remained the much-loved symbol of a generation and played a major part in the broadcast celebrations marking the 60th anniversary of the end of World War II in 2005. She was created a dame in 1975.

LYON, BEN (1901–1979). Ben Lyon was an American actor who had a successful career in film. During World War II, he and his wife, **Bebe Daniels**, settled in the United Kingdom and became well-known **comedy** radio broadcasters, first in *Hi Gang!* from 1940–1949 and subsequently in *Life with the Lyons*, which ran on radio and later on television until 1960, when Daniels's health began to decline.

LYONS, MICHAEL (1949–). Sir Michael Lyons is a former chairman of the **BBC Trust**. He was appointed to the position on 1 May 2007, succeeding **Michael Grade**, who left the **British Broadcasting Corporation (BBC)** to become executive chairman of Independent Television. Lyons had been a prominent figure in the British Labour Party, holding a number of key positions. A House of Lords all-party select committee was critical of the way individuals were appointed to the BBC, claiming that the British government exercised too much influence in the process, an allegation Lyons dismissed. The duration of a chairmanship is normally four years, and the incumbent can seek reappointment for a further term. In September 2010, however, Lyons announced that he would not be seeking reappointment in 2011, citing increasing work responsibilities outside the BBC. He was succeeded by Lord Patten of Barnes (**Chris Patten**).

LYTTELTON, HUMPHREY (1921–2008). Educated at Eton College and Camberwell School of Art, Humphrey Lyttelton saw war service from 1941–1946, in the Grenadier Guards. During this time he became proficient on the trumpet and, in 1947, joined George Webb's Dixielanders. The following year, he formed his own band and signed with Parlophone Records in 1949. In that same year, partnered with clarinetist Wally Fawkes ("Trog"), he founded the *Daily Mail* cartoon strip *Flook*, a project he continued to work on until 1953. In 1956, Lyttelton's band supported Louis Armstrong in London and produced the first British jazz record to become a hit, *Bad Penny Blues*.

Lyttelton simultaneously developed other career strands, including work in radio. Beginning in 1967, he hosted **BBC Radio 2's** *Best of Jazz* and, in 1972, commenced hosting the **comedy** radio **series** *I'm Sorry I Haven't a Clue*, which was heard at various times on BBC Radio 2 and later on **BBC Radio 4**. The program reached cult status, largely due to Lyttelton's sometimes outrageous chairmanship. Known mostly by the nickname "Humph," he was much loved both as a musician and broadcaster, although outside the professional spotlight he was an intensely private man. After his death following surgery for an aortic aneurism, there were numerous tribute programs, including *Humphrey Lyttelton Day*, broadcast by Radio 4 on 15 June 2008.

See also MUSIC; QUIZ SHOWS.

MACCOLL, EWAN (1915–1989). Songwriter, singer, and writer **Ewan MacColl** was born in Lancashire as Jimmy Miller. As a young man, he joined the Communist Party, a member of which he remained until 1960, and throughout the 1930s he worked on experimental theater projects with **Joan Littlewood**, whom he later married. During the 1930s, MacColl appeared— as Jimmy Miller—in some of the Manchester radio **features** under the aegis of **E. A. Harding**. He was married three times in his life, ultimately to Peggy Seeger; in the late 1950s, they collaborated with **Charles Parker** on the creation of the *Radio Ballads*, fusing song, location actuality, and the spoken word to create a new form of radio feature.

MACGREGOR, SUE (1941–). Raised in South Africa, Sue MacGregor trained as a reporter on *The World at One* before presenting *Woman's Hour* from 1972–1987, when she joined the *Today* program, where she stayed for more than 17 years, becoming the program's longest-serving presenter when she left in 2002. Until 2010, she hosted the **BBC Radio 4** book program *A Good Read*, and she also presents *The Reunion* on the same network. MacGregor was made a Commander of the Most Excellent Order of the British Empire in 2002, for her contributions to broadcasting.
See also NEWS; WOMEN.

MACKENZIE, KELVIN (1946–). From 1998–2005, Kelvin Mackenzie was chairman and chief executive of the **Wireless Group** and owner of **talkSPORT** and 13 regional and **local radio** stations in Britain. A former editor of the *Sun* newspaper, he has always been a controversial media figure, and in 2003, Mackenzie launched an unsuccessful attempt at suing **Radio Joint Audience Research**, jointly owned by the **British Broadcasting Corporation** and the **Commercial Radio Companies Association**, for allegedly operating a corrupt audience measurement system, which, he claimed, underestimated talkSPORT's reach. He also sought to change the method of measurement from that of diaries to electronic monitoring. The sale of the Wireless Group to Ulster Television in May 2005 is said to have profited Mackenzie personally by approximately £6 million.

See also COMMERCIAL RADIO.

MACNEICE, LOUIS (1907–1963). Distinguished as a poet, Louis Mac-Neice worked for the **British Broadcasting Corporation** beginning in 1940, producing many remarkable radio **features**, initially created out of his own writing in support of the war effort. Of these, the most important were *Alexander Nevsky* (1941), based on the film by Serge Eisenstein, and *Christopher Columbus* (1942), which marked the 450th anniversary of the crossing to America. This featured Laurence Olivier in the title role and an original score by William Walton. Postwar, MacNeice's most famous work was the poetic **drama** *The Dark Tower*, which was first heard on the **BBC Home Service** in January 1946, with a second production in 1956, starring Richard Burton. The work was an allegory concerning fate and free will, and the title was taken from the poem *Childe Roland to the Dark Tower Came*, by Robert Browning.

See also RADIO POEMS.

MACONIE, STUART (1961–). Stuart Maconie is a **disc jockey**, presenter, author, and critic specializing in popular culture and **music**. He has principally worked on **BBC Radio 1**, **BBC Radio 2**, and **BBC Radio 6 Music**. From 1994–2001, he presented *The Treatment*, a satirical **news** review on **BBC Radio 5 Live**. From 1995–1997, he presented *Collins and Maconie's Hit Parade* with Andrew Collins on BBC Radio 1. Maconie joined BBC Radio 2 in 1998, presenting a range of programs, and in April 2007, he began hosting a program with **Mark Radcliffe** on weekday evenings until April 2010, when the slot was taken over by **Jo Whiley**. In 2011, *The Radcliffe and Maconie Show*, produced by **Smooth Operations**, transferred to BBC Radio 6 Music in an afternoon program slot. Other commitments for Maconie on Radio 6 Music have been *The Freak Zone* and *The People's Songs*, a **series** that explored British social history through music. The series subsequently spawned a book by Maconie of the same name.

MACPHERSON, SANDY (1897–1975). Real name Roderick Hallowell Macpherson, Sandy Macpherson was originally organist at the Empire Cinema in Leicester Square. He succeeded **Reginald Foort** as **British Broadcasting Corporation** staff organist in 1938, the quiet Canadian tones of his presentation endearing him to millions. Born in Paris, Ontario, Macpherson served in the Canadian Forces during World War I, and thereafter he worked as a cinema pianist, before gaining employment as an organist on the Loew circuit. In 1928, he came to London and began his 10-year tenure at Leicester Square.

Macpherson was a prolific radio entertainer, and at the outset of World War II, he virtually sustained radio broadcasting for the first few days, broadcasting no less than 45 programs in two weeks. It was MacPherson who may be said to have created the radio request program, linking millions of servicemen and servicewomen with their families via his melodic organ playing and gentle, cozy style of presentation. By July 1952, he had made 6,000 programs. He subsequently had long-running shows on the **Light Programme**, among them *From My PostBag* and *The Chapel in the Valley*. He died on his 78th birthday.

See also MUSIC.

MACPHERSON, STEWART (1908–1995). Stewart MacPherson, a Canadian broadcaster, came to Britain a year after his namesake, Sandy Macpherson, began broadcasting for the **British Broadcasting Corporation (BBC)**. Originally an ice hockey commentator, he worked as a BBC war correspondent, commentating on the Arnhem campaign from the air and later gaining a popular following as host of a number of successful radio programs, among them *Down Your Way* (of which he was the first presenter), *Ignorance Is Bliss*, and *Twenty Questions*. His style was fast moving, and his sporting commentaries conveyed a unique sense of excitement. In 1949, he received the vote for "Voice of the Year" during the **National Radio Awards**.

Despite his success in U.K. radio, MacPherson was unsettled in Britain and decided to accept an offer by **Edward R. Murrow** for a job as **news** and **sports** commentator at a Columbia Broadcasting System (CBS) radio station in Minneapolis in the United States. British listeners had such affection for him that, upon his departure from the BBC, King George VI and Queen Elizabeth invited him to record his last *Twenty Questions* program at Buckingham Palace.

MacPherson's time in Minneapolis was not a success, and when CBS sold the station in 1960, he accepted a post with a sports organization in his native Winnipeg, moving back into broadcasting shortly thereafter, when a new television station opened in the city. One of his first actions was to revive the *Twenty Questions* format on the station. He retired in 1974, and died in April 1995.

MADDEN, CECIL (1902–1987). After a period spent working in theater management in Paris, Cecil Madden joined the **British Broadcasting Corporation (BBC)** Talks Department in 1933, and became responsible for the **outside broadcasting** elements of the new magazine program *In Town To-*

night. He became a senior producer with the new **Empire Service** and, in 1936, moved into television, preparing for the first high-definition television service.

With the outbreak of World War II and closure of BBC television, Madden returned to radio, and in 1940, he was made head of overseas entertainment. It was Madden who conceived of the idea for the **Allied Expeditionary Forces Programme**. During the war years, he was responsible for discovering many artists who would become well-known stars in the United Kingdom, including Petula Clark and the Beverley Sisters.

When U.K. television resumed transmissions in June 1946, Madden returned to his post as programs organizer, and it is for this work that he is oftentimes referred to as one of the founding fathers of British television. He was awarded the title Member of the Most Excellent Order of the British Empire in 1952 and retired from the BBC in 1964, although he continued to lead an active and creative life until his death in May 1987.

MAGIC. Magic radio is a brand operated throughout the United Kingdom by the **Bauer Radio Group**, with **music** stations in the English regions and London.

MAIN WILSON, DENNIS (1925–1997). Dennis Main Wilson was a distinguished producer of light entertainment programs for both radio and television mostly associated with his success in sound on *The Goon Show* and *Hancock's Half Hour*. He joined the **British Broadcasting Corporation** in 1941 and, during World War II, attended the Royal Military Academy, becoming an army captain and landing at Juno Beach on D-Day. Returning to radio in 1951, he began working on *The Goon Show* and, in 1954, produced the first of no less than 68 episodes of *Hancock's Half Hour*. Three years later, Main Wilson moved to television production work, where, among numerous programs, he was responsible for Johnny Speight's *'Til Death Us Do Part*. Despite continuing success in the medium, it was for his radio years that he was prideful.

See also COMEDY; SERIES.

MAIR, EDDIE (1965–). Eddie Mair is a radio journalist and presenter from Scotland who began his broadcasting career on the Dundee station Radio Tay. Joining the **British Broadcasting Corporation** in 1987, as a subeditor for **Radio Scotland**, he later moved into presentation for the station. In 1993, he hosted *Breakaway*, a weekly travel and leisure program on **BBC Radio 4**. Mair joined **BBC Radio 5 Live** when it opened in 1994 and was the first host of the BBC Radio 4 *Broadcasting House* program upon its launch in April

1998. He remained in this capacity until 2003, when he took over the presentation of the *PM* program. He has won a number of **Sony Radio Academy Awards**, including the **news** journalist award in 2005.

See also CURRENT AFFAIRS.

MAN BORN TO BE KING, THE. Between December 1941 and October 1942, a 12-part **serial** was broadcast on Sunday evenings during *Children's Hour*, causing considerable controversy within the **British Broadcasting Corporation (BBC)** and the wider context of morality. *The Man Born to Be King* was written by novelist Dorothy L. Sayers and told the dramatized story of the life of Christ. When BBC executives wanted to alter her script, Sayers tore up her contract but was mollified when **Val Gielgud**—with whom she had worked successfully in the past—was appointed as producer. Later, at a press conference, Sayers read extracts from the work; she included passages that angered many due to her use of slang language. Many complaints were received, and the issue was even debated in the House of Commons. Scripts were adjusted, and the transmission demonstrated a work of great power and importance. The sequence was repeated many times in its original broadcast form, in 1949, 1951, and 1965, and broadcast again in a new production, freshly adapted by Raymond Raikes as the **BBC Radio 4** *Classic Serial* in 1975.

See also DRAMA; RELIGIOUS PROGRAMS.

MAN IN BLACK, THE. A renamed version made in 1949, of the original **series** *Appointment with Fear*, starring **Valentine Dyall** as the eponymous narrator, who began each episode with the words, "This is your storyteller, the Man in Black, bringing you another . . . Appointment with Fear." With its new name, the series was revived in 1955, and directed by John Kier Cross.

See also DRAMA; MYSTERY PROGRAMS.

MANSELL, GERARD (1921–2010). Gerard Mansell was an executive of the **British Broadcasting Corporation (BBC)** who is most remembered for reshaping BBC radio in 1967, renaming the networks **BBC Radio 2**, **BBC Radio 3**, and **BBC Radio 4** at the time of the creation of **BBC Radio 1**. He joined the BBC in 1951, as part of the foreign **news** department and, in 1961, became head of the General Overseas Service's **talks** and **features**. Mansell was in charge of the **BBC Home Service** from 1965–1969, bridging the network's time of rebirth in 1967 as BBC Radio 4. This was part of a process, undertaken with **Frank Gillard**, that saw the abolition of the old names **Light Programme**, **Third Programme**, and Home Service and the creation of the new popular music station, BBC Radio 1. The move was controversial and accompanied by the ending of the radio features department.

It was Mansell who oversaw the creation of the Radio 4 news program *The World at One*. He was also involved in the creation of the document *Broadcasting in the Seventies*, which caused considerable controversy in its radical restructuring of BBC radio. From 1972–1981, he was director of External Services, and in 1982, Mansell wrote a history of the **BBC World Service** entitled *Let Truth Be Told*. He was awarded the honor of Commander of the Most Excellent Order of the British Empire in 1979, retired from the BBC in 1981, and received a gold **Sony Radio Academy Award** for his contributions to British radio in 1988.

MANSFIELD, DAVID (1954–). David Mansfield was appointed chief executive of **GCap Media** in May 2005, when **Capital Radio** and **Great Western Radio** merged. He resigned from the post in September of that same year. Prior to this, he was chief executive of Capital Radio beginning in July 1997, having joined the company in 1993, as commercial director. He had begun his career as a marketing executive at Scottish Television and Grampian Sales in 1977. Following a number of management roles, Mansfield joined Thames Television in 1985, as marketing controller. He served as deputy director of sales and marketing, where he was responsible for the day-to-day sales operation of the company until leaving to join Capital Radio in 1993.

See also COMMERCIAL RADIO.

MANX RADIO. Officially "Radio Manx Ltd.," Manx Radio is a **commercial radio** station broadcasting on and for the Isle of Man. It is notable for having been the first legal commercial radio station, having begun broadcasting on 29 June 1964, more than 10 years prior to the creation of independent local radio throughout the rest of the United Kingdom. Since the Isle of Man maintained its own government and laws, Manx was not subject to the same regulations concerning commercial radio as the remainder of the United Kingdom. The station broadcasts mainly in English, although there are some programs in the Manx language, and during the Isle of Man Motorcycle T.T. race once a year, there are also occasional programs in French and German.

MARCONI COMPANY. Initially established in 1897, by **Guglielmo Marconi**, as the Wireless Telegraph and Signal Company, and carrying Marconi's name beginning in 1900, as Marconi's Wireless Telegraphy Company, it was at the Marconi Company's **Chelmsford** headquarters that the great experiments of 1920 were carried out, culminating in the historic transmission of a recital by singer Dame Nellie Melba in June of that year. In 1921, the company received a license from the postmaster-general to transmit publicly from a small station at **Writtle**, near Chelmsford, with the call sign 2MT, and transmissions commenced in February 1922, led by **Peter Eckersley**. Shortly thereafter, the Marconi Company began broadcasting from **Marconi House** in London's Strand, using the call sign 2LO. In November of that year, the station became the starting point for the newly formed **British Broadcasting Company**.

MARCONI HOUSE. Situated in the Strand in London, Marconi House had been purchased by the **Marconi Company** in 1912, as its business was expanding and its existing London premises in nearby Kingsway became inadequate. The first 2LO transmitter was housed on the site of the former Gaiety Theatre, from where the initial broadcasts of the **British Broadcasting Company (BBC)** took place on 14 November 1922. The transmitter went through a number of adjustments and improvements, and was subsequently replaced with a larger and more powerful version, situated at **Selfridges** on Oxford Street. In April 1923, the BBC moved to new premises at **Savoy Hill**, where the organization remained until the opening of **Broadcasting House** in 1932.

MARCONI, GUGLIELMO (1874–1937). Hailed by many as the father of wireless, Guglielmo Marconi's principal experiments were conducted in the United Kingdom, including the famous transmission in 1901, when it was claimed that a transmission of the Morse code for the letter "S," sent from a station in **Poldhu**, Cornwall, was received at St John's, Newfoundland, making it the first transatlantic electronic communication and gaining Marconi worldwide fame. (Some scholars have questioned whether the signal was indeed received as history states.)

Marconi was born in Bologna, Italy, and from an early age had followed the experiments of James Maxwell, Heinrich Hertz, and Oliver Lodge in electrical science and the existence of radio waves. In 1895, he succeeded in sending a wireless signal more than a mile on his father's estate at Pontecchio in Italy. Frustrated by the lack of interest shown in his native land, he traveled to England the following year and was granted the world's first patent for a system of wireless telegraphy. In July 1897, he formed the Wireless Telegraph and Signal Company, renamed Marconi's Wireless Telegraphy Company in 1900 (*see also* MARCONI COMPANY).

In 1900, Marconi's most famous patent, for "tuned or syntonic telegraphy," was taken out, and then came the Poldhu experiment, which was crucial in its demonstration that wireless waves were not affected by the curvature of the earth. While serving as a commissioned officer for the Italian army during World War I, Marconi investigated the development of **short-wave**, which he continued into the 1930s. During his lifetime, he received many honors, including, in 1909, the Nobel Prize for Physics; in 1914, he was appointed Honorary Knight Grand Cross of the Royal Victorian Order in the United Kingdom.

MARCONI-STILLE SYSTEM. In 1924, German inventor Curt Stille created a machine capable of recording sound on steel wire, a version of which was bought in 1931, by Louis Blattner, who brought it to England and developed it as the **Blattnerphone**. Blattner sold his machine to the **British Broadcasting Corporation (BBC)** that same year, but the **Marconi Company** was also in the process of purchasing the U.K. rights to Stille's original patents. Marconi and the BBC jointly produced a number of steel tape recorders as the "Marconi-Stille System," with the intent to broadcast to various different time zones with the creation of the **Empire Service** in 1932.

MARINE, AND C., BROADCASTING (OFFENCES) ACT 1967. Often abbreviated as the Marine Broadcasting Offences Act, this legislation became law in the United Kingdom at midnight on Monday, 14 August 1967. Its purpose was to extend the powers of the 1949 Wireless Telegraphy Act beyond the territorial land mass and territorial waters of the United Kingdom, to cover airspace and bodies of water. At the time that the bill was introduced to the British Parliament in 1966, there were radio stations and proposals for television stations outside British licensing jurisdiction with signals aimed at Britain. The existing stations, for instance, **Radio Caroline** and **Radio London**, were broadcasting using unallocated wavelengths from vessels moored on the coast of the British Isles.

At the time, the only legal licensed broadcaster in the United Kingdom was the **British Broadcasting Corporation (BBC)**, and the Labour government, led by Harold Wilson, was opposed to any form of **commercial radio** competition, although commercial television had been licensed in Britain since September 1955. The government claimed that World War II military installations would be misappropriated; wavelengths would be allocated to other broadcasters; and recorded **music** would be played without authorization, while ignoring copyright and royalty regulations. Other charges were that the vessels were a danger to shipping and that signals could interfere with aircraft and police, fire, and ambulance services. When the bill became law on 14 August 1967, all but one of the offshore stations (Radio Caroline) ceased broadcasting. Within weeks, the BBC's new popular music station, **BBC Radio 1**, began broadcasting from London.

See also PIRATE RADIO.

MARSHALL, HOWARD (1900–1973). Howard Marshall was one of the most distinguished commentators at **British Broadcasting Corporation (BBC) outside broadcasts**, including sporting and national events. Coming from a print journalism background, in 1928, he became the BBC's assistant **news** editor, and during the 1930s and 1940s, he was known for his cricket commentaries. Marshall also described the coronations of 1937 and 1953 for radio listeners and, between those two events, from 1940–1943, served as director of public relations for the Ministry of Food, and as a war correspondent from 1943–1945. He was among the broadcasters who described the Normandy D-Day landings in 1944.

See also WARTIME BROADCASTING.

MARY WHITEHOUSE EXPERIENCE, THE. A topical sketch show first broadcast on **BBC Radio 1** in 1989. Among its principle performers were **David Baddiel**, **Hugh Dennis**, and **Steve Punt**. The program was ironically named after Mary Whitehouse (1910–2001), a campaigner against what she viewed as a decline in morality and standards, particularly on British television. The show ran for more than four **series**, plus one "special," for a total of 44 episodes, from March 1989 to December 1990. It is seen, both in terms of style and personnel, as a forerunner of *The Now Show*. It transferred to television and ran in two series of six episodes each in 1991 and 1992.

See also COMEDY.

MASCHWITZ, ERIC (1901–1969). Eric Maschwitz joined the **British Broadcasting Company** at **Savoy Hill** in 1926 and was editor of *Radio Times* from 1927–1933, when he became director of variety programming. Thus, he was responsible for light entertainment during what many have called the "golden age" of radio. Programs included *In Town Tonight* and *Scrapbook*. Maschwitz was a multitalented man, successful as a songwriter (among many others he wrote the lyrics for "These Foolish Things") and novelist (using the pseudonym "Holt Marvell" he cowrote the detective novel *Death at Broadcasting House* with **Val Gielgud**).

MASON, MICHAEL (1924–2014). Michael Mason was an innovative and adventurous **features** producer who was best known for the production of epic-scale **documentary series**, most notably *The Long March of Everyman* and *Plain Tales from the Raj*. After military service, he read English at Cambridge, before joining the **British Broadcasting Corporation (BBC)** in 1965. His first production was *A Bayeaux Tapestry* in 1966, to mark the 900th anniversary of the Battle of Hastings. The program employed what were to become Mason's trademarks: the mix of voices, **music**, and sound, and, in particular, vox-pop inserts.

The Long March of Everyman, considered to be Mason's masterpiece, was a 26-part series of 45-minute programs broadcast weekly on **BBC Radio 4** beginning in November 1971. They told the story of the people of Britain through letters, diaries, grave inscriptions, songs, and poems, with voices as near as possible in social character to the original author. The mixing was undertaken by the **BBC Radiophonic Workshop**.

The scale of Mason's ambition sometimes created tensions with BBC controllers, but his work touched a chord with listeners, a remarkable example being *Plain Tales from the Raj* (1974), a kaleidoscopic evocation of the last years of the old British Empire, built around field recordings of veterans of British rule in India. The original programs drew large audiences and prompted a second series and a book. Mason retired in 1984.

MATHESON, HILDA (1888–1940). Hilda Matheson was one of the true founders of radio journalism at the **British Broadcasting Company/ Corporation (BBC)**. During World War I, she had worked for MI5, prior to which she had been political secretary to Nancy Astor. She was recruited by **John Reith** in 1926, as the BBC's first director of **talks**, and Matheson transformed the output, bringing some of the greatest cultural and intellectual voices of the time to the air, including H. G. Wells, George Bernard Shaw, and Vita Sackville-West, who became her lover.

It was Matheson who understood for the first time that there is a specific skill and art to direct presentation on radio. In 1931, she resigned from the BBC, after clashing with Reith regarding the issue of the censorship of a talk on James Joyce. She went on to oversee the African Survey, continuing her work with MI5/MI6 at the outbreak of World War II and running the Joint Broadcasting Committee. In 1940, debilitated by overwork, her health failed, and she died during surgery.

See also WOMEN.

MATTHEW, BRIAN (1928–). Originally trained as an actor, Brian Matthew became widely known as a presenter on the **Light Programme** during the 1950s. He hosted *Saturday Skiffle Club* beginning in 1957 and remained as host when the show broadened its remit as *Saturday Club*, and subsequently fronted another **music**-based program, *Easy Beat*, taking into account the growth of popular music at a time when the **British Broadcasting Corporation** was making few concessions to youth culture. A broadcaster of great longevity, Matthew returned to the same Saturday morning slot many years later, when he began broadcasting *Sounds of the '60s* on **BBC Radio 2** in 1990. The program was still airing to a faithful audience in 2014.

See also DISC JOCKEY (DJ).

MAXWELL, CHARLES (1910–1998). Charles Maxwell began his radio career in prewar **commercial radio** as one of the first announcers on **Radio Luxembourg**, and he was also associated with **Radio Normandy**. Working with **Bob Danvers-Walker** and **Roy Plomley** at Radio Normandy, he helped develop the station's brief persona **Radio International**, broadcasting to British troops in France during the first months of World War. Maxwell later joined the **British Broadcasting Corporation** as a producer, working on a number of highly successful radio programs, among them the hit **comedy** show *Take It from Here*.

MCCULLOCH, DEREK (1897–1967). Derek McCulloch—"Uncle Mac" to generations of children—had suffered severe injuries in World War I and subsequently lost a leg in a road accident. Notwithstanding, his career in children's radio entertainment was long and distinguished. He joined the **British Broadcasting Company (BBC)** in 1926, as an **announcer**, and became organizer of *Children's Hour* in 1933, followed by director in 1938. McCulloch became known for his closing farewell at the end of programs— "Goodnight children—everywhere"—he introduced during World War II. He was also the voice of Larry the Lamb in the *Children's Hour* **series** *Toytown*. Although he left the staff of the BBC in 1950, he returned to broadcast *Children's Favourites* on Saturday mornings from 1954–1964. In addition, McCulloch chaired *Nature Parliament*, a program that had been his own idea.

See also CHILDREN'S PROGRAMS.

MCINTYRE, IAN (1931–2014). Ian McIntyre joined the **British Broadcasting Corporation (BBC)** as a **talks** producer in 1957, and was involved with the **current affairs** program *At Home and Abroad*. During the 1960s, he worked at Conservative Central Office in Edinburgh and stood unsuccessfully for parliament in 1966. During the late 1960s, McIntyre was an occasional presenter of **Third Programme/BBC Radio 3 documentaries**, and he became the main presenter of the flagship **BBC Radio 4** current affairs series *Analysis* between 1970–1975, presenting 91 editions. McIntyre worked closely with producer **George Fischer** on this and other talk programs during this period. He was appointed controller of Radio 4 in 1976, moving to Radio 3 as controller in 1978 and retiring from the BBC in 1987. McIntyre was a champion of Reithian values within the BBC and wrote an important biography of **John Reith**. He died in April 2014, at the age of 82.

MCWHINNIE, DONALD (1920–1987). Donald McWhinnie was a major figure in the development of adventurous **drama** while serving as assistant head of the **British Broadcasting Corporation's** Radio Drama Department in the 1950s. He worked on the production of works by key European dramatists, among them **Samuel Beckett**.

MEDIACITYUK. MediaCityUK is a development by Peel Media located beside the Manchester Ship Canal in Salford and Trafford, Greater Manchester, chosen by the **British Broadcasting Corporation (BBC)** as its new North of England base in 2006. Two years prior, the corporation had proposed a major policy of decentralization from London, choosing the site as its preferred option; development of the site commenced in 2007, and a phased BBC relocation took place in the summer of 2011. By March 2013, other tenants included ITV Studios and ITV Granada.

BBC Radio 5 Live is based at MediaCityUK, and some programs for **BBC Radio 3**, **BBC Radio 4**, and **BBC Radio 6 Music** are also originated there; BBC Radio Manchester is based within the development, as well as a considerable portion of the BBC's television operations. The **BBC Philharmonic**, already based in Manchester, was rehoused within MediaCityUK and has its own dedicated audio studio. By 2014, there were nine BBC business departments housed within the complex: BBC North, BBC North West, BBC Breakfast, BBC Children's, BBC Radio 5 Live, BBC Research, BBC Sport, BBC Learning, and the BBC Philharmonic.

In October 2011, the University of Salford relocated its media teaching and research departments to MediaCityUK, and the site also contains facilities for a number of radio and television **independent production** companies.

MEDIA.INFO. An online site offering up-to-date information relating to British media, including websites, addresses, a blog, and consistently updated facts, figures, and **news** about the changing audio industry. Formerly Media U.K., it rebranded in March 2014 and adopted its current name. **James Cridland** is managing director.

MEDIUMWAVE (MW). *See* AMPLITUDE MODULATION (AM).

MEET THE HUGGETTS. A **comedy series** that ran from 1953–1961, based on characters that had first appeared in the film *Holiday Camp* in 1947. On radio, as on film, Joel and Ethel Huggett were played by **Jack Warner** and Kathleen Harrison. A succession of six young actresses played their voluptuous daughter Jane.

"MELBA" BROADCAST. One of the most important events in the early history of British radio was the broadcast—on 15 June 1920—of a song recital by Australian prima donna Dame Nellie Melba (1861–1931). The 30-minute transmission from the **Marconi Company** on New Street in **Chelmsford** was commissioned by Lord Northcliffe, proprietor of the *Daily Mail* newspaper. In the days preceding the event, the paper enthusiastically promoted the concert, and at 7:10 p.m., after a studio announcement, Melba ran through the scale during a sound check, what she referred to as her "Hallo to the world." The concert itself was scheduled to begin at 7:15 p.m., and Melba punctually sang "Home Sweet Home," followed by "Nymphes et Sylvains" (in French) and "Addio" from *La Boheme* (in Italian). This was to have been the official end of the recital; however, there had been some technical problems during the third song, and Melba was persuaded by the engineer in charge of the broadcast, **H. J. Round**, to sing an encore. She, in fact, sang several more songs, including "Chant Venitien" and a repeat performance of "Nymphes et Sylvains," ending with the first stanza of "God Save the King."

Although Melba's greatest years were behind her by the time of the Chelmsford broadcast, she was still a household name and extremely popular with a wide audience. "Home Sweet Home" was one of her most famous songs, and its inclusion at the start of this recital had an enormous impact. The concert was a great success, and the Marconi Company received more than 400 immediate reception reports from throughout the world, including Northern Persia, Madrid, The Hague, Sweden, Norway, and Berlin, as well as from a large number of ships equipped with radio receivers, en route to various ports. The day after the event, the *Daily Mail* reported, "Art and science joined hands, and the world listening in must have counted every minute of it precious."

MELODIES FOR YOU. Originally broadcast on **BBC Radio 2** on Sunday mornings, a long-running program of light classical **music**. It moved to an evening slot in 1994. In 2007, the program was merged with *Your Hundred Best Tunes*, while retaining its original title. The last transmission was on 28 August 2011, after nearly 50 years on the air.

MEN TALKING. In prewar broadcasting, one of the problems facing producers within the **British Broadcasting Company/Corporation (BBC)** was ridding their **talk** programs of scripted speech, while preserving control of the content, particularly in areas of contentious or controversial ideas. In 1937, producer Roger Wilson created a talk **series** entitled *Men Talking*, based on a series in the United States, *The Chicago Round Table*. The talks were unrehearsed and unscripted, and speakers were chosen for their expertise on particular subjects, as well as their ability to be at ease and voice opinion. The nature of the program style, "controlled" by a chairman, was popular and instrumental in eradicating barriers between the elitism the BBC was sometimes accused of and the working-class sector of its audience.

MERRY-GO-ROUND. Two programs have carried this title. One was a **children's program** on **Radio Luxembourg** in 1954. Far more important, however, was the wartime program of the same name, a **comedy series** that featured material gathered from the three branches of the armed forces. Having initially been targeted at forces in the Mediterranean and Middle East, in January 1945, it expanded its remit more globally. Postwar, *Merry-Go-Round* was divided into three force-specific shows, *Stand Easy* (army), *Much-Binding-in-the-Marsh* (air force), and *Waterlogged Spa* (navy). Many future stars of radio appeared in these shows, most notably **Charlie Chester** in *Stand Easy* and **Eric Barker** in *Waterlogged Spa*.

MESSITER, IAN (1920–1999). Ian Messiter was a light entertainment radio producer who joined the **British Broadcasting Corporation** in 1942. He was instrumental in developing the careers of **Bernard Braden** and Barbara Kelly, and devised the program that was a major initial vehicle for their talents, *Leave Your Name and Number*. Messiter also worked on *It's That Man Again*, *The Piddingtons*, and *Twenty Questions*, on which it was his task to sack a drunken **Gilbert Harding**. He was said to be the most prolific inventor of radio and television game shows in the world, but, by far, his most famous creation was *Just a Minute*, based on experiences as a boy at Sherborne School in Dorset.
See also COMEDY; QUIZ SHOWS; SERIES.

METCALFE, JEAN (1923–2000). Originally joining the **British Broadcasting Corporation (BBC)** as a typist, Jean Metcalfe's warm voice was noticed by a radio producer on the telephone, and she successfully auditioned as an **announcer**. During World War II, she became the most popular presenter on the request program *Family Favourites* and stayed with the show after the war, when it became *Two-Way Family Favourites*. It was here that she met her future husband, Cliff Michelmore, on the air; she was presenting from London while he was hosting the other link of the program from Hamburg. It was 18 months before they actually met, in 1949, and they married the following year. In 1955, Metcalfe was voted *Daily Mail* Broadcasting Personality of the Year. She also presented *Woman's Hour* and, after some years away from broadcasting, returned to host national radio's first counseling program, *If You Think You've Got Problems*, from 1971–1976.
See also WARTIME BROADCASTING; WOMEN.

MIALL, LEONARD (1914–2005). Leonard Miall worked for the **British Broadcasting Corporation (BBC)** from 1939–1974, both as a broadcaster and an administrator. As part of the Corporation's European Service during the early years of World War II, he was in charge of broadcasts in German (he had studied in Germany and was fluent in the language). At the end of the war, he worked in Luxembourg as part of the Psychological Warfare Division of the Supreme Headquarters Allied Expeditionary Force, rejoining the BBC as a foreign correspondent in Czechoslovakia and subsequently in the United States.

Miall later moved into television administration as assistant controller of Programme Services, and he ended his BBC career as controller of overseas and foreign relations. He also helped establish the **Commonwealth Broadcasting Association**. After his retirement, Miall worked as a researcher of broadcasting history, becoming a consultant research historian at the BBC, and wrote newspaper obituaries on broadcasting personalities.

See also WARTIME BROADCASTING.

MIDDLETON, CECIL HENRY (1887–1945). In 1931, the **British Broadcasting Corporation** contacted the Royal Horticultural Society, seeking an expert in gardening matters who would also be able to make regular broadcast. The result was C. H. Middleton, whose regular program *The Week in the Garden* became immensely popular; "Mr. Middleton," as he was known, quickly attained the status of national personality. In 1934, he created the Sunday **series** *In Your Garden*, which continued throughout World War II and which he was still presenting at the time of his death in 1945.

MIDGET RECORDER. Two recording devices using this name were employed by sound broadcasters in Great Britain during the 1940s and 1950s, and both machines revolutionized **outside broadcasting**.

(1) "Midget Portable" or "Riverside Portable." As D-Day approached, the **British Broadcasting Corporation (BBC)** realized that it would be a period of the war unprecedented in its mobility, and for its correspondent to be in a technical position to report accurately on current events they would need to be equipped with personal recording devices that were fully portable. The answer to this need came in the form of the "Midget Portable" or "Riverside Portable," developed by BBC engineers, in conjunction with Marguerite Sound Studios. The machines weighed 35 pounds and recorded sound onto a double-sided 10-inch disk. The freedom provided by this machine gave BBC correspondents the ability to report for the nightly program *War Report*. It also facilitated some of the most remarkable eyewitness accounts of the war from such broadcasters as **Richard Dimbleby**, **Frank Gillard**, Stanley Maxted, and **Godfrey Talbot**. Their use of the device brought the actual sounds

of warfare into British homes for the first time. Between 1944–1945, 72 machines were manufactured. This technology forever changed the way **news** was reported.

(2) EMI "Midget" Tape Recorder. This first truly portable tape recorder was first produced by Electrical and Musical Industries in about 1950. It was a product of the miniaturization brought about by the development of integrated circuits and used early transistors, rather than the more bulky and unreliable **valves** (tubes). The compact portability of the machine was also enabled by the small electric motor. Initially used for news gathering, it was famously the tool that unlocked location and actuality for radio **feature** makers, including the legendary *Radio Ballads* made by **Charles Parker** and **Ewan MacColl**. It was the precursor of the **Uher**.

MILLIGAN, SPIKE (1918–2002). Spike Milligan was a comic genius whose best-known radio creation was *The Goon Show*, a program of surreal, anarchic humor that changed attitudes toward radio **comedy** from the time of its first appearance on the **Light Programme** in the 1950s. Born in India as Terence Milligan, the son of an army officer, he served in Italy and Tunisia in World War II, during which time he met **Harry Secombe**, later another key member of the Goons. In 1951, the two joined forces with two other former servicemen, **Michael Bentine** and **Peter Sellers**, and *The Goon Show* team was complete. The program ran for six years.

Milligan was a sensitive man, given to bouts of deep depression. He had been shell-shocked in the war and suffered a number of nervous breakdowns caused by, among other things, the sheer stress of having to write scripts for *The Goon Show* under the considerable pressure of a weekly deadline. He had a huge influence on British comedy, combining **music** hall ideas with surreal absurdity, blended with a fascination for language. Milligan was awarded the title Commander of the Most Excellent Order of the British Empire and, in 2000, an honorary knighthood, although he had refused to swear allegiance to the queen.

See also SERIES.

MILNE, ALASTAIR (1930–2013). Alastair Milne entered broadcasting as a trainee in 1954 and was mentored by television producer Grace Wyndham-Goldie. Having worked as a producer of influential television programs for the **British Broadcasting Corporation (BBC)**, he succeeded **Ian Trethowan** as director-general in 1982, the first television producer to be appointed to the role. It was a time of considerable government interference in BBC policy, under Margaret Thatcher, an interference that was often supported by members of the BBC Board of Governors, including the chairman, **Marmaduke Hussey**. Thus, Milne frequently found himself in conflict with both the government and his own board regarding the BBC's independence, on one occasion calling the governors a "bunch of amateurs." He was a strong defender of the **license fee** as a means of funding the BBC. Milne was forced to resign from the BBC in 1987. His autobiography was published in 1988. After leaving the corporation, he remained critical of various aspects of its hierarchy and some programming policies of the early years of the 21st century, which he regarded as "dumbing down" editorial content. He died on 8 January 2013, after suffering a series of strokes.

MITCHELL, DENIS (1911–1990). Although born in the United Kingdom, Denis Mitchell's family moved to South Africa when he was six years old. He gained his first radio experience writing scripts for the South African Broadcasting Corporation (SABC). Initially interested in **drama**, he was attached to an entertainment unit during World War II. At the end of hostilities, he joined the staff of SABC.

It was during this time that Mitchell became fascinated by the concept of the **documentary** approach, in particular the witness of "real" people. He met **D. G. Bridson** during a visit to South Africa and, on his advice, returned to the United Kingdom in 1949, where, a year later, he became **features** producer for the **British Broadcasting Corporation (BBC)** in Manchester. His work was characterized by the voices of people seldom heard in radio at the time—the homeless, the unemployed, and criminals. He would often work alone, meeting people on the streets by chance and recording them in their own surroundings, rather than in the studio.

Beginning in 1955, Mitchell took his techniques and interests to television. In 1962, he left the BBC to form Denis Mitchell Films, making documentaries on social issues for most of the major television companies.

MOIR, JAMES (1941–). As controller of **BBC Radio 2** from 1996–2004, James Moir successfully implemented a strategy to attract a new audience to the network, while continuing to provide programs that appealed to its existing—more mature—listenership, creating a radio brand that consistently increased its position as the most listened-to radio station in the United Kingdom. Perceiving that the necessary realignment of **BBC Radio 1** with a younger target audience would disenfranchise some of its older audience, Moir redeveloped BBC Radio 2, taking on many of the former BBC Radio 1 presenters and creating a station that proved unassailable in terms of listenership during the early years of the 21st century.

Ironically, Moir's background prior to his 1996 appointment was exclusively in television. Joining BBC TV's Light Entertainment Department in 1963, as a production trainee, he became a production manager six months later, subsequently making his way through the roles of producer (1970) and executive producer (1980) to become head of the variety department of the Light Entertainment Group (January 1982). Moir became head of the group in 1987, and was appointed deputy director of Corporate Affairs for the **British Broadcasting Corporation** in 1993. He resigned from his post at BBC Radio 2 in 2004 and was succeeded by his deputy, **Lesley Douglas**. He then became a nonexecutive director of **Celador Radio Broadcasting**. In recognition of his work in radio, Moir was awarded a fellowship at the **Radio Academy** in 1998.

MONDAY NIGHT AT SEVEN/EIGHT. In April 1937, the **British Broadcasting Corporation** began to air a **series** of shows that were a blend of variety and magazine content entitled *Monday at Seven*. The program ran for an hour and later became *Monday Night at Seven* (beginning in October 1938). Afte a schedule change in November 1939, the program became *Monday Night at Eight*, and with basically an unchanged format, the show ran through eight series until March 1948. The tradition of this popular program was revived from 1959–1962, in *Monday Night at Home*, initially presented by **René Cutforth**.

MOORE, RAY (1942–1989). One of **BBC Radio 2's** most popular presenters in the early morning schedule, Ray Moore had a wry Liverpool humor. He began his career as a presenter of the 1966 **Light Programme** show *Pop North*. A heavy smoker, he developed throat cancer, which forced his retirement in 1988, a year before his death from the disease.
    See also DISC JOCKEY (DJ); MUSIC.

MORLEY, SHERIDAN (1941–2007). The son of actor Robert Morley and grandson of actress Dame Gladys Cooper, Sheridan Morley was an author, critic, director, actor, and broadcaster. In his varied career, Morley made major contributions to arts broadcasting in Britain, both in television and radio. He presented the **BBC Radio 4** program *Kaleidoscope* for a time, as well as the **BBC Radio 2** *Arts Programme* from its start in 1990 until 2004, when he took over the presenter's role on *Melodies for You*, also for Radio 2. Morley's final appearance in this role came in November 2006, three months before his death.

MORRIS, CHRIS (1962–). Chris Morris is an actor, satirist, and writer known for his surreal and often black humor. His work has included *On the Hour*, developed with **Armando Iannucci** as a parody of **news** programs. His work has frequently provoked controversy, and Morris has been dismissed from various radio stations, including Radio Cambridgeshire, Radio Bristol, and **Greater London Radio**. In 1994, **BBC Radio 1** aired *The Chris*

Morris Music Show, and during that same year, he worked with Peter Cook on a series of improvised conversations entitled *Why Bother?* on **BBC Radio 3**. Between 1979–1999, Morris directed, cowrote, and presented *Blue Jam* for three series for BBC Radio 1.

See also COMEDY.

MP3. At the turn of the 20th century, the potential for the creation of MPEG Audio Layer 3, or MP3, made the download and transfer of sound files from the Internet a major issue for the global **music** industry. Controversy arose when copyrighted songs were illegally distributed from websites. In 2004, the technology began to directly impact radio via Apple's MP3 player, the **iPod**. Downloadable radio became a growing phenomenon, and numerous sites appeared, offering the service in various degrees of professionalism. In Britain, the **British Broadcasting Corporation** began experimenting with downloadable programs in the early spring of 2005, with the first program being offered on its websites in the form of **BBC Radio 4's** cultural discussion program *In Our Time*.

MRS. DALE'S DIARY. A daily **drama serial** of immense following at the peak of its reputation, *Mrs. Dale's Diary* began on the **Light Programme** in January 1948. It revolved around the daily diary of a fictional doctor's wife, who recounted happenings in her family, living in "Parkwood Hill," South London. Mrs. Dale was first played by Ellis Powell. A familiar part of the program was its improvised harp theme, performed by Sidonie Goossens. A number of changes were introduced throughout the years in an attempt to keep the serial relevant. In February 1962, the title was changed to *The Dales*, and the family moved to the Home Counties. At the same time, the famous harp theme was replaced by a more contemporary and less reflective signature tune, written by Ron Grainer. A little more than a year later, Ellis Powell was replaced as Mrs. Dale by former film actress, singer, and dancer Jessie Matthews. The program continued after the birth of **BBC Radio 2** and finally ended in April 1969, after 21 years on the air.

See also SOAP OPERAS.

MUCH-BINDING-IN-THE-MARSH. Growing out of the tripartite forces program *Merry-Go-Round*, *Much-Binding-in-the-Marsh* was based on a fictional Royal Air Force station, changed in its postwar incarnation into a country club. It began in January 1947, and starred **Richard Murdoch** and **Kenneth Horne**, who also cowrote the show. **Sam Costa**, Maurice Denham, and Dora Bryan also appeared in a number of episodes of the **series**, which ran until 1953 (although by this time the title had been abbreviated to simply *Much-Binding*). In 1948, Murdoch wrote a monthly spin-off chronicle accompanying the program in *Strand Magazine*. Also famous was the theme song, written and sung by Murdoch and Horne. It was repeated as late as the 1980s. The show was said to be a favorite among members of the British Royal Family, as well as among certain politicians, including Conservative prime minister John Major.

See also COMEDY; WARTIME BROADCASTING.

MUIR, FRANK (1920–1998). Brought up in London's East End, Frank Muir began writing for radio during World War II. Having served as an airman, at the end of hostilities, he joined the **British Broadcasting Corporation** as a **comedy** writer, working with comedian **Jimmy Edwards**. It was **Ted Kavanagh** who first teamed Muir's talents with those of **Denis Norden** in 1947, beginning a long partnership that produced, among other hits, *Take It from Here*. Moving into television, the pair never abandoned their radio roots, and Muir later developed a new radio **series** as writer and presenter of *Frank Muir Goes into. . .* , produced by another long-term collaborator, Simon Brett. Muir and Norden regularly appeared on radio panel games, most notably *My Word* and *My Music*. The Frank Muir and Denis Norden Archive at the University of Sussex contains more than 600 of their scripts, deposited there in 2000, by Norden himself and Muir's son, Jamie.

MULTIPLEX. The term *multiplex*, used within telecommunications and for computer systems, refers to a group of signals or digital data streams combined through a shared medium, making it possible to transfer several video or audio channels simultaneously via the same frequency channel, together with various related or complementary services. **Digital Audio Broadcasting** uses multiplexing to transmit rafts of services nationally, regionally, and locally.

MURDOCH, RICHARD (1907–1990). Richard Murdoch worked on *Band Waggon* with **Arthur Askey**, and later on *Merry-Go-Round*, where he began his partnership with **Kenneth Horne**, which continued on *Much-Binding-in-the-Marsh*. In 1962, he began the **Light Programme series** *The Men from the Ministry*, initially with Wilfrid Hyde-White and subsequently with Deryck Guyler. Murdoch continued working until the end of his life and was appearing on *Just a Minute* a year before his death.

See also COMEDY.

MURPHY, FRANK (1889–1955). Frank Murphy, who would later give his name to one of the great British radio manufacturing companies, was, from an early age, a gifted student of mathematics. After attending Oxford, he worked for the **Post Office** and Western Electric as an engineer, prior to serving in communications during World War I. In 1919, he met (Charles) Rupert Casson, a young copywriter. They formed the Engineering Publicity Service, an advertising company serving clients in the field of engineering. Murphy Casson, as the company became known, was successful, but Murphy found it unfulfilling; in 1928, he withdrew to begin his own radio manufacturing company. By 1936, Murphy Radio, based in Welwyn Garden City, was acknowledged as one of the leaders in the field, based on Murphy's personal insistence on the two cardinal virtues of reliability and value for money. Murphy sets were not always the most stylish, but they were durable and consistently high performing.

Murphy was a man of high principles, and in 1937, he resigned from the board of his flourishing radio business to develop a new venture of good-quality furniture aimed at a mass market. The venture failed, and despite various subsequent attempts at developing new ideas, including immigration to Canada in 1947, Murphy ended his life working a round of occasional jobs, including taxi driving and teaching mathematics at a Toronto high school.

MURRAY, JENNI (1950–). Jenni Murray was a regular presenter of **BBC Radio 4's** *Woman's Hour* beginning in 1987. Born in Barnsley, Yorkshire, she earned a degree in French and **drama** from Hull University, and joined BBC Radio Bristol in 1973. After a number of subsequent posts in television, she joined BBC Radio 4 as a presenter on the *Today* program in 1985. She has also presented the BBC Radio 4 media magazine program *The Message* and worked as a print journalist for a number of major national U.K. newspapers. In 1999, Murray received the award Most Excellent Order of the British Empire for her contributions to broadcasting, and she was made a Dame Commander of the British Empire during the Queen's birthday honors in 2011.

See also NEWS; WOMEN.

MURRAY, PETER (1925–). One of Britain's most popular and experienced **disc jockeys** of the postwar era and a successful television personality, Peter Murray came from a theater background. He joined **Radio Luxembourg** in 1950 and remained with the station until 1955, during which time he hosted numerous programs, including *Top Twenty*. He also worked for the **British Broadcasting Corporation**, presenting *Pete's Party* for the **Light Programme** and sharing a good-natured on-air rivalry with fellow Light Programme presenter **David Jacobs**. When **BBC Radio 1** was launched in 1967, Murray was one of the original team, moving in 1969 to **BBC Radio 2**, where, for more than 10 years, he presented *Open House*. In 1983, he was dropped from the schedule but immediately joined the **London**

Broadcasting Company, where he continued his career for several more years. He occasionally returned to the stage for acting roles. On television, he hosted *Six-Five Special* and later *Top of the Pops*.

See also COMMERCIAL RADIO; MUSIC.

MURROW, EDWARD R. (1908–1965). One of the world's great broadcasters from the time period was Edward R. Murrow. Through his graphic descriptions of London air raids and their effects during World War II, he gave millions of Americans a true sense of the impact of the conflict at a time when Great Britain stood very much alone against the forces of Nazi Germany. His nightly introduction, "This . . . is London," became a familiar trademark in the same way that **Stuart Hibberd's** voice intoning the same words was instantly identifiable.

Murrow later flew on Royal Air Force bombing raids, and he was—exceptionally for a non-British citizen—awarded the Most Excellent Order of the British Empire for his war reporting. He had been a participant in the founding of the Columbia Broadcasting System, serving as its director of **talks** from 1935–1937, European director from 1937–1946, and, postwar, director of public affairs from 1946–1947. In 1961, he was appointed by President John F. Kennedy as director of the United States Information Agency, where part of his responsibility was the output of **Voice of America**.

See also NEWS; WARTIME BROADCASTING.

MUSIC. There is a long tradition of patronage of "live" music in British radio, dating back to the earliest broadcasts. This has been due, in part, to the role played by the **British Broadcasting Corporation (BBC)** as a public service organization, and partly because of regulatory issues that restricted the amount of music played from commercial recordings. The BBC has fostered—and continues to maintain—a large number of orchestras. (*See* BBC CONCERT ORCHESTRA; BBC NORTHERN DANCE ORCHESTRA; BBC PHILHARMONIC; BBC SINGERS; BBC SYMPHONY ORCHESTRA.)

During the 1920s, 1930s, and 1940s, the corporation augmented these with dance bands and smaller ensembles. (*See* BBC DANCE ORCHESTRA; BBC REVUE ORCHESTRA; BBC VARIETY ORCHESTRA.) Until World War II, the use of records in BBC programs was often seen as merely a substitute for live music, with a few notable exceptions. Contrary to BBC policy, the **commercial radio** stations broadcasting from the continent during the 1930s existed on a diet of commercial records. These stations and their musical output exposed the BBC to criticism for its somewhat staid musical policy, particularly on Sundays, when the Reithian (*See* REITH, JOHN CHARLES WALSHAM) idea of the "Lord's Day" informed an output in which popular music had no place.

Examination of program schedules from prewar radio stations in Great Britain shows the strong influence of light orchestral music rather than jazz, although dance orchestras increasingly established "swing" in the repertoire, and the coming of American bands during wartime created a strong appetite for such music. At the same time, the necessity of linking members of the military forces with loved ones at home saw the growth of such record request programs such *Family Favourites*, creating personalities out of presenters, including Cliff Michelmore and **Jean Metcalfe**.

After the war, the BBC was slow to respond to the growth of the new popular music, and during the 1950s and 1960s, in particular, it became increasingly out of touch with trends in youth culture. During this time, the main source of popular music on radio aimed at the young was **Radio Luxembourg**, which established its *Top Twenty* program in 1948, but even this was based on sheet music sales rather than records, and it was not until 1952, with the establishment of the first pop chart in *New Musical Express* magazine, that it overtly became a program of the best-selling records in the United Kingdom. During the 1960s, the crisis in British music radio came to a head with the establishment of **pirate radio** stations, for example, **Radio Caroline** and **Radio London**, transmitting from ships moored outside U.K. territorial waters and broadcasting a type of American-style music radio previously unheard by British audiences. Given that this coincided with the explosion of 1960s youth popular music culture, the effect was dramatic and drove the BBC to create generic radio stations in 1967, including, for the first time, a network specifically aimed at the youth audience, **BBC Radio 1**.

In September 1946, the BBC created a consciously elitist cultural network on the **Third Programme**, broadcasting not only classical orchestral music, but challenging **drama** and discussions. In 1967, this became **BBC Radio 3**, which continues to be the largest purveyor of live concert music in the world. More recently, it has widened its musical brief to include world music and jazz. Classical music has continued to play a large part in radio in Britain on other stations; in 1992, **Classic FM** became the first national commercial station in the United Kingdom, maintaining its success with a policy of light classical music scheduled in the style of popular music radio. Establishing jazz as a popular format has been somewhat more problematic, and commercial stations seeking an all-jazz format have often been forced to modify their playlists to embrace a less niche form of content.

From the establishment of land-based commercial radio in 1973 until changes in regulation in 1990, independent local radio was legally committed to the support of live music through agreements with the Musicians' Union. After 1990, this commitment ceased, and at the same time, output on such stations became increasingly playlist bound. "Appointment to listen" specialist shows gave way to an overall station "sound," formats aimed at a specific demographic identified in station policy. The development of digital playout systems, with playlists created by computers, further divorced presenters from their audiences, somewhat reversing one of music radio's major contributions to the medium: the personality **disc jockey (DJ)**.

The creation of personalities in popular music radio within Britain—DJs—began somewhat spasmodically in the late 1920s and 1930s, with the work of such broadcasters as **Christopher Stone** and his colleague, **Doris Arnold**, one of the first female DJs. During this era, records were usually played on BBC programs by way of reviewing new material, and announcements frequently included details, for instance, record label and number. Prewar band leader **Jack Jackson** developed innovative ways of interacting with commercial recordings in his shows, using **comedy** material from radio programs to form a dialogue with the music. These techniques were highly influential and subsequently developed by a number of other presenters. It was, however, with the arrival of the offshore stations in the 1960s that DJs were truly established as a major element of U.K. radio. Presenters like **Kenny Everett**, **John Peel**, **Johnnie Walker**, and "**Emperor Rosko**" became major personalities in the youth culture of the time and brought U.S.-style music radio to British audiences for the first time, creating a refreshing, inventive, and often creative style of broadcasting. Many of these presenters were signed by the BBC with the creation of Radio 1, the first voice on the network being former Radio Caroline and Radio London presenter **Tony Blackburn**. There have also been strong followings for **women** DJs the likes of **Anne Nightingale** and **Jo Whiley**.

Alternatives to the niche programming of music radio have also existed: *Sing Something Simple*, a gentle program of light vocal music, was, for many years, broadcast on late Sunday afternoons on the **Light Programme/ BBC Radio 2** as a 30-minute medley by Cliff Adams and his singers, while Radio Luxembourg's *Smash Hits* program from the 1950s used the conceit of inviting listeners to request their most hated records for destruction. During the first years of the 21st century, popular music radio in Great Britain faced new challenges with the growth of technology permitting the download of music from the Internet and a decline in radio listening among younger audiences. At the same time, the range and quality of music radio throughout the genres remained impressive.

MYERS, JOHN (1959–). John Myers is a radio executive, consultant, and presenter. Until 2014, he was chairman of the **Radio Academy Awards**. Myers began his radio career as a station assistant on BBC Radio Cumbria in 1980, moving to Red Rose Radio as a presenter in 1982, and subsequently to Radio Tees in 1984. In 1989, he became program controller and breakfast presenter for the Red Rose Gold station. In 1993, Myers became managing director of **Border Radio Holdings**, and the following year, he created the **Century Radio** brand. He was appointed chief executive of **Guardian Media Group** Radio in 1999, developing **Real Radio, Smooth Radio,** and Rock Radio.

In 2009, Myers was asked by the Labour government to produce a report on the future of **local radio**. Some of his recommendations were incorporated into the Digital Economy Act of 2010 and led to a number of mergers within the **Heart** and Smooth Radio networks. In 2011, he began a review of BBC Local Radio, which was published in February 2012. He served as chief executive of the **Radio Academy** from April 2011 to June 2012.

See also COMMERCIAL RADIO.

MYSTERY PROGRAMS. By its very nature, radio is a medium of the imagination, and this has lent it the capacity to engage the mind in **dramas** that explore realms of mystery in terms of crime and the supernatural. In the former genre, there have been numerous programs in which detective stories have been played out to great effect, not least the Sherlock Holmes tales by Sir Arthur Conan Doyle, with Basil Rathbone as one of the earliest radio interpreters. **Samuel Beckett's** radio dramas play in the shadows of the medium, which also lends itself to adaptation; the Saturday drama slot on **BBC Radio 4** has been a popular place in the schedule for such programs, both in terms of original dramas and dramatizations. **BBC Radio 4 Extra** regularly repeats mystery stories from the archives of the **British Broadcasting Corporation**. These include the *Charles Paris Mysteries*, based on the work of Simon Brett; the *Inspector Alleyn Mysteries*, adapted from the writings of Ngaio Marsh; and many adaptations of Agatha Christie, among them the *Miss Marple* and *Hercule Poirot* stories. Famous among British mystery **series**, invested with a vein of horror, was the strand *Appointment with Fear*, which ran during the 1940s and 1950s, starring **Valentine Dyall** as the central figure, the Man in Black.

N

NATIONAL PROGRAMME. On 9 March 1930, the **British Broadcasting Corporation** streamlined its radio services by creating the National Programme, which, as its name suggests, carried a full service nationwide. To complement this, the **Regional Programme** was born that same year, creating the opportunity for geographical variation. This system of networking continued until September 1939, when both programs were absorbed into the newly named **BBC Home Service**.

NATIONAL RADIO AWARDS. Established in 1950, and running for five years, the National Radio Awards were sponsored by the *Daily Mail* and were the first awards for broadcasters in Britain. The first radio awards, presented by Lady Rothermere, went to the following:

Outstanding Actor	James McKechnie
Outstanding Actress	Gladys Young
Voice of the Year	**Richard Dimbleby**
Outstanding Variety Series	*Educating Archie*

In the second ceremony, by now opened up to television, in addition to radio, held in 1952, the radio awards went to the following:

Personality of the Year	**Wilfred Pickles**
Outstanding Radio Program	*Take It from Here*

In 1953, the following awards were handed out:

Personality of the Year	**Gilbert Harding**
Outstanding Actor	Howard Marion Crawford
Outstanding Actress	Gladys Young

Most Popular Musical Entertainer	Tom Jenkins
Most Entertaining Program	*Educating Archie*
Most Promising New Program	*The Al Read* Show

The fourth series of awards, issued in January 1954, produced the following results for U.K. radio:

Personality of the Year	Gilbert Harding
Outstanding Actor	James Mckechnie
Outstanding Actress	Marjorie Westbury
Most Popular Musical Entertainer	Tom Jenkins
Most Entertaining Program	**The Archers**, *Take It from Here*
Most Promising New Program	*The Name's the Same*

The fifth and final year of the awards came in January 1955. Radio prizes went to the following:

Personality of the Year	**Jean Metcalfe**
Outstanding Actor	Richard Williams
Outstanding Actress	Marjorie Westbury
Most Popular Musical Entertainer	Cyril Stapleton
Most Entertaining Program	*The Archers*
Most Promising New Program	*Hello Playmates*

NATIONAL RADIO CENTRE (NRC). Created by the **Radio Society of Great Britain** at **Bletchley Park**, Buckinghamshire, and formally opened on 11 July 2012, NRC is an educational facility chronicling—with practical demonstrations, films, and interactivity—the history and development of wireless technology. From the earliest 19th century experiments to the projected future of the medium, visitors are encouraged to adopt a "hands-on" approach to understanding the nature of radio in its various forms via experiments, interactive displays, and broadcasting.

NAUGHTON, BILL (1910–1992). Born in County Mayo, Ireland, but brought up in Bolton, Lancashire, Bill Naughton is an important example of a writer whose work has transferred successfully from radio to film and television. He is noted for his graphic and realistic stories describing working-class life in postwar Britain. His first piece of radio was *Timothy*, broadcast on the **BBC Home Service** in 1956. Naughton was a member of an elite group of new writers who were given opportunities by the development of the **Third Programme** in the 1950s and early 1960s. (Others included **Samuel Beckett**, Harold Pinter, and John Osborne.)

Notable among more than 15 radio plays was *Alfie Elkins and His Little Life*, produced by **Douglas Cleverdon**, which was ultimately to become the film *Alfie*, starring Michael Caine, in a role originally created by Bill Owen on the Third Programme in 1962. Other "cross-overs" have been *All in Good Time* (**BBC Radio 3**, 1973), which became the film *The Family Way*, and *My Flesh, My Blood*, which later became a successful stage play and film as *Spring and Port Wine*.

NAVY LARK, THE. A spoof of life in the Royal Navy that became one of the most popular U.K. radio **comedy series** of all time, as well as being the longest-running radio comedy (prior to *Week Ending* gaining the distinction) from 1959–1977. Set onboard "HMS *Troutbridge*," the series was successful less because of its innovative writing and production than for the brilliance of its ensemble of actors and the quality of the characterization. The three leading characters were "The No. 1," initially played by Dennis Price and, after the first series, Stephen Murray; "Sub-Lieutenant Phillips," played with suave idiocy by Leslie Phillips; and Chief Petty Officer Pertwee, played by Jon Pertwee. Other parts were in the hands of Richard Caldicott, Heather Chasen, Michael Bates, Ronnie Barker, and Tenniel Evans. The program was created by Laurie Wyman.

NAVY MIXTURE. A wartime **series** that began in February 1943, on the **General Forces Programme**. It provided early exposure for many variety artists who would later become household names in postwar Britain, among them Peter Brough, **David Jacobs**, and **Jimmy Edwards**. The last series started in July 1947 and ended in November of that same year. Elements of the program were incorporated and revived into a new format, which became the successful **comedy** series *Take It from Here*.

See also WARTIME BROADCASTING.

NELSON, TREVOR (1964–). Trevor Nelson's radio career began in 1985, when he worked as a **disc jockey** for **pirate radio** station Kiss. When the station gained a broadcasting license in 1990, becoming **Kiss FM**, he became its director, as well as presenter. In 1996, he joined **BBC Radio 1**, subsequently broadcasting programs on **BBC Radio 1Xtra** and **BBC Radio 2**, produced by the production company **Somethin' Else**. In 2002, Nelson was the recipient of the award Member of the Most Excellent Order of the British Empire for his contributions to the Millennium Volunteers program, an initiative established with public funding to help young people between the ages of 14 and 24. He received a special gold lifetime achievement award for his services in broadcasting at the 2010 **Sony Radio Academy Awards**.

See also MUSIC.

NETWORK CHART SHOW. A program created by **Unique Broadcasting Company** as a rundown of the United Kingdom's top-selling records. It was notable in that it was the first syndicated show on independent local radio (ILR). It began in 1984, hosted by **Capital Radio's** David Jensen, and, beginning in 1985, was sponsored by the Nescafé coffee company. Broadcast on Sunday evenings, the program was consumed by almost the entire ILR network during a period when consolidation of ownership had not been approached as an issue, thus creating the first real national commercial competition for the **British Broadcasting Corporation**. At its peak, the *Network Chart Show* claimed to have reached 20 percent of people ages 10 to 24 in the nation. It was also broadcast by a number of other countries.

See also MUSIC.

NETWORK THREE. This **British Broadcasting Corporation** service was introduced in 1957, on the **Third Programme** frequency. The idea behind it was to provide a daytime service that would draw an audience that might consider the high-culture evening schedule of the Third Programme too intimidating.

See also BBC RADIO 3; MUSIC.

NEWMAN, ROB (1964–). Rob Newman, a writer, comedian, and political activist, was, for a number of years, the writing and performing partner of **David Baddiel**, with whom he worked alongside **Steve Punt** and **Hugh Dennis** to create the **BBC Radio 1 comedy series** *The Mary Whitehouse Experience* in 1989–1990, a program that subsequently transferred to television. After he split with Baddiel, Newman's profile diminished, and toward the end of the 20th century he reemerged as a politically active figure whose subsequent work has shown a strong social conscience.

NEWS. The first news to be broadcast by the **British Broadcasting Company (BBC)** was also the first program aired by the corporation, when **Arthur Burrows** read a bulletin on 14 November 1922, from **Marconi House**. It would, however, be several years before the BBC had complete freedom to develop a news policy unrestricted by agreements with newspaper proprietors and press agencies. During the **General Strike** of 1926, it was required, by necessity, to develop independent sources of news, but this was short-lived.

It was with the coming of World War II that major breakthroughs occurred that would define the future of newsgathering and use of location-based reporters as a key factor in the process (*see* WARTIME BROADCASTING). The program *War Report* was particularly significant in this respect. It was the necessities of the situation and requirement for portability and durability of reporters' equipment during the Allied advances after D-Day that shaped news programs thereafter. In more recent military conflicts, the use of bi-media reporters, "embedded" with troops in situations directly linked to action, has provided material of an immediate nature to both radio and television, using satellite technology to provide coverage virtually instantaneously.

Technology has continued to play a major part in the way news is gathered, both within the BBC and in other news organizations. With the advent of **commercial radio**—in particular the first station, the **London Broadcasting Company (LBC)**, as well as **Independent Radio News**, in October 1973—news styles of radio journalism developed, with the growing use of reporters from ethnic backgrounds and so forth. In 2014, LBC extended its coverage beyond its original London profile via the **Digital Audio Broadcasting** network, becoming the United Kingdom's first dedicated commercial radio news and information station.

Forms of news presentation have varied throughout the history of U.K. radio; during World War II, the major BBC bulletin was at 9:00 p.m., and it was during this time that newsreaders began to identify themselves by name, guarding against the possibility of their material being confused with propaganda broadcasts. In recent years, the concept of such rolling news services as the one provided by **BBC Radio 5 Live** have provided an alternative to the set-piece bulletins and news programs heard on **BBC Radio 4** or on-the-hour short summaries aired on many music stations. The continuing technological advances in Web usage have provided radio broadcasters with further mechanisms for the dissemination and complementary development of news stories.

See also CURRENT AFFAIRS; DOCUMENTARY.

NEWS HUDDLINES, THE. A highly popular and long-running topical **comedy** program that aired on **BBC Radio 2** from 1975–2001. Presented by **Roy Hudd**, the show was made up of sketches, songs, and satirical comments on **news** and **current affairs**. Two notable cast members were **Chris Emmett** and **June Whitfield**, the latter joining the program in 1984. In the history of radio comedy, *The News Huddlines* was second only to *Week Ending* in terms of longevity, and in 1994, it became the longest-running radio comedy program with an audience. Its style included elements of British **music** hall in its humor, built as it was around Hudd's comedy style, with its roots in traditional variety. The show ended with a Christmas special in 2001.

NEWS QUIZ. A long-running topical game show that began in 1977. Panelists commented on **current affairs** in an amusing format, devised by John Lloyd. The program was subsequently adapted for television as *Have I Got News for You*.
   See also QUIZ SHOWS.

NEWSBEAT. A 15-minute program of hard and soft **news** created by **BBC Radio 1** in 1974, with the aim of engaging its youth audience in **current affairs**. Always fast moving, the format was highly successful and enduring.

NEWSHOUR. A long-running program of international **news** and **current affairs** broadcast on the **BBC World Service**. It is also heard in the United States via certain Public Broadcasting Services. *Newshour* was first broadcast in 1988, initially from **Bush House**, but later from **Broadcasting House** in London, where it is transmitted live twice, in separate editions aimed at different areas of the world. The program is considered to be the flagship of the BBC World Service's news output.

NICHOLS, JOY (1925–1992). Joy Nichols was an Australian-born actress and comedian who became widely known to British radio audiences as one of the stars of the **comedy series** *Take It from Here*. Given her first British radio opportunity by **Charles Maxwell**, she first appeared in *Navy Mixture* in 1947, with **Jimmy Edwards**. The following year, with the launch of *Take It from Here*, Nichols became known for her singing skills, as well as her comedy. In 1952, she left the show to have a baby, returning briefly before leaving permanently in 1953, at which time she was replaced by **June Whitfield** and singer Alma Cogan. That same year, she recorded the popular song *Little Red Monkey* with Edwards and Dick Bentley, which was much requested for a time on *Children's Favourites*. Nichols later went to live with her family in the United States, ultimately leaving show business.

NIGHT THOUGHTS. A **radio poem**, or "radiophonic poem," as its author called it, written by David Gascoyne (1916–2001) and first broadcast on the **Third Programme** on 7 December 1955, with **music** composed by Humphrey Searle. Produced by **Douglas Cleverdon**, the cast included Robert Harris, Hugh David, David William, Frank Duncan, Alan Reid, Peter Claughton, Norman Shelley, Robert Marsden, Gladys Young, Jill Balcon, and Leonard Sachs. Gascoyne later spoke of the pain of writer's block the commission produced in him and the compassionate tolerance of Cleverdon, who enabled him to complete the work at his own pace. The result was one of British radio's great masterpieces.

NIGHTINGALE, ANNE (1943–). Formerly a newspaper journalist, Brighton-born Anne (Annie) Nightingale joined **BBC Radio 1** in 1970, becoming the network's first female **disc jockey**. Her *Sunday Request Show* ran from 1982–1994 and gained something of a cult following. In 1996, she was seriously injured in a mugging incident in Cuba. Nightingale has continued her association with BBC Radio 1 into the 21st century and works on several other **British Broadcasting Corporation** networks, including on the **BBC Radio 4** shows *Woman's Hour*, *Pick of the Week*, and *Front Row*. In the 2001 New Year Honors list, she received the award Member of the Most Excellent Order of the British Empire for her contributions to radio broadcasting and, in 2004, was inducted into the **Radio Academy** Hall of Fame.
See also WOMEN.

NME RADIO. NME Radio was an on-air extension of *NME Magazine*, formerly *New Musical Express*, and began broadcasting in 2008. It was owned by IPC Media, with a license granted to DX Media. This was taken over by Town and Country Broadcasting in 2010, which relaunched the station. It was principally heard on **Digital Audio Broadcasting multiplexes** in various parts of the United Kingdom but abruptly ceased broadcasting in February 2013, and returned its license to the **Office of Communications**.
See also MUSIC.

NORDEN, DENIS (1922–). With his writing partner, **Frank Muir**, Denis Norden created many of the most famous British radio comedies, including *Take It from Here* and *Breakfast with Braden*. He also became increasingly known as a broadcaster in his own right and regularly appeared on such radio game shows as *My Word* and *My Music*. In television, Norden was host of *It'll Be Alright on the* Night, a successful occasional **series** of programs that exposed television fluffs and errors.
See also COMEDY.

NORMAN AND HENRY BONES. A long-running **series** of stories about two boy-detectives, sons of the Reverend Henry Bones, created by Anthony C. Wilson, a schoolmaster. The first in the series, *Mystery at Ditchmoor*, aired on **Children's Hour** in July 1943, produced by Josephine Plummer. The two boys were played by Charles Hawtrey (Norman) and Peter Mullins (Henry). Mullins was later replaced by Patricia Hayes.

See also CHILDREN'S PROGRAMS; DRAMA.

NORMAN, R. C. (1873–1963). Ronald Collet Norman was chairman of the **British Broadcasting Corporation (BBC)** from 1935–1939. He had a good relationship with **John Reith** and proved to be an intelligent and knowledgeable chairman. He had worked in local politics, most notably with the London County Council from 1907–1922. After leaving the BBC, Norman served with a number of cultural institutions in Britain, including the National Trust.

NORTON, GRAHAM (1963–). Graham Norton is an Irish entertainer and broadcaster known for his television and radio work. When **Jonathan Ross** resigned from the **British Broadcasting Corporation** in July 2010, Norton took over his Saturday morning program on **BBC Radio 2**.

NOW SHOW, THE. First broadcast in 1998, *The Now Show* is a **comedy series** that satirizes the **news** of the week through a series of sketches and stand-up routines, presented by **Steve Punt** and **Hugh Dennis**. It is a successor to *The Mary Whitehouse Experience*, in which Punt and Dennis were also heavily featured. The program was named Best British Radio Panel Show/Satire at the 2008 Comedy.co.uk Awards.

O

OFFICE OF COMMUNICATIONS (OFCOM). OFCOM was created in December 2003, when the previous regulators, the **Radio Authority** and the Independent Television Commission, were abolished. The aim was to establish an overarching regulatory body in response to the perceived convergence of media in the digital age. Thus, by its own definition, Ofcom is the "regulator for the U.K. communications industries, with responsibilities across television, radio, telecommunications, and wireless communications services." Its remit is to balance choice and competition in the media industries with the duty to "foster plurality, inform citizenship, protect viewers, listeners and customers, and promote cultural diversity." The office also takes an active role in encouraging the development of new electronic media and communications.

See also COMMERCIAL RADIO.

OGILVIE, F. W. (1893–1949). Sir Frederick Wolff Ogilvie was director-general of the **British Broadcasting Corporation (BBC)** from 1938–1942, succeeding **John Reith**. His background was that of an economics academic, having been vice chancellor of Queen's University in Belfast prior to his appointment. Ogilvie was forced to defend the BBC's independence during the early war years, when various elements in both the press and government began questioning the future of the BBC. Overseas programs increased during his time as director-general, but there were issues relating to delays in implementation and overspending, and he was jointly replaced in 1942, by **R. W. Foot** and **Cecil Graves**. One criticism of Ogilvie was that he lacked certain leadership qualities; Reith writes of him in his autobiography, "I was quite sure he was not the man for the BBC." After his time with the corporation, Ogilvie became principal of Jesus College in Oxford and a vocal critic of the postwar BBC.

OLIVER, VIC (1897–1965). Vic Oliver was of Austrian aristocratic stock, the son of Baron Victor von Samek. In 1922, he relinquished his hereditary title. Oliver was an extremely accomplished musician, playing the violin and piano, and even touring the United States as a concert pianist in 1927. He later began to develop **comedy** routines involving his **music** and, in so doing, became an influence on later acts, for instance Victor Borge. He became part of the wartime team of *Hi Gang!* with **Ben Lyon** and **Bebe Daniels**. After the war, Oliver continued to blend comedy and music, forming the British Concert Orchestra and acting as master of ceremonies for *Variety Playhouse*. He was married to Sir Winston Churchill's daughter Sarah, but the couple divorced in 1945.

See also SERIES; WARTIME BROADCASTING.

ON THE HOUR. A **comedy series** on **BBC Radio 4** that parodied **news** and **current affairs** broadcasting. It ran on the network between 1991–1992, and subsequently spawned a television version entitled *The Day Today*. Fronted by **Chris Morris**, it is an example of the partnership between Morris and **Armando Iannucci**. Although a satire, the program's straight-faced imitation of contemporary news styles produced some complaints from listeners, who were convinced that it was not a parody. At the 1992 British Comedy Awards, *On the Hour* was named Best Radio Comedy and, during that same year, received the Writers' Guild of Great Britain award for comedy/light entertainment.

ONE MINUTE, PLEASE. A popular panel game devised by **Ian Messiter** and the forerunner of *Just a Minute* It first aired in August 1951. The initial broadcast had **Roy Plomley** serving as chair, with panelists that included **Gilbert Harding** and **Kenneth Horne**. One of the favorite team members was cartoonist **Gerard Hoffnung**, who first became known to British audiences on the program.

See also COMEDY; QUIZ SHOWS; SERIES.

ONEWORD RADIO. A national digital radio station dedicated to books and literature-based talk launched in 2000. It suffered when **BBC Radio 7** subsequently began broadcasting, using a similar format, and the station went through a period of stagnation. In 2005, it was jointly acquired by **Unique Broadcasting Company Media** and Channel 4, after which there was an attempt at regeneration, as the station moved to new studios and launched fresh programming. From the start, Oneword Radio's output had mostly been in the genre of "talking books." It ceased broadcasting in January 2008.

OPERATION YEWTREE. A police investigation initiated by allegations of sexual abuse against broadcaster **Jimmy Savile** after his death in 2011, and others. The Metropolitan Police launched the investigation following an Independent Television program, *Exposure: The Other Side of Jimmy Savile*, was broadcast on 3 October 2012. Police research resulted in the publication of a report into Savile's alleged crimes, *Giving Victims a Voice*, which was published in January 2013. In addition to Savile, the operation was concerned with claims against various other individuals, particularly in the media and entertainment industries. It remains ongoing.

OPPORTUNITY KNOCKS. A well-known talent show that began on the **Light Programme** in February 1949, before moving to **Radio Luxembourg** in 1950. It was hosted by **Hughie Green**, who devised the program, produced by **Dennis Main Wilson** for the **British Broadcasting Corporation** and Gordon Crier for Radio Luxembourg, where it was sponsored by Horlicks. With the coming of Independent Television, the program was transferred to television, where it enjoyed great success for many years.

See also COMMERCIAL RADIO.

ORAM, DAPHNE (1925–2003). Daphne Oram was a British composer and musician who specialized in electronic sound. She was a cofounder of the **BBC Radiophonic Workshop** and created a technology for creating electronic sounds called **Oramics**. Oram joined the **British Broadcasting Corporation (BBC)** in 1942, and following a visit to the French network Radiodiffusion-Télévision Française (RTF) in Paris during the 1950s, she campaigned within the BBC for the development of electronics as a sound resource. With colleague **Desmond Briscoe**, she created sound designs and scores for a number of key productions, among them **Samuel Beckett's** *All That Fall* (1957). Briscoe and Oram established the BBC Radiophonic Workshop in 1958.

Frustrated by the lack of interest in her field within the BBC, Oram resigned in 1959 and created her Oramics studios for electronic composition in Kent, from where she produced a range of work for radio, television, and film, as well as installations and exhibitions. A large archive of her work is housed at the University of London's Goldsmith's College. It was launched in 2008, with a symposium and a series of concerts at London's Southbank Centre.

ORAMICS. Between 1957–1962, composer and musician **Daphne Oram** developed a technology for electronic composition that she called Oramics. This device consisted of a large, rectangular metal frame that provided a table-like surface traversed by 10 synchronized strips of clear, sprocketed 35-millimeter film. The musician drew shapes on the film to create a mask, which modulated the light received by photocells. Oram used the term *Oramics* as a brand name for both her studio in Kent and the business interests that she developed there.

See also BBC RADIOPHONIC WORKSHOP.

ORIGINAL 106. This station name relates to two broadcasting organizations. In September 2005, a new **commercial radio** license was awarded for the Solent region of the United Kingdom, to serve the area bounded by Bournemouth and Southampton. The franchise was hotly contended but given to Original 106. Original 106 was 95 percent owned by CanWest Mediaworks, a wholly owned subsidiary of the CanWest Global Communications Corporation and Seven Broadcast of Canada. The station offered "adult alternative radio aimed at 40 to 59-year-olds" and was scheduled to begin broadcasting in 2006. In October 2008, it was replaced by the *Coast*, which, in turn, was rebranded as a **Jack FM** station in 2011.

The name "Original 106" also applies to an independent radio station in Scotland broadcasting to Aberdeen and Aberdeenshire. It received the last new **frequency modulation (FM)** license to be awarded by the **Office of Communications** in January 2007, and launched in October of that same year. In September 2009, the station was bought by a consortium led by Adam Findlay.

ORION MEDIA. A **commercial radio** group created in June 2009, by **Phil Riley,** through the purchase of a number of radio stations in the Midlands formerly owned by **Global Radio.** After Global acquired **GCap Media** in 2007, the Office of Fair Trading debated whether the group should be required to sell some of its stations in the West Midlands to restore competition within the radio industry in the region. Riley purchased **BRMB**, Mercia, Wyvern, Beacon in the West Midlands, and Heart 106 in the East Midlands, forming Orion Media. In January 2011, Heart 106 was relaunched as Gem 106, and the four West Midlands stations were renamed "Free Radio." In January 2012, BRMB, Birmingham, became Free Radio Birmingham. Mercia was renamed Free Radio Coventry; Warwickshire, Wyvern was rebranded as Free Radio Herefordshire; Worcestershire became Free Radio Shropshire; and Beacon became Black Country.

OTHER PEOPLE'S HOUSES. See SOS.

OUTSIDE BROADCASTS (OB). Both the **British Broadcasting Corporation (BBC)** and **commercial radio** operators were involved in the development of OBs. From the earliest days of radio, the desire of broadcasters to move beyond the bounds of the studio led to some adventurous experiments. In fact, the precursor of OBs could be said to be the prewireless relays of the Electrophone Company, based on Gerard Street in London, beginning as early as 1894. The principle here was that of a live performance from a theater, concert hall, or church, which was then relayed via telephone line to subscribers. There was, however, no real radio production in the sense that it would become known. The first BBC OB was in January 1923, from Covent Garden. Beatrice Harrison made her famous **Cello and the Nightingale** broadcast in 1924, and the BBC's Outside Broadcasts Department was formally constituted in 1925.

Sports commentary began in January 1927, when the England–Wales rugby match was broadcast "live" from Twickenham. A week later, the first soccer match commentary to be broadcast came from Highbury and featured Arsenal against Sheffield United. There was some doubt in those early days that a listener would be able to follow the action without some form of aid, and for a time a representation of the playing area was included in *Radio Times*, divided into numbered squares. As commentary proceeded, a second voice called out the number of the square corresponding to the point of action on the pitch.

Difficulties in sports commentaries have, for the most part, been less significant than initially feared, largely due to the skill of a new breed of broadcaster that emerged with the new form. Even snooker has been attempted and notably resulted in the first woman commentator, Thelma Carpenter, herself an amateur champion at the sport, who was engaged by the BBC to provide commentary on a match in 1936.

Also during the 1930s, such commercial stations as **Radio Normandy** and agencies including the **J. Walter Thompson Organization** mounted variety shows that were recorded for transmission from continental locations. Among the most successful of these was *Radio Normandy Calling*.

Portability of recording developed up to and throughout World War II and enabled the BBC's war correspondents to provide graphic descriptions of events and places that had hitherto been impossible to relay to audiences at home. In addition, many "live" transmissions of events like the coronation of King George V led to a considerable enrichment of the texture of British radio.

OVALTINEY'S CONCERT PARTY. One of the most significant **children's programs** ever broadcast on U.K. radio, the *Ovaltiney's Concert Party* was first broadcast from **Radio Luxembourg** in December 1934, featuring **Jack Payne** and his band and child impersonator **Harry Hemsley**. Young listeners could join the League of Ovaltineys, and weekly messages were sent to members in code. The program aired on early Sunday evenings until Radio Luxembourg closed down at the outbreak of World War II but returned when the station reopened, with a similar format and using its famous theme song, "We Are the Ovaltineys," possibly the best-known and most successful British advertising jingle ever created:

We are the Ovaltineys, little girls and boys. Make your request, we'll not refuse you. We are here just to amuse you. Would you like a song or story, will you share our joys? At games or sports we're more than keen. No merrier children could be seen, because we all drink Ovaltine, we're happy girls and boys.

P

PAIN, NESTA (1905–1995). After a brilliant academic career, gaining a first in classics at Liverpool University and then going on to Somerville College in Oxford to undertake a Ph.D. in comparative philology, Nesta Pain married at the age of 21 and had her only child. During this time she became closely involved with Liverpool Playhouse and wrote two plays. In 1942, having separated from her husband, she moved to London with her 15-year-old daughter and joined the **British Broadcasting Corporation**, where she began writing and producing programs for both the External Services and domestic audiences.

In 1947, Pain became part of the Features Department, working under **Laurence Gilliam**, where she stayed for 12 years, writing, producing, and directing a wide range of material and becoming a passionate advocate of the radio **feature**. In 1957, she was responsible for persuading John Mortimer to write his first radio play, *The Dock Brief*, which won a **Prix Italia** that same year.

Pain was seconded to television in 1956 but continued to work in radio features until 1964, when she resigned. A year later, the department was closed. She took a part-time post as a scriptwriter/producer and continued to produce a range of acclaimed programs, including a serialized life of Queen Victoria. Upon her retirement, she was impeded by poor eyesight, although she remained mentally active and creative until her death. She remained a champion of the radio feature, claiming that it was the "one unique form that radio has achieved in its short history."

See also DOCUMENTARY; WOMEN.

PANEL GAMES. *See* QUIZ SHOWS.

PANETTA, FRANCESCA (1977–). Francesca Panetta is a radio and digital audio producer who works as special projects editor in the multimedia department of the *Guardian* newspaper, as well as a program and innovative sound maker through the independent company Phantom Productions. She began her career with the **British Broadcasting Corporation** as a trainee sound assistant, working on programs for **BBC Radio 3** and **BBC Radio 4**, prior to joining the *Guardian's* newly formed audio department in 2006. In this role, and as an independent, Panetta produced a number of award-winning programs, podcasts, and multimedia works, including the Hackney Podcast and **Hackney Hear**, both developed in and around the eponymous London borough. Hackney Hear, a **smartphone** application that uses the **Global Positioning System (GPS)**, was developed from 2010, and utilizes triggers from locations to stimulate audio that is experienced by the phone user as he or she moves through specific places. Panetta has subsequently extended the concept to other locations within the United Kingdom and internationally.

See also DOCUMENTARY; FEATURE; WOMEN.

PARFITT, ANDY (1958–). Andy Parfitt's appointment to the post of controller of **BBC Radio 1** in March 1998 occurred as a result of his predecessor, **Matthew Bannister's**, appointment as director of BBC radio previous year. He had begun his career with the **British Broadcasting Corporation (BBC)** in 1980, as a studio manager, before an attachment to the **British Forces Broadcasting Service** in the Falkland Islands. Parfitt returned to the BBC in 1984 and became a producer for **BBC Radio 4**, working on arts and magazine programs. In 1989, he was a part of the launch team of the original **BBC Radio 5**, becoming the network's assistant editor.

In 1993, Parfitt moved to Radio 1 as chief assistant to the controller, being successively promoted to the posts of editor of commissioning and planning, and then managing editor, before succeeding Bannister. In 2002, he oversaw the conception and launch of **BBC Radio 1Xtra**, a new digital radio service for fans of new black **music**. In December 2008, Parfitt's BBC role expanded when he took on the position of controller of popular music. In July 2011, it was announced that he would leave the BBC after 13 years with Radio 1. He was succeeded by **Ben Cooper** and took a job as executive director of talent for the advertising agency Saatchi and Saatchi. Parfitt is also chair of the charity Youth Music, and he has been awarded a fellowship at the **Radio Academy**.

PARK, RICHARD (1948–). Richard Park began his radio career in 1966, as a **pirate radio disc jockey** for the offshore station **Radio Scotland**. When **BBC Radio 1** opened in 1967, he joined the station as a presenter before moving to **Radio Clyde** during the 1970s, working in **music** and **sports**, eventually becoming head of entertainment. In 1987, Park became program controller at **Capital Radio** in London, where he was responsible for hiring **Chris Tarrant** and developing new presentation talent. In 2001, he left Capital to set up his own consultancy, Park Management, and was radio consultant for **Emap**. During the first decade of the 21st century, he continued to present programs on **London Broadcasting Company** and **talk-SPORT**, in addition to making a number of television appearances. When **Ashley Tabor** created **Global Radio** in 2007, Park was employed as director of broadcasting and named group executive director. He is a fellow of the **Radio Academy**.

See also COMMERCIAL RADIO.

PARKER, CHARLES (1919–1980). Charles Parker was a highly influential producer best remembered for his eight *Radio Ballads*, which he made between 1958–1964, with **Ewan MacColl** and Peggy Seeger. After war service as a submarine commander, he earned a degree from Queen's College in Cambridge in 1948. That same year, he joined the North American Service of the **British Broadcasting Corporation (BBC)** and then became a producer in External Services.

In 1954, Parker became senior **features** producer for the BBC Midland Region in Birmingham and began experimenting with the new portable **Midget** tape recorder, manufactured by Electrical and Musical Industries. The first result of this experimentation was *The Ballad of John Axon*, broadcast in 1958. Seven other ballads followed. Parker's funding was withdrawn in 1964. He continued to work with MacColl to produce the 14-part **series** *The Song Carriers*.

In 1972, Parker was forced into early retirement, although he continued to produce radio in a "guest" capacity until 1976. Thereafter, he fostered his already considerable interest in social-action theater, producing some of the first multimedia work for Arnold Wesker's Centre 42 and becoming a founding member of Banner Theatre of Actuality in 1974, where he attempted to extend the concept of the radio ballad form to the stage and other media.

Parker became a highly sought-after lecturer on the university circuit, vigorously expounding his views on oral history and mass communication. He had also assembled a vast archive, which, upon his death, was deposited at the Central Library in Birmingham.

See also CHARLES PARKER ARCHIVE TRUST; CHARLES PARKER DAY.

PARSONS, NICHOLAS (1923–). Nicholas Parsons is a radio and television presenter and actor. He is widely known for his hosting of panel games, in particular, his chairmanship of the **BBC Radio 4 quiz show** *Just a Minute*, which he has presented since its inception in December 1967. He was first discovered by **Carroll Levis** and appeared on his radio show, going on to become a familiar face and voice on U.K. radio and television, as well as contributing to numerous charities, for which he received the honor of Commander of the Most Excellent Order of the British Empire in 2014.

PASTERNAK, MICHAEL. *See* "EMPEROR ROSKO" (1942–).

PATTEN, CHRIS (1944–). Christopher Francis Patten, Baron Patten of Barnes, better known as Chris Patten, was chairman of the **BBC Trust** from 2011–2014, the first person to chair the newly formed trust, which replaced the Board of Governors of the **British Broadcasting Corporation (BBC)**. Prior to his time with the BBC, he was active in Conservative Party politics and was Britain's last governor and commander in chief of Hong Kong, ahead of its handover to the People's Republic of China in 1997. In May 2014, Patten resigned his position as chair of the trust on grounds of ill health, a year before his official term of office was due to end. He was replaced in an acting capacity by Diane Coyle, former economics editor for the *Independent* newspaper, and subsequently on a permanent basis by **Rona Fairhead**.

PAUL TEMPLE. Created in April 1938, by Francis Durbridge, as an eight-part adventure **serial** in the **British Broadcasting Corporation's** Midland region, the show was originally called *Send for Paul Temple*, and it was such a success, with its sophisticated format—that of an intellectual and attractive married couple working as amateur sleuths to defeat crime—that it ran for a full 30 years, finally ending in the spring of 1968. For 25 of those years, it was produced by the same man, Martyn C. Webster. During its lifetime, six actors played Paul Temple, and two actresses played his wife, "Steve."
See also DRAMA.

PAYNE, JACK (1899–1969). Jack Payne was a successful band leader who made his first broadcast as conductor of the Hotel Cecil dance band in 1924 and became so popular that the **British Broadcasting Company** invited him to form its first dance orchestra, the **BBC Dance Orchestra**, which he led from 1928–1932, during which time he became a household name. In 1932, he resigned from his BBC post to take his own band on tour, but he continued to be a major radio personality, fostering many vocalists with his band during the prewar years.

In the late 1930s, when dance bands in both Great Britain and the United States were swamping the popular **music** market, Payne formed his own theatrical agency, although with the outbreak of war, he formed a new band and became popular as a troop entertainer. After the war, he became a successful radio presenter, including on *Say It with Music*, the title being taken from his own theme tune, which ran for three years, from 1954–1957, on the **Light Programme**.

PC 49. The subtitle of this extremely popular postwar **British Broadcasting Corporation series** was "Incidents in the Career of Police Constable Archibald Berkeley-Willoughby." The concept—original for its time—was that the central character was an upper-class police constable, a former public schoolboy, playing against the stereotype of members of the U.K. police force who came from more working-class stock. The eponymous hero was played by Brian Reece, and the program was created from an idea by Australian crime journalist Alan Stranks. Each episode was a self-contained adventure in its own right, and the show proved so popular in its six years on the air, from 1947–1953, that it spawned spin-offs of a number of books, two films, and cartoon representations, most notably in the boys' *Eagle* comic, which continued to publish the exploits of PC 49 until March 1957, exactly four years after the last radio series.

See also DRAMA.

PEACH, LAWRENCE DU GARDE (1890–1974). After an academic career in his native Sheffield, which included a Ph.D. in 1921, Lawrence du Garde Peach became increasingly interested in **drama** for specific target markets. Beginning in 1923, he began to explore the possibilities afforded by the new medium of radio. Particularly fascinated by the opportunities in the area of children's drama, he contributed many dramatized historical and biographical programs for *Children's Hour*. Moving through various fields of endeavor—including politics—Peach continued his involvement in drama both on the provincial stage and on radio. Moreover, during the 1950s, he wrote more than 20 children's titles for educational publisher Wills and Hepworth, for their Ladybird imprint. After writing more than 400 radio plays for broadcast for the **British Broadcasting Company/Corporation** throughout the 1920s and beyond, Peach may hold the claim for the most prolific radio playwright in British radio history.

See also CHILDREN'S PROGRAMS.

PEASE, JOSEPH (1860–1943). Joseph Albert Pease, Lord Gainford of Headlam, was the first chairman of the **British Broadcasting Company (BBC)**. He had worked in the family coal and iron business prior to entering the British Parliament, where he served in Lloyd George's Liberal government as postmaster-general. He was chairman until 1927 and, after his time with the BBC, worked for the Federation of British Industries.

PEEL, JOHN (1939–2004). Born John Robert Parker Ravenscroft in Heswall, near Liverpool, John Peel first worked in radio as a **disc jockey (DJ)** for WRR in Dallas in the early 1960s. Returning to Britain at the height of the North Sea **pirate radio** boom, he joined **Radio London** before coming to

BBC Radio 1 upon its creation in August 1967. He remained on the station for the remainder of his life, the only survivor of its original DJ lineup. Peel was famous and much loved for his championing of new bands throughout his career, including Joy Division, the White Stripes, and the Undertones, whose song "Teenage Kicks" remained his all-time favorite record. He had earlier given studio time in his *Peel Sessions* to emerging stars of a previous generation, including David Bowie, Captain Beefheart, and Marc Bolan. Peel uniquely remained an icon to youth culture—even at the age of 65—while becoming a favorite of middle-class England with his weekly **BBC Radio 4** program *Home Truths*. In 1998, he received the Most Excellent Order of the British Empire award and, in 2003, was given a place in the **Radio Academy** Hall of Fame. He died while on a working holiday in Peru in October 2004.

See also MUSIC.

PEOPLE ARE FUNNY. A **series** produced by Ross Radio Productions for Pye Radio for **Radio Luxembourg** beginning in November 1953. It ran for 72 weeks in two series, the second beginning in August 1955. Performed in front of a live audience, the program was a fast-moving audience participation **comedy** show directed by one of the United Kingdom's most energetic pioneers and champions of **commercial radio, John Whitney**.

PERKINS, JOHN (1945–). Managing director of **Independent Radio News (IRN)** from 1989–2009, John Perkins began his radio journalism career in 1974, at Radio City in Liverpool, as the new station's political reporter, after working as a reporter for various daily newspapers. He moved to the London all-**news** station **London Broadcasting Company (LBC)** the following year and was one of the presenters chosen for LBC's experiment in U.S.-style rolling **news** format. In 1978, Perkins joined IRN, where he worked as home affairs editor and industrial editor. In 1982, he was appointed managing editor of LBC and IRN and, in 1986, became editor of IRN. His appointment as managing director of IRN came three years later.

Perkins's time at IRN coincided with a number of major developments in distribution and funding; he oversaw the introduction of satellite distribution of the service and funding by commercials rather than cash payments. This proved to be the turning point for the organization, which had been dogged by financial problems since its inception. IRN went on to become one of the world's most successful radio news broadcasters, producing substantial profits and returning millions of pounds each year to client stations in the form of "loyalty bonuses." Perkins retired in November 2009.

PETTICOAT LINE. A program conceived by **Anona Winn** and **Ian Messiter** in January 1965, as a feminist panel discussion, in a sense a version of the *Any Questions?* format. It ran until 1979 and featured such panelists as Renee Houston, Katharine Whitehorn, Marjorie Proops, and Jane Asher.
See also WOMEN.

PHILIPS-MILLER RECORDING SYSTEM. In 1931, after a number of experiments into sound on film, Dr. J. A. Miller developed a system that became the basis of the Philips-Miller recording process, with tape and equipment manufactured by Philips in Eindhoven, the Netherlands. This was a sound-only system to be used as a radio recording medium. The requirements of quality and instant playback were fulfilled at a stroke with this superior technical advancement, which was picked up during the prewar years by both the **British Broadcasting Corporation** and commercial companies, with the most widespread use initially being among the latter.

The idea of film that required processing before broadcast clearly prevented the instant use of recorded work in playback form. This was circumvented in the Philips-Miller system by having a groove or pattern cut in a cellulose base of film, coated with gelatin, on which was placed a skin of black mercuric oxide three microns thick. A v-shaped cutter recorded sound signals by tracing a pattern in the oxide, leaving a transparent track down the center of the film. This optical pattern could be "read" by a photoelectric cell. The result, manufactured and sold by the trade name Philimil, was the highest-quality recorded sound known before World War II.

With advances in magnetic tape developments after the war, particularly as a result of German quality improvements, the Philips-Miller Recording System was no longer relevant and fell into disuse.

PHONE-IN. A term coined in the United States in 1968 and first heard as a phrase in the United Kingdom in 1971. BBC Radio Nottingham has been claimed to be the first U.K. station to hold a phone-in, in 1968. During the 1970s, with the growth of **local radio**, the genre became a staple of output, being cheap and frequently controversial. This also fueled the development of the "shock-jock" style of presenter, who would debate—often violently and abusively—with his callers. The technique was explored on **London Broadcasting Company** and **talkSPORT** by such presenters as **Brian Hayes** and **James Whale**. On national radio, the first **BBC Radio 4** phone-in was *It's Your Line* in the 1970s, followed in 1989 by *Any Answers?*, which had previously been a letters-only response to *Any Questions?*

PICK OF THE POPS. A record program two hours in length that began on the **Light Programme** in October 1955, introduced by **Franklin Engelmann** and billed as a choice of "current popular gramophone records." Engelmann was soon replaced by **Alan Dell** and then **David Jacobs** in a late-night Saturday slot. In 1961, **Alan Freeman** became the host, and a new formula emerged of new releases in the first hour and the top 10 in the second, broadcast in reverse order. During this time the show moved to Sunday afternoons and was absorbed into **BBC Radio 1** when the station was created in 1967. In later incarnations, broadcast by **BBC Radio 2** on Saturday afternoons, the program moved toward a retrospective format, and when Freeman finally retired, the show, now made by the **independent production** company **Unique Broadcasting**, was hosted by Dale Winton, featuring two top 10 lists from past years.

In September 2010, Winton left the program to pursue other broadcasting commitments and was succeeded by **Tony Blackburn**. The show had previously been prerecorded, but Blackburn and his producer, Phil Swern, introduced a policy of broadcasting live beginning in January 2011. The only exceptions are when the presenter is on holiday or has other commitments, in which case the program is prerecorded. This differs from the general Radio 2 convention, in which stand-in presenters are employed at such times. The current format is to broadcast two separate charts from past years, one during each hour.

See also DISC JOCKEY (DJ); MUSIC.

PICKLES, WILFRED (1904–1978). Wilfred Pickles, a Halifax-born man who moved into regional radio in 1931, made radio history in two principal ways. First, during World War II, he read the **news** despite having a strong North Country accent, thus breaking the mold of the somewhat formal **British Broadcasting Corporation (BBC)** news-reading style. Second, and more significantly, his highly popular **series** *Have a Go* gave the microphone on location to the people who came to the show, creating an ad-lib program of considerable oral history significance through local storytelling within the format of a **quiz show**. With his wife Mabel as prize-giver—"What's on the table, Mabel?" was a catchphrase—the program became a national institution. As a broadcaster, Pickles was extremely versatile, with the ability to sing and tell stories, as well as perform stand-up comedy, pantomime, straight acting, and newsreading.

Pickles was also a beloved broadcaster to young people, and for more than 20 years, from 1942–1963, he captivated Northern children with his *Pleasant Journey* **talks** on *Children's Hour*. His work, and that of others in the North Region of the BBC, went a long way toward the democratizing of British radio. Significantly, in his 1949 autobiography, *Between You and Me,* he writes, "I wish the men who make the restrictive decisions at the BBC could get out and meet the people." With his slogan, "presenting the people to the people," Pickles broke through some of the social barriers that British public service broadcasting had created and, in so doing, became one of its best-loved personalities in radio.

See also CHILDREN'S PROGRAMS.

PIDDINGTONS, THE. In 1949 and 1950, Australian Sidney Piddington and his wife, former actress Lesley Pope, brought *The Piddingtons* to British radio, indulging in what they referred to as "their own kind of mystery." The **series** involved a wide range of mindreading stunts, many incredibly complex and skillful. Part of the mystery was the way in which the program was achieved; each show ended with the words, "Telepathy or not telepathy? You are the judge." Publicity for the show was considerable, and public debate on the Piddingtons's methods was rife. Producer **Ian Messiter** kept his peace about the trick of it. Prior to their **British Broadcasting Corporation** series, the couple had presented their act on Australian radio beginning in 1947.

PIRATE RADIO. A term used to denote a form of sound broadcasting contravening licensing regulations either within the country of origin or reception, or both. In the United States, pirate radio stations are sometimes called "bootleg" stations. Although there seems to be no specific historical point to which the use of the term *pirate* can be traced, it appears to have been used beginning in the earliest days of broadcasting. Long before the term was used in this context, it had been used in the field of publishing to describe illegal reprints of published works.

In the United Kingdom, the term was used in the 1930s to describe the activities of **Radio Luxembourg**. This station was considered a "pirate" internationally, rather than some of the other continent-based stations broadcasting to Britain, therefore contravening the monopoly of the **British Broadcasting Corporation**; while stations like **Radio Normandy**, **Radio Toulouse**, and others were broadcasting in English and aimed at U.K. audiences, they were doing so with the agreement and support of continental radio stations with legitimate wavelengths. Radio Luxembourg, however, was illegally using a wavelength that had been assigned to another potential broadcaster, Warsaw Radio, which had been allocated the frequency by international agreement but had yet (November 1933) to begin broadcasting on it.

Hence, a U.K. precedent for the term was established, equating it with "theft." This definition was again applied by the Harold Wilson Labour Party government of the 1960s in its decision to close down such offshore radio stations as **Radio Caroline**, **Radio London**, and others (*see* MARINE, AND C., BROADCASTING (OFFENCES) ACT 1967). In Britain, licenses were required to transmit and receive; thus, these stations were pirates, and with it being illegal to listen to unlicensed stations, listeners and broadcasters alike were breaking the law.

Advocates of such stations referred to them as "free" radio, and a number of these stations, which began illegally, have subsequently become licensed, government-approved organizations. (One example is the London-originating **music** station **Kiss FM**.) Pirate radio in Britain has frequently been seen as a catalyst for change, providing a revivifying force that has often generated a reevaluation of traditional radio services and, in most cases, an absorption of techniques, styles, technology, and personnel into the mainstream. A number of U.K.-based ethnic "pirates" have demonstrated a consumer need that has resulted in the legitimization of their activities and granting of a government license, particularly in the field of **community radio**. Nonetheless, in late fall of 2005, the government media industry regulator, the **Office of Communications**, confirmed its intention to prohibit any such stations from broadcasting.

"Pirate" radio can also be seen as touching on other areas, for instance, national and international propaganda. For example, the traditional voice of Hanoi, the Voice of Vietnam, had a U.S.-sponsored anticommunist counterpoint in the Voice of Free Vietnam. The use of the Internet and the ease with which Internet radio stations are able to function has increasingly overtaken the idea of terrestrial "pirate" radio stations, although the element of danger and innovation implied by the term in its most positive form continues to have a powerful impact on radio in general.

See also COMMERCIAL RADIO.

PITTAS, CHRISTOS (1945–). Born in Alexandria, Egypt, from Greek parents, composer Christos Pittas grew up in Cyprus, where he began his musical studies. In 1970, he came to England as a student and has since lived mostly in London. His works often explore forms that combine sound, movement, and speech. Since 1971, Pittas has worked extensively for the **British Broadcasting Corportion's** Radio Drama Department, composing original musical scores for numerous productions and working with a large number of directors, including Ian Cotterel, Martin Jenkins, and **John Theocharis**. He also specializes in radio interpretations of the classical repertoire, including *The Theban Trilogy* by Sophocles (director, David Spencer, 1983) and *The Birds* by Aristophanes (John Theocharis, 1990).

PLAIN TALES FROM THE RAJ. A major **documentary series** produced by **Michael Mason** for **BBC Radio 4** and broadcast in 1974. Noted for its innovative kaleidoscopic techniques, the series chronicled the final years of Britain's colonial control in India and was built around interviews with veterans of the end of the British Empire, from Field Marshal Sir Claude Auchin-leck, the last commander in chief of the preindependence Indian army, to writer and comedian **Spike Milligan**, born in Poona and the son of a serving British soldier. The scale of the programs was epic, and they drew large audiences. A second series was commissioned as a result and a book published based on series one.

See also FEATURE.

PLANET ROCK. A station currently owned by **Bauer Radio** and originally launched in 1999, on **Digital Audio Broadcasting**. In February 2008, the current owner, **GCap Media**, announced plans to close the station, and on 4 June 2008, it was announced that Planet Rock would be sold to a private consortium led by Malcolm Bluemel, who began seeking a new buyer for the station in September 2012. On 6 February 2013, Planet Rock was bought by Bauer Radio. Throughout its existence it has won many awards, including, in 2012, Digital Station of the Year at the **Sony Radio Academy Awards**.

See also COMMERCIAL RADIO; MUSIC.

PLOMLEY, ROY (1914–1985). Initially working as a small-parts actor, Roy Plomley joined **Radio Normandy** in 1936, as an **announcer**. He went on to produce and present much of the **International Broadcasting Company's outside broadcast** output, most notably the touring stage variety show *Radio Normandy Calling*. Plomley was involved with the establishment of short-lived **Radio International** during the first months of World War II and narrowly escaped capture, returning to England, where he established his most enduring creation, *Desert Island Discs*, for the **British Broadcasting Corporation** in 1942. As a radio panel show host, he chaired *We Beg to Differ* and *One Minute, Please* on the **Light Programme** and, from 1946–1949, was master of ceremonies of the same network's *Accordion Club*.

See also COMMERCIAL RADIO; DISC JOCKEY (DJ); QUIZ SHOWS.

PLOWDEN, BRIDGET (1910–2000). A public servant who had a considerable influence on the development of education, in particular at the primary level, Bridget, Lady Plowden, became involved in broadcasting administration and regulation in 1970, initially as a deputy chairman of the **British Broadcasting Corporation's** Board of Governors. The current chairman, **Charles Hill**, had hoped that she would succeed him, but instead, in 1975, she became chairman of the **Independent Broadcasting Authority**, where she became deeply interested in the program output of both Independent Television and fledgling **independent local radio**. Plowden was well liked in this role and made it a policy to visit new stations as they went on the air.

PLOWRIGHT, PIERS (1937–). One of the most distinguished **features** producers of his generation, Piers Plowright was educated at Christ Church in Oxford. He joined the British Council in 1963 and worked as radio and television officer in Khartoum, Sudan, from 1964–1967. In 1968, he joined the **British Broadcasting Corporation's (BBC)** English by Radio Department, working from **Bush House** in London. An attachment to BBC Radio Drama in 1973 led to a permanent post for Plowright the following year as executive producer for the **BBC Radio 2 serial** *Waggoners' Walk*. He remained with the program until 1978, when he became a producer of plays and features, with responsibility, beginning in 1980, for short stories and features on **BBC Radio 3**, while maintaining production work on **BBC Radio 4**.

Between 1982–1990, Plowright was one of two features producers to work in the Drama Department, winning the **Prix Italia** for his radio **documentaries** *Nobody Stays in This House Long* (1983), *Setting Sail* (1986), and *One Big Kitchen Table* (1988). Beginning in 1990, he was a senior features producer in Features, Education, and Arts Radio (a department that changed its name several times before his retirement from the BBC in 1997). In 1998, Plowright was made a fellow of the Royal Society of Literature. After retiring from program making, he continued to present occasional features and **talks** on Radio 3 and Radio 4, also maintaining an active role as a freelance lecturer and writer.

See also DRAMA; SERIALS; SOAP OPERAS.

PLUGGE, LEONARD (1889–1981). Captain Leonard Plugge, for many, was the founding father of **commercial radio** in Britain. His father was a Belgian citizen of Dutch descent. Plugge was educated in London and Brussels, and gained a degree in civil engineering at University College in London. During World War I, he joined the Royal Naval Volunteer Reserve, transferring in 1918 to the air force, where he became a captain, a title he used in civilian life for the rest of his career. He remained with the air force until 1921, working on the technical side and representing the air force at aeronautical control commissions in Berlin and Paris, for which he was elected a fellow of the Royal Aeronautical Society in 1921.

From 1923–1930, Plugge worked in London for the Underground Railways group of companies, and during this time he became fascinated with the possibilities of the new medium of radio. In 1924, he traveled France and Italy by train, exploring the concept of portable radio reception. In 1926, he was the first person to have a radio installed in a private car, and the following year Plugge announced plans to tour Europe with a colleague, each in their own car, with the intention of examining the possibility of keeping in touch with one another by wireless,, predicting the creation of the car telephone, which would come 40 years later.

In 1925, Plugge set up an experimental transmission from the Eiffel Tower in Paris, broadcasting a 15-minute fashion **talk** sponsored by the London store **Selfridges**. Since the broadcast received no publicity, it went virtually unnoticed. Plugge, however, was a born entrepreneur, and during the early 1930s, while experimenting with the concept of the car radio, he was traveling through Normandy in France and arranged a meeting with Fernand Legrand—who was, at that time, himself exploring the possibilities of wireless transmissions from the town of Fécamp. Thus was born the successful partnership that created **Radio Normandy** and ultimately the network that was the **International Broadcasting Company**. Plugge had been assisted in his initial research into continental stations by his early work, paid for by the **British Broadcasting Company/Corporation (BBC)**, which would later publish program details from **international radio** stations in the BBC journal *World Radio*.

Plugge pronounced his name "Plooje"—although when he carried out a 1935 general election campaign under a "Free Radio" ticket, his slogan became, "Plug(ge) in for Chatham." He won the seat, although he lost it in the general election of 1945. This marked the end of his period of influence, with the closure, prewar, of his commercial interests in France and the loss of his French holdings.

It has been claimed that his name is the origin of the term *record plugger*, being a promoter of commercial recorded material for radio; however, this has not been proven. Plugge married in 1934 and had two sons and a daughter. In 1972, he moved to Hollywood, California, and died there of a heart attack in February 1981.

PM. A **news** magazine program that runs from 5:00 p.m. to 6:00 p.m. on weekday evenings, bridging the **BBC Radio 4** schedule from afternoon to evening. The show first went on the air in 1970. Its format has changed very little throughout the years, with its dual presenter style and blend of heavy and light news items.

PODCASTING. *See* MP3.

POLDHU. In 1900, **Guglielmo Marconi** came to Cornwall and set up an experimental wireless station on cliffs above Poldhu cove, on the Lizard Peninsula. The design of the station was predominantly by Sir **John Ambrose Fleming**. The exposed location of the station resulted in considerable storm damage, and the first experimental signals traveled only a short distance. On 12 December 1901, however, the first transatlantic wireless signal was sent from here and picked up 1,800 miles away, on Signal Hill, St.

John's, Newfoundland, where Marconi had established an aerial, held airborne by kites, and a receiving station. The prearranged signal sent was Morse code for the letter "S."

In 1903, the site was visited by the prince and princess of Wales, and the nearby Poldhu Hotel (now a retirement rest home) continues to be a place of pilgrimage for radio enthusiasts. The original wireless station buildings were demolished in 1937, when the **Marconi Company** erected a commemorative granite obelisk that stands on the edge of the cliff close to the site.

POST OFFICE. The role of the Post Office, originally the General Post Office (GPO), in British radio has been considerable. From the earliest days, the power of the postmaster-general (PMG) as arbiter of content and licenser of broadcasters, listeners, and, initially, receivers ensured that government policies relating to broadcasting were firmly administered and controlled. After the **"Melba" broadcast** of 15 June 1920, from **Chelmsford**, the PMG at the time, the Rt. Hon. Albert Illingworth, announced to the House of Commons that further experimental broadcasts would be suspended because of "interference with legitimate services," the phrase being used to refer to complaints from officials at the newly established air traffic control system installed at London's Croydon airport. Thus, the Post Office was the controller and guardian of frequency use, even prior to the creation of the **British Broadcasting Company (BBC)**.

The GPO issued licenses for listeners and introduced a stipulation in 1922 that holders of such licenses could only listen to BBC programs on British-made equipment manufactured by a member company of the BBC and approved by the Post Office. Such receivers carried a circular stamp of approval, with the logo "BBC/PMG" and a registration number. With the growth of homemade sets, rules were laid down by the Post Office that each of the constituent parts of the receiver should bear the stamp of approval. When the company became the **British Broadcasting Corporation** in 1927, this regulation was no longer necessary, although the Post Office continued to control licensing.

The direct involvement of the PMG continued until 1969, when a Supplemental Royal Charter (Cmnd. 4194) was granted, following a Post Office Act of the same year, which transferred the powers of the PMG with regard to broadcasting to the newly created government post of the minister of posts and telecommunications.

See also CHARTER.

POSTE PARISIEN. The first European radio station to be entirely owned by a newspaper (*Le Petit Parisien*), Poste Parisien was housed in state-of-the-art studios off the Champs Elysees in Paris during its prime in the 1930s, having started broadcasting as La Poste Petit Parisien in July 1923. Its transformation into an ultra-modern studio complex, together with the development of a 60-kW transmitter capable of U.K. reception, resulted from the flotation of the station in October 1929, which raised 5,500,000 French francs.

In partnership with the **International Broadcasting Company**, Poste Parisien gradually expanded its U.K. transmissions to 18 hours per week by the outbreak of World War II. Recordings of the station's French output from the period include a station call signal of a gong, identical to the sound later used by **Radio Luxembourg**.

See also COMMERCIAL RADIO.

POTTER, GILLIE (1888–1975). Gillie Potter, whose real name was Hugh Peel, was an educated and sophisticated humorist who specialized in an English "upper-class" persona (using the epithet of "Lord Marshmallow of Hogsnorton"). Although he was a highly successful stage artist, his style was particularly suited to radio, and he frequently broadcast 15-minute studio **talks**, without a "live" audience. Potter made his radio debut in 1931, and his style, with its love of language and wordplay, quickly endeared him to pre-war audiences and the **British Broadcasting Corporation**, which found in his witty style a counterpoint to the broader **music** hall acts. He made his last radio **series**, *Mr. Gillie Potter*, in 1952. During the early 1960s, Potter retired to Bournemouth, and his last broadcast appearance was as part of the panel game show *Sounds Familiar* in 1970.

See also COMEDY.

POTTER, STEPHEN (1900–1969). Stephen Potter worked as a writer and critic, producing a series of studies of literary figures, including D. H. Lawrence and Samuel Taylor Coleridge, before joining the **British Broadcasting Corporation (BBC)** as a writer/producer in the Features Department in 1938, later rising to become head of **features** and poetry. During the World War II, he produced a number of features and **documentaries** on literary themes and also relating to the current conflict, before developing a series of satirical programs with Joyce Grenfell under the collective title *How*. These dealt with everyday issues in a humorous way, with such titles as *How to Give a Party* and *How to Talk to Children*. There were 29 *How* programs, starting in 1943. In 1946, *How to Listen to Radio* was the first program heard on the BBC's newly created **Third Programme**.

Potter's lightness of touch as a producer helped the genre of the radio feature develop a new impressionistic style, using natural dialog and minimal sound effects. Among notable successes were his *Professional Portraits* and *New Judgments*, as well as his production of Nevill Coghill's version of

Chaucer's *The Canterbury Tales*. In 1947, Potter began working on a new book, which became *The Theory and Practice of Gamesmanship*. It became such a success that he left the BBC to concentrate on his writing, and a series of sequels followed.

POWELL, ALLAN (1876–1948). Sir Allan Powell, chairman of the **British Broadcasting Corporation (BBC)** from 1939–1946, was responsible for maintaining the BBC's independence during the difficult war years. It was Powell who dismissed **F. W. Ogilvie** as director-general, replacing him with **Cecil Graves** and **R. W. Foot**, and subsequently **William Haley**.

POWER BEHIND THE MICROPHONE, THE. A remarkably prophetic book, written by **Peter Eckersley** in 1942, that extended the concept of "wired" radio, as developed during the 1930s, through **relay exchanges** to a vision of a system that only came to fruition in Britain at the start of the 21st century through the establishment of cable transmission systems. It is worth quoting from Eckersley's work, predicting as it does the digital revolution in the context of living standards in the United Kingdom, which would not manifest itself for another half-century:

> I have a dream about the future. I see the interior of a living-room. The wide windows are formed from double panes of glass, fixed and immovable. The conditioned air is fresh and warm. . . . Flush against the wall there is a translucent screen with numbered strips of lettering running across it . . . these are the titles describing the many different "broadcasting" programmes which can be heard by just pressing the corresponding button. . . . Not a hint of background noise spoils the sound even though some of the performances take place half across Europe, the quality is so lovely that reproduction criticizes every detail of the playing and speaking.
>
> Of course it is only a dream, but not so completely fantastic as some might imagine. It could all be done by using wires rather than wireless to distribute programmes. Let a cable, no thicker than a man's finger, be laid along the streets, outside the houses, and the main part of the installation is completed. The cable would only contain two or three conductors, and tappings would be made on to these for branch feeders to bring the service into the houses. The branch ends in the houses would be connected to house receivers. The street cables would be taken to transmitters, which would inject programmes into them. (Eckersley, *The Power behind the Microphone*, 1942.

PRIESTLAND, GERALD (1927–1991). Joining the **British Broadcasting Corporation (BBC)** as a graduate trainee in the **news** division in 1948, Gerald Priestland received numerous overseas postings as a reporter, including in Asia, Europe, the Middle East, and the United States, where he interviewed Martin Luther King Jr. shortly before the civil rights leader's assassination. He soon moved into television, returning to the United Kingdom but taking on the host role for *Newsdesk* on **BBC Radio 4** in 1970, a post he retained for four years.

A breakdown in the mid-1970s, brought on by his experiences during his coverage of the Vietnam War, led Priestland to a profound religious faith, and in 1976, he became a Quaker. In 1977, he became the BBC's religious affairs correspondent and created an unprecedented response from the public through his **series** *Priestland's Progress*, in which he brought religious faith to a mass audience and prompted a postbag of more than 20,000 letters. Priestland became a popular voice on the ***Today*** program, and even after his retirement, he was heard weekly in the *Pause for Thought* spot on **Terry Wogan's** morning **BBC Radio 2** program.

PRIESTLEY, J. B. (1894–1984). John Boynton Priestley was a prolific writer, and his plays—both on the stage and on the radio—were successful beginning in the mid-1930s. Prior to World War II, however, he had held no great regard for radio. This would change with a **series** of **talks**, begun in June 1940, as an attempt by the **British Broadcasting Corporation** to counter the propaganda broadcasts of **William Joyce**. Priestley wrote and presented the series, entitled *Postscript*, which went out after the 9:00 p.m. **news** on Sunday evenings. These broadcasts were characterized by both their content—a straightforward honesty and communicable determination that touched the national mood in a way similar to Winston Churchill's broadcasts—and Priestley's style, a bluff, North Country voice that spoke directly to listeners. Priestley's Socialist politics at one point offended Conservative sensibilities in October 1940, and he was removed from the air, to be briefly reinstated in January 1941. The talks that aired during these months were later collected and published in the book *All England Listened* (1967).

PRIVATE DREAMS AND PUBLIC NIGHTMARES. An experimental program written by **Frederick Bradnum** and produced by **Donald McWhinnie** in 1957. Described as a "radiophonic poem," it used new technology—sound and **music** produced by electronic and other nonconventional means distanced from human "players" in what McWhinnie referred to as a "science of making sound patterns." The show was part of an impetus within the **British Broadcasting Corporation (BBC)** that, within a few months, led to the creation of the **BBC Radiophonic Workshop**. Among the actors involved in the production was **Andrew Sachs**, who, more than 20 years later, would undertake his own experiment in using sound as narrative in his wordless play ***The Revenge***.

See also DRAMA.

PRIX EUROPA. This European tri-medial festival and competition is held in Germany and was launched in 1987. Today, it hosts radio, television, and online entries from European broadcasters. The festival is also a meeting place for debate, discussion, and networking among radio producers from different cultures. It is held each October in the Berlin-Brandenburg region of Germany. In 1997, the event merged with the Berlin Prix Futura, which had been launched in 1969.

PRIX ITALIA. The Prix Italia is the oldest and most prestigious international competition for radio, television, and related media. It awards prizes for productions in the fields of **drama, documentary** (including both cultural and **current affairs**), the performing arts, and **music**. The competition was founded in Capri in 1948, and it is hosted on an annual basis by a major Italian city. Only members of the Prix Italia are permitted to enter the competition; membership is made up of 80 public and private radio and television companies, representing 42 countries from five continents. Its general assembly meets annually to select a president from its membership.

PROGRAM SHARING. A concept of exchanging program material between **independent radio** stations in operation from 1976–1990. It was first administered by the **Independent Broadcasting Authority (IBA)** and subsequently by the **Association of Independent Radio Contractors (AIRC)**. Programs from local stations throughout Great Britain were centrally copied and offered to other companies, free of charge. The scheme helped overturn prejudice against the fledgling commercial industry by disseminating programs.

The funding for the enterprise—advertising, copying, and distribution costs—came from a controversial tax raised by the IBA called secondary rental. The range of work was considerable and demonstrated a notable difference in programming to that permitted after the 1990 Broadcasting Act, when regulations were relaxed and effectively ended most creative speech and arts coverage on **commercial radio** in Britain.

PUNT, STEVE (1962–). Steve Punt is a writer and performer who began his association with radio while still at university, when he started writing for *Week Ending*. With his long-term collaborator, **Hugh Dennis**, and **David Baddiel**, he was recruited to create and perform a satirical sketch and stand-up program for **BBC Radio 1** called *The Mary Whitehouse Experience*, which was transferred to television after three years. For **BBC Radio 2**, Punt and Dennis wrote and performed *It's Been a Bad Week*, as well as, for **BBC Radio 4**, *The Now Show*. In 2011, Punt hosted a new **quiz show** for Radio 4 called *The 3rd Degree*.

See also COMEDY; SERIES.

PURVES, LIBBY (1950–). Libby Purves presented **BBC Radio 4's** conversation program *Midweek* beginning in 1983. After joining the **British Broadcasting Corporation** in 1971, as a studio manager, at the age of 28, she joined **Brian Redhead** as copresenter on the *Today* program, becoming the show's first woman presenter. She was also the first person to broadcast "live" from Beijing, hosting *Today* from there in 1978. Other programs have included *The Learning Curve* and a number of **documentaries**. Purves has also been a print journalist, and she has written travel books, works on childcare, several novels, and a book in praise of radio entitled *Radio: A True Love Story* (2002).

PYE, WILLIAM GEORGE (1869–1949), AND PYE, HAROLD JOHN (1901–1986). William and Harold Pye, father and son, together created one of the most prestigious British radio manufacturing firms, which ultimately became known as "Pye of Cambridge." William had started his own business in 1896, as a scientific instrument manufacturer. During World War I, the Pye company made optical and electrical instruments for the armed services. After the war, with the coming of the **British Broadcasting Company** and radio broadcasting, it began manufacturing receivers.

In 1923, William's son Harold joined the company and the following year was made a partner. Harold was an excellent engineer and salesman, and he was able to design sets that proved attractive to consumer needs, paying particular attention to the receiver cabinets as furniture. During this period, the famous Pye "Fretwork Sunrise" began to appear on the cabinets of Pye sets. Harold had noticed the motif on a colleague's cigarette case and used it to great effect beginning in 1927. It was used for 10 years and briefly reappeared on a 1948 model. It remains an iconic image of U.K. radio manufacture in the 1930s.

Meanwhile, William was maintaining his instrument business and, in 1929, sold the radio branch to Charles Orr Stanley. The company continued to trade as Pye Radio and, after 1937, Pye Ltd., while William's original company, W. G. Pye and Co., continued under William's leadership until 1936. When William retired in 1936, he sold his interest to Harold, who ran the company until 1947, developing, as in the previous war, a working relationship with the government in the manufacture of military equipment. He then sold this company to Pye Ltd., and thereafter, although the Pye name continued for many years, the family no longer controlled it. Harold retired at the early age of 46.

QUEEN'S HALL. Almost adjacent to **Broadcasting House** in London, standing where a modern hotel now resides, together with what was, until 2010, the **British Broadcasting Corporation's** office block, Henry Wood House (prior to the absorption of these offices into the newly developed Broadcasting House), Queen's Hall was used for the promenade concerts until being destroyed by bombs in May 1941. It was here that the **BBC Symphony Orchestra** gave its first concert, in October 1930, under the leadership of Arthur Catterall.

See also MUSIC.

QUERY PROGRAMME. Said to be the first radio **quiz show**, the *Query Programme* ran for a **series** of eight editions beginning in May 1926. Listeners were to place a series of named radio performers in their correct *Radio Times* billings. Weekly winners were invited to spend an evening at London station 2L0.

QUIGLEY, JANET (1902–1987). Janet Quigley was involved as a producer in many important wartime and postwar **British Broadcasting Corporation (BBC)** radio initiatives. Prior to her BBC career, she had worked in publishing and with the Empire Marketing Board. Her first job with the corporation, which she joined in 1936, was in the Talks Department, where she was assigned the task of researching topics for **talks** that would appeal to **women**. One of her major initiatives during this time was the 12-part **series** *Towards National Health*, broadcast in 1937, covering fitness and nutrition.

Quigley worked on *Women at War*, which began in October 1941, initially designed for women serving in the armed forces. She also produced the lighter series *Kitchen Front*. In 1944, she was awarded the honor of Member of the Most Excellent Order of the British Empire for her work on wartime talks. Quigley left the BBC a year later to marry but returned in 1950 as editor of *Woman's Hour*. In 1956, she was promoted to Talks Department management, where, in 1957, with Isa Benzie, she was instrumental in the creation of the flagship **news** program *Today*. She also helped create *In Touch*, a program for the blind.

Quigley referred to what she called radio's capacity for "indirect propaganda" as a means of conveying valuable social messages, and her ability to impose this quality on the programs with which she was associated during a span of 30 years can be seen as one of her greatest contributions to the medium. She retired in 1962 but continued to write for radio, serializing more than 20 books for *Woman's Hour*.

See also CURRENT AFFAIRS; WARTIME BROADCASTING.

QUIZ SHOWS. In Britain, the birth of the radio quiz can arguably be said to be in 1926, with *Query Programme*, although it was not until 1937 that the concept was further explored. *Monday Night at Seven* contained an element entitled *Puzzle Corner*, and in 1938, *Children's Hour* carried a series of spelling contests between teams from different parts of the country, chaired by **Freddy Grisewood** and entitled *Spelling Bee*. The genre has subsequently developed to the extent that it is not possible to chronicle all programs; however, it is notable that during the immediate prewar years and from 1939 onward, there was a proliferation of quiz programs feeding a growing appetite among the British radio audience.

Among these, contained within the 1944 program, *Merry-Go-Round* was the first quiz show to offer a cash prize, Double or Quits Cash Quiz. **Alastair Cooke** chaired *Transatlantic Quiz* in 1945, and this was followed by *Round Britain Quiz* in 1947, still being broadcast as the longest-running quiz show on British radio. The trend continued with the popular schools quiz *Top of the Form*, which ran on the **Light Programme** from 1948–1986. *What Do You Know?*, which began in 1953, under the chairmanship of **Franklin Engelmann**, evolved into *Brain of Britain* with Robert Robinson in 1967. The most popular of all radio quizzes, however, remains *Have a Go*, which began airing in 1946, with **Wilfred Pickles**, and ran until 1967. Another perennial favorite has been *Just a Minute*, which also started in 1967.

In many ways, **BBC Radio 4** has been the natural home of literary panel games and quizzes, typified by *Quote . . . Unquote*, which began in 1976, and continues to run in **series**, with its creator, Nigel Rees, as chair. **Comedy** and parody versions of the quiz show format have included *Does the Team Think?* and *I'm Sorry I Haven't a Clue*.

QUOTE . . . UNQUOTE. A long-running panel **quiz show** broadcast on **BBC Radio 4**, at one time airing on **BBC Radio 2** and also the **BBC World Service**. It was devised by Nigel Rees, who also presented the program, which had its first broadcast in 1976.

R

RADCLIFFE, MARK (1958–). Mark Radcliffe began his radio career at Piccadilly radio, a **commercial radio** station in Manchester, before moving to **BBC Radio 5 Live** and, in 1991, **BBC Radio 1**, where he worked with his long-time collaborator, Marc Riley, and the dual pseudonym "Mark and Lard." The duo won three **Sony Radio Academy Awards**. In 2004, Radcliffe began working for **BBC Radio 2**, later hosting the folk **music** program, as well as, for a time, a weekday evening slot with **Stuart Maconie**, a show that was critically acclaimed and won a Sony Radio Academy Award for best radio show in 2009. In 2010, the program was reduced to three nights a week, and in 2011, it was transferred to a weekday afternoon slot on **BBC Radio 6 Music**. In 2013, Radcliffe took over as host of Radio 2's weekly folk program from **Mike Harding**. Radcliffe has also worked as a radio producer; in 1983, he produced sessions for the **John Peel** show featuring such artists as Billy Bragg. He has also produced **comedy** for **BBC Radio 4**, most notably *Count Arthur Strong's Radio Show*.
    See also DISC JOCKEY (DJ).

RADIO ACADEMY. The Radio Academy was formed as a registered charity in 1983, for the "encouragement, recognition, and promotion of excellence in U.K. broadcasting and audio production." Administered through a board of trustees, it established a range of events throughout the year, including the annual Radio Festival, the **Radio Production Awards**, and, from 1983–2014, the **Sony Radio Academy Awards** and subsequently the **Radio Academy Awards**. In addition, the academy created regular master classes for young people intending to make a career in radio, as well as local events throughout the country. In November 2014, it abruptly announced the closure of its executive unit and dismissal of its staff, with the exception of its chief executive officer. It also announced that the Radio Academy Awards would no longer continue in their existing form, stating the academy's intention to create a new event celebrating British radio.

RADIO ACADEMY AWARDS. Started in 1983, during the same year as the foundation of the **Radio Academy**, the Radio Academy Awards were considered by many to be the most prestigious awards in the U.K. radio industry. The categories for the awards were decided by an annual committee, with the aim of including the main areas, from **music**, **news**, and speech, to **radio drama**, **comedy**, and **sports**, and not discriminating against station size or niche categories. Judging was undertaken by panels of professionals from the radio industry and related academic institutions, as well as critics.

Until 2013, the awards were named for their first sponsor, Sony, initially as the Sony Radio Awards and subsequently as the **Sony Radio Academy Awards**. In August 2013, Sony announced the end of its sponsorship agreement with the Radio Academy after 32 years. The awards were then named the Radio Academy Awards, as the search for a new sponsor was undertaken. This was not forthcoming, and in November 2014, the academy announced that there would be no awards in 2015. At the same time, **Ben Cooper**, chair of the Radio Academy, issued a statement, stating, "I'm confident and determined that as an industry we can create an exciting and modern event that retains the gravitas of over 30 years of Awards." At publication, details of this event—and the future of the academy—were not available.

See also RADIO PRODUCTION AWARDS (RPAS); STUDENT RADIO ASSOCIATION (SRA).

RADIO ARANJUEZ. *See* EAQ MADRID.

RADIO ATHLONE. An Irish radio station that presents a unique case in the history of prewar **commercial radio** broadcasting to the United Kingdom: a state-run broadcaster, initially partially funded by **license fees** and partially by customs duties. It opened in 1933 and, from the start, operated a U.K. concession, initially granted to Radio Athlone Publicity and subsequently—briefly—to the **International Broadcasting Company**, before, in May 1935, the Irish government made a decision that non-Irish advertisers would not be permitted to sponsor programs. Thereafter, the only sponsored programs on the station became those supported by the Hospitals Trust, which were advertised by 1937, in *Radio Pictorial*, as being one hour per night, seven nights a week. At the same time, transmitter power had been increased from an already powerful 60 kW to 100 kW, the most that was permitted to Ireland according to international agreement. By the end of that year, the station was being billed as Radio Eireann, although program output remained unchanged until the outbreak of war.

RADIO AUTHORITY (RA). Created by the 1990 Broadcasting Act to replace the **Independent Broadcasting Authority**, the RA was designed to be the regulator of radio broadcasting in Great Britain outside the **British Broadcasting Corporation**. This included local and national **commercial radio**, as well as the regulation and licensing of student and hospital broadcasting and **restricted service license** stations. Its first chair was Lord Chalfont, and its first chief executive was **Peter Baldwin**. The RA was intended to be a "light-touch" regulator, but as the decade proceeded, commercial broadcasters sought a further easing of regulation and greater opportunities for consolidation. In the 2003 Broadcasting Act, the RA was deemed to be no longer appropriate to the converging digital world of modern media and, in December 2003, replaced by the wider-reaching regulatory powers of the **Office of Communications**.

RADIO BALLADS. This groundbreaking concept of **feature** making grew out of the partnership between the husband and wife folk team of **Ewan MacColl** and Peggy Seeger and **British Broadcasting Corporation** producer **Charles Parker**. There were eight "Ballads," as follows (with transmission dates):

The Ballad of John Axon	2 July 1958
Song of a Road	5 November 1959
Singing the Fishing	16 August 1960
The Big Hewer	18 August 1961
The Body Blow	27 March 1962
On the Edge	13 February 1963
The Fight Game	3 July 1963
The Travelling People	17 April 1964

The programs not only developed a new narratorless technique of **documentary** storytelling, using new mobile recording technology, they also gave a direct voice to working-class communities, elevating their stories to a kind of radio "art." The best known of the eight programs is *Singing the Fishing,* which won the **Prix Italia** in October 1960.

RADIO CAROLINE. The brainchild of Ronan O'Rahilly, the first of the U.K. **pirate radio** stations of the 1960s, and extremely important in the development of postwar British radio, Radio Caroline shaped the **music** radio revolution that led to the creation of **BBC Radio 1** by the **British Broadcasting Corporation** and, ultimately, the launch of **commercial radio** in Britain in October 1973. The station began broadcasting on 29 March

1964, from a ship moored off the Thames Estuary. Its first voice was that of **Simon Dee**. After merging with Radio Atlanta shortly thereafter, the original ship sailed the coast to the Isle of Man, where it became Radio Caroline North, while Atlanta became Radio Caroline South.

When the offshore stations were outlawed by the **Marine, and c., Broadcasting (Offences) Act 1967**, Caroline alone defied the ban, with **Johnnie Walker** and Robbie Dale continuing to broadcast, giving the station legend status. Administration was established in Holland, and the Caroline brand has continued in various guises despite sinkings, changes in ships, raids by the U.K. Department of Trade and Industry, and hurricanes. In 2004, it was once again heard through the new medium of satellite radio, a continuing icon in U.K. radio, even when reduced to little more than a famous name.

See also DISC JOCKEY (DJ).

RADIOCENTRE. RadioCentre is the industry body for **commercial radio** in the United Kingdom. It was established in July 2006, with the merging of the **Commercial Radio Companies Association** and the Radio Advertising Bureau. It is joint owner—with the **British Broadcasting Corporation**—of **Radio Joint Audience Research** Ltd. and the online audio system **Radioplayer**. Its first chief executive was **Andrew Harrison**, who was succeeded in the role by **Siobhan Kenny** in 2013.

RADIO CITY. There have been two stations by this name. In the early summer of 1964, during the period of **pirate radio** expansion, a World War II fort located nine miles off the east coast of England, on the Shivering Sands sandbank, was occupied by a company run by David Sutch ("Screaming Lord Sutch") and launched later that same year as Radio City. During its short existence, the station was involved in various controversies, including a murder.

And second, when land-based independent local radio was approved in 1972, a number of station licenses were granted after the initial franchises of the **London Broadcasting Company**, **Capital Radio**, and **Radio Clyde**. One of these was Radio City in Liverpool, on the air since 1974 and broadcasting to Merseyside, Cheshire, and parts of Wales and Lancashire. The station's first controller was **Gillian Reynolds**, who, in taking on the post, became the first female controller in U.K. **commercial radio**.

RADIO CLYDE. A Glasgow independent local radio station that became the first **commercial radio** operation to be established outside London when it began broadcasting in December 1973. Run by James Gordon, later Lord Gordon of Strathclyde, it became, with Radio Forth, the foundation of **Scottish Radio Holdings**. Particularly in its early days, the station was noted for its **drama** and **talks** production, by the hand of—successively—Hamish Wilson and Finlay Welsh. Currently owned by **Bauer Radio**, output is divided between two stations, Clyde 1 and Clyde 2.

RADIO CÔTE D'AZUR. A French radio station originally based in the Municipal Casino at Juan-les-Pins. It was one of those used by the **International Broadcasting Company (IBC)** to carry programs to the United Kingdom in English. Although the station itself changed its name to Radio Méditerranée for domestic transmissions, the IBC, broadcasting to the United Kingdom beginning in 1934, kept the title "Radio Côte d'Azur (Juan-les-Pins)" as a more evocative brand, advertising output in *Radio Pictorial* and inviting listeners to "tune in on Sundays to the Sunny South." Shortly before the outbreak of World War II, however, the station's domestic name was also being used for its international output, with an increasing amount of English-language programming.
See also COMMERCIAL RADIO.

RADIO DATA SYSTEM (RDS). A transitional technology for **frequency modulation (FM)** usage that grew out of developments made by Swedish engineers in 1976. The main benefits of the RDS (RBDS in the United States) were that radios using the system would automatically retune to locate the strongest FM signal, while carrying the Enhanced Other Networks (EON) feature, enabling travel broadcasts to be detected and permitted to interrupt received programs. This was particularly useful for car radios. The system also permitted display of station information. Designed for use with FM **analog**, much of the RDS technology was incorporated into U.K. digital radio as this new platform gradually began to supersede FM transmissions.

RADIODNS. RadioDNS is a technology that connects broadcast radio and the Internet, permitting enhanced and interactive services. It is intended for use on hybrid radios—radio receivers with both broadcast and Internet radio capabilities.

RADIO EIREANN. *See* RADIO ATHLONE.

RADIO FUN. A comic paper produced by Amalgamated Press for children, published from 15 October 1938 to 18 February 1961, as a companion to another of its comics, *Film Fun.* Toward the end of its existence, it was renamed *Radio Fun and Adventure.* It featured comic strip interpretations of many radio personalities, including **Arthur Askey, Tommy Handley,** and **Richard Murdoch.** An annual was also produced, containing the same illustrated formats in omnibus form.

See also JOURNALS.

RADIO INDEPENDENTS GROUP (RIG). A nonprofit trade body funded through membership fees and other fundraising events, representing the interests and needs of the United Kingdom's independent radio production industry. Founded in February 2004, RIG currently represents two-thirds of the industry. In addition to representing its members' needs in negotiations with the **British Broadcasting Corporation, commercial radio** groups, the government, and other groups, the group offers support, resources, information, access, training, and legal advice. It aims to bring together the knowledge of those working in the independent radio production sector and support this part of the industry. RIG is coorganizer—with the **Radio Academy**—of the **Radio Production Awards**.

See also INDEPENDENT PRODUCTION.

RADIO INTERNATIONAL. After the closure of **Radio Normandy** in 1939, the **International Broadcasting Company** used its resources and transmitter without the support of sponsorship by advertising to create programs for the British Expeditionary Forces in France until it was closed down by a joint British and French government ruling on 3 January 1940. During its short life, it predated the **BBC Forces Programme**, which commenced within days of its demise.

See also COMMERCIAL RADIO; PLUGGE, LEONARD (1889–1981).

RADIO JOINT AUDIENCE RESEARCH (RAJAR). RAJAR was established in 1992, to operate a single-audience measurement system for the U.K. radio industry. The company was wholly owned by the **British Broadcasting Corporation (BBC)** and initially the **Commercial Radio Companies Association (CRCA)**, subsequently the **RadioCentre**. The structure is that of a "deadlocked" company, board decisions requiring the agreement of both parties.

In addition to BBC and CRCA representation, membership of the board recognizes the interests of the advertising community, which is represented by the Institute of Practitioners in Advertising. In recent years, there has been much discussion within the British industry relating to the adjustment of RAJAR's methods of monitoring an increasingly complex market. The traditional method of audience measurement has been through the issue to listeners of personalized diaries, to be completed according to the individual's listening habits. There has been increasing pressure from some areas for the introduction of a system of electronic metering.

RADIO LEICESTER. Radio Leicester was the first **local radio** station in Britain run by the **British Broadcasting Corporation**, commencing transmissions on 8 November 1967, under the management of **Maurice Ennals**.

RADIO LONDON. Not to be confused with **British Broadcasting Corporation's** BBC Radio London, launched in 1970, prior to being rebranded as **Greater London Radio** in 1988, Radio London was one of the seminal **pirate radio** stations, operating from the North Sea. It began broadcasting on 23 December 1964. Transmitting from the *M.V. Galaxy*, a former U.S. minesweeper moored off Frinton-on-Sea, Essex, the station was the major competitor of **Radio Caroline** and became the platform for many U.K. **disc jockeys** who went on to become household names in radio, including **John Peel**, **Tony Blackburn**, and **Kenny Everett**. Also known as "Big L" and "Wonderful Radio London," it closed down in August 1967, when the **Marine, and c., Broadcasting (Offences) Act** went into effect in the United Kingdom.

See also COMMERCIAL RADIO; MUSIC.

RADIO LUXEMBOURG. A famous station that went on the air from the Villa Louvigny in Luxembourg city in late 1933, after a series of test transmissions that had begun in March of that same year. It originally broadcast on a wavelength of 1,190 meters, and its policy—together with that of **Radio Normandy** and other stations operated by the **International Broadcasting Company**—was to beam sponsored programs at Britain, attacking the public service monopoly of the **British Broadcasting Corporation (BBC)**. The station targeted Sunday listeners denied entertainment by the BBC's **Sunday broadcasting policy** and, at its peak in the mid-1930s, achieved huge audiences with such programs as *Ovaltiney's Concert Party* and *The Palmolive Program*.

Radio Luxembourg closed down on 21 September 1939, shortly after the outbreak of hostilities. Because of its strategic significance, the station, with its giant transmitter, situated on the Junglinster Plateau, was used by both German and Allied forces at various times during World War II. It was used as a relay for the transmission of the propaganda broadcasts of **William Joyce,** and following the station's liberation by American forces on 10 September 1944, it initiated programming aimed at the retreating German army using the station name "Radio Twelve-Twelve," after the U.S. 12th Army, which was operating the programs.

Radio Luxembourg reopened its commercial English-language transmissions on 1 July 1946, and on 2 July 1951, it switched to its famous wavelength of 208 meters, medium wave. The 1950s proved to be a second golden age of sponsorship for the station; it once again offered populist listening to an audience to which the BBC did not cater. With the coming of **pirate radio** in the 1960s and the BBC's creation of **BBC Radio 1** in 1967, Radio Luxembourg's audience began to decrease. In August 1990, it launched a new satellite channel but finally closed for good on 30 December 1992.

See also COMMERCIAL RADIO; MUSIC.

RADIO LYON. Radio Lyon began broadcasting to its French community in 1924, but licensed English-language transmissions began under the title "Radio Lyons" in the autumn of 1936. The U.K. agency was Broadcast Advertising of London, with a program department at the commercial recording studios of Vox. Thus, it was one of the few independent commercial operations of the time outside of the activities of the **International Broadcasting Company**, **Wireless Publicity**, or the **J. Walter Thompson Organization**.

The station's output had many original features, including the marketing of its chief **announcer**, Tony Melrose, as the "golden voice of Radio Lyons." Adopting a visual pun on its name in the symbol of two lions on its program publicity material, it also created an early version of a **music** chart in 1937, when it broadcast a list of the 12 most popular tunes requested by listeners. It continued its transmissions in English until the start of World War II.

See also COMMERCIAL RADIO.

RADIO NEWSREEL. *Radio Newsreel* was initially started in July 1940, as a daily program for North America, and the **British Broadcasting Corporation** initiated a Pacific edition in October of that same year and an African version in October 1941. It was first broadcast to British audiences in November 1947, and continued to be broadcast to domestic audiences until April 1970, thereafter continuing on the **BBC World Service**. Its theme tune, "Imperial Echoes," became famous.

See also NEWS.

RADIO NORMANDY. The fruit of a speculative partnership between entrepreneur **Leonard Plugge** and Fernand Legrand, a businessman from Fécamp, on the Normandy coast, Radio Normandy was the first station to beam regularly sponsored programs from the continent to Britain. In so doing, it formed the foundation of Plugge's **International Broadcasting Company (IBC)**, which flourished throughout the 1930s. First transmissions were under its non-Anglicized name, "Radio-Normandie," on 11 October 1931, on 246 meters, medium wave.

In 1935, a wavelength change to 1,304 meters greatly improved British reception, although the station never achieved the nationwide coverage of **Radio Luxembourg's** giant transmitter. Indeed, the marketing branch of the

IBC made a virtue of this, claiming to potential advertisers that they deliberately targeted the "prosperous south" of the country. The station gave early opportunities to a number of young broadcasters who would go on to achieve success elsewhere, among them **Bob Danvers-Walker** and **Roy Plomley**. It developed a sophisticated policy of **outside broadcast** recording, most notably the touring variety show *Radio Normandy Calling*.

For some months after the outbreak of World War II, the IBC sought to reinvent the station as a service for British troops under the title **Radio International**. On 3 January 1940, however, this closed down, and after the war, changes in French media regulation made it impossible for the station to resume its transmissions.

See also COMMERCIAL RADIO; MUSIC.

RADIO NORMANDY CALLING. In 1938, at the height of the prewar **commercial radio** boom in Britain, the **International Broadcasting Company** created a traveling show, recorded on location at various venues throughout the United Kingdom. The aim, particularly in the north of the country, was to raise awareness of **Radio Normandy**, which was less well known in the region than **Radio Luxembourg** because of relative transmitter power. It was presented by **Roy Plomley** and had a theme sung by the "Belles of Normandy":

> Radio Normandy calling you,
> Bringing you **music** from out the blue,
> Laughter and rhythm, so when you hear . . . (bell rings)
> You know it stands for Radio Normandy coming through,
> With lots of enjoyment for all,
> So be sure to listen to
> *Radio Normandy Calling.*

The program existed in both on-air and off-air versions, the latter being used solely as a promotional vehicle, from which specific acts were selected for the broadcast version, once a week.

RADIOLYMPIA. *See RADIO SHOW.*

RADIO PARADE MOVIES. In 1933, British International Pictures, based at Elstree, made a **feature** film that included many of the top radio variety stars of the time. Entitled *Radio Parade of 1933*, it clearly borrowed from U.S. films of the time, including some of those made by Busby Berkeley, as well as Hollywood's *Big Broadcast* **series**. Unfortunately, the film no longer exists. A restored version of the sequel, *Radio Parade of 1935*, remains and contains an innovative color sequence and a host of major radio personalities.

The film is noteworthy in that its main plot revolves around a staid **British Broadcasting Corporation** run by an autocrat (Will Hay impersonating **John Reith** under the name of "Garland").

RADIO PARIS. Beginning broadcasting in 1921, to a French domestic audience, Radio Paris was carrying some programs made by the **International Broadcasting Company** in early 1933, but shortly thereafter, the stake with the U.K. company seems to have ended. Thereafter, the station became involved with the early radio aspirations of a group of entrepreneurs led by the newspaper the *Sunday Referee* and Radio Publicity (Universal). Broadcasting on **longwave**, it became a popular broadcaster of English-language programming until December 1933; however, this output had been threatened by a French government decision to take the station out of private hands and turn it into a state-run enterprise.

At this time, a new station was being developed in Luxembourg, and negotiations led to a shift of U.K. programming, transmitted on Sundays, from Paris to Luxembourg. In early December 1933, output was broadcast on both stations simultaneously, with the chief **announcer, Stephen Williams**, encouraging listeners to retune to the new wavelength, guided by the sound of his voice, and leading to the creation of **Radio Luxembourg's** first U.K. output. Radio Paris opened under state control on 17 December. British transmissions from the station ceased.

See also COMMERCIAL RADIO; MUSIC; PIRATE RADIO.

RADIO PICTORIAL. A populist magazine that began as a **journal** of general broadcasting "gossip" in January 1934. By August of that year, it was carrying full details of **commercial radio** broadcasts from the continent, despite a British ban on newspaper publicity for the services. At first, there were articles relating to **British Broadcasting Corporation** programs and personalities, but these diminished as the decade proceeded. With the coming of war and ending of the programs it publicized, the magazine also ended its life, with the final edition appearing on 8 September 1939.

RADIOPLAYER. Radioplayer is an online device born of a partnership between the **British Broadcasting Corporation (BBC)** and U.K. Commercial Radio, offering **webcasting** of British radio. Its slogan is, "U.K. radio in one place." UK Radioplayer Ltd. is a nonprofit company founded by the BBC, **Global Radio, Guardian Media Group** Radio, **Absolute Radio**, and **RadioCentre** to develop a player that could offer audiences a simple and consistent online listening experience in both public service and commercial formats. Thus, in addition to BBC content, Radioplayer enables audiences to discover and listen to live and on-demand radio from the **Office of Communications** licensed U.K. radio stations.

See also BBC IPLAYER RADIO.

RADIO POEMS. Radio and poetry have long been linked, and there has been a large number of commissions for radio poems—works specifically designed to be interpreted by and through the medium. In many cases, these have been linked to **drama**, while in others, the genre has been used to illuminate **features**. **British Broadcasting Corporation** producer **Douglas Cleverdon** was particularly active in this field, fostering and developing relationships with leading poets during the 1940s and 1950s, including David Jones, David Gascoyne, and Dylan Thomas. Perhaps the most famous radio poetic drama was Thomas's *Under Milk Wood*, produced by Cleverdon in 1954. Other poets who have been attracted to the medium have included **Louis MacNeice**, Michael Symmons Roberts, George Macbeth, Katrina Porteous, and Julian May.

RADIO PRODUCTION AWARDS (RPAS). Organized by the **Radio Academy** and the **Radio Independents Group**, these awards are designed to recognize and celebrate the work of U.K.-based radio and audio producers. Where the **Radio Academy Awards** recognize programs, stations, and broadcasters, the RPAs honor the achievement of individual producers and production companies, demonstrated by a body of work created and delivered during the previous year. The awards are open to all U.K.-based radio and audio producers. These include independents; freelancers; and staff of and contributors to **British Broadcasting Corporation (BBC)** networks, BBC local and regional stations, **Office of Communications**–licensed **commercial radio** and **community radio** stations, **Student Radio Association**–affiliated student radio stations, and **Hospital Broadcasting Association**–affiliated radio stations. Entries are also welcome from audio producers working primarily in the digital sector on output for commercial or nonprofit audio streams and podcasts.

RADIO SCOTLAND. An offshore **pirate radio** station that began broadcasting from a former lightship, the LV *Comet*, anchored at various locations off the Scottish coastline. Radio Scotland began broadcasting on 31 December 1965, with a presentation team that included **Richard Park** and **Stuart Henry**. The station's owner, Tommy Shields, had repeatedly lobbied for the British government to grant the station a legal license on the grounds that it was serving parts of Scotland that were beyond the range of **British Broadcasting Corporation** stations. These attempts were unsuccessful, and with the introduction of the **Marine, and c., Broadcasting (Offences) Act 1967**, the station closed on 14 August of that year. The station is not to be confused with **BBC Radio Scotland**.

RADIO SHOW. The first U.K. radio exhibition took place in the Horticultural Hall in London from 30 September to 7 October 1922. In March 1923, the *Daily Mail* Ideal Home exhibition included a display and demonstration of equipment, and by 1925, with the new technology now established as a major business, an exhibition at the Royal Albert Hall featured 122 stands mounted by 63 suppliers. This led to the establishment of an annual radio show staged beginning in 1926, in the Empire Hall in Olympia, London, by the Radio Manufacturers Association, and subsequently in partnership with the **British Broadcasting Company (BBC)**.

"Radiolympia," as it was originally known, and, after its transfer to the Earls Court complex, "The Radio Show," was, for 40 years (aside from the war years), the showcase for the British industry, covering television beginning in 1936, in addition to sound broadcasting. Programs were broadcast live from the exhibition throughout its history, including, in 1934, *Variety from Olympia*, with **Henry Hall** and the **BBC Dance Orchestra**, and a special edition of *In Town Tonight*. The annual event even had the theme tune "Listen to Your Radio" composed in its honor in 1937.

The first postwar Radiolympia took place in 1947. As the Radio Show, it continued to be a major annual week of celebration of the medium, until in 1966, when the BBC decided it was no longer appropriate. There was one revival, in 1988, when more than 93,000 people visited the "BBC Radio Show" at Earls Court.

RADIO SOCIETY OF GREAT BRITAIN (RSGB). Originally formed as the London Wireless Club in July 1913, the RSGB is the national society for amateur radio operators, representing the interests of 60,000 licensed radio amateurs in the United Kingdom. It also provides a voice for its members with the U.K. government and the regulatory body the **Office of Communications (Ofcom)**. During World War II, the RSGB was recruited into the government department MI8, the Radio Security Service, and played a role in intercepting undercover enemy transmissions. In 2006, the society worked with Ofcom to revise the U.K. amateur radio license, including an abolition of its annual **license fee** and the removal of the previous requirement to log all transmissions. In July 2012, the RSGB formally opened the **National Radio Centre** at **Bletchley Park**, Buckinghamshire.

RADIO THEATRE (BROADCASTING HOUSE). A large studio with the capacity for an audience of several hundred people originally called the Concert Hall. The first performance held there was of the Caterall Quartet on 15 October 1932. Designed by Val Myer as a venue for the performance and recording of classical **music**, it has had a number of uses, including, during World War II, as an emergency dormitory for staff of the **British Broadcasting Corporation**. Radio Theatre features fine art deco design details that include scenes from Greek mythology. During the refurbishment of **Broadcasting House** in the early 21st century, a new elevated floor was installed to provide easier access from street level. This resulted in the design reliefs over the original doorways and along the side walls being visible at a lower level than before. Since the theater reopened in 2007, it has been used for the recording of pop and rock music concerts and staging of **comedy** and variety shows. It also serves as a conference venue.

RADIO TIMES. In 1923, in response to a boycott by the British Newspaper Proprietors' Association, **John Reith** launched *The Radio Times*, subtitled "The Official Organ of the **British Broadcasting Company (BBC).**" The first edition of this weekly listings magazine was published on 28 September 1923. From the start, it contained a range of features, letter pages, competitions, and advertisements. It also developed a tradition of commissioned art covers, marking special occasions, the seasons of the year, anniversaries, and so forth.

When first published, the schedules were printed from Sunday to Saturday, following Reith's view of Sunday—the first day of the week—as being the "Lord's Day." This continued until October 1960, when the broadcasting week became reflected in the journal's pages as running from Saturday to Friday. Until the end of 1936, the magazine was called *The Radio Times*; in its 8 January 1937 edition, however, it received a major style overhaul, at which point the word *The* was dropped from its title and the **journal** was thereafter known as simply *Radio Times*.

With the advent of television, the journal began to accommodate television schedules, and there have been a number of attempts throughout the years to integrate radio and television programs. Since 1989, radio programs have been grouped at the back of the magazine, and the brief has increasingly widened to include non-BBC programming and digital stations. In spite of the predominance of television within its pages in recent years, the magazine retains its original title.

See also LISTENER, THE; RADIO PICTORIAL; WORLD RADIO.

RADIO TOULOUSE. Radio Toulouse played a key part in the story of English-language commercial broadcasts from the continent in that it was the first station to broadcast sponsored programs regularly to Great Britain from France, in 1928, shortly after the illegal boosting of its transmitter strength. These were record programs, sponsored by Vox and presented by **Christopher Stone**. Thereafter, irregular English-language programming came from the station, although in early 1933, the **International Broadcasting Company (IBC)** was broadcasting *The IBC Half Hour* from the station on a regular basis.

In 1933, the station was destroyed by fire and did not reopen until 1937, when it recommenced transmissions from a greatly improved site. The U.K. concession moved to the W. E. D. Allen Agency. The company benefited from the expertise of **Peter Eckersley**, who had become a business associate. Somewhat surprisingly, the opening of the new English service in 1937 began with an inaugural address by Winston Churchill, followed by a talk by Eckersley. Program listings continued in *Radio Pictorial* until May 1938, at which point traces of U.K. transmissions disappeared.

See also COMMERCIAL RADIO; MUSIC.

RAY, TED (1906–1977). Born Charles Olden in Wigan, Ted Ray grew up in Liverpool and learned his **comedy** trade on the **music** hall stage, where his act, wisecracking interspersed with violin playing, carried the sobriquet "Fiddling and Fooling." He began his radio career in 1939 and, in 1949, gained his own half-hour radio show, *Ray's a Laugh*, which the **British Broadcasting Corporation** used as a replacement for *It's That Man Again*. The program ran for more than 10 years. Ray was also a regular member of the off-the-cuff comedy **quiz show** *Does the Team Think?* His theme tune was "You Are My Sunshine."

RAY'S A LAUGH. A **comedy series** that was centered on **Ted Ray** and a cast that included Kitty Bluett, Patricia Hayes, and Kenneth Connor, and ran from 1949–1961 on the **Light Programme**. The first series contained no less than 64 episodes and featured a young **Peter Sellers**, who later cited Ray as one of his great comedic influences.

READ, AL (1909–1987). Al Read was a comedian who came from a Lancashire background and was, until he broke into radio **comedy**, the latest generation in his family's meat pie manufacturing business. After becoming resident comedian on *Variety Fanfare* in 1951, he quickly became a popular favorite with audiences for his comedy of social observation, largely drawn from Lancashire working-class life. *The Al Read Show* ran throughout the late 1950s and into the 1960s on the **Light Programme**.

READ, MIKE (1947–). Mike Read is a **disc jockey**, writer, and broadcaster who began his radio career at the reading **commercial radio** station Radio 210 in 1976, where he co-presented a program with **Steve Wright** prior to joining **Radio Luxembourg** in 1977. He began his association with **BBC Radio 1** in 1978 and remained with the station in various capacities until 1991, during which time he spent five years as host of the breakfast program. Upon leaving Radio 1, Read worked for a number of **Gold** stations and, in subsequent years, has presented for **Classic FM** and Jazz FM, as well as many other regional and local stations. He later worked for **Magic** 1548 in the North of England and Radio Berkshire.

Outside radio, Read has a wide range of interests, including poetry, **music** composition, and literary history. He has published a range of books on these subjects, including a biography of poet Rupert Brooke.

REAL RADIO. A network of stations established during a period of years beginning in October 2000, partly from the **Century Radio** brand, and developed under the control of **Guardian Media Group (GMG)** Radio and subsequently **GCap Media** and **Global Radio**. The stations, in Wales, the North West of England, the North East of England, South Yorkshire, West Yorkshire, and Scotland, broadcast a range of material, including **music**, **news**, **sports**, and conversation, aimed at an audience ages 30 to 40. In June 2012, Global Radio bought GMG Radio, thus acquiring the Real Radio network, although the stations continued to be operated separately pending a regulatory review into the sale. In October 2012, the British government announced that Global's takeover would not be investigated on grounds of plurality. In May 2013, the Competition Commission published a report looking into the acquisition of GMG Radio, declaring that Global must dispose of some of its other broadcasting assets, a decision Global appealed. In February 2014, Global announced that it would rebrand Real Radio stations as **Heart**, using the latter's brand name and networked programming under license, with the exception of Real Radio Yorkshire and Real Radio North Wales, which would be sold to **Communicorp**.

See also COMMERCIAL RADIO.

REDHEAD, BRIAN (1929–1994). With a background in print journalism, Brian Redhead came to **BBC Radio 4's** flagship morning program *Today* in 1975. Although known for his confident and often combative style of interviewing—particularly politicians—he was keenly interested in comparative religion, in particular, Christianity, and often presented programs relating to this subject. He was chair of the *Radio 4 Debates* beginning in 1989 and, nine years before his debut on the *Today* program, host of *A Word in Edge-*

ways, starting in 1966. Born on Tyneside, Redhead retained a passionate commitment to the North of England, an engagement reflected in his election, shortly before his death, as chancellor of Manchester University.

See also NEWS.

REGIONAL PROGRAMME. The concept of a regional service for the **British Broadcasting Company** came from the corporation's chief engineer, **Peter Eckersley**, in 1924, but the Regional Programme did not begin until 21 October 1929; during this time, the 2LO transmitter moved to the **Brookmans Park Transmitting Station**, and London Regional was born. Other regional services were created in the Midlands (1931), Scotland (1932), West and Wales (1933), and Northern Ireland (1934), providing a localized alternative to the **National Programme**, which had begun under that name in 1930. The Regional and National programmes merged on 1 September 1939, to become the **BBC Home Service**. After the war, regional programs returned but as opt-outs from the main Home Service.

See also BBC RADIO 4.

REITH LECTURES. The **British Broadcasting Corporation** inaugurated the Reith Lectures in 1947, naming them after the first director-general, **John Reith**. Each year, the corporation invites a leading figure to deliver a series of lectures, with the aim of advancing public understanding and debate about significant issues of public interest. The lecture series is broadcast on **BBC Radio 4**, and the first was given in 1948, by Bertrand Russell. Chronologically, speakers and topics have been as follows:

1948	Bertrand Russell	*Authority and the Individual*
1949	Robert Birley	*Britain and Europe*
1950	John Zachary Young	*Doubt and Certainty in Science*
1951	Lord Radcliffe	*Power and the State*
1952	Arnold Toynbee	*The World and the West*
1953	Robert Oppenheimer	*Science and the Common Understanding*
1954	Sir Oliver Franks	*Britain and the Tide of World Affairs*
1955	Nikolaus Pevsner	*The Englishness of English Art*
1956	Sir Edward Appleton	*Science and the Nation*
1957	George Kennan	*Russia, the Atom, and the West*
1958	Bernard Lovell	*The Individual and the Universe*

1959	Peter Medawar	*The Future of Man*
1960	Edgar Wind	*Art and Anarchy*
1961	Margery Perham	*The Colonial Reckoning*
1962	Prof. George Carstairs	*This Island Now*
1963	Dr. Albert Sloman	*A Universe in the Making*
1964	Sir Leon Bagrit	*The Age of Automation*
1965	Robert Gardiner	*A World of Peoples*
1966	J. K. Galbraith	*The New Industrial State*
1967	Edmund Leach	*A Runaway World*
1968	Lester Pearson	*Peace in the Family of Man*
1969	Dr. Frank Frazer Darling	*Wilderness and Plenty*
1970	Dr. Donald Schon	*Change and Industrial Society*
1971	Richard Hoggart	*Only Connect*
1972	Andrew Schonfield	*Europe: Journey to an Unknown Destination*
1973	Prof. Alastair Buchan	*Change without War*
1974	Prof. Ralf Dahrendorf	*The New Liberty*
1975	Dr. Daniel Boorstin	*America and the World Experience*
1976	Dr. Colin Blakemore	*Mechanics of the Mind*
1977	Prof. A. H. Halsey	*Change in British Society*
1978	Rev. Dr. E. Norman	*Christianity and the World*
1979	Prof. Ali Mazrul	*The African Connection*
1980	Ian Kennedy	*Unmasking Medicine*
1981	Prof. Laurence Martin	*The Two-Edged Sword*
1982	Prof. Denis Donoghue	*The Arts without Mystery*
1983	Sir Douglas Wass	*Government and the Governed*
1984	Prof. John Searle	*Minds, Brains, and Science*
1985	David Henderson	*Innocence and Design*
1986	Lord McCluskey	*Law, Justice, and Democracy*
1987	Prof. Alexander Goehr	*The Survival of the Symphony*
1988	Prof. Geoffrey Hosking	*The Rediscovery of Politics*
1989	Jacques Darras	*Beyond the Tunnel of History*

1990	Rabbi Dr. Jonathan Sacks	*The Persistence of Faith*
1991	Dr. Steve Jones	*The Language of the Genes*
1992	no lecture series	
1993	Edward Said	*Representation and the Intellectual*
1994	Marina Warner	*Managing Monsters*
1995	Sir Richard Rogers	*Sustainable City*
1996	Jean Aitchison	*The Language Web*
1997	Patricia Williams	*The Genealogy of Race*
1999	Anthony Giddens	*Runaway World*
2000	**Chris Patten**	*Respect for the Earth*
	Sir John Brown	
	Thomas Lovejoy	
	Gro Harlem Brundtland	
	Vandana Shiva	
	HRH The Prince of Wales	
2001	Tom Kirkwood	*The End of Age*
2002	Prof. Onora O'Neill	*A Question of Trust*
2003	V. S. Ramachandrian	*The Emerging Mind*
2004	Wole Soyinka	*Climate of Fear*
2005	Lord Broers	*The Triumph of Technology*
2006	Daniel Barenboim	*In the Beginning Was Sound*
2007	Jeffrey Sachs	*Bursting at the Seams*
2008	Prof. Jonathan Spence	*Chinese Vistas*
2009	Michael Sandel	*A New Citizenship*
2010	Martin Rees	*Scientific Horizons*
2011	Aung San Suu Kyi/ Baroness Manningham-Buller	*Securing Freedom*
2012	Niall Ferguson	*The Rule of Law and Its Enemies*
2013	Grayson Perry	*Playing to the Gallery*
2014	Dr. Atul Gawande	*The Future of Medicine*

REITH, JOHN CHARLES WALSHAM (1889–1971). Sir John, later Lord Reith of Stonehaven, was born in Stonehaven, the son of a Scottish Presbyterian minister. Following his education at Glasgow Academy and Gresham's School in Norfolk, he served an engineering apprenticeship with the North British Locomotive Company. Reith was a major in the Royal Engineers during World War I from 1914–1915, when he was badly wounded. In 1919, he became general manager of William Beardmore and Co., an engineering firm in Glasgow, and shortly thereafter, at the age of 33, he was appointed general manager of the newly formed **British Broadcasting Company (BBC)**.

From the start, Reith held a high-minded vision that the BBC's role was to inform, educate, and entertain; this concept would shape the development of public service broadcasting in Britain ever after. Within seven months, he launched the *Radio Times* as the **journal** of the new organization, circumventing boycotts from the Newspaper Proprietors' Association. One of Reith's great achievements of the early years was enabling the BBC to negotiate the events of 1926, when Britain was hit by the **General Strike** and newspapers ceased publication. He saw a great opportunity to demonstrate the immediacy and **news** power of radio.

When the company changed to a corporation under Royal Charter on 1 January 1927, Reith became its first director-general, a post he retained until 1938. He was knighted in 1927. Reith was a complex man whose concepts created the term *Reithian*, a word still used to describe the ideology that inspired his attitude toward public service broadcasting. Aspects of his paternalistic attitude and an autocratic style of management brought him considerable criticism. In particular, his Sabbatarian policy during the prewar years of the BBC, forbidding light entertainment on Sundays, created opportunities for **commercial radio** entrepreneurs using continental station bases to directly attack the BBC's monopoly (*see also* SUNDAY BROADCASTING POLICY).

It was at the bidding of Prime Minister Neville Chamberlain that Reith left the BBC in 1938, to become chairman of Imperial Airways. Although his post-BBC years were filled with achievement and recognition—he was created baron in 1940 and was chairman of the Commonwealth Telecommunications Board from 1946–1950, during which time (1948) the BBC inaugurated the **Reith Lectures** in his honor—there remained a sense that he felt betrayed by the direction that British broadcasting took after his departure from a position of direct influence. Reith wrote two volumes of autobiography: *Broadcast over Britain* (1924) and *Into the Wind* (1949). He also kept a diary, which was subsequently published.

RELAY EXCHANGES. The development of relay exchanges—organizations specializing in the dissemination of radio programs via telephone wires as opposed to wirelessly from transmitters—was a crucial factor in the advance of **commercial radio** in Britain before World War II. Their existence is also significant in that they predated by many years the development of cable broadcasting in the United Kingdom.

The idea of sending material through a telephone wire for public—as opposed to private—consumption, had been present beginning in the 1890s (*see* ELECTROPHONE). With the development of radio on a mass audience scale in the late 1920s and early 1930s, the idea of wired relays, under license to the **Post Office** as controller of the lines, became a key issue in British radio. One of the most enthusiastic supporters of "wired broadcasting" was the first chief engineer for the **British Broadcasting Company (BBC)**, **Peter Eckersley**. After his departure from the BBC in 1929, Eckersley worked strenuously at developing the medium, one of the benefits of which was that the vagaries of signal fade and strength could be eliminated; this was particularly useful in blocks of flats and other poor reception areas.

Eckersley's experiments gave prospective listeners a choice of four programs on a subscription basis. With the BBC offering two—the **National Programme** and **Regional Programme**—there was room for competition on an equal technical quality basis. This—and the fact that a subscription to a relay service was cheap and therefore attractive to the poorer sectors of society—was of major significance to the issue of commercial competition from the continent. The BBC sought to reach an agreement with two of the relay companies—Standard Radio Relay Services and Radio Central Exchanges—that they would relay only BBC programs. The scheme was thwarted by the Post Office, however, with the argument that "it would be unfair to impose restrictions on relay subscribers [that] were not imposed on the private owners of wireless sets."

Major relay subscription areas were established in Leicester, Derby, Nottingham, Sheffield, Middlesborough, Newcastle, and Carlisle. For obvious reasons of reception, Wales—North and South—was "wired," and the city of Hull boasted the most extensive wired network in Europe. The growth of relay services in Britain during the first half of the 1930s was remarkable. In 1931, there were 132 exchanges, with 43,889 subscribers. In 1932, there were 194 exchanges, with 82,690 subscribers. From this almost doubling of subscribers, the growth in subsequent years was startling. In 1935, there were 343 exchanges, with 233,554 subscribers. By 1939, the number of relay exchanges had fallen, partly because of a vigorous campaign against the services by radio receiver manufacturers. In December of that year, there were 284 exchanges, with 270,596 subscribers. Nonetheless, taking into account the number of listeners per household, relay services were, by this time, reaching a total audience of 1,033,677. With World War II came the end of relay exchanges, and in spite of pressure from enthusiasts like Ecker-sley (*see POWER BEHIND THE MICROPHONE, THE*), it would be more than 60 years before the concept of wired—or cable—transmission was re-adopted in Britain.

RELAY STATIONS. When the **British Broadcasting Company** estab-lished its first eight stations between 1922–1924, it achieved a geographical spread of the United Kingdom, which it quickly sought to enhance by the establishment of a series of relay stations, responsible only for transmitting program material, rather than originating it. These stations were, in chrono-logical order of opening, as follows:

Sheffield (6FL)	16 November 1923
Plymouth (5PY)	28 March 1924
Edinburgh (2EH)	1 May 1924
Liverpool (6LV)	11 June 1924
Leeds/Bradford (2LS)	8 July 1924
Hull (6KH)	15 August 1924
Nottingham (5NG)	16 September 1924
Stoke-on-Trent (6ST)	21 October 1924
Dundee (2DE)	12 November 1924
Swansea (5SX)	12 December 1924

By 1939, the number of **relay exchanges** had fallen, partly due to a vigorous campaign against the services by radio receiver manufacturers. In December of that year, there were 284 exchanges, with 270,596 subscribers. Nonethe-less, taking into account the number of listeners per household, relay services were, by this time, reaching a total audience of 1,033,677. With World War II came an end to the exchanges, and in spite of pressure from enthusiasts, like **Peter Eckersley** (*see POWER BEHIND THE MICROPHONE, THE*) it would be more than 60 years before the concept of wired—or cable—trans-mission was readopted in Great Britain.

RELIGIOUS PROGRAMS. The relationship between British broadcast-ing—particularly the **British Broadcasting Company/Corporation (BBC)**—and religious content is a complex one. From its earliest days, the BBC saw as part of its role as a public service broadcaster the need to include religious—that is to say Christian—instruction and to this end it worked in partnership with a Churches Advisory Board, which, in turn, exercised con-siderable control on program policy and content. In the 1920s and 1930s, the strict **Sunday broadcasting policy** introduced by **John Reith** and overseen by such bodies ensured that material was strictly monitored to reflect the sacredness of the day, exposing the BBC to criticism from broader social groups and competition from **commercial radio** interests.

There were also discussions and disputes as to what representation other churches beyond the traditional Church of England should have in broadcasting. In recent years, religious educational programs have been somewhat modified to take into account a more humanist and ethical approach to a changing society, but many program slots with BBC schedules continue to reflect the historical placement of material containing—in the broadest sense—religious instruction. These include *Thought for the Day* within **BBC Radio 4's** *Today* program and *Pause for Thought* on **BBC Radio 2's** breakfast show. Other long-term programs have included *Daily Service* and *The Epilogue*. As part of its policy, the BBC published *The BBC Hymn Book* for many years, and **BBC Radio 3** continues to broadcast *Choral Evensong* live from a major church or cathedral each week.

Controversy has included the problems of religious broadcasting during wartime and issues raised by religious **drama**, for example, the 12-part **series** dramatizing Dorothy L. Sayers's *The Man Born to Be King*. Less controversial has been the long-running *Festival of Nine Lessons and Carols*, broadcast on both radio and television from King's College Chapel in Cambridge each Christmas, for many a staple of the holiday season. Today the BBC includes programs of moral ethical issues within a broader religious remit, as well as material that reflects the multicultural nature of modern Britain.

In its early years, independent local radio was strictly regulated by the **Independent Broadcasting Authority** to include religious programming within its public service responsibility; however, this was interpreted with more freedom than within the BBC, and while content was closely monitored by the regulator, during the 1980s, such programs as *All Faiths*, from the Bournemouth station Two Counties Radio (2CR), provided popular blends of **music** and multicultural content that were inclusive rather than exclusive and appealed to a wide range of listeners. With the further relaxation of regulations, most religious programming has disappeared from commercial radio, while a number of community stations are run by specific religious and ethnic groups. In addition, there are several commercial stations broadcasting online and on **Digital Audio Broadcasting** that cater to evangelical Christian and other ethnic and multicultural religious groups and faiths.

RESTRICTED SERVICE LICENSE (RSL). The concept of the RSL radio station was created by the **Radio Authority**, regulator of U.K. **commercial radio** from 1990–2003. It has subsequently been developed by the regulatory successor, the **Office of Communications (Ofcom)**. The RSL was part of the widening of public access to radio broadcasting, and successful licensees are permitted to run a radio station, usually for as many as 28 days, either on **frequency modulation (FM)** or **amplitude modulation (AM)** on low power. The scheme is particularly attractive to charities, festivals, and other specific events. More extended versions are available for such institutions as hospitals and student organizations. It also permits those planning to apply for a full-time license, for example, potential **community radio** stations, to test audiences within their target area. RSLs are issued at Ofcom's discretion, subject to frequency availability and adherence to various specified basic rules and technical criteria.

REVENGE, THE. A 30-minute radio play without words written and performed by **Andrew Sachs** and produced by **Glyn Dearman** in 1978, and first broadcast on **BBC Radio 3**. The program was recorded in various locations using **binaural recording**, a technique whereby two microphones are placed in the position of the human ears to replicate as near as possible the reality of listening, particularly when heard through stereo headphones. The plot of the play involved a man on the run who gets revenge on his enemy by finding him and drowning him. Sachs, a ubiquitous radio actor, used the concept to demonstrate that there were ways in which radio **drama** could escape the confines of studio/script-based limitations. Critics of the play pointed out that while such an experiment was capable of telling a story through sound effects and incoherent human vocalization, the subtler aspects of motive and characterization proved to be beyond such techniques. *The Revenge* has been rebroadcast many times since its first transmission, particularly on **BBC Radio 4 Extra**.

REYNOLDS, GILLIAN (1935–). Gillian Reynolds was a well-known radio critic who began her career in the field in 1967, as radio critic for the *Guardian* newspaper. In 1974, she was the founding program controller of the Liverpool independent local radio station **Radio City**, making her the first woman controller of a **commercial radio** station in the United Kingdom. Thereafter, she became radio critic for the *Daily Telegraph* and one of the most respected voices in British radio criticism. Reynolds was chairman of the **Charles Parker Archive Trust** at Birmingham Central Library, a role in which she was succeeded by **Tim Blackmore** in 2011. She served for five years on the Consultative Committee of the National Sound Archive and became the first fellow of the **Radio Academy** in 1990. In 1999, Reynolds was made a Member of the Most Excellent Order of the British Empire for her contributions to journalism.

See also WOMEN.

RIDERS OF THE RANGE. Created by **Charles Chilton** as the first U.K.-made radio **series** in the western genre. Broadcast on the **Light Programme** from 1949–1953, the series was based on known information relating to the history of the American West. Chilton also scripted a "spin-off" cartoon series in the children's comic book the *Eagle*. The **music** for the program was created by the Four Ramblers, one of whom, Val Doonican, went on to achieve fame in a solo singing career.

RILEY, PHIL (?–). Phil Riley is owner of **Orion Media** in the West Midlands, a group he created in 2009, from the purchase of a number of stations in the region from **Global Radio**. He began his career in radio at **BRMB** in Birmingham in 1980 and subsequently directed a number of stations in the Midlands, north of England and London. In 1994, Riley joined the newly created **Chrysalis** and was chief executive of the group from 1999–2007, when he oversaw the sale of Chrysalis to Global Radio. He was active in the development of **Digital Audio Broadcasting** and is a fellow of the **Radio Academy**.

See also COMMERCIAL RADIO.

ROBINSON FAMILY, THE. Initially billed as a "day-to-day history of an ordinary family" (changing by its end to an "everyday story of everyday people," thus predating *The Archers'* billing as an "everyday story of country folk"), *The Robinson Family* was the first exploration of the genre of the daily **serial** by the **British Broadcasting Corporation**, starting in July 1945. To create a sense of authenticity, the production team, writers, and actors were not billed. It was broadcast at 2:45 p.m. each afternoon on the **BBC Home Service** and ended its run on Christmas Eve 1947.

See also DRAMA; SERIES; SOAP OPERAS.

"ROMANY". Rev. George Bramwell Evens (1883–1943) was a Methodist minister whose roots lay in gypsy stock, and in October 1932, he began a popular **series** of "walks" in the studios of the **British Broadcasting Corporation** North Region, in Manchester. The *Out with Romany* programs were initially only heard in the North of England, but beginning in 1938, they were broadcast on the **National Programme**. In these simulated nature walks, Evens was joined by two children, Muriel Levy and Doris Gambell, and a spaniel named "Raq." The programs became extremely popular and spawned a series of books by Evens.

See also CHILDREN'S PROGRAMS.

ROSEN, MICHAEL (1946–). Michael Rosen is a children's novelist and poet, and a regular broadcaster on British radio and television. After studying at Wadham College in Oxford in 1969, he became a graduate trainee at the **British Broadcasting Corporation**. He has subsequently worked on a freelance basis. In addition to presenting a range of radio **documentary features**, Rosen regularly hosts *Word of Mouth* on **BBC Radio 4**.

ROSS, JONATHAN (1960–). One of the most recognizable entertainers in U.K. media, Jonathan Ross's hosting of his highly successful Saturday morning program on **BBC Radio 2** from 1999–2010 complemented his television work for the **British Broadcasting Corporation (BBC)**, and in 2005, an independent panel commissioned by *Radio Times* voted him the most successful radio broadcaster in Britain. Born in the East End of London, his first radio work was in 1987, when he stood in for two weeks on **BBC Radio 1**. The following year, Ross joined Richard Branson's **Virgin Radio** station, where his producer was **Chris Evans**. Meanwhile, he continued to make freelance appearances on the **BBC Radio 4** program *Loose Ends* from 1987–1989.

In 1998, Ross returned to Virgin Radio with *The Jonathan Ross Show*, working with his producer, Andy Davies, for the first time. The format, of producer and presenter sharing on-air banter, proved popular, and when Radio 2 controller **James Moir** brought him to the network, the format transferred with Ross and achieved new heights of critical and audience success. In 2000, Ross won a **Sony Radio Academy Award** for **music** presentation; other awards have included Radio Program of the Year and Radio Personality of the Year at the annual **Television and Radio Industries Club** in 2000 and 2001, respectively.

Ross's on-air comments both on radio and television frequently caused controversy, and beginning in 2009, his Radio 2 program was prerecorded 24 hours before transmission. This followed a guest appearance on **Russell Brand's** show on the same network, during which the two men left lewd messages, during a prerecorded program, on the answering machine of actor **Andrew Sachs** relating to Sachs's granddaughter. Brand resigned from the program as a result, and Ross was suspended without pay for 12 weeks. The BBC was fined £150,000 for the broadcast, and the controller of Radio 2, **Lesley Douglas**, also resigned. In January 2010, Ross decided not to renew his contract with the BBC. His place on Radio 2 was taken by **Graham Norton**, who also took over Ross's Friday night television show.

See also COMMERCIAL RADIO; DISC JOCKEY (DJ).

ROUND BRITAIN QUIZ. Starting in 1947, and continuing on **BBC Radio 4**, *Round Britain Quiz* is the longest-running radio **quiz show** in Britain. Teams from various U.K. regions play in head-to-head tournaments in a series of multipart questions. The winner of the 2014 **series** was Scotland.

ROUND THE HORNE. A famous **comedy series** written by a team of writers led by **Barry Took** and **Marty Feldman**, and including Brian Cooke, Johnnie Mortimer, and Donald Webster. It was the successor to *Beyond Our Ken*. Both programs revolved around **Kenneth Horne** and *Round the Horne*, which ran on the **Light Programme** from March 1965 to June 1968. At its peak, 15 million listeners a week were tuning in to hear a blend of innuendo, camp, familiar catchphrases, and wordplay from a regular team that featured **Kenneth Williams**, Betty Marsden, Hugh Paddick, and Bill Pertwee. In 2002, a stage version, *Round the Horne Revisited*, devised by Cooke, re-created the program, with actors impersonating the original players with considerable success.

ROUND, HENRY JOSEPH (1881–1966). H. J. Round was a highly gifted radio engineer and inventor who joined the **Marconi Company** in 1902. After working in the United States for the company, where he devised the elements of direction finding, he returned to Britain to work personally with **Guglielmo Marconi**, before further travel to Ireland and South America in 1912, where he operated two wireless stations on the upper reaches of the Amazon, redesigning them to operate on two separate wavelengths by day and by night, the first time that deliberate use had been made of wavelength differences to solve problems of transmission.

World War I featured Round in distinguished service, working in communications, most notably when through his wireless operations, the movements of the German fleet prior to the Battle of Jutland were detected. He also designed the first telephony transmitters and receivers for airborne use. He received the Military Cross for his services in 1918. After the war, he helped set up the experimental station at **Chelmsford** and engineered the first public broadcast entertainment on 15 June 1920, a recital by Australian prima donna Dame Nellie Melba (*see* "MELBA" BROADCAST). When, two years later, the **Writtle** experiments led to the establishment of 2LO at **Marconi House** in London, the transmitter was designed by Round.

Other contributions were the creation of the artificial echo system and the Sykes-Round microphone. In 1931, Round set up a private practice as a research consultant, and he continued to work, largely on the defense applications of wireless, both for the Admiralty and the Marconi Company. He filed 117 patent applications during his lifetime, the last of which was recorded in 1962, when he was 81.

ROYAL BROADCASTS. The first broadcast by a reigning British monarch was at the opening of the British Empire Exhibition in 1924, when George V spoke to the assembled crowds. He was preceded by Prince George (later George VI), who made the infamous speech that became a central part of the film *The King's Speech.* The first Christmas broadcast by a member of the British Royal Family was on 25 December 1932, when King George V spoke to an estimated audience of 20 million people throughout the British Empire. The broadcast was made possible through the use of **shortwave** broadcasting and engineering advances made by the **British Broadcasting Corporation** through the development of its newly established **Empire Service**. The event began a long tradition of Christmas Day broadcasts by the reigning monarch that continue on radio and television in modern times.

The monarchy has also used radio to communicate with its subjects at other key times, notably in 1936, when, on 11 December, Edward VIII made his famous abdication speech. At the outbreak of World War II, George VI spoke to the nation in a broadcast that lasted six minutes; although his vocal impediment is evident, the speech helped him make a triumphant connection with the people and cemented the bond between monarch and country, as well as enhancing the reputation of radio as a tool of immediate communication during such times. As a young princess, Queen Elizabeth II made her first public speech via radio on 13 October 1940, with an address to the children of the Commonwealth, many of them living away from home due to war. Her younger sister, Princess Margaret, joined in at the end. The Queen also broadcast on the occasion of her 21st birthday and at her coronation, on 2 June 1953.

Other broadcasts have reflected dark times in the history of the country and the Royal Family and have included the speech made by the queen on 5 September 1997, following the death of Diana, Princess of Wales. In more recent times, many of these types of royal broadcasts have been made through the medium of television, but the tradition of the Christmas broadcasts continues on both radio and television.

Added to the direct communication from the monarch have been numerous broadcasts relating to the British Royal Family, including live relays of the coronation of 1953—a key moment in the development of the television audience—and the funeral of Diana, Princess of Wales.

RUSSELL, AUDREY (1906–1989). Born in Dublin and trained as an actress, Audrey Russell joined the London Fire Brigade shortly before World War II broke out and worked actively in this capacity throughout the London blitz. Based near **Broadcasting House**, she came to the notice of the **British Broadcasting Corporation (BBC)** after being interviewed on the effects of air raids. She was invited to make a **series** of broadcasts on the work of the

Auxiliary Fire Service, which resulted in a secondment to the Air Ministry, from where she broadcast a series of **talks** on the work of the Women's Auxiliary Air Force.

In 1942, the BBC appointed Russell as traveling reporter for the magazine program *Radio Newsreel*, with the specific task of touring Britain, reporting on the effects of war from various parts of the country. She became an accredited war correspondent and sent dispatches from Belgium, Holland, Norway, and Germany. After the war, she became a reporter for the **BBC Home Service**, although her great skill—and love—was for commentary rather than reportage.

In 1947, Russell was part of the **outside broadcast** team covering the wedding of Princess Elizabeth, which led to her becoming one of the key members of commentary teams covering state occasions for the BBC; she worked on relays from the Festival of Britain in 1951, and went on the first of many royal tours in 1952. She was in Westminster Abbey, commentating on the coronation of Queen Elizabeth II in 1953, and went on to cover numerous other events of national significance, including the funeral of Winston Churchill in 1965 and the Silver Jubilee of 1977. Russell was the only woman to become an accredited war correspondent during World War II and the first female **news** reporter on the Home Service. She became a freeman of the city of London in 1967 and was appointed a Member of the Royal Victorian Order in 1976.

See also ROYAL BROADCASTS; WOMEN.

S

6 MUSIC. *See* BBC RADIO 6 MUSIC.

7DIGITAL. 7digital Group is a digital music and radio platform that develops global streaming of radio and audio. In June 2014, **Unique Broadcasting Company Media** merged with 7digital to form the 7digital Group.

SACHS, ANDREW (1930–). Andrew Sachs is a German-born actor who came to Britain with his parents in 1938. He has been heavily involved with creative radio throughout his career; notable in the 1950s was **Frederick Bradnum's** *Private Dreams and Public Nightmares*, made by the **BBC Radiophonic Workshop**. Sachs's work as a narrator made him one of the best-known voices on British radio and television, and he appeared in numerous radio **dramas**, **series**, and poetry programs. In 1978, he wrote and performed *The Revenge*, a play without words for radio, as an example of the possibilities of radio drama breaking free of heavily script-based productions. The play, which was 30 minutes in duration, was made using binaural stereo on location. It has been repeated many times.

In October 2008, the **British Broadcasting Corporation (BBC)** apologized to Sachs for prank telephone calls regarding Sachs's granddaughter, Georgina Baillie, broadcast on **BBC Radio 2** by **Russell Brand** and **Jonathan Ross** during Brand's prerecorded radio show. Ross was suspended from the BBC, Brand and Radio 2 controller **Lesley Douglas** resigned, and the BBC was fined £150,000.

SAGA RADIO. Saga Radio grew out of the Saga brand, created in the 1950s by Sidney De Haan, who identified a growth market for providing products and services to older members of the community—initially the retired population. Beginning with the holiday market, Saga diversified into magazine publication (1984) and insurance and investment (1987).

It was the success of *Saga Magazine* that encouraged the company to explore the possibilities of radio at a time when the U.K. **commercial radio** sector was about to enter a period of change and growth. Pursuing preliminary work on an application for the first national commercial license (*See* CLASSIC FM), the company went on to undertake its own research, leading to the establishment of Saga Radio in 1994. Market research showed that radio services for listeners ages 50 and older were lacking, and given that this age group was clearly identified as Saga's brand target, the group moved forward in the application process for a number of licenses. These included the West Midlands, Yorkshire, and East Midlands licenses. In 1999, Saga appointed Ron Coles as its director of radio, and subsequently the group invested heavily in digital radio, with both its Saga Radio regional stations and its digital-only Primetime Radio national station.

In 2006, the stations were sold to the **Guardian Media Group**, which relaunched them alongside its Smooth stations as **Smooth Radio**. The Saga Radio brand ceased to exist on 23 March 2007, with the Smooth Radio brand launching two days later, on 26 March. There are six of these stations, three of each now owned by **Global Radio** and **Communicorp** as a franchise.

SARONY, LESLIE (1897–1985). Leslie Sarony was a well-known song-writer and entertainer who enjoyed considerable success during the 1920s and 1930s as a stage and recording artist, and, in 1935, formed, with pianist Leslie Holmes, the variety double act they called "The Two Leslies." In November 1936, they created an occasional **comedy series** entitled *Radio Pie*, which Sarony himself devised, featuring a cast of well-known variety performers, including **Tommy Handley** and Anne Ziegler. It proved to be so popular that a stage version toured Britain in 1939, to considerable acclaim.

Holmes retired in 1946, and Sarony continued the act for three more years with Michael Cole, before returning to solo variety work in the late 1940s. He continued to work until near the end of his life, in demand as a "straight" character actor in stage productions ranging from the work of **Samuel Beckett** and Shakespeare to a film role in *Chitty Chitty Bang Bang*. In 1983, Sarony appeared in his second royal variety performance, less than two years before his death from cancer in February 1985.

SATURDAY CLUB. A live program of popular **music** hosted by **Brian Matthew** that began on the **Light Programme** in 1957, as *Saturday Skiffle Club*, and continued until 1969. It was initially one of the few shows on **British Broadcasting Corporation** radio that catered to a youth market. The show featured a blend of interviews, records, and "live" sessions with leading artists and bands, and it was responsible for introducing many U.S. artists to U.K. radio audiences; in 1960, the program featured sets with Gene Vincent and Eddie Cochran, and in June 1966, to celebrate its 400th edition, guests included Cliff Richard and the Shadows, Billy Fury, Marianne Faithfull, **Humphrey Lyttelton**, and the Beatles.

SATURDAY LIVE. Launched in 2006, with **Maria Williams** as executive producer and **Fi Glover** as presenter, *Saturday Live* is a popular weekend radio program, airing on **BBC Radio 4** at 9.00 a.m. on Saturday mornings. It won the gold **Sony Radio Academy Award** for best U.K. speech program in 2008. **Richard Coles** took over as the program's main presenter in March 2011, and in May 2012, the show was extended from one hour to 90 minutes.

SATURDAY SKIFFLE CLUB. A precursor of the broader-ranging *Saturday Club* that grew out of the U.K. trend that involved young people making their own **music**. **Brian Matthew**, who continued to host the program after its name change, introduced many professional artists in the field, including Chas McDevitt and Nancy Whiskey, who had a major hit with their version of *Freight Train*, and other groups of the era, among them the Vipers and Johnny Duncan and the Blue Grass Boys. The program was produced by Jimmy Grant. In April 1958, **Radio Luxembourg** capitalized on the trend by introducing *Amateur Skiffle Club*.

SAVEEN, ALBERT (1915–1994). Working under his surname, Saveen was a highly successful ventriloquist and the first to have his own **series** on radio—a **Light Programme** show called *Midday with Daisy May*. He was originally a printer; a cockney who developed a sophisticated presentation style with his doll "Daisy May," Saveen had suffered lung damage during the war and later said it was the effect of this that inadvertently led him to create the voice he used in his ventriloquist act.

See also EDUCATING ARCHIE.

SAVILE, JIMMY (1926–2011). A former Yorkshire miner, Jimmy Savile's extrovert style was first heard on **Radio Luxembourg**, before he moved in 1968 to **BBC Radio 1**, where he presented *Savile's Travels*, a highly popular program that was transferred to **commercial radio** in 1989. He became widely known as a television personality and was knighted in 1990, for his services to charity. After his death, however, a television **documentary** explored claims of sexual abuse, leading to a criminal investigation that uncovered hundreds of allegations during a span of 60 years. A number of public bodies—including the **British Broadcasting Corporation**—were subjected to examination, and in January 2013, a joint report by the National Society for the Prevention of Cruelty to Children and the Metropolitan Police stated that 450 people had made complaints against Savile and that the ages of complainants ranged from eight to 47 years. In the meantime, a broader investigation into the actions of the British media, **Operation Yewtree**, was launched in October 2012, involving enquiries into sexual abuse claims against a number of high-profile living individuals and media personalities, in addition to Savile.

SAVOY HILL. The first permanent home of the **British Broadcasting Company (BBC)**. Two Savoy Hill was part of a building owned by the Institute of Electrical Engineers (IEE) on the Thames Embankment, adjacent to the Savoy Hotel. The IEE leased the building to the BBC, and the building was the scene of some of the most important early radio experiments, notably in **drama**. The BBC, in the form of 2LO, moved into Savoy Hill on 2 February 1923, and broadcasting began from the premises on 1 May of that year. Photographic images of the studios show broadcasting in a more elegant time; one of the studios was modeled on the lounge of Eastbourne's **Grand Hotel**, itself the origin of a famous **series** of light orchestral **music** programs that ran into the 1970s. Because of the building's proximity to the Savoy Hotel, a number of the dance bands employed by the hotel became regular broadcasters, most notably the **Savoy Orpheans**. The last program, *The End of Savoy Hill*, produced by **Lance Sieveking**, took place on 14 May 1932, ending with a final announcement by **Stuart Hibberd**, after which an unidentified voice from the new headquarters was heard, ensuring complete continuity: "This is **Broadcasting House** calling."

SAVOY ORPHEANS. The Savoy Orpheans became the most famous of the Savoy Hotel dance bands to perform at Savoy Hill during the 1920s, becoming major radio and recording stars. The band recorded prolifically from its formation in 1923 until 1927, initially under Debroy Summers, who led the first direct relay from the hotel on 11 October 1923, with Cyril Ramon Newton and finally pianist Carroll Gibbons.

SCOTT, ROGER (1943–1989). After a stint as a merchant seaman, Roger Scott began his broadcasting career on U.S. and Canadian radio stations during the 1960s, before joining the renowned biscuit factory radio station United Biscuits Network. In 1973, he was a member of the original on-air team at **Capital Radio**, where his afternoon shows gained significant audiences, with an emphasis on such **features** as *Three O'Clock Thrill* and *Hitline*. After 15 years, Scott moved from Capital to **BBC Radio 1** in 1988 (although he had appeared on **British Broadcasting Corporation** radio in the early 1970s using the pseudonym "Bob Baker"). His devotion to the **music** he played and eschewing of the cult of personality gained him a loyal fan base, and Scott broadcast his *Saturday Sequence* and *Late Night Sunday* programs until shortly before his early death from throat cancer.
See also COMMERCIAL RADIO; DISC JOCKEY (DJ).

SCOTTISH RADIO HOLDINGS (SRH). SRH grew out the third **commercial radio** license to be granted in the United Kingdom, when **Radio Clyde** went on the air in December 1973, serving Glasgow. The first two London stations—**London Broadcasting Company** and **Capital Radio**—had suffered troubled starts a few months earlier and endured some initial financial problems. Clyde, on the other hand, was an immediate success.

In 1990, U.K. radio ownership rules were relaxed, enabling the two main Scottish stations, Radio Clyde and Radio Forth, to merge in 1991, creating SRH. In 1995, the company expanded into print, buying newspaper and magazine interests in Ireland, Northern Ireland, and Scotland. In the meantime, its radio division continued to expand, acquiring Today FM, Ireland's independent national station, and the Dublin-based FM104. SRH's radio division comprised 22 **analog** services, one digital service, and six digital licenses. In June 2005, the group was acquired by **Emap** Radio.

SCRAPBOOK. A highly popular and valuable **series** of historical **documentaries** that was the first of its kind, starting in December 1933, with *Scrapbook for 1913*. The premise behind the series was that each program would be based on one year, which would then be examined historically through archives, **music**, and reconstruction. The programs were researched by journalist Leslie Baily, who devised the idea and also created two books based on the series, which ran until 1974. The 40th anniversary of the founding of the **British Broadcasting Company** was marked in 1962, by *Scrapbook for 1922*. The programs were presented by **Freddy Grisewood**.

SECOMBE, HARRY (1921–2001). Harry Secombe was famed for his work on the groundbreaking radio **comedy series** *The Goon Show*, on which his stock character was "Neddy Seagoon." The program, on which he worked with **Spike Milligan**, **Peter Sellers**, and **Michael Bentine**, was first broadcast in 1949, and ran for nine years. Secombe later moved into television and film, and was an accomplished singer. He was knighted in 1981.

SELFRIDGES. A large department store on London's Oxford Street, founded in 1909, by American retail magnate Harry Gordon Selfridge (1864–1947). From 1924–1929, the building housed the **British Broadcasting Company's** 2LO transmitter and aerials. The transmitter had formerly been situated at **Marconi House** on the Strand. In another link to the early days of broadcasting, in 1925, a fashion **talk** sponsored by Selfridges was broadcast in English from the studio on the Eiffel Tower in Paris, organized by Captain **Leonard Plugge**, a pioneer of early commercial broadcasting who went on to establish the **International Broadcasting Company** and

Radio Normandy's English-language transmissions. Thus, the store can claim to have been involved in both public service broadcasting and **commercial radio**, almost from their inception, in Britain.

SELLERS, PETER (1925–1980). Born in Southsea, on the south coast of England, Peter Sellers was one of the United Kingdom's most gifted comic actors, enjoying considerable success in film in later years. Nonetheless, it was as a member of the revolutionary *The Goon Show* for which he is best remembered in terms of radio. Drafted into the Royal Air Force (RAF) at the age of 18, Sellers's ambition to become a pilot was thwarted by his poor eyesight. Thus, he became an official RAF concert entertainer. Seeking to develop a career in this field after World War II, he contacted producer Roy Speer, who engaged him for the 1948 program *Showtime*. This, in turn, led to *The Goon Show*. A number of comic recordings followed, and Sellers subsequently participated less in radio as his film career burgeoned.

See also COMEDY.

SERIALS. The serial genre can be divided into two forms: dramatized and nondramatized. The former was the first to be broadcast by the **British Broadcasting Company (BBC)**. From September 1923 to February 1924, the BBC transmitted a serialized reading of an adventure novel for boys by Herbert Strang entitled *Jack Hardy*. In December 1925, the BBC ran a three-part serial entitled *The Mayfair Mystery*, which was in the form of a competition, inviting listeners to find the correct solution to a detective story for a prize of £100. The first adult serialized reading was *At the Villa Rose*, read in five episodes by Campbell Gullan in July 1926.

The first **drama** serial was Hilda Chamberlain's *Ghostly Fingers*, broadcast in three parts on the evenings of 23 and 28 August 1926, with parts one and two being transmitted on the first of those evenings; however, it was not until June 1935 that the first true dramatized radio serial in the modern sense was broadcast by the **British Broadcasting Corporation**. This was *The Mystery of the Seven Cafes*, produced by A. W. Hanson and featuring **Norman Shelley** in the central role. By the time World War II broke out, **commercial radio** was developing the genre of the popular radio serial, inspired by the experiences of such U.S. agencies as the **J. Walter Thompson Organization**.

After the war, a number of children's serials gained large audiences, including *Norman and Henry Bones* and *Toytown*. Crossover programming between generations was achieved with the 1950s science fiction serial *Journey into Space*, while *Mrs. Dale's Diary*, later renamed *The Dales* starting in 1948, appealed to a largely female daytime audience. This was replaced by *Waggoners' Walk* in 1969, which ran until 1980. The most successful serial on U.K. radio is *The Archers*, a daily serial with an omnibus edition broadcast on Sundays. This began in 1950 and continues today. In 1997, the **BBC World Service** created a serial for an international audience entitled *Westway*, which, despite considerable success with global listeners, was axed in a round of cost-cutting measures in 2005.

See also SOAP OPERAS.

SERIES. The genre of the radio series was first successfully developed in the United States. The concept was—and remains—a program that operates on a regular basis—usually weekly—using the same formula of personnel, style, and content, broadcast at the same time on the same day. **Comedy** series and **quiz shows** have historically conveniently fallen into this category. For comedy, the most durable format—one that was to form the blueprint for many that followed—was first created by *Band Waggon* in 1938. This, however, was not the first comedy series; that honor goes to *Radio Radiance* (1925), featuring **Tommy Handley**. That same year, the **British Broadcasting Company (BBC)** broadcast the first series of popular **music** programs, entitled *Winners*. Throughout the 1930s, **commercial radio** capitalized on the concept of familiarity and habit in the radio audience, and virtually every program on these stations was made as a series. At the same time, social issues were being addressed in such BBC series as *Time to Spare*, which focused on the plight of the unemployed.

There have been—and continue to be—series in every genre on U.K. radio; in the field of **news** and **current affairs**, **BBC Radio 4** has long provided in-depth coverage through programs like *Analysis* and *From Our Own Correspondent*, weekly series of informed comment and reportage. Comedy series have included many classic programs, among them *The Goon Show*, *Round the Horne*, and *Take It from Here*. The long-running *I'm Sorry I Haven't a Clue* owes much of its success to the personalities of its participants, while series of readings, for instance, the daily *Book at Bedtime*, have become institutions. Daily programs include the **news** programs *Today* and *The World at One*, as well as *Woman's Hour* and *You and Yours*, all on Radio 4.

SHAPLEY, OLIVE (1910–1999). Olive Shapley was a highly imaginative and creative **documentary** program maker and broadcaster who spent 40 years working for the **British Broadcasting Corporation (BBC)** in both radio and television. Joining the Corporation in 1934, after gaining an education at Oxford, she worked with some of the most significant names in broadcasting. Starting on *Children's Hour*, in Manchester, she became North Region controller of the program.

Shapley became part of the thriving left-wing Features Department developed by **E. A. Harding** and, between 1937–1939, made a number of social-action documentaries, for example, *Miners' Wives*, *They Speak for Themselves*, and *The Classic Soil*. This last program, written by Joan Littlewood, compared the living conditions of the Manchester working class with those described by Frederick Engels 100 years earlier. In 1939, she married John Scarlett Alexander Salt, director of programs in Manchester, and resigned from her staff position because of the ruling that married couples were not permitted to work for the BBC together.

As soon as World War II was declared, however, Shapley returned as a freelancer and made memorable programs about the effect of war on ordinary people's lives. Among her documentaries after the outbreak of war were *Women in Europe* and *Women in Wartime*. From 1942–1945, Shapley and her husband lived and worked in New York, where she continued to contribute material for *Children's Hour* and created **Letter from America**, which was subsequently taken over by **Alistair Cooke**.

After the war and her return to the United Kingdom, and the death of her husband in 1947, Shapley became involved in the creation of **Woman's Hour**, a program with which she was associated for more than 20 years, both as producer and presenter. She was also part of early postwar British television, and in 1952, she married Christopher Gorton, a textiles executive in Manchester. He died in 1959.

Shapley continued to work in radio and television until her retirement in 1973. Thereafter, she worked and campaigned on a range of social action issues and traveled widely. In 1996, she published her autobiography, *Broadcasting a Life*.

See also FEATURE; WOMEN.

SHELLEY, NORMAN (1903–1980). Having made his early radio reputation in Australia and New Zealand, Norman Shelley first broadcast for the **British Broadcasting Corporation (BBC)** in 1926, and by the end of the 1930s he had become known as one of U.K. radio's most versatile and respected actors, becoming an original member of the BBC's wartime repertory company. He was a regular reader on **Book at Bedtime**, and later in life he appeared for a time on **The Archers**, playing "Colonel Danby" until the time of his death.

Shelley's most famous part, however, was that of Winston Churchill. On 4 June 1940, Churchill had made his famous speech saying, "We will fight them on the beaches" to the House of Commons. The British Council had wanted Churchill to record the speech for broadcast as propaganda to the United States, but Churchill refused to read it again, suggesting that someone else should read it in his stead. Shelley was approached and recorded it, later claiming that Churchill was pleased with the impersonation. Many listeners in the United States apparently believed that they were listening to Churchill himself. Stories later began to circulate that Shelley was responsible for more broadcasts during which he purported to be Churchill. The veracity of this remains widely debated.

SHENNAN, BOB (1962–). Bob Shennan began his radio career at Hereward Radio in 1985, as a journalist, having graduated with a degree in English from Cambridge. He joined the **British Broadcasting Corporation (BBC)** as a trainee producer in Radio Sport in 1987, going on to become a senior producer in 1989, followed by editor of Radio Sport in 1992. After elevation to the post of head of Radio Sport in 1994, Shennan assumed responsibility for BBC television and radio **sports** coverage in 1997. In 2000, he was appointed controller of **BBC Radio 5 Live**, with responsibility for all aspects of the network's output. Upon the resignation of **Lesley Douglas** as controller of **BBC Radio 2** in 2008, Shennan was appointed as her successor.
See also MUSIC.

SHORTWAVE (SW). Prior to the development of the global possibilities for radio programming afforded by the Internet, SW broadcasting remained, for many years, the main means of long-distance sound transmission. **Guglielmo Marconi** had experimented with the medium, although the first engineer to use it for broadcast was Frank Conrad of Westinghouse in the United States.

The long-distance capability of SW relates to a section of the ionosphere containing reflective properties, causing signals in the range of one to three megahertz to "bounce." This layer was named the "Kennelly–Heaviside Layer," after American Arthur Kennelly (1861–1939) and Briton Sir Oliver Heaviside (1850–1925), who had independently discovered the existence of the layer 55 to 95 miles above the Earth's surface. It subsequently became known as the "E-Layer."

Playing a major part in the dissemination of the **BBC World Service**, SW broadcasting provided a crucial element in the technical development of international broadcasting by the **British Broadcasting Corporation**, and during the postwar period, it was widely used for propaganda purposes. It was for this reason that many large-scale SW stations were state controlled or national broadcasters rather than privately run companies, although some of these continue to use the medium in a limited manner. Since the end of the Cold War and the diminishing amount of jamming of signals by hostile powers, SW transmission and reception have improved, although there has been a steady decline in general usage since 2000.
See also ANALOG.

SIEPMANN, CHARLES (1899–1985). Born in England, where he spent the first half of his life, Charles Siepmann later moved to the United States, where his influence on media affairs matched that of his prewar years with the **British Broadcasting Corporation (BBC)**. He joined the newly established BBC within a year of its creation under **charter**. Beginning in 1927, as the deputy director of adult education, Siepmann became director of the department in 1929. In 1932, when the department was merged with **talks**, he took on the role of director of the combined units, creating a period of considerable creativity in the genre.

Internal departmental tensions led to Siepmann's move to a newly created post of director of regional relations. The importance of this was twofold; although the **Regional Programme** had been established in technical terms, it was the first time that the social and cultural implications of broadcasting had been explored on a regional level, and Siepmann came to understand the significance of local and regional planning, which would profoundly affect the long-term future of broadcasting in the United Kingdom.

From 1936–1939, Siepmann was director of program planning. Thereafter, after gaining American citizenship, he worked for the U.S. government as a consultant to the Federal Communications Commission and authored an important report entitled *Public Service Responsibilities of Broadcast Licensees*, a critique of program and advertising practices on a number of U.S. stations. The work remained highly controversial. From 1946 until the end of his career, Siepmann was involved in academia in the United States, remaining a staunch believer in the public service ideals he had upheld during his time with the BBC.

SIEVEKING, LANCE (1896–1972). Prior to his radio career, Lance Sieveking served as a pilot in World War I and was shot down in 1917. Joining the **British Broadcasting Company (BBC)** in 1924, he first worked as assistant to the director of education, before progressing to become the first head of **outside broadcasts** for BBC radio. His approach to the problems of presenting **sports** on radio was innovative and imaginative; the first such event was the 1927 Twickenham encounter between England and Wales. Having personally hired the commentator, H. B. T. Wakelam, Sieveking placed a blind rugby enthusiast next to him to enable him to focus his commentary on an audience without the benefit of vision.

Later moving into the field of radio **drama**, Sieveking was prolific both in production and adaptation. He had found a genre that fascinated him philosophically. In his 1934 book *The Stuff of Radio*, he writes,

> It is interesting to reflect that practically all the things which go to make up the daily broadcast programmes existed before broadcasting was invented, and are now being transmitted just as they stand, very much as the

water which existed before water companies is now being transmitted to the water companies' subscribers. . . . No, there is only one true stuff of radio. One kind of thing, one genre of arranged sounds, that is peculiarly, particularly, and integrally *the* stuff of radio. The radio-play and the "**feature**-program" are of this genre.

Well-known broadcaster and cricket commentator **John Arlott** later called Sieveking "probably the most creative pioneer of British broadcasting."

SILVEY, ROBERT (1905–1981). One of the pioneers of U.K. radio audience research, Robert Silvey originally worked for the London Press Exchange from 1929–1936, and was involved in researching listenership for early **commercial radio** interests in Great Britain. In October 1936, he joined the **British Broadcasting Corporation (BBC)** to set up Listener Research (later Audience Research), of which he remained head until his retirement in 1968.

Silvey devised two research strategies: a continuous survey of listening, which provided estimates of audience size for individual programs, and "panels" of listeners (and later viewers), who were sent questionnaires on a weekly basis to obtain their opinions on selected programs. The survey, involving interviewing a representative sample of the audience regarding their listening—and viewing—for the previous day, ran beginning in December 1939 and continued long after Silvey's retirement.

Silvey and **Stephen Tallents**, with whom he worked, encountered considerable suspicion from some BBC staff about audience measurement, with many believing that it would lead to a tyranny of chasing audience figures and result in less quality programming. After he left the BBC, Silvey lectured widely in the United States, Canada, and Europe on audience research and involved himself with the work of Amnesty International. He was awarded the honor of Most Excellent Order of the British Empire in 1960, and in 1974, he published *Who's Listening? The Story of BBC Audience Research*.

SIMON, ERNEST (1884–1968). Sir Ernest Emil Darwin Simon, Lord Simon of Wythenshawe, was chairman of the **British Broadcasting Corporation (BBC)** from 1947–1952. Having begun his political life as a Liberal member of parliament in 1923, he joined the Labour Party in 1946, and was granted a peerage in 1947. Lord Simon supported the view that **BBC chairmen** and governors should be granted greater executive responsibility. Unlike previous chairmen, he adopted a highly proactive policy of spending a substantial part of his working week in his office at **Broadcasting House**. He was a founder of the *New Statesman* magazine and an important figure in the rebuilding of postwar Britain. His home city was Manchester, with which he maintained close connections, chairing the city council there until 1957.

SIMONS, JOHN (?–). John Simons is a radio executive, broadcaster, and programming director who works for **Guardian Media Group (GMG)** Radio, now owned by **Global Radio**. He began his career on Radio Tees, where he worked from 1983–1985, when he moved to BBC Radio Nottingham. In 1994, Simons joined **John Myers** as part of the team that launched **Century Radio**, helping to develop the network as the brand became successful. In 1997, he joined Talk Radio but left in 1998, when **Kelvin MacKenzie** took over the station. Simons subsequently joined the **London Broadcasting Company** and then **BBC Radio 2**. In 2000, he was reunited with Myers when he became group program director for GMG Radio. In 2004, he was awarded a gold **Sony Radio Academy Award** for Programmer of the Year. In December 2006, Simons was honored with a **Radio Academy** fellowship.

See also COMMERCIAL RADIO.

SIMPSON, ALAN. *See* GALTON, RAY (1930–), AND SIMPSON, ALAN (1929–).

SIMS, MONICA (1925–). A distinguished producer and editor of *Woman's Hour* from 1964–1967, Monica Sims was controller of **BBC Radio 4** from 1978–1983. During her long career, she was also head of children's television programs and a member of the British Board of Film Classification. Sims has received the award Most Excellent Order of the British Empire.

See also CURRENT AFFAIRS; WOMEN.

SING SOMETHING SIMPLE. A show that began on the **Light Programme** in July 1959. The format was simple and unchanging; created by musical arranger Cliff Adams (1923–2001), it revolved around his choir—the Cliff Adams Singers—who presented a half-hour of continuous song, characterized by a gentle, sentimental nostalgia. The singers were accompanied by accordionist Jack Emblow, and the formula proved enduringly popular for an older generation of listeners. Starting on Fridays, the program soon moved to a Sunday afternoon slot, where it continued on **BBC Radio 2** until Adams's death in 2001.

See also MUSIC.

SINGING THE FISHING. A **feature** by **Charles Parker**, **Ewan MacColl**, and Peggy Seeger that first aired in August 1960, and was the most famous of the *Radio Ballads* produced by this team from 1958–1964. It fully established the radio ballad as a new form. The third in the **series**, it took as its subject Britain's herring fishing communities and featured the singing of Norfolk fisherman Sam Larner. The program took nearly four months to make and used 250 reels of taped actuality and interviews. Upon transmission, *Singing the Fishing* was critically lauded and won the **Prix Italia** award for radio in October 1960. It was subsequently broadcast in 86 countries and issued as a commercial recording.

See also FEATURE.

SKY NEWS RADIO. The radio department of Sky News, a service provided by British Sky Broadcasting. It was launched in June 1999 and, in March 2009, became the main supplier of **news** to **Independent Radio News**, providing a service to the majority of **commercial radio** stations in the United Kingdom. In addition, Sky News Radio supplies bulletins to a large number of student, community, and hospital radio stations in Britain. It also provides a service to the **British Forces Broadcasting Service** and radio stations in Ireland, Spain, Cyprus, the United Arab Emirates, South Africa, and Australia.

SLOCOMBE, MARIE (1912–1995). Marie Slocombe is credited with creating the **BBC Sound Archive** in 1936, when, as a temporary secretary, she was told to dispose of some used recordings, which she considered to be of historical value. In 1941, she was appointed as the first sound recordings librarian and introduced a structured indexing system. Slocombe expanded the archive and began to actively acquire recordings from throughout the world, including those involving wildlife and **music**; she was responsible for the **British Broadcasting Corporation's (BBC)** acquisition of the birdsong collection of **Ludwig Koch**. As a member of the English Folk Dance and Song Society, she also ensured that folk music, oral history, and dialect were well represented and collaborated with the Leeds University Dialect Survey to accomplish this. After her retirement from the BBC, Slocombe continued her interest in folk music, editing the newsletter of the English Folk Dance and Song Society for some years.

SMARTPHONE. A smartphone is a cell phone that offers advanced features and applications. The development of technology has enabled smartphones to include many of the features previously carried by more traditional desktop and laptop computers, notably Wi-Fi and Web browsing capabilities. This has had a major impact on mobile radio listening, with both the **British Broadcasting Corporation** and **commercial radio** creating applications to enable access to U.K. stations (*see also* WEBCASTING). The devices have also enhanced listener interactivity, notably through texting and e-mail, as well as the ability to participate in "**phone-ins**" to stations while on the move. According to **Radio Joint Audience Research** figures, listenership via this method grew considerably between 2010–2013, by which time approximately 20 percent of U.K. radio listening was through smartphone apps.

SMASH HITS. A **Radio Luxembourg** program from the 1950s that revolved around the premise of listeners' least-liked records. Members of the audience would write requests for a record to be destroyed on air, stating their reasons. After the record was played one time, it would be "smashed." The **series** proved to be highly popular, first broadcast in December 1952, and running in various forms until 1956.

See also MUSIC.

SMASH HITS RADIO. Broadly based on a now-defunct pop **music** and teen interest magazine of the same name, Smash Hits Radio was a station that initially broadcast in the **Digital Audio Broadcasting (DAB)** and Freeview television formats, opening in 2002. Playing contemporary hits, it was operated by **Bauer Radio**, with a convention that eschewed the use of presenters. Between 2007–2008, it was removed from a number of DAB and television channels but remained available on Freeview until August 2013, when it also ceased broadcasting online.

See also COMMERCIAL RADIO.

SMITH, MIKE (1955–2014). Mike Smith was a radio and television presenter associated with **BBC Radio 1** and **Capital Radio**. After working for **Hospital Radio** in **Chelmsford**, he joined Radio 1 in 1975, in a freelance capacity, working principally on promotions. In 1978, Smith joined Capital, becoming host of the breakfast show in July 1980. In 1981, he met his future wife, television presenter Sarah Greene, and a year later, he returned to Radio 1 to present early morning shows. In May 1986, after hosting various programs, Smith presented the breakfast show, continuing in the role until 1988. He became widely known as a television presenter, was an accomplished pilot, and participated in motor racing. In 2003, he moved away from presentation, setting up his own company, Flying TV, which provided aerial filming facilities from helicopters. Smith died in August 2014, following major heart surgery.

See also DISC JOCKEY (DJ); MUSIC.

SMOOTH OPERATIONS. Smooth Operations was created as an **independent production** company in 1992, by Nick Barraclough, who was later joined by former **British Broadcasting Corporation (BBC)** radio producer **John Leonard**. Programs produced by the company for BBC radio have included the *Radio 2 Folk Show*, *Radcliffe and Maconie*, *The New Radio*

Ballads, and ***Count Arthur Strong's Radio Show!*** In 2006, Smooth Operations was sold to **Unique Broadcasting Company (UBC)**, with Leonard remaining as managing director and Barraclough leaving to pursue a career as a freelance presenter and producer. In 2014, UBC and Smooth Operations merged with digital music company **7digital**, which is working to develop global streaming radio services.

SMOOTH RADIO. Smooth Radio opened in 1990, initially as 102.2 Jazz FM, based in London, with a second station opening in Manchester in 1994. This was rebranded in 2004, as Smooth FM, with the London station rebranding in 2005. In 2007, the owners, **Guardian Media Group (GMG) Radio**, bought the **Saga Radio** network and rebranded it as Smooth Radio. Following the Digital Economy Act of 2010, Smooth merged its English stations into a single quasi-national broadcaster. In June 2012, GMG Radio was taken over by **Global Radio**, which thus took charge of the Smooth Radio brand.
    See also COMMERCIAL RADIO; MUSIC.

SNAGGE, JOHN (1904–1996). John Snagge joined the **British Broadcasting Company (BBC)** after traveling from Oxford in 1924. His first role was that of station director of the Stoke-on-Trent station, but in 1928, he became an **announcer** at **Savoy Hill**. Among many other BBC posts, he was associated with **outside broadcasts** during the 1930s and is best remembered for his radio commentary on the Varsity Boat Race, which he performed from 1931–1980. Snagge's remark during a moment of confusion in the 1949 race, "I don't know who's ahead—it's either Oxford or Cambridge," remains a favorite. Beyond this, he was the voice of the BBC during many key historical moments, announcing, for example, the D-Day landings, V-E Day, V-J Day, and the deaths of King George VI and Queen Mary. In the years before his final retirement from broadcasting in 1981, Snagge made in excess of 100 programs for BBC Radio London under the title *John Snagge's London*.

SOAP OPERAS. An early example of what might be called "soap opera" on U.K. radio was ***Young Widow Jones***, broadcast on **Radio Luxembourg** on a daily basis in 1938. Also on Radio Luxembourg briefly in 1939 was *Stella Dallas*, based on characters in a U.S. movie of the same name, which stars Barbara Stanwyck. The first **British Broadcasting Corporation (BBC)** program in the genre was ***Front Line Family***, broadcast on the General Overseas Service from April 1941 until the end of World War II. Beginning in July 1945, it was retitled as ***The Robinson Family*** and redesigned for a domestic audience on the **Light Programme**.

During the postwar years, particularly prior to the mass take-up of television in the early 1950s, soap operas increasingly found their place on U.K. radio; *Mrs. Dale's Diary* was first heard in January 1948, and *At the Luscombes* started being broadcast by the **BBC Home Service** West Region in September 1948. In 1950, *The Archers* began airing in the Midland Region of the BBC. *Mrs. Dale's Diary* ended in April 1969, having been renamed *The Dales* in 1962; this was replaced by *Waggoners' Walk*, a **serial** that ran on **BBC Radio 2** until 1980. When the BBC decided to axe the program, **Capital Radio** attempted to take it over, but this was rejected.

More recent soap operas have included *Westway*, broadcast on the **BBC World Service** with some popular audience success until funding cuts took it off the air in 2005, and *Silver Street*, broadcast on the **BBC Asian Network** from 2004 to March 2010, when the serial was axed, again due to cost-cutting policies. *The Archers* remains on the air, the most successful soap opera in U.K. radio history.

See also DRAMA.

SOMERVILLE, MARY (1897–1963). Born in New Zealand, Mary Somerville was educated in Scotland and Oxford, and while at college, she met **John Reith**, who was running the **British Broadcasting Company (BBC)**. Somerville, a passionate believer in education and a mature student at Oxford, wrote to Reith in February 1925, offering her services to the BBC on a voluntary basis to help develop the use of radio in schools to supplement what she saw as the overly rigid scholasticism of the education system. As a result, she was appointed schools assistant in July 1925, working under J. C. Stobart, the company's director of education.

Thereafter, Somerville devoted her career, despite poor health, to the development of radio as an educational tool, fusing the ideals of scholarship with the techniques of the new medium. In 1929, she became responsible for the broadcasting of programs to schools and, by 1950, had risen to the post of controller of **talks** (home sound), becoming the first woman to attain the post of controller in the BBC.

See also WOMEN.

SOMETHIN' ELSE. Somethin' Else is a production company founded in 1991, working in the fields of interactivity, radio, and television. Its radio division is one of the largest independent program makers in the United Kingdom, producing content for **BBC Radio 1**, **BBC Radio 2**, **BBC Radio 3**, **BBC Radio 4**, and **BBC Radio 5 Live**. Aside from working with the **British Broadcasting Corporation**, the company has made programs for **Absolute Radio**.

See also INDEPENDENT PRODUCTION; RADIO INDEPENDENTS GROUP (RIG).

SONY RADIO ACADEMY AWARDS. These awards have been seen by the U.K. radio business as the industry's equivalent of the British Academy of Film and Television Arts awards for film and television in the United Kingdom or the Academy Awards (Oscars) for film in the United States. First presented as the Sony Radio Awards in 1983, the aim from the start was to recognize excellence in British radio. In a later agreement between Sony U.K. and the **Radio Academy**, the country's main industry organization, the names of the two institutions were combined in the title. The awards took the form of a nominations event in which short-listed entries were announced, followed a month later by a banquet, usually in the Grosvenor House hotel on London's Park Lane, at which time the actual winners were announced. In August 2013, Sony announced the end of its sponsorship agreement with the Radio Academy after 32 years. In 2014, the awards were therefore renamed the **Radio Academy Awards**.

SOS. In 1933, the **British Broadcasting Company (BBC)** ran a **series** of programs, presented by writer S. P. B. Mais, that were eyewitness accounts of unemployment. The series came from the Talks Department and ran in tandem with a complementary series, *Other People's Houses*. It was followed a year later by another 12-part series of programs on unemployment entitled *Time to Spare*. The programs were controversial and drew strong responses from all sides. At the same time, they remain landmarks in the development of public service broadcasting in the United Kingdom. These were the first attempts by the BBC to examine and analyze social issues in human terms.

SOS MESSAGES. These messages, requesting relatives to establish contact with a sick or dying relative, have been broadcast by **British Broadcasting Company/Corporation** since 1923, as part of its public service remit. The format is unchanging and follows a strict pattern of words. Once a familiar part of **BBC Home Service** and **BBC Radio 4** continuity, increasingly sophisticated communication technology has rendered the service less necessary, although broadcast announcements of this type continue to be heard.

SOUND ARCHIVES. *See* BBC SOUND ARCHIVE; BBC TRANSCRIPTION SERVICES; BRITISH LIBRARY SOUND ARCHIVE.

SOUND WOMEN. Sound Women is a networking and development group for **women** working in U.K. audio and radio, founded in 2011, by producer and trainer **Maria Williams**, who is also its managing director. The objective of the group is to build confidence, networking, and leadership skills among women within—and seeking to be part of—the audio industry and enable them to reach their full potential. The organization works with the industry to build opportunities for women and runs a mentoring scheme, offering training workshops and commissioning new research into women working in audio.

SPORTS. The development of radio as a medium for sports commentary was initially seen as problematic. In early soccer commentaries, it was felt that listeners would require a visual aid to assist them in picturing the action of the game; a numbered grid, representing the playing area, was placed in the *Radio Times*, and as the commentator was describing the play, another voice would call out the number of the square in which the action was taking place. In addition, full radio sports coverage required the development of technical resources and, crucially, agreement with the Press Association. It was with the creation under **charter** of the **British Broadcasting Corporation (BBC)** in 1927, that this agreement was achieved, and organized coverage of sporting events was launched on radio, with a flurry of events.

In January of that year came both the first commentary of a rugby international (England versus Wales) and a soccer match (Arsenal versus Sheffield United.) In March 1927, the first horse racing commentary was broadcast, of the Grand National Steeplechase. In April, the first commentary of the Oxford versus Cambridge boat race on the River Thames in London began a long tradition that continued well into the era of television coverage of the event, and in the same month came the first coverage of the major soccer event on the U.K. sports calendar, the FA Cup Final (Cardiff City versus Arsenal). This was followed in May by the first commentary on a cricket match (Essex versus the New Zealand touring team) and, in June, the first Wimbledon tennis tournament.

The establishment of radio as a medium for sports coverage involved the creation of a new kind of broadcaster, with both specialist knowledge and the ability to describe—often at high speed—the action as it developed before them. Such broadcasters included **George Allison**, (soccer), **Eamonn Andrews** (boxing), **John Snagge** (the boat race), and **Raymond Glendenning** (horse racing). In addition to **outside broadcasts**, a number of magazine programs fed the appetite for sport, including *Sports Report*, which began in 1948. The necessity to cover extended sporting events, for instance, cricket, with matches lasting between three and five days, led to all-day commentaries, for example, *Test Match Special*, which has covered every international test match since 1957 and featured many famous broadcasters, including

John Arlott and **Brian Johnston**. For some, the service is controversial, as it adopts **BBC Radio 4's longwave** service, displacing regular programs, in addition to being carried by a digital service.

A number of sports-specific stations have developed in recent years, including **BBC Radio 5 Live**, which carries sport, in addition to a general rolling **news** format, and its digital companion station BBC Radio 5 Live Sports Extra, activated when two or more major sporting events are taking place concurrently. Moreover, the **commercial radio** station **talkSPORT** carries a male-biased national schedule of commentary and **phone-in** content.

STOLLER, TONY (1947–). Tony Stoller was a key figure in **commercial radio** regulation for many years, following an early career in regional newspapers. He held senior posts in the radio division of the **Independent Broadcasting Authority** for five years, after moving in 1974, from the position of marketing services manager of the *Liverpool Daily Post and Echo*. After a time as the first director of the **Association of Independent Radio Contractors**, the trade organization for commercial radio companies, he was managing director of Thames Valley Broadcasting (Radio 210) in Reading for four years.

Stoller was chief executive of the **Radio Authority**, which, prior to the creation of the **Office of Communications (Ofcom)**, licensed and regulated commercial radio services in the United Kingdom. In April 2003, he became Ofcom's external relations director, responsible for building the organization's structure and presence in the Home Nations and creating a climate among stakeholders and opinion leaders that enabled Ofcom to carry out its regulatory duties, both nationally and internationally. In 2003, Stoller was awarded the title Commander of the Most Excellent Order of the British Empire for his services in the field of broadcasting, and he retired in 2005. His history of independent radio in the United Kingdom, *Sounds of Your Life*, was published in 2010.

See also COMMUNITY RADIO.

STONE, CHRISTOPHER (1882–1965). Christopher Stone has been called the first British broadcaster to make a profession of playing records full-time on the radio. He began doing so for the **British Broadcasting Corporation (BBC)** in 1927, and later moved to **commercial radio** in the 1930s, where he became increasingly popular on **Radio Luxembourg**.

Stone was educated at Eton College and Christ Church in Oxford. In 1914, he enlisted in the Middlesex Regiment and, the following year, was commissioned in the Royal Fusiliers. He was awarded the Distinguished Service Order and the Military Cross for his service in World War I. It was in July

1927, while acting as joint editor—with his brother-in-law, Compton Mackenzie—of the magazine the *Gramophone*, that Stone became associated with radio record programs. The key to his success was his casual approach and spontaneity; at a time when virtually all speakers and presenters on radio worked from scripts, he insisted on a conversational ad-lib approach. In his own words, "I never had any words written down. I insisted on being free to meander along in my own fashion and tell a few personal stories prompted by the records I played." This style quickly endeared him to British radio audiences, tired of more formal presentation, and he gained a large following.

Stone was lucratively involved in many sponsorship deals and recorded promotional material for many commercial services. As a result of this, and his continuing association with Radio Luxembourg, he was blacklisted by the BBC, although after the war, with the climate of commercial radio from Europe changed, he returned to the corporation for a time, working on a number of charity appeals and raising £100,000 in four years.

Stone was also a successful writer, the author of eight novels and *Christopher Stone Speaking*, a nonfiction work written in 1933, in which he expresses his own views relating to the current state of radio, including the debate relating to the BBC and commercial interests.

See also DISC JOCKEY (DJ).

STREET, ARTHUR GEORGE (1892–1966). A. G. Street, as he was known on the air, was a Wiltshire-born farmer who turned to writing articles on farming affairs in the late 1920s and subsequently wrote a number of books, including more than 30 novels and cameos about country life. His autobiography of his early years farming in Britain and Canada, *Farmer's Glory*, was published in 1932. That same year, Street made his first broadcast, quickly becoming a popular commentator on **current affairs** in general and rural life in particular. He was particularly liked for his gruff, down-to-earth turn of phrases and opinions. After the war, he became a regular member of the panel for the new current affairs opinion program *Any Questions?*, which originated in the **British Broadcasting Corporation's** West Region of Bristol.

STUDENT RADIO ASSOCIATION (SRA). An organization set up to support and act on behalf of U.K. student radio stations associated with or linked to places of education. It was formed in January 2002, when a previous representative body, the National Association of Student Broadcasting, which had been established in August 1988, was dissolved. In 2014, there were 65 stations in the SRA, which receives support from industry partners, including the **Radio Academy**. The SRA runs the Student Radio Awards, which is supported by **BBC Radio 1** and **Global Radio**, as well as an annual conference.

SUNDAY BROADCASTING POLICY. During the 1930s, a significant aspect of **British Broadcasting Corporation (BBC)** broadcasting strategy was its Sunday policy. In this, perhaps as much as anywhere else in corporation affairs of the time, thinking inspired by the upbringing and attitudes of **John Reith** influenced public service broadcasting. The issues raised by the corporation's Sunday broadcasting policy were of profound importance to the development of U.K. broadcasting between 1930–1939.

Reith, the son of a man who became moderator of the General Assembly of the Free Church of Scotland, fervently believed all his life that Sunday was an institution that "belonged to the maintenance of a Christian presence." He stated his position on Sunday broadcasting within two years of the creation of the **British Broadcasting Company**, in his book *Broadcast over Britain* (1924):

> The surrender of the principles of Sunday observance is fraught with danger, even if the Sabbath were made for man. The secularizing of the day is one of the most significant and unfortunate trends of modern life of which there is evidence . . . it is a sad reflection on human intelligence if recreation is only to be found in the distractions of excitement.

To understand how this attitude related to Sunday programs on BBC radio, it is only necessary to examine a Sunday listings page from an edition of *Radio Times* of the era. For example, the **National Programme** page for Sunday, 5 April 1935, shows that transmissions began at 10:30 a.m., with a weather bulletin for farmers, followed by a 15-minute interlude. Then there was part one of the *St. Matthew Passion*, a program of classical orchestral **music**, and a chamber recital by a string quintet. Most of the afternoon was devoted to the second half of the *St. Matthew Passion*, followed by a **talk** for children entitled *Joan and Betty's Bible Story*. After this came program 10 in the **series**, *Heroes of the Free Church*. This took the time to 5:10 p.m., at which point came *How to Read an Epistle*, prior to a performance of Richard Brinsley Sheridan's play *The Rivals*. Thereafter, the diet of religious talks and chamber music resumed until close down, with a *Religious Epilogue* at 10:45 p.m.

This paternalistically inspired Sabbatarianism on the part of the legal monopoly broadcaster opened the BBC to criticism, which first came from entrepreneur **Leonard Plugge**. Plugge's actions in the development of **commercial radio** broadcasting from continental stations directly attacked "BBC Sunday," and the creation of **International Broadcasting Company** programs from **Radio Normandy** and other stations inspired others, for instance, **Wireless Publicity**, who developed **Radio Luxembourg** in 1933. The competition was centered on breaching the BBC's monopoly at its most vulnerable point—on Sundays.

For many working-class people of the time, Sunday was the only day of rest in an otherwise grueling week. Wages were poor, unemployment was high, and the international situation was threatening and depressing. Capitalizing on this, the commercial enterprises provided a diet of populist entertainment that drew audiences away from the BBC. Indeed, only the outbreak of World War II ended this threat to the corporation's monopoly, which otherwise could have changed the face of British broadcasting permanently.

See also RELIGIOUS PROGRAMS.

SWANN, MICHAEL (1920–1990). Sir Michael Meredith Swann, Lord Swann of Coln St. Denys, was one of the most popular chairmen of the **British Broadcasting Corporation (BBC)**. Unlike his predecessor, **Charles Hill**, he did not involve himself in program decisions and thus maintained a good working relationship with directors-general **Ian Trethowan** and **Charles Curran**. Under his chairmanship, which lasted from 1973–1980, the BBC navigated its way through some potentially difficult times, including the aftermath of the report of the **Annan Committee** and **license fee** negotiations.

SYKES COMMITTEE. A government committee set up in 1923, under the chairmanship of Sir Frederick Sykes, the Sykes Committee was charged with examining issues of finance, organization, and control relating to the future of British broadcasting. The group's discussions were heavily influenced by the initial development of wireless in the United States, which had been free and chaotic. The **Post Office** pressed for a disciplined structuring of wavelengths and usage.

The Sykes Committee considered whether advertising should be permitted within the British system, deciding that, although it should not be an established practice in general terms, certain forms of "sponsorship" should be allowed, whereby commercial concerns could support concerts and should be acknowledged on the air for doing so. This was hardly implemented in the early **British Broadcasting Company (BBC)**.

Other issues considered by the committee related to concerns voiced by the Newspaper Proprietors' Association, which was concerned on behalf of its members about the development of **news** on the BBC, which it saw as infringing on its interests. A further recommendation of the committee was that the BBC should receive an increased share of revenue derived from the **license fee** and collected by the Post Office from the public.

See also COMMITTEES OF ENQUIRY; CRAWFORD COMMITTEE (CMND. 2599).

T

TABOR, ASHLEY (1980–). The son of Michael Tabor, a bookmaker and racehorse owner, Ashley Tabor founded **Global Radio** in 2007, when he bought the **Chrysalis** group. By 2014, he was the company's executive president and the youngest radio station owner in Europe. Amongst the brands in his empire are **Classic FM, Heart, Capital Radio, London Broadcasting Company, Choice, Gold,** and **Xfm.**
See also COMMERCIAL RADIO.

TAKE IT FROM HERE. A show that ran on the **Light Programme** from 1948–1960, as the first completely new **comedy series** to emerge after World War II. It was written by **Frank Muir** and **Denis Norden**, and starred **Jimmy Edwards, Joy Nichols,** and Dick Bentley. The first producer was **Charles Maxwell**, who had worked for **Radio Luxembourg** before the war. Nichols left the program in 1952, and was ultimately replaced by **June Whitfield** and singer Alma Cogan. One of the new elements that entered the program with the coming of Whitfield was the long-running saga of "The Glums," with Bentley playing "Ron" and Whitfield as "Eth." For the 13th and last series, the writing was taken over by Eric Merriman and Barry Took.

TAKE YOUR PICK. A **comedy** quiz program produced by Star Sound Studios for **Radio Luxembourg** from 1953–1960, by which time it had been transferred to television. Originally sponsored by Beecham's Pills, its host was Michael Miles.
See also QUIZ SHOWS; SERIES.

TALBOT, GODFREY (1908–2000). After an early career working in the newspaper business in Manchester, Godfrey Talbot joined the **British Broadcasting Corporation (BBC)** in 1937, as press officer for the North Region. With the coming of World War II in 1939, he transferred to London, where he initially worked as a copyeditor. With the need for BBC war reporters established, Talbot delivered his first reports during the London Blitz and, proving his value as a broadcaster, was sent in 1942 to follow General

Bernard Montgomery and the Eighth Army and report on its advance from El Alamein to Tripoli. He was mentioned in dispatches and received a military Most Excellent Order of the British Empire for his work.

After the war, Talbot was responsible for organizing the BBC's **news** gathering operation; one of his suggestions was the use of a series of specialist correspondents, with one attached to Buckingham Palace, a post to which he himself was appointed, becoming the first BBC court reporter. He became the "voice" on radio for many state occasions and reported on Princess Elizabeth's 1951 Canadian tour. Talbot retired in 1969, although he continued to be heard on occasional broadcasts and commentaries.

See also WARTIME BROADCASTING.

TALKS. The idea of scripted talks, usually by key intellectual figures in their respective fields, was a genre championed by **John Reith** within the **British Broadcasting Company (BBC)** beginning **in** its earliest days. The traditional prescribed length was 15 to 20 minutes, and the earliest of these was by E. B. Towse, in December 1922. As with those given by **Oliver Lodge** and **J. B. Priestley**, talks were frequently given in **series** and became regular "appointment to listen" programs. Specialist themes developed in literature, film, and **music**, and transcripts often appeared in the *Listener*. H. G. Wells and C. S. Lewis were frequently employed to give talks. Many were aimed at children, among them *The Zoo Man* and *Out with Romany* (*see* "ROMANY").

Illustrated talks, for instance, the series *Talking about Music*, have sometimes crossed over from one network to another, while such personalities as **Charles Hill** in *Radio Doctor* and **C. H. Middleton**, with his gardening talks, gained major audiences prewar and postwar, respectively. The traditional length of a radio talk evolved to 15 or 20 minutes; however, postwar, literary critic Lionel Trilling gave a talk on the **Third Programme** that lasted for 65 minutes—thought to have been the longest uninterrupted broadcast by one voice. One of the greatest—and longest-running—series of talks has been *Letter from America* by **Alastair Cooke**. **BBC Radio 3** later revived the concept of the talk in a weekly series of five linked 15-minute written programs, often presented by writers or thinkers, entitled *The Essay*.

TALKSPORT. Using a logo styled as talkSPORT, this broadcaster is a national **analog commercial radio** station transmitting from London and providing 24-hour **sports** radio coverage. The station first launched on 14 February 1995, as Talk Radio UK, broadcasting a schedule of **phone-in** programs and "chat." It began to foster an interest in sports content in 1997, when it won the rights to broadcast British Football League coverage. In November 1998, Talk Radio UK was purchased by TalkCo Holdings, the chairman and chief executive of which was **Kelvin MacKenzie**. This brought about a radical restructuring of output and a culling of staff and presenters. In 1999, TalkCo underwent a rebranding, becoming the **Wireless Group**, which relaunched the station as Talksport in January 2000. It was bought by the Ulster Television Group in 2005, which subsequently adopted the change of logo.

See also COMMERCIAL RADIO.

TALLENTS, STEPHEN (1884–1958). A distinguished civil servant for much of his career, Stephen Tallents was a public relations expert who played an important role in the development of publicity and the early development of audience measurement in the **British Broadcasting Corporation (BBC)**. Joining the corporation from the General Post Office in 1935, as controller of public relations, he had aspirations to succeed **John Reith**, although when Reith left the BBC in July 1938, the appointment went to someone else. In May 1940, Tallents was made responsible for the overseas services of the BBC but was forced to resign in September 1941, because of internal conflicts.

TAPE RECORDING. The possibility of recording programs had been explored relatively early on by radio engineers; during the 1920s, visits were made to view German experiments in the use of tape, but the quality was not deemed of a sufficient standard to warrant further development. Producers at the **British Broadcasting Company/Corporation (BBC)** held two points of view: Some believed that "live" broadcasting was better in that it produced stronger and sharper performances from artists and speakers. Others, for example, **Lance Sieveking** and **Val Gielgud**, saw creative and practical possibilities in what was known as "bottled" programs. The introduction of the **Empire Service** in 1932, broadcasting to differing time zones, made recording essential, and the means of answering the requirement came with the use of steel tape and the **Blattnerphone/Marconi-Stille System**.

This system was later superseded by **disc recording**, using technology devised in Britain by **Cecil Watts**, and also, for a time, by the **Philips-Miller Recording System**. It was not until World War II that staff at the **BBC Monitoring Service** came to understand the great advances made by German sound engineers in the use of magnetic tape. In 1945, the BBC acquired a German army Magnetophon Tonschreiber B magnetic tape recorder, and this, together with other acquisitions, led to experimentation that moved the corporation toward the gradual adoption of tape as the preeminent recording medium, a system that would last into the digital age.

The creation of the **Midget Recorder** by Electrical and Musical Industries in the 1950s—and subsequently other portable machines, for instance, the **Uher**—gave journalists and producers a combination of quality and flexibility that had previously been lacking. Quarter-inch tape recording—principally at speeds of 7.5 inches per second (IPS) or 15 IPS, using flexible oxide-covered plastic tape, easily edited with a chinagraph pencil and razor blade—became the stock-in-trade for a generation of broadcasters. Tape machines of this type could still be found in some BBC studios into the 21st century.

TARRANT, CHRIS (1946–). Although principally a television presenter and game show host, Chris Tarrant's tenure as breakfast show **disc jockey** on London's **Capital Radio** (1987–2003) earned him induction into the **Radio Academy's** Hall of Fame in December 2003. In addition, his work on the program was honored with a Gold Award at the **Sony Radio Academy Awards**, as well as another Gold Award in 2001, for career achievement. Moreover, Tarrant was named Radio Personality of the Year in 1990.

See also COMMERCIAL RADIO; MUSIC.

TELEGRAPHY ACTS. The early evolution of British broadcasting was established out of regulations that predated it in its transmitted form. A series of government acts in the late 19th and early 20th centuries established rules that contained the foundations of a regulated broadcasting system. The first telegraph companies in Great Britain were privately owned; during the 1860s, it became increasingly clear that commercial and government business would rely more and more on telegraphic communications. In the 1863 Electric Telegraph Act, clauses 21 and 49 established the origins of state control. The role of the postmaster-general was initially seen to be dominant.

The 1868 Electric Telegraphy Act empowered the **Post Office** to create, acquire, and operate telegraph business, in addition to existing privately operated ones, wherever required by the public interest. A year later, the 1869 Telegraph Act gave the Post Office further power, stating, "The Postmaster-General, by himself or by his deputies, and his and their respective servants and agents, shall, from and after the passing of this Act, have the exclusive privilege of transmitting telegrams within the United Kingdom of Great Britain and Ireland." **Guglielmo Marconi's** systems of wireless transmission were becoming widely adopted by 1903, when the Berlin Convention set out an agreement, signed by the major powers, establishing a plan for universal compulsory intercommunication, by which no wireless station was permitted to refuse the reception of a signal from another station using another system of transmission. This was seen as being of particular importance during times of war or national or international emergency. Great Britain was not in a position to sign the agreement, because the country lacked legislation that would enable it to enforce the articles of the convention.

The Wireless Telegraphy Act of 1904 accordingly contained an Explanatory Memorandum enabling British delegates to sign relevant documents at a second Berlin Convention in 1906. This important act took into account the already-dominant view that the new medium would develop quickly and widely. It gained for the state wide powers for the regulation of wireless telegraphy, while enabling the individual enthusiast to develop interests in wireless for private use. From this time onward, however, it was compulsory for each operator of wireless telegraphy to possess an official license.

TELEVISION AND RADIO INDUSTRIES CLUB (TRIC). Formed in 1931, TRIC was founded to "promote mutual understanding and goodwill amongst those engaged in the audio, visual, communication, and allied industries." Membership embraces the communication, entertainment, manufacturing, and service sectors, from program makers and broadcasters to radio producers and radio makers. The organization hosts the annual TRIC Awards.

TEST MATCH SPECIAL (TMS). Radio's international cricket commentary service, which proudly boasts "ball-by-ball" commentary of every test match series that has taken place in England since 1957, in addition to coverage of many games played overseas (since 1990). The preservation of its continuous service during matches has frequently provided the **British Broadcasting Corporation (BBC)** with scheduling problems, as wavelengths have changed throughout the years. *TMS* is currently broadcast on **BBC Radio 4's longwave** frequency, and **BBC Radio 5 Live's** Sports Extra digital service. Throughout the years, the program has been characterized by the personalities of its presenters, **John Arlott**, **Brian Johnston**, Fred Truman, Christopher Martin-Jenkins, and others. The mix of styles has produced a unique blend of professionalism and schoolboy humor that is somehow peculiarly English and eccentric.

See also SPORTS.

THEOCHARIS, JOHN (1932–). John Theocharis was born and educated in cosmopolitan Alexandria. In his early 20s, he worked at the local radio station, broadcasting in Greek, English, and French. He taught in Ethiopia and published his early poetry in Athens. His love of English literature and theater brought him to London, where he won a scholarship to the Royal Academy of Dramatic Art. Theocharis subsequently joined the **BBC World Service**. His production for the BBC Greek Service of a long-lost play by

Menander (the first in any medium) drew the attention of **Martin Esslin**. Theocharis was appointed senior producer and features editor, capacities in which he served on **BBC Radio 3** and **BBC Radio 4** for more than 20 years.

Dividing his time between **drama** and **features**, he found the cross-fertilization of the two disciplines a great source of inspiration. Theocharis directed many modern British and continental plays (among the latter *Outside the Jeweler's* by Pope John Paul II), as well as classical **drama** and numerous Greek tragedies. As editor, he ran the BBC Radio Drama Features unit for several years and made a large number of major features, including such drama-**documentaries** as *The Lady Chatterley Trial* and his coproduction of *The Chicago Conspiracy Trial* (which won the New York Festivals International Radio Award).

Favoring original sounds and treating radio as a visual medium whenever possible, Theocharis has recorded features in many parts of Europe, and as a freelance director since 1992, he has made documentaries and dramas for numerous broadcasters worldwide. For many years he also served as radio jury member/chairman for Prix Futura, **Prix Europa**, and the International Prix Marulic, as well as a regular BBC representative at the International Features Conference.

THERMIONIC VALVE. *See* VALVE.

THESE YOU HAVE LOVED. The title of this long-running **music** program, devised and presented for many years by **Doris Arnold**, was taken from Rupert Brooke's poem *The Great Lover*. It began in November 1938, and established Arnold as the first female **disc jockey** in the United Kingdom. The content was that of extracts of classical and light classical music, requested by listeners, and the show became extremely popular during World War II, as a link between armed forces personnel and their loved ones at home. The program went through many **series**, and Arnold herself broadcast her 300th edition in March 1951. She continued to host the program, which ran intermittently through the 1960s; however, for the final five years of its existence, from 1972–1978, it was presented by **Richard Baker**. The last edition was appropriately broadcast on 11 November (Armistice Day) of that year.

THIRD PROGRAMME. As part of the **British Broadcasting Corporation's (BBC)** postwar reorganization, the Third Programme was established on 29 September 1946, as a cultural channel specializing in classical **music**, **drama**, experimental works, and "highbrow" **talks** and **features**. Thus, it was the first totally new radio network to be created after World War II. Its tone and ambition were summed up by poet Henry Reed, who stated, "[It acknowledges] that some listeners are fools and some are not, and that we cannot wait for the fools to catch up with their betters." That said, among its lighter items was a much-loved **series** by **Stephen Potter** and **Joyce Grenfell** called *How To. . . .* The first episode of this program was transmitted on the network's opening night with *How to Listen.* Shortly after its inception, the station was taken off the air for 16 days in February 1947, as the result of a fuel crisis that hit Britain. After initially only broadcasting in the evenings, it gradually increased its output, although its focus was frequently blurred by the "bolting on" of other services—**Network Three**, the Music Programme, and Third Network. In 1967, the Third Programme became **BBC Radio 3**, and in recent years, successive controllers have sought to widen its appeal through the introduction of jazz and world **music**.

THOMAS, HOWARD (1909–1986). Howard Thomas was, in the latter part of his career, one of the key founding figures in U.K. commercial television, which began in 1955. Prior to this, however, he had maintained a long and successful career in radio, including working for both the **British Broadcasting Corporation (BBC)** and the prewar commercial sector. Working for the London Press Exchange (LPE) beginning in 1937, he started writing scripts for the BBC and, in 1938, set up the Commercial Radio Department of the LPE, writing and producing many of the programs for **Radio Luxembourg** and **Radio Normandy** himself. In 1940, having been rejected for military service due to poor eyesight, Thomas took a staff post with the BBC; throughout the years of World War II, he produced more than 500 programs, including *Sincerely Yours* featuring **Vera Lynn**. He also created *The Brain's Trust* and was personally responsible for the selection of panel members.

In 1944, disillusioned with the BBC, Thomas resigned and subsequently developed his second highly successful career as a film and television producer, initially with Pathé Pictures, the subsidiary of the Associated British Picture Corporation. In 1955, when the company was invited by the Independent Television Authority to apply for a weekend contract to service the North and Midlands, he formed ABC Television and continued to work in commercial television until his retirement in 1979, at the age of 70. He received the title Commander of the Most Excellent Order of the British Empire in 1967.

THOMPSON, JOHN (?–). Coming from a publishing background, John Thompson was the first director of radio at the **Independent Broadcasting Authority** from 1972–1987, when he was succeeded by his deputy, **Peter Baldwin**.

See also COMMERCIAL RADIO; INDEPENDENT LOCAL RADIO (ILR).

THOMPSON, MARK (1957–). Mark Thompson rose through the ranks of the **British Broadcasting Corporation (BBC)** to senior management after starting out as a production trainee in 1979. After a range of television jobs, he became director of Nations and Regions in 1996, and director of television in 2000. After two years as chief executive of Channel Four Television, from 2002–2004, Thompson returned to the BBC as director-general after the resignation of **Greg Dyke.** He left the BBC in 2012, to become chief executive of the New York Times Company and was succeeded by **George Entwistle.**

TIME TO SPARE. See SOS.

TIMPSON, JOHN (1928–2005). John Timpson was a popular radio broadcaster of the 1970s and 1980s who developed as an author of the English countryside after his retirement from the **British Broadcasting Corporation.** He presented the *Today* program from 1970–1976 and 1978–1986. While on *Today*, Timpson was widely known for his on-air relationship with **Brian Redhead.** He was chairman of the **BBC Radio 4 series** *Any Questions?* from 1984–1987 and subsequently made a number of series as a freelancer for the network, including *Timpson's England.*
　See also NEWS.

TODAY. **BBC Radio 4's** flagship morning **news** and **current affairs** magazine program for 50 years running. Its form and character have, however, changed during that time. Beginning on the **BBC Home Service** in 1957, conceived by a team that included **Janet Quigley** and **Isa Benzie,** *Today's* original format was that of a light magazine show. Since that time, it has become more of a hard news program with a political agenda, reflected in the range of its presenters, from the avuncular **Jack de Manio** to the aggressive style of **John Humphrys.** The program's uncompromising agenda has, on occasion, led to tensions with politicians and political parties, none more so than in 2003, when **Andrew Gilligan's** report on information gained from the government weapon's inspector, Dr. David Kelly, regarding government claims of Iraqi military capability, led to the Hutton Report and the ultimate resignation of senior **British Broadcasting Corporation** figures.
　See also TIMPSON, JOHN (1928–2005).

TOOK, BARRY (1928–2002). Barry Took was a comedian, scriptwriter, and successful presenter both on radio and television. In 1951, he won a radio talent show as a comedian, and his skill as a scriptwriter of **comedy** radio soon showed itself in such programs as *Beyond Our Ken.* His greatest achievement, however, was that show's successor, *Round the Horne*, which he cowrote with **Marty Feldman**. Took was also host of the **BBC Radio 4** program *News Quiz* for some years.

See also SERIES.

TOPICAL TAPES. The Topical Tapes project grew out of the **British Broadcasting Corporation's** Overseas Regional Service at **Bush House**, which directed material to specific areas of the world via direct transmission and tape and cassette distribution. The service began in November 1962, and provided subscribers with a weekly service of English-language topicality to supplement the services available by **shortwave** transmission. Approximately 12 weekly magazine programs were produced on such subjects as development, international business, books, and science, and they were distributed to—and broadcast by—more than 35 countries (more than 100 stations in the United States alone). The subject matter was always topical in that the material was designed to remain relevant for approximately two weeks, the time being governed by the longest estimated time taken for tapes posted in London to reach the furthest recipients, in the South Pacific. The service was closed down in March 1996, due to a funding crisis, after almost 34 years.

TOP OF THE FORM. Commencing in 1948, on the **Light Programme**, *Top of the Form* was a schools' **quiz show** in which teams of four from U.K. secondary schools competed in a knockout competition featuring general knowledge questions. It was a highly successful format and ran until 1986.

See also SERIES.

TOP TWENTY. A program that aired on **Radio Luxembourg** beginning in 1948, serving as the earliest chart show broadcast on radio for British audiences. It was also significant in that it was transmitted on Sundays, which had frequently been seen as a day inappropriate for such broadcasting. *Top Twenty* continued in various forms until the closure of Radio Luxembourg in 1992, but it's most radical change came in 1952. Prior to this point, the program—although using records as illustration—was a representation of the top 20 sheet **music** sales in U.K. popular music. As purchasing moved away from sheet music toward the growing consumption of gramophone records, fueled by the developing popular music industry of the 1950s and 1960s, record sales became the significant unit of interest. In 1952, with the creation, in *New Musical Express* magazine, of the first weekly printed chart of record sales, the program switched its emphasis to reflect the development.

TORCH, SIDNEY (1908–1990). Starting his musical career as an organist, Sidney Torch became conductor of the Royal Air Force Concert Orchestra during World War II and thereafter became widely known as a composer of light orchestral **music**. In 1953, he worked with the **British Broadcasting Corporation (BBC)** to devise *Friday Night Is Music Night*. Torch also conducted the **BBC Concert Orchestra** for nearly 20 years on the **Light Programme**, later **BBC Radio 2**, until his retirement in 1972. He broadcast on countless occasions, including frequent celebrity concerts and relays from the Royal Festival Hall in London, as part of the BBC's regular light music festivals. He was awarded the honor Member of the Most Excellent Order of the British Empire in 1985.

TOYTOWN. An extremely popular and long-running **children's program** that was first broadcast as part of *Children's Hour* in July 1929, with **series** running intermittently until February 1963, by which time its parent program had already been axed by **Frank Gillard**. Originally taken from the book *Tales from Toytown* by S. Hulme Beaman, the stories were adapted for radio by **Derek McCulloch**, who also narrated the programs and played the central character, "Larry the Lamb." There were 36 stories in all, and the program's much-loved signature tune was "Parade of the Tin Soldiers."

TRAIN, JACK (1902–1966). Jack Train was a genuine radio personality, created by radio, and a versatile and popular user of the medium. Prior to his first work in the medium, he had appeared in the West End review *Many Happy Returns* in 1928, the same year as his radio debut, and worked with comedians Nervo and Knox of the "Crazy Gang" vaudeville act for five years. Train first came to major public attention in 1939, as one of the stars of *It's That Man Again*, in which he played a variety of rich comic characters. He had a considerable gift for mimicry and was a multivoiced entertainer perfectly suited to the fast-moving, character-based format of the show.

After the war, Train hosted record programs for the **Light Programme** and was a long-term panel member of *Twenty Questions*, where his ability to improvise without a script once again made him a favorite of radio audiences. He also appeared in numerous films, including one that developed the success of his radio **quiz show**, *The Twenty Questions Murder Mystery*.

TRANSISTOR. The development of the transistor as a replacement for the **valve** within radio receivers had a major effect on the portability of the medium. Originally created in 1947, by research scientists at the Bell Laboratories in the United States, the device consisted of the addition of a second contact point to a crystal diode, with a pointed "**cat's whisker**" touching its surface. The application of this miniaturized form of amplification was initially slowed by the difficulty of manufacturing the invention. After early experimentation, the Japanese company Totsuko (later to become Sony) began work on the use of transistors during the 1950s and, in March 1957, produced the first true "pocket" radio, the TR-63. During the 1960s, social changes in Great Britain and the growing youth market for popular **music** created a large demand for mobile radio technology, and what became known as the "Transistor Age" was born. By 1963, 36 percent of radios sold in Britain were imported from Japan, and the tiny sets of the time enabled teenagers to tune in to their music anywhere, escaping the dominance of television.

TRAVIS, DAVE LEE (1945–). Born David Griffin, Dave Lee Travis trained as a designer and took a part-time job as a club **disc jockey** in his native Manchester, where he changed his name to Dave Lee Travis. Becoming known as simply "D. L. T.," he joined **Radio Caroline** South in September 1965, transferring to the North station in 1967, where he remained until passage of the **Marine, and c., Broadcasting (Offences) Act** in August of that year. He joined **BBC Radio 1** and stayed with the station until 1994, when he resigned on the air in protest of the changes to the network being instigated by the controller, **Matthew Bannister**. In the meantime, in 1990, it was revealed that Travis's **BBC World Service** record program, *A Jolly Good Show*, received the largest postbag of any English-language program on the network.

After leaving Radio 1, Travis joined the **Classic Gold Network**, presenting a long-running morning program and working on a number of syndicated shows for other stations. In 2006, he joined the **Magic** network. In November 2012, he was arrested in connection with **Operation Yewtree**, a police operation investigating historic sexual offences, charges he denied. He was acquitted of 12 of these charges in February 2014 but retried on two in September 2014.

See also COMMERCIAL RADIO; MUSIC.

TRETHOWAN, IAN (1922–1990). Sir Ian Trethowan was managing director of **British Broadcasting Corporation (BBC)** radio from 1970–1976, and thus the incumbent of the significant *Broadcasting in the Seventies* paper. During his time with the corporation, **BBC Radio 4** gained its first woman newsreader (Sheila Tracy). In 1977, Trethowan succeeded Sir **Charles Curran** as director-general of the BBC. His background was in print journalism, and his first job was as an office boy for the *Daily Sketch* at the age of 16. He joined the BBC from Independent Television News as a parliamentary commentator in 1963. His time as director-general coincided with a period of considerable difficulty for the BBC, with shrinking income from **license fees** and government criticism via the report of the **Annan Committee**. Trethowan is remembered as being a warm and genial person of considerable intelligence. He survived a heart attack in 1979 and stayed in the post of director-general until 1982, at the age of 60, subsequently serving as a board member for numerous other organizations, including Thames Television and the British Council. His death in 1990 was from motor neuron disease.

See also WOMEN.

"TUNE IN". A song recorded by **Jack Payne** and his band that became the theme tune of **Radio Luxembourg** from its inception in 1934. "Tune In" also commercially issued, with some success. In common with a number of the station's other elements, it was revived when Radio Luxembourg returned to civilian output after World War II. Its refrain was,

> Tune in, Tune in,
> Just sit in your easy chair
> And through the air to anywhere
> Tune in, keep tuning in.

TUSA, JOHN (1936–). John Tusa is an arts administrator and broadcast journalist. From 1980–1986, he was managing director of the **BBC World Service**. He began his career as a trainee with the **British Broadcasting Corporation (BBC)**, before developing as a presenter and journalist on some of BBC television's main **news** and **current affairs** programs. Tusa also frequently broadcast on BBC radio, and beginning in October 2009, for three months, he presented a daily **BBC Radio 4** series called *Day by Day*, a program that used archive sound recordings to track events from 1989, including the fall of the Berlin Wall. He received a knighthood in June 2003.

See also WORLD TONIGHT, THE.

TWENTY QUESTIONS. A variation of the well-known parlor game *Animal, Vegetable, Mineral, Twenty Questions* started in 1947 and ran until 1976, on the **Light Programme**, also going out on **Radio Luxembourg** for a time. The show was produced in front of a live audience, and the first chairman was **Stewart MacPherson**, later replaced by **Gilbert Harding**, who was eventually dismissed from the program for being drunk on the air. Long-term panelists included **Anona Winn**, **Richard Dimbleby**, and **Jack Train**.

See also QUIZ SHOWS; SERIES.

TYDEMAN, JOHN (1936–). After actively developing his interest in theater while at Cambridge, John Tydeman joined the **British Broadcasting Corporation (BBC)** in 1959, spending 25 years in the Radio Drama Department and rising to become its head in 1986. As radio director, his chief interest was in fostering contemporary dramatists and new talent. In this capacity, Tydeman was responsible for discovering Joe Orton and producing his first play, *Ruffian on the Stair*. Tydeman won the **Prix Italia** in 1970, followed by the Prix Futura in 1979 and 1983. In 1994, he was honored at the **Sony Radio Academy Awards** for his contributions to radio.

Since his retirement from the BBC in 1994, Tydeman has remained actively involved with radio **drama**, working throughout the world, including in the United States, where he directed for National Public Radio, working closely with poet Archibald MacLeish and playwright Edward Albee. He also directed plays for audiobooks on CD and cassette, and twice served as chairman of the Prix Italia radio drama jury. Tydeman received the award Most Excellent Order of the British Empire in 2004 for his work in British radio drama and, in 2010, was honored with a Lifetime Achievement Award at the **Radio Production Awards**.

UHER. For more than 30 years—until the advent of high-quality cassette recording and subsequently digital recording—the German Uher portable tape machine was the mainstay of professional radio interviewing and **news** reporting. Strong, robust, and simple to use, the Report series had a number of tape speeds, although for professionals, 7.5 inches per second was the preferred speed for broadcast quality. Set to this speed, the five-inch tape reels produced 15 minutes of recording. The machine was standard issue when **British Broadcasting Corporation local radio** began in 1967.

UK RADIO DEVELOPMENTS (UKRD). UKRD was formed in August 1990, to invest in British **commercial radio**. In 2009, it became a majority shareholder in **The Local Radio Company**, and by 2014, the group owned 16 stations.

ULLSWATER COMMITTEE. The purpose of the Ullswater Committee, under the chairmanship of Lord Ullswater, appointed in 1935, was to "consider the constitution, control, and finance of the broadcasting service in [Great Britain] and advise generally on the conditions under which the service, including broadcasting to the Empire, television broadcasting, and the system of wireless exchanges, should be conducted after the 31st December 1936." The significance of the date was the expiration of the **British Broadcasting Corporation**'s **(BBC) charter**, and it came at a crucial time, given the competition from **commercial radio** interests in the form of populist programming from such organizations as **Radio Luxembourg** and the **International Broadcasting Company**.

Ullswater mostly ratified and confirmed the previous status of issues relating to the BBC's structure and character, renewing the charter for a further 10 years. It did, however, criticize the corporation for its program content in certain areas, notably its heavy **Sunday broadcasting policy**, and concerns were voiced that the BBC did not consult the political parties on major issues as much as it should and that there were signs that the corporation was beginning to usurp certain areas of political patronage.

See also COMMITTEES OF ENQUIRY.

"UNCLE CARACTACUS". *See* LEWIS, CECIL (1898–1997).

"UNCLE MAC". *See* MCCULLOCH, DEREK (1897–1967).

UNDER MILK WOOD. A "play for voices" written by Dylan Thomas, first produced by **Douglas Cleverdon** for the **Third Programme** in January 1954. Thomas had died two months earlier. Had he lived, he would have played the part of First Voice himself. Instead, the part was given to Richard Burton, whose performance in the role has become legendary. The play, which runs for 90 minutes, grew out of a 1945 radio **talk** Thomas had given on the Welsh Regional Home Service entitled *Quite Early One Morning*, which begins: "Quite early one morning in the winter in Wales, by the sea that was lying down still and green as grass after a night of tar-black howling and rolling." Many of the characters in his talk ultimately found their way into the finished work. In the play, which evolved tortuously during a period of years and owes its existence almost entirely to Cleverdon's persuadings, Thomas created a work that is at once a poem and a definition of the radio listening experience. Taking place during the course of one day in a fictional Welsh village, the piece was commissioned not by the Radio Drama Department of the **British Broadcasting Corporation**, but by the Features Department. The **music** was created by Thomas's boyhood friend, composer Daniel Jones.
See also RADIO POEMS.

UNIQUE BROADCASTING COMPANY/UBC MEDIA GROUP. Formed in 1989, UBC was a pioneer of sponsored programs for independent local radio. Founded by **Noel Edmonds**, Simon Cole, and **Tim Blackmore**, the company grew and expanded, eventually—as UBC Media—becoming the leading **independent production** company in the United Kingdom. In 1992, the **British Broadcasting Corporation** began experimenting with independent production for radio, and UBC soon won contracts with all five networks. In 1999, the company floated on the U.K. stock market as UBC Media Group and used the investment to expand into digital broadcasting. In August 2005, Edmonds cashed in his stake in the company for £1.35 million.

Since 2006, UBC has moved away from radio station ownership and **Digital Audio Broadcasting**, to focus more on content production and software relating to interactivity in media. In June 2014, UBC Media Group and 7digital merged to create a new global **music** and radio platform with the new name 7digital Group.
See also COMMERCIAL RADIO.

UNIVERSAL PROGRAMMES COMPANY (UPC). UPC was the production wing of the **International Broadcasting Company (IBC)**, and its role was to package sponsored programs in Britain, for transmission from the IBC's continental stations. UPC was based at 37 Portland Place—just 200 yards from **Broadcasting House**—during the 1930s.

See also COMMERCIAL RADIO; PLUGGE, LEONARD (1889–1981).

UNIVERSAL RADIO PUBLICITY. Formerly known as Radio Publicity Ltd., this pioneering independent producer of sponsored programs is known to have been active as early as 1929, when it produced a program of dance **music** on **Radio Paris**, sponsored by Revelation Suitcases. After the company's name change in October 1930, it also broadcast nightly sponsored shows on Irish radio.

See also COMMERCIAL RADIO; RADIO LUXEMBOURG.

V

VALVE. Invented by Sir **John Ambrose Fleming** in 1904, and patented the following year, the two-electrode radio rectifier, also known as the thermionic valve, vacuum diode, kenetron, Fleming valve, and, in the United States, vacuum tube, would be of crucial significance in the development of radio and amplification of received signals within sets. The term *valve* was used by Fleming because the device only allows electrical current to pass in one direction. This piece of technology enabled electrons to flow from the negatively charged cathode to the positively charged anode; as the current within the tube is moving from negative to positive, incoming signals' oscillations are rectified into a detectable direct current. Although Fleming's invention predated the creation of wireless networks by almost two decades, the valve was initially neglected due to its cost and the development of the cruder but cheaper **"cat's whisker."** By the 1950s, the large, fragile valve was giving way to the new technology of the **transistor**, although while it ceased to be a part of radio receivers, it continued to be used in transmitters.

VARIETY BANDBOX. A weekly Sunday evening show devised by **Cecil Madden**. It was originally designed for the armed forces and began airing in December 1942, on the **Overseas Programme**, transferring in February 1944, to the **General Forces Programme**, where demand soared for its star-studded entertainment. Sunday variety on **British Broadcasting Corporation (BBC)** radio was, until World War II, a rare thing, and British audiences had to turn to the **commercial radio** stations, for instance, **Radio Luxembourg** and **Radio Normandy**, for such fare.

Once established in the public consciousness, *Variety Bandbox* achieved numerous seasons spanning several years. The final edition was broadcast on 28 September 1952, by which time it had moved to a Monday evening slot on the **Light Programme**. Among the stars who took part in the program during the 10 years of its existence were Issy Bonn, Reg Dixon, Arthur English, **Frankie Howerd**, Margaret Lockwood, **Al Read**, Max Wall, and Bernard Miles. In its final **series**, the resident orchestra was that of Cyril Stapleton.

See also COMEDY; WARTIME BROADCASTING.

339

VARIETY DEPARTMENT. Variety provision within the **British Broadcasting Corporation (BBC)** originally came under the same heading as **drama**; however, this changed in 1933, when a specific Variety Department was created under the directorship of **Eric Maschwitz**, editor of *Radio Times*. The role of the department was to fill BBC airtime with a little less than 18 hours of vaudeville, operetta, light **music**, dance music, and **comedy**. The first **series** to come out of the new department was *In Town Tonight*. The department grew quickly and was housed in a number of BBC premises during its existence, including **Broadcasting House**, St. George's Hall, and Aeolian Hall. Many popular shows originated here, including such legends as *It's That Man Again*, *Variety Bandbox*, *Band Waggon*, *Ack-Ack Beer-Beer*, and *Garrison Theatre*.

See also WARTIME BROADCASTING.

VARIETY FANFARE. Billed as "heralding variety in the North," the **series** ran for a time as *Fanfare*, changing its name in July 1949, after which time it ran for several more months, featuring such comedians as **Cyril Fletcher** and **Frankie Howerd**, as well as musical acts, including harmonica player Tommy Reilly and singer Betty Driver.

VARIETY PLAYHOUSE. A Saturday evening **series** that began airing in May 1953, initially hosted by **Vic Oliver** on the **BBC Home Service**. It ran until 1963, and during its lifetime many of the top names in British light entertainment appeared on the program. The mix was varied; the first show featured—among others—Jean Sablon and Benny Hill, and subsequent programs featured appearances by such artists as violinist Campoli, singer Billy Eckstine, and actor Sir Donald Wolfit. Its content, spanning a period of 10 years, reflected changes in entertainment trends during the era.

VAUGHAN-THOMAS, WYNFORD (1908–1987). A friend of Dylan Thomas, Wynford Vaughan-Thomas shared the poet's delight in words and applied it to the art of the radio commentator, giving his work a Celtic lyrical quality in which his Welshness was always a factor. Among many famous broadcasts, his commentary from a Lancaster bomber flying over Berlin in 1943 became famous, as did his other war reports, for instance, when he described General Bernard Montgomery crossing the Rhine and transmitted from the Hamburg studio used by **William Joyce** shortly after Joyce had made his final broadcast. Vaughan-Thomas was later a familiar voice at state and royal occasions, serving as part of the radio commentary team at the 1981 wedding of Prince Charles and Lady Diana Spencer. A man who loved the landscape of Britain, he presented the monthly program *The Countryside in . . .* until his death at the age of 79.

See also WARTIME BROADCASTING.

VIC SAMSON, SPECIAL INVESTIGATOR. Broadcast in a short-lived **series** on **Radio Luxembourg** beginning in mid-August 1939, *Vic Samson, Special Investigator* was the first daily adventure **serial** aimed at children and preempted the **British Broadcasting Corporation's** *Dick Barton, Special Agent* by seven years. The eponymous hero worked for Scotland Yard and was assisted by his schoolboy brother, Bob. The series disappeared with the closure of Radio Luxembourg at the onset of World War II and was never revived.

See also DRAMA.

VERY HIGH FREQUENCY (VHF). *See* FREQUENCY MODULATION (FM).

VIKING RADIO. A **commercial radio** station based in Hull that commenced broadcasting in 1984, and was notable for being the first to divide its **frequency modulation (FM)** and medium wave services, providing alternative services for its listeners, a trend that would later become common practice on independent local radio stations. At the time, however, this was only on weekends to provide an alternative service for **sports** fans. The station completely split its frequencies in 1989, with the launch of its Classic Gold service. In 2008, Viking FM, as it was by then known, was purchased by **Bauer Radio**.

See also COUNTY SOUND.

VINE, JEREMY (1965–). Jeremy Vine is a television and radio broadcaster who took over the role of host of the **BBC Radio 2** lunchtime program from **Jimmy Young** in 2003. After university, he spent a short time at Metro Radio, before joining the **British Broadcasting Corporation** in 1987. In 2005 and 2011, Vine was named speech broadcaster of the year at the **Sony Radio Academy Awards**. He continues a dual career on radio and television.

See also CURRENT AFFAIRS; NEWS.

VIRGIN RADIO. Originally owned by entrepreneur Richard Branson, Virgin Radio became the U.K.'s first national pop **music** station when it began broadcasting on 30 April 1993, as Virgin 1215. Its policy was that of playing quality rock, featuring a high proportion of album tracks, which has remained the backbone of its output.

In 1997, **Capital Radio**, exploiting the climate of radio deregulation that permitted groups to consolidate into multistation ownership, attempted to buy Virgin Radio from Branson. The issue was referred to the U.K. Monopolies and Mergers Commission. Before a ruling could be made on the purchase, Ginger Media Group, owned by **Chris Evans**, stepped in and bought the station. Subsequently purchased by **Scottish Radio Holdings** in 2005, the station became the subject of considerable renewed speculation regarding its ownership.

Broadcasting to most of Great Britain was via medium wave, and the development of digital radio was clearly significant for a station like Virgin; it was accordingly part of the **multiplex** launched by **Digital One** in the spring of 1999. Technical innovation—an issue of considerable interest to the station's core audience—has always been part of Virgin Radio's policy; its Web presence is extremely sophisticated, and it was one of the early sites to experiment with online broadcasting. It has also used satellite platforms to reach an increasingly global audience. In March 2005, it was the first U.K. **commercial radio** station to offer a "podcasting" of a daily show. The Virgin Radio brand has more recently been identified with a number of stations worldwide under license from the Virgin Group. In September 2008, Virgin Radio UK became **Absolute Radio**.

VOCALION CONCERT. A half-hour record program that was significant as the first **commercial radio series** to be advertised (in the *Sunday Referee*). Featuring records on the Broadcast label, it ran from October 1931 to January 1932, initially on **Radio Toulouse** and subsequently on **Radio Paris**. There is, however, evidence that versions of the program were broadcast earlier than that, with **British Broadcasting Corporation** reception reports dating from 1929.

VOICE OF AMERICA (VOA). Funded by the U.S. government, this service began in 1942, initially only broadcasting in German. It grew to include 44 languages, including English, and had a large listenership in Britain immediately after World War II and during the 1950s. One reason for its popularity in the United Kingdom—apart from its commentary during the postwar age of uncertainty brought about by the Cold War—was the fact that British audiences had developed a taste for the more relaxed style and accents of U.S. presenters during the war. The service itself grew out of a perceived need in that in 1939, the United States was the only world power without a government-sponsored international radio service. Today VOA is a multimedia service that reaches 100 million listeners globally.

See also WARTIME BROADCASTING.

VOICE OF THE LISTENER AND VIEWER (VLV). A pressure group founded as Voice of the Listener in 1983, by Jocelyn Hay, to campaign for the preservation of Reithian (*see* REITH, JOHN) standards in radio broadcasting. It was initially created in opposition to a proposal to transform **BBC Radio 4** into a rolling **news** format network. Once established, it became clear that other issues in broadcasting required a consumer organization to act and speak on behalf of listeners. Formed during a period when radio was moving into an era of deregulation, VLV was a strong lobbyist of parliament during the passage of the 1990 Broadcasting Act. The word *viewer* was added to the title the following year, broadening the brief to television.

VOIGT, PAUL (1901–1981). One of the leading inventors of sound equipment, Paul Voigt was born on 9 December 1901, just three days before the first transatlantic signal by **Guglielmo Marconi**. Born in London by German parents, he was educated at Dulwich College, and even as a child Voigt was fascinated by the mechanics of wireless. He joined the southeast London electronics firm J. E. Hough, manufacturing gramophone records and machines, and later moving into radio set manufacture.

Voigt became a specialist in microphones, amplifiers, and above all, loudspeakers. After his employers went out of business in 1933, he formed Voigt Patents and concentrated on manufacturing loudspeakers for such public arenas as cinemas and dance halls. He was among the pioneers who predicted the later growth of **music** radio and recordings in the home. Near the end of World War II, he suffered a breakdown and decided to move to Canada to continue his work on loudspeakers. Immigrating in April 1950, Voigt found work with the Canadian Radio Authority. In his last years, he almost completely neglected audio, becoming involved in the theory of electromagnetic induction, some of Albert Einstein's work, and whether the speed of light was an invariable constant or slowed toward the extremes of the universe; however, it is for his technical work in the areas of sound production and reception that he is most remembered.

W

WAGGONERS' WALK. After the demise of *Mrs. Dale's Diary*/*The Dales*, **BBC Radio 2** sought to introduce a more socially relevant daily **serial** that would reflect modern life. The result was *Waggoners' Walk*, which was broadcast Monday through Friday from 1969–1980 (2,824 episodes). **Piers Plowright** was one of its first producers.

See also DRAMA; SOAP OPERAS.

WALKER, JOHNNIE (1945–). Johnnie Walker has been one of the major figures in the development of **music** radio in the United Kingdom since his time on **pirate radio** station **Radio Caroline**. When the **Marine, and c., Broadcasting (Offences) Act 1967** went into effect on 14 August 1967, Walker and fellow Caroline **disc jockey** Robbie Dale defied the legislation and continued broadcasting past the midnight deadline. It was reputed that more than 20 million people were listening throughout Europe.

From 1969–1976, Walker worked for **BBC Radio 1**, where he gained a reputation for his knowledge of and respect for the music he played on his programs, pioneering such new names as Steve Harley, Lou Reed, Fleetwood Mac, and Steely Dan. Often outspoken and controversial, he left Radio 1 in 1976, after a disagreement with the station controller, **Johnny Beerling**, and moved to San Francisco, where he recorded a weekly program broadcast on **Radio Luxembourg**.

In the first years of the 1980s, Walker returned to the United Kingdom, and after periods on **local radio** in the West of England, he worked on **BBC Radio 5** before joining **BBC Radio 2** to take over the early evening drive-time program upon the retirement of **John Dunn** in 1998. He moved to a Sunday evening slot in 2006, later moving to a mid-afternoon opening for a two-hour show that featured music and performers from the 1970s.

See also COMMERCIAL RADIO.

WALTERS, JOHN (1939–2001). An award-winning **British Broadcasting Corporation (BBC)** producer and broadcaster, John Walters began as an artist and teacher, later becoming a musician, working with the Alan Price

Set, and even playing on the same bill as the Beatles in their final British stage appearance. He joined **BBC Radio 1** at its creation in 1967. Two years later, Walters began his long association with **John Peel**, a partnership that lasted more than 20 years. His wry and witty sense of humor and turn of phrase made him a popular broadcaster in his own right. For a time, he hosted his own programs, *Walters Weekly* (which became *Walters Week*) on BBC Radio 1 and *Largely Walters* on **BBC Radio 4**, in addition to creating a **series** of comic monologues featured in programs by other broadcasters. He left the BBC staff in 1991.

WAR REPORT. *War Report* was first broadcast by **British Broadcasting Corporation (BBC)** radio after the nine o'clock **news** on D-Day, 6 June 1944, and it continued nightly until 5 May 1945. From the initial landings until the final defeat of Nazi Germany, it gave millions of listeners a nightly picture of the progress of the war through the eyes of the men seeing it live. Using the new recording technology of the **Midget Recorder**, which was relatively lightweight and portable, such BBC correspondents as **Richard Dimbleby**, **Frank Gillard**, **Wynford Vaughan-Thomas**, and **Godfrey Talbot** relayed vivid word pictures to the waiting audience in Great Britain. Reports usually reached the listener within 24 hours of having been recorded. Among the most famous reports was Dimbleby's moving account of the liberation of the Belsen concentration camp. The necessities created by the policy decision to cover the last stages of the war in such a way forever changed radio as a **news**-gathering medium.

See also CURRENT AFFAIRS; WARTIME BROADCASTING.

WARNER, JACK (1895–1981). Jack Warner (real name Horace John Waters) was the brother of **Elsie and Doris Waters**. Having initially trained as an engineer just prior to the outbreak of World War I, he worked as a mechanic in Paris and gained a good working knowledge of French. From 1914–1918, Waters worked as a driver with the Royal Flying Corps, based in France, after which he returned to his work as a mechanic, this time in England. During the war, he began working as an entertainer at concert parties, but he was older than 30 before he became a professional entertainer.

In 1935, Waters made his West End debut, at which point he changed his name to Warner; however, it was with his role on the radio show *Garrison Theatre* in 1939 that his fame was assured. After the war, he played Joe Huggett in the successful radio **comedy** show *Meet the Huggetts*. Thereafter, an increasingly successful career in television and film beckoned, and he reached a new audience as PC George Dixon in the popular television series *Dixon of Dock Green*, which ran from 1955–1976. With no formal training,

Warner's great gift was sincerity, a quality heard and understood by the radio microphone, establishing him as a major British star with an affectionate following.

WARTIME BROADCASTING. The role of the **British Broadcasting Corporation (BBC)** during World War II is important and must be considered from two perspectives: home front and overseas broadcasting. By the time hostilities had commenced, the corporation had found time to clearly establish its policy, including, where appropriate, evacuating and/or relocating certain services. Within days of the announcement, a "Supplementary Edition" of *Radio Times* was published, carrying the banner, "Broadcasting Carries On."

Because a depleted workforce on the domestic scene was augmented by many who found themselves in an unfamiliar situation, morale was a crucial issue, and the BBC created a number of new programs to cater to this environment, for instance, ***Workers' Playtime*** and *Music While You Work*. Other programs supported the government's "Dig for Victory" campaign, including *The Kitchen Front, Back to the Land*, and *The Radio Allotment*. In the early days, **J. B. Priestley's** *Postscript* program, broadcast after the Sunday evening **news**, countered the decrease in morale caused by the broadcasts of **William Joyce**, and in the last year of the war, Allied progress throughout Europe was monitored by the nightly *War Report* program.

The **Variety Department** created a range of light entertainment programs, many of which would become radio legend, for example, ***Band Waggon*** and ***It's That Man Again***. A new, relaxed style began to emerge in programming, partly caused as the war continued by the influx of U.S. and Canadian broadcasters, who, together with the BBC, created a tripartite forces broadcasting service that gave U.K. domestic audiences—who could also listen—a taste of a new style of radio.

At the same time, some felt that BBC programs were becoming more vulgar and catering to a lower common denominator than before. The **BBC Forces Programme** was requested to use material aimed at the elevation of standards and provision of more informative content; this led to the creation of *The Brain's Trust*, which, with a weekly postbag of up to 4,000 letters, became the first "serious" program to attract a mass audience.

As with domestic programming, the BBC's overseas output had been primed for the event of war for several years. Countering German propaganda broadcasts became an increasing concern of the British government beginning in 1933, when the Nazis came to power, and the BBC was asked to respond, which it did in 1938, with the creation of the **BBC Arabic Service**, as well as services in Spanish and Portuguese. Between 1940–1941, the BBC increased its overseas output threefold. A special service to North America was created that demonstrated to the United States the true situation in a beleaguered Great Britain, with such dramatized **documentary** programs as *The Stones Cry Out*.

During this time, services also began in every major European language. In 1941, as the expanding provision dictated the need for more space, the BBC took over the **Bush House** studios, formerly used by the **J. Walter Thompson Organization's commercial radio** division. This became the headquarters of the BBC European Service and went on to become—for many overseas listeners even after the war—the true home of BBC radio. It was from Bush House, on the BBC French Service, that Charles de Gaulle made his first broadcast—on 18 June 1940—four days after the fall of Paris. The French Resistance was thus created, with a force estimated to be 56,000 strong.

It is hard to overestimate the importance of the role of the BBC during World War II. The corporation had entered the war somewhat demoralized, with areas of its output under siege from such commercial interests as the **International Broadcasting Company** and **Radio Luxembourg**. By 1945, the BBC was an organization commanding global respect. This may be measured by the fact that in September 1939, it was transmitting in seven languages. By 1945, there were more than 40 services, and the staff of the BBC had more than doubled.

WATERS, ELSIE (1893–1990), AND DORIS WATERS (1899–1978). Elsie and Doris Waters made up one of the most famous and popular **comedy** double acts in British variety and, as their onstage personas, "Gert and Daisy," two cockney women, appeared in every medium. Two sisters, they never married and lived together all their lives. Their first radio broadcast was in 1929, which led to a record contract. For one of their commercial recordings, they created the characters for which they were forever known; the recording was played on the air by **Christopher Stone**, and a highly successful career ensued. It was said that the East London working-class sound of the act appealed to an audience alienated by the Reithian **British Broadcasting Corporation's** policy of standard English presentation.

In March 1934, the Waters sisters appeared on *Henry Hall's Guest Night*, and two months later they appeared in their first Royal Variety Performance. The act was a particular favorite of Queen Elizabeth, later the Queen Mother. During World War II, they regularly appeared on programs like *Workers' Playtime*. After the war, they both received the award Most Excellent Order of the British Empire, and "Gert and Daisy" continued to perform until the 1970s.

WATTS, CECIL (1896–1967). Cecil Watts was a musician who had worked in **music** during the early days of 2LO. His major contribution, however, was the invention of direct **disc recording**, a technology he devised to replay rehearsals to his band but was adopted as a revolutionary instant recording device by program makers. To manufacture the number of discs required, which he and his wife Agnes called the Marguerite Sound System [later Marguerite Sound Studios] (MSS), based on a name that came from both sides of their family, he established a factory on London's Shaftesbury Avenue, then on Charing Cross Road, and subsequently at Kew.

The demand first came from **commercial radio**, although the **British Broadcasting Corporation** began to buy the Watts discs in quantity in April 1934. For the first time in the history of radio, broadcasters had access to an instant, cheap, and durable playback system, and the recording of program material was immeasurably enhanced. Watts later developed a means of cleaning discs during playback, a device he called the "Dust Bug."

WEATHER BROADCASTS. Weather reports and bulletins have been a staple part of radio since its creation, usually—although not exclusively—as an addendum to **news** summaries. The first **British Broadcasting Company (BBC)** weather forecast was a shipping forecast broadcast on behalf of the British Meteorological Office on 14 November 1923, and the first daily forecast was transmitted on 26 March 1923. Since then the relationship between the Met Office and British broadcasting has continued.

Of particular fascination to British listeners has been the shipping forecast, which is broadcast on **BBC Radio 4** four times a day, separate from bulletins, and includes forecasts and weather reports for the sea areas surrounding the coasts of the British Isles. The forecast has a strict and formal structure, limited to 370 words, and its rhythmic and repetitive style has gained a listenership much wider than its intended audience of mariners and other specialists. It begins with "And now the shipping forecast, issued by the Met Office on behalf of the Maritime and Coastguard Agency at xxxx today." The forecast goes on to name and report on conditions in British sea areas, for instance. Rockall, Malin, Hebrides, Bailey, and Fair Isle. These names, relating to often remote and elemental places, have proved to hold an interest for listeners independent of content and meaning, and the shipping forecast has even prompted responses from poets, artists, and composers.

The development of new technology has made BBC weather reporting widely available in various formats beyond traditional transmissions; the BBC Weather website was launched in 1997, and in addition to U.K. weather, it carries reports and forecasts from throughout the world, in addition to special weather-related **features**. In May 2013, the BBC launched its mobile weather app for **smartphones**, with data supplied by the Met Office.

WEBCASTING. Also known as Internet radio, webcasting is an audio service transmitted via the Internet. It should be distinguished from on-demand file sharing and podcasting, which involve downloading rather than continuous streaming. In the latter sense, webcasting resembles the listener experience provided by traditional "live" broadcasting. Many webcasts are run by radio stations as simultaneous transmissions of orthodox programming, although numerous niche "Internet-only" stations are also available. From the broadcasters' point of view, the Internet provides a means of reaching audiences beyond the normal range of terrestrial transmitters. Thus, a **local radio** station serving a particular city or region potentially becomes available to a global audience, a phenomenon that is becoming popular among listeners with an interest in a particular place while being geographically separated from it. Nevertheless, some broadcasters limit the availability of broadcasts geographically due to copyright concerns.

Listening is often carried out through a computer, although manufacturers have increasingly started introducing sets that resemble traditional broadcast receivers, as well as hybrid devices capable of combining Internet listening facilities with **frequency modulation (FM)** and **Digital Audio Broadcasting** capabilities. The trend for Internet listening has been facilitated by the development of broadband and Wi-Fi capabilities in the domestic environment. Since 2010, there has been a considerable increase in Internet listening via cell phones, with figures taken by **Radio Joint Audience Research** in 2013 showing that 20.3 percent of the U.K. adult population aged 15 years and older listen to radio through this media, as opposed to the third quarter of 2010, when only 12.8 percent of U.K. adults listened to online radio on their **smartphones**.

See also BBC IPLAYER RADIO; RADIOPLAYER.

WEEK ENDING. *Week Ending*, which aired on **BBC Radio 4** on Friday evenings beginning in 1970, was the longest-running British radio **comedy** program. Produced by Simon Brett and **David Hatch**, it was originally written by Pete Spence. The program had 27 producers and more than 65 writers, among them Jimmy Mulville, Griff Rhys Jones, and **Douglas Adams**. Growing out of the tradition of Oxbridge satire, the show frequently found itself on dangerous ground, as in 1980, when journalist and broadcaster Derek Jameson attempted—and failed—to sue after a biting sketch that attacked him for his alleged lack of intellect. The show finally ended in 1998.

See also SERIES.

WESTERN BROTHERS. Kenneth (?–1963) and George (?–1969) Western were a double act that satirized the British upper classes. Known as "The Wireless Cads," they were actually cousins and had solo careers until they first met in 1925, when they formed one of the most successful acts onstage and on the radio. They broadcast from the 1930s onward, including during and after World War II, although the peak of their fame and success was undoubtedly during the 1930s, when they were featured in cabaret, variety, and radio. Their monologues and routines frequently used the paternalistic **British Broadcasting Corporation (BBC)** as a target, with such items as "O Dear, What Can the Matter Be, No One to Read Out the News," "The Old School Tie," and "We're Frightfully BBC." The style was that of a languid, unison drawl, and onstage they wore evening dress and monocles.

See also COMEDY.

WESTERN HOUSE. A building located close to **Broadcasting House** under lease by the **British Broadcasting Corporation (BBC)**. It has housed the offices and studios of **BBC Radio 2** and **BBC Radio 6 Music**, as well as a number of other radio studios. Western House also provides a number of recreational facilities for use by BBC staff.

WHALE, JAMES (1951–). A controversial and aggressive **talk** show host, James Whale developed a style similar to some of the U.S.-based "shock jocks," engaging in belligerent debates with **phone-in** callers and frequently verbally attacking their views on the air. First heard on Metro Radio in the 1970s, he moved to Radio Aire in 1981, where his program was also televised by Yorkshire TV. After leaving radio to concentrate on television, he returned to work on the national talk station **talkSPORT**, where, in 2005, he broadcast a late-night phone in.

In May 2008, Whale was sacked and the radio station fined £20,000 by the **Office of Communications** for "seriously breaching the due impartiality rules at the time of an election" on the air. In August 2008, he began broadcasting on an occasional basis for **London Broadcasting Company**, deputizing for other broadcasters. In March 2013, after a period spent presenting the drive-time program, Whale was replaced and his contract with the station not renewed. He later presented shows on a number on **British Broadcasting Corporation local radio** stations.

WHAT DO YOU KNOW?. A **quiz show** created by John P. Wynn for the **Light Programme** and chaired by **Franklin Engelmann**. Contestants competed for the title "Brain of Britain." The program was first broadcast in 1953, and was transferred to television in 1958, under the title *Ask Me Another*. In 1967, the radio version was renamed *Brain of Britain*.

WHEELER, CHARLES (1923–2008). Joining the **British Broadcasting Corporation (BBC)** in 1947, after military service in the Royal Marines, Charles Wheeler went on to become the BBC's longest-serving foreign correspondent, a role he fulfilled until his death. In addition to becoming a familiar face on television, he presented a number of distinguished programs for **BBC Radio 4** and was a regular contributor to the network's long-running series *From Our Own Correspondent*. Wheeler was knighted in 2006, for his contributions to overseas broadcasting and journalism. After his death, the publication *British Journalism Review* established the annual Charles Wheeler Award for outstanding contributions to broadcast journalism.

See also CURRENT AFFAIRS; NEWS.

WHILEY, JO (1965–). Jo Whiley is a **disc jockey** and presenter of programs on both radio and television. She is widely known for programs on **BBC Radio 1** and later **BBC Radio 2**. Her first job in radio was with Radio Sussex, and after completing a year at City University studying journalism, she gained a job as a researcher for **BBC Radio 4**, which ultimately led to her first presentation role. From September 1993 to March 2011, Whiley worked for Radio 1, hosting a range of programs. In July 2008, the program she was then presenting was fined for misleading listeners, after a staff member took part in an on-air competition, claiming to be a member of the public.

In September 2009, Whiley left Radio 1's weekday output and moved to a weekend slot as part of a major adjustment in the station's schedule. Her last program for Radio 1 aired on 27 March 2011, and beginning on 4 April 2011, she presented an evening show on Radio 2, succeeding a program hosted by **Mark Radcliffe** and **Stuart Maconie**.

See also MUSIC; WOMEN.

WHITBY, TONY (1929–1975). Tony Whitby was controller of **BBC Radio 4** in the early 1970s, involved in the development of many significant programs during his time with the network, including *Kaleidoscope* and *I'm Sorry I Haven't a Clue*.

WHITE, PETER (1947–). Peter White, blind since birth, has been the main presenter of the **BBC Radio 4** program for the visually impaired, *In Touch*, which he joined in 1974. He began his radio career in 1971, with Radio Solent in Southampton. Since 1995, he has been the **British Broadcasting Corporation's** disability affairs correspondent. Between 1995 and 2005, White wrote four **series** of autobiographical **talks** for Radio 4. He also presented numerous programs for television and, in 1999, published his autobiography, *See It My Way*. He is part of the presentation team for the Radio 4 consumer program *You and Yours*. In 1988, White was made a Member of the Most Excellent Order of the British Empire, and in 2001, he was honored as Speech Broadcaster of the Year at the **Sony Radio Academy Awards**.

WHITFIELD, JUNE (1925–). A highly popular actress particularly known for her **comedy** work on radio and television, June Whitfield first appeared in a leading role on the long-running program *Take It from Here*, on which she became popular for her portrayal of "Eth" in the regular sketch **series** *The Glums*. Prior to this she worked with **Wilfred Pickles** and appeared on the panel game *Twenty Questions*. She has maintained a highly successful career in television but, in 1984, returned to radio as part of *The News Huddlines*, alongside **Roy Hudd** and **Chris Emmett**, which ran until 2001. Whitfield received a Lifetime Achievement Award at the British Comedy Awards in 1994 and was awarded the honor Commander of the Most Excellent Order of the British Empire in 1998.

See also WOMEN.

WHITLEY, JOHN HENRY (1866–1935). John Whitley became chairman of the **British Broadcasting Corporation (BBC)** in 1930, succeeding **George Clarendon**. Coming from a family cotton business, he became a member of parliament and subsequently speaker of the House of Commons. Following a dispute between Clarendon and **John Reith**, a document was drawn up that established the rights and duties of the chairman and the members of the Board of Governors. This became known as the Whitley Document and instituted a status quo whereby the BBC presented a unified face to the outside world. Reith and Whitley maintained a good relationship, and Whitley died in office.

See also WHITLEY, OLIVER (1912–2005).

WHITLEY, OLIVER (1912–2005). Oliver Whitley, son of **John Whitley**, joined the **British Broadcasting Corporation (BBC)** in 1935 and, in 1939, was attached to the **BBC Monitoring Service**, which was, at that time, expanding into a 24-hour operation monitoring 150 foreign **news** bulletins per day. Whitley resigned in 1941 and spent wartime service in the navy. He rejoined the BBC after the war in 1946 and was immediately seconded to the Colonial Office to advise on the development of broadcasting in British overseas territories. Whitley returned in 1949, as head of the General Overseas Service; in 1955, he was appointed assistant controller of the Overseas Service.

In 1958, Whitley left **Bush House** and took up the post of appointments officer and then controller of staff training and appointments. He became chief assistant to **Hugh Greene** during the latter's tenure as director-general of the BBC and served on the Board of Management. He ended his career with the corporation as the first managing director of External Services, a post he held from 1969 until his retirement in 1972.

WHITNEY, JOHN (1930–). John Whitney became involved in radio in 1951, when he founded Ross Radio Productions, producing programs for **Radio Luxembourg**. A particular success from this time was *People Are Funny*. A passionate advocate of **commercial radio**, in 1964, Whitney co-founded the Local Radio Association, an organization created to encourage the introduction of self-funding radio in the United Kingdom. He was founding managing director of **Capital Radio** from 1973–1982, at which time he was appointed director-general of the **Independent Broadcasting Authority**, a post he held until 1989. Whitney was chairman of the **Association of Independent Radio Contractors** from 1973–1975, and again in 1980. Among his numerous executive posts, he has been chairman of the **Sony Radio Academy Awards** and **Radio Joint Audience Research**.

WILLIAMS, GWYNETH (1953–). Gwyneth Williams became controller of **BBC Radio 4** in September 2010, when she succeeded **Mark Damazer** in the post. She grew up in South Africa and attended St. Hugh's College in Oxford, joining the **BBC World Service** as a trainee in 1976. During the 1980s, Williams worked on Radio 4's *The World Tonight*, before becoming deputy editor of **current affairs** programs. In 1994, as editor of policy and social programs, she launched current affairs programs on **BBC Radio 5 Live**. She subsequently became head of radio current affairs and editor of the **British Broadcasting Corporation's Reith Lectures**. In 2007, Williams returned to the World Service as director of English networks and **news**, responsible for the service's English-language programming, a post she held until 2010.

WILLIAMS, KENNETH (1926–1988). A highly talented actor, Kenneth Williams is best remembered for his camp portrayal of an array of bizarre **comedy** characters, in particular in *Beyond Our Ken* and *Round the Horne*. A great and much-loved raconteur, he was a regular and brilliant member of the *Just a Minute* team for nearly 20 years. He had earlier worked with **Tony Hancock** on *Hancock's Half Hour*. Williams was a complex person with a serious side that embraced a great love of poetry and art.

WILLIAMS, MARIA (1967–). Maria Williams is founder and managing director of **Sound Women** and also an independent trainer and executive radio producer. She began her career as a researcher/producer at the **British Broadcasting Corporation (BBC)** in Birmingham in 1990. While there she researched the award-winning program *Never the Same Again* for **BBC Radio 4**. Williams subsequently worked for **BBC Radio 1**, **BBC Radio 1Xtra**, **BBC Radio 3**, **BBC Radio 4**, **BBC Radio 5 Live**, **BBC Radio 6 Music**, and *CBeebies Radio*. From January 2004 to February 2006, she was deputy editor of *Woman's Hour* and, from then until May 2008, executive producer of *Saturday Live*, a program she created and launched, and which won gold at the **Sony Radio Academy Awards** for Best Speech Program in 2008. In 2014, Williams coordinated the Sport Relief fundraising event for BBC radio.

See also CURRENT AFFAIRS; DOCUMENTARY; WOMEN.

WILLIAMS, STEPHEN (1908–1994). Stephen Williams was an important figure in **commercial radio** history before and after World War II. After spending time at **Radio Normandy**, he worked for **Radio Paris** at the time of the transfer of output to the fledgling **Radio Luxembourg** in December 1933. It was Williams who was responsible for the launch and early development of the station.

During World War II, he became the broadcasting officer for the Entertainments National Service Association. Among the programs he worked on during this time were *Variety Bandbox* and *It's All Yours*. Returning to Luxembourg in January 1945, Williams became the first postwar director of the station when it was relaunched. In 1948, he joined the **British Broadcasting Corporation (BBC)**, where, for 14 years, he produced *Have a Go*. He was also involved in the establishment of BBC Radio Enterprises in the mid-1960s.

WILTON, ROBB (1881–1957). Referring to himself as a "**comedy** character actor," Robb Wilton was already a star of **music** hall and repertory theater by the time he made his first radio appearance—on 2LO—in 1922. Born in Liverpool, he developed a rich strain of Northern English humor that centered on a bumbling bureaucratic inefficiency. Wilton became a major radio star in the late 1930s, and throughout the war years the British public found solace in his sketches and routines, which revolved around "muddling through"; he captured the mood of the nation by creating this loveable persona. His last radio appearance was on *Blackpool Night* in August 1956. He died in May of the following year.

WINN, ANONA (1907–1994). Born in Australia, Anona Winn first trained as a pianist and then as an opera singer (under Dame Nellie Melba) prior to coming to Great Britain. She first broadcast on radio in 1928, in *Fancy Meeting You*. Widely known as a singer, composer, impressionist, and actress, she had made more than 300 broadcasts by the mid-1930s and fronted her own dance band, Anona Winn and Her Winners. Postwar, her considerable fame rested mostly on her role as a panelist on *Twenty Questions* beginning in 1947, as well as her presentation of *Petticoat Line* beginning in 1965 (a program she also devised).

See also QUIZ SHOWS; SERIES; WOMEN.

WIRELESS GROUP. Wireless Group, the company that owned the national commercial speech station **talkSPORT**, as well as 13 regional and **local radio** stations, was run by **Kelvin MacKenzie**, a former editor of the *Sun* newspaper, from 1998–2005, when the group was purchased by Ulster Television for £98.2 million.

See also COMMERCIAL RADIO.

WIRELESS PUBLICITY. Founded as a production house in 1936, by **Radio Luxembourg**, in premises on London's Thames Embankment, Wireless Publicity was created, like its rival companies, the **Universal Programmes Company** and **Universal Radio Publicity**, to package sponsored programs for the station. As with its parent company, it was revived after the war, and in 1954, its name was changed to Radio Luxembourg, London.

See also COMMERCIAL RADIO.

WOGAN, TERRY (1938–). Born in Limerick, Ireland, Terry Wogan's first role in radio was with Radio Telefis Eireann as a newsreader/**announcer**. After two years working in **documentary features**, he moved into light entertainment as a **disc jockey** and presenter of **quiz shows** and variety programs. Wogan's first job with **British Broadcasting Corporation (BBC)** radio was presenting the **Light Programme music** show *Midday Spin*, and when **BBC Radio 1** started, he presented *Late Night Extra* on weekday evenings. He later presented the afternoon program on **BBC Radio 2**, taking over the breakfast show in April 1972.

Wogan left radio for a period to concentrate on television, including *Wogan*, a chat show that ran for seven years on BBC 1 TV, three nights a week. It is, however, as a radio presenter that Wogan has been most celebrated. In 1993, he returned to Radio 2 to once again present the breakfast show, this time retitled *Wake Up to Wogan*. A series of honors followed. In 1994, he won the **Sony Radio Academy Award** for the Best Breakfast Show; in 1997, he received the award Most Excellent Order of the British Empire in the New Year's Honors List; and in 2005, he was awarded an honorary knighthood, in addition to receiving the award for Radio Broadcaster of the Year at the Broadcasting Press Guild Awards.

Wogan retired from his role as host of the Radio 2 breakfast show in December 2009 and was succeeded by **Chris Evans**. He returned to the network in February 2010, to host a weekly two-hour Sunday morning program with an audience in **Radio Theatre** at **Broadcasting House**. This ran for four **series**, before the format was changed to more orthodox studio-based production.

WOMAN'S HOUR. Founded by **Norman Collins**, creator of the **Light Programme**, in October 1946, *Woman's Hour* originally occupied the 2:00 p.m. to 3:00 p.m. afternoon slot, a time conceived as being the one hour during the day when **women** at home would have time to themselves. The program's format—a **series** of magazine items and studio interviews on matters relating to women—has essentially remained the same, although the content has been altered to reflect the changing role of women in society.

In 1990, **BBC Radio 4** moved the program—amidst considerable controversy—to a morning slot in its schedule, where it has remained. Although its first presenter was male, the program has subsequently been presented by a series of women, including **Jean Metcalfe, Marjorie Anderson, Sue MacGregor**, and **Jenni Murray**. The later structure of the program has allowed for the last 15 minutes to feature a **drama serial**. In April 2014, *Woman's Hour* celebrated its 60th anniversary.

WOMEN. Beginning in the first days of U.K. broadcasting and the creation of the **British Broadcasting Company (BBC)**, the role and perception of women as broadcasters and listeners alike has at once been crucial and frequently contradictory. In the latter case, there was a long-held view informing policy among broadcasters that a man's place was in the workplace, while a woman's was in the home, making her an available audience for programs of a particular type and style. Early examples of men's attitudes toward women within the medium show that women were frequently patronized and marginalized both as staff members and consumers of radio, attitudes that reflected the Victorian roots from which the first broadcasters emerged.

The first programs specifically aimed at female listeners featured content suggested by the Women's Advisory Committee, and the coming in 1946 of the long-running *Woman's Hour* involved an evolution of styles and attitudes. Hosted by a succession of highly distinguished broadcasters, including **Jean Metcalfe, Marjorie Anderson, Sue MacGregor**, and **Jenni Murray**, the show has continued to evolve. At the same time, the existence of such a program has been sporadically criticized as a form of compartmentalizing women's issues and ideas. The perception of a stereotypical image of the woman listener was carried over into a number of broadcasting **journals**, including *Radio Pictorial*, during the 1930s.

A number of **serials** and **soap operas**, for example, *Young Widow Jones*, *Mrs. Dale's Diary*, and *Waggoners' Walk*, demonstrated media perceptions of women in society during various stages of British broadcasting history. In the field of light entertainment, **Mabel Constanduros** was significant during the 1930s for creating a unique voice for British radio **comedy**. Likewise, **Elsie and Doris Waters**, in the personas of their cockney characters, "Gert and Daisy," established themselves as a radio institution that survived for more than 40 years.

The first woman announcer to introduce a program was Sheila Borrett, in July 1933. A month later, the **news** was read by a woman for the first time, although this was discontinued soon thereafter. It was not until 1974 that the news on **BBC Radio 4** was read by a woman (Sheila Tracy), and shortly afterward, Sandra Chalmers and **Gillian Reynolds** became managers of **British Broadcasting Corporation** radio and **commercial radio** stations, respectively. Other distinguished broadcasters included **Audrey Russell** in the field of live commentary and **Doris Arnold** in **music** presentation.

Early and highly influential women producers included **Olive Shapley**, **Nesta Pain**, and **Hilda Matheson**, who were innovators and developers of radio techniques that were subsequently widely adopted. Nevertheless, the official prejudices within the BBC meant that there was little equality; for instance, if a female staff member married a male who also worked for the BBC, the woman was required to resign from her post. The history of women in U.K. radio provides many examples of inequalities, while demonstrating the major part played in all areas, including production, presentation, technical work, and management. In the modern BBC, **Helen Boaden** and **Lesley Douglas**—as controllers of BBC Radio 4 and **BBC Radio 2**, respectively— have significantly contributed to the development of radio in the United Kingdom, and **Jenny Abramsky's** role as director of radio and music has been instrumental in steering BBC policy through major changes in the way radio is made and consumed. Outside the BBC, the diversity of women's roles in modern society has been reflected in many ways, including feminist **community radio** stations, lesbian radio, and local Asian radio.

In general presentation, **Anne Nightingale** and **Jo Whiley** have achieved real status and authority in popular music presentation, while Jenni Murray has presented both news and specialist media programs, as has **Libby Purves**. Beginning in 1925, **Mary Somerville** helped develop the BBC's policies relating to educational broadcasting, and **Bridget Plowden**, in her role as chairman of the **Independent Broadcasting Authority**, was a key figure in the evolution of commercial radio within the United Kingdom.

As the 21st century has progressed, the role of women in production—particularly in the field of creative **feature** making—has developed, and the work of such program makers as **Francesca Panetta** has partnered the development of new technology with a poetic sensibility. Others, like **Nina Garthwaite**, with the creation of such interest groups as **In the Dark**, have championed **documentary** making in both long and short forms. Women have also started to occupy more roles in management (**Gwyneth Williams** took over the controllership of Radio 4 in 2010), although more opportunities need to be created in this area, particularly in the commercial sector. **Sound Women**, formed in 2011, by **Maria Williams**, has taken a practical approach to supporting women in the radio and audio industries, aiming to build confidence, develop networking and leadership skills, and bring women together to explore and compare experiences to enable them to realize their full potential.

WOOD NORTON. A medieval mansion in Worcestershire that was purchased by the **British Broadcasting Corporation (BBC)** in 1939, to relocate its broadcasting operations away from urban sites during wartime. A dozen studios were built, and within a year, Wood Norton had become one of the largest broadcasting centers in Europe, averaging 1,300 radio programs a week. It was also, for a time, a monitoring station, with linguists tuning in to overseas broadcasts. After the war, Wood Norton became the BBC's engineering training center. Purpose-built facilities on the grounds are still used for this.

WORD OF MOUTH. A program broadcast on **BBC Radio 4** about the English language and the way it is spoken. It was first broadcast in 1992, with **Frank Delaney** as presenter and **Simon Elmes** as producer. The show was subsequently presented by **Michael Rosen**.

WORKERS' PLAYTIME. In 1940, the minister for labour, Ernest Bevin, requested that the **British Broadcasting Corporation (BBC)** devise a program that would support and cheer workers in factories supporting the war effort. The result was *Workers' Playtime*, which began as a weekend show in May 1941, and moved into a thrice-weekly slot in October that year, when Bevin himself introduced the program. Hosted by Bill Gates, the program comprised variety "turns"—most notably **Elsie and Doris Waters**, who were regulars throughout the show's lifetime in their characters of "Gert and Daisy"—and two pianos, and it was always transmitted as an **outside broadcast** from a factory canteen, the location of which was kept secret for security reasons during the war years, the announcement only telling the listener that it came from a "works somewhere in England." *Workers' Playtime* long outlived its original intention, the final edition under the original name coming from a factory in Hatfield Heath in October 1964, when guests introduced by Gates included Anne Shelton, **Cyril Fletcher**, and Val Doonican.

See also WARTIME BROADCASTING.

WORLD AT ONE, THE. Created by Andrew Boyle, launched in October 1965, and hosted in its early years by **William Hardcastle**, *The World at One*, a daily half-hour **news** magazine program on the **BBC Home Service** that continues on **BBC Radio 4**, is an example of a policy encouraged by **Frank Gillard**, during his time as director of sound broadcasting at the **British Broadcasting Corporation**, and **Gerard Mansell** of moving speech output away from scripted contributions and into the field of live debate.

See also CURRENT AFFAIRS; NEWS.

WORLD RADIO. Almost as soon as radio began in an organized form in the United Kingdom, early adopters of receiver technology sought to experiment by exploring the airwaves in an attempt to locate additional and more distant radio stations. Within the context of this climate, the **British Broadcasting Company (BBC)** founded *World Radio*, initially the *Radio Supplement*, in 1925, two years after its domestic, *Radio Times*. Subtitled the *Official Foreign and Technical Journal of the BBC*, its purpose was to foster awareness of international radio, and the **journal** contained articles and listings, together with wavelengths and broadcasting times. As the **British Broadcasting Corporation** moved toward its new **Empire Service**, the journal was expanded in 1932, in spite of objections from the trade press.

The interest in international listening during the 1920s and early 1930s gave *World Radio* its purpose; compared to *Radio Times*, its circulation was extremely modest. In 1930, *Radio Times* had 1,334,063 listeners, while *World Radio* had 153,595. In 1931, *Radio Times* had 11,575,151 listeners, while *World Radio* had 181,513. And in 1932, *Radio Times* had 1,825,951 listeners, while *World Radio* had 157,545. The year 1931 proved to be the high point in sales for *World Radio*, and thereafter sales diminished. The journal ceased publication in 1939.

It is a curious and ironic fact that in the first years of the 1930s, *World Radio* was carrying listings for stations that themselves were supported by sponsorship, broadcasting from the continent into the United Kingdom. As a BBC journal, this was inappropriate, while at the same time, the corporation had commercial factors to consider in the sale of its magazines. Although most of the listings were terse and factual, a study of the pages of *World Radio* will occasionally reveal a sponsor's message, and toward the end of the journal's life, it was carrying full details of **Radio Normandy** programs.

It is no coincidence that **Leonard Plugge**, while developing his **commercial radio** interests, had gained a contract from the BBC itself to "supply, translate, and sub-edit foreign wireless programs" for *World Radio*.

WORLD RADIO NETWORK (WRN). Based in Britain, WRN was created in 1992, by three former **British Broadcasting Corporation** staff members who wanted to take advantage of emerging technologies to improve the distribution of international **shortwave (SW)** radio. The company's first contract was to deliver programs from Vatican Radio to listeners via the Astra satellite. WRN then began to create its own branded radio channels, carrying daily scheduled programs, many from international SW broadcasters. These channels were distributed to listeners via **analog** and later digital satellite, cable, Internet, and local **amplitude modulation (AM)/frequency modulation (FM)** relays, enabling listeners to hear international radio in greatly improved audio quality, particularly in comparison to SW.

Channels were themed according to language, and WRN developed services in English, German, French, Russian, and Arabic. International broadcasters will find in WRN a conduit for the daily or weekly dissemination of their programs in high-quality audio; these include Radio Netherlands, China Radio International, Radio Canada International, Deutsche Welle, and Radio Australia. Distribution has continued to develop as new technologies have appeared, among them podcasting, **Digital Audio Broadcasting**, and mobile telephony.

In recent years, the company has taken advantage of its aggregation and distribution infrastructure to offer a wide range of transmission services to other broadcasters. It also developed an extensive brokerage service, buying time on SW and AM and FM transmitters on behalf of clients. Today, as WRN Broadcast, the company continues to work with both radio and television organizations to enable the delivery of content to specific audiences worldwide. In April 2009, WRN Broadcast acquired TSI Broadcast to further enhance its services in this field.

WORLD TONIGHT, THE. Broadcast on **BBC Radio 4**, *The World Tonight* is a long-running **current affairs** program broadcast at 10:00 p.m. on weekday nights, featuring **news**, analysis, and commentary on domestic and world issues. The program boasts an impressive list of distinguished journalists/presenters, including **Robin Lustig**, Anthony Howard, Richard Kershaw, and **John Tusa**.

WRIGHT, STEVE (1954–). Joining **BBC Radio 2** in April 1996, as part of the redesign of the station instigated by the controller, **James Moir**, Steve Wright initially presented two weekend shows, on Saturday and Sunday mornings, but later moved to weekday afternoons, while continuing with his *Sunday Love Songs* program. Born in Greenwich, London, he first joined the **British Broadcasting Corporation** as a researcher and record librarian, leaving in 1975, to briefly work in European radio. Thereafter, Wright made programs for the **London Broadcasting Company** and then Thames Valley Radio (Radio 210) in 1976. Three years later, he was at **Radio Luxembourg** and then joined **BBC Radio 1** in January 1980, where he presented various shows.

In January 1994, after a highly successful stint as the afternoon program host, Wright took over the breakfast show, where he remained until 21 April 1995, when he resigned in dramatic fashion in protest of the reforms of the network being undertaken by Controller **Matthew Bannister**. He has won a wide range of awards for his work in U.K. **music** radio.

See also DISC JOCKEY (DJ).

WRITTLE. Situated near **Chelmsford**, in Essex, home of the **Marconi Company**, the village of Writtle was the location of the first regular public broadcast program in the United Kingdom, which commenced in February 1922. The circuit was almost identical to that of a standard Marconi telephone, and the transmitter fed a four-wire aerial 250 feet long and 100 feet high, originally radiating on a wavelength of 700 meters. The equipment was housed in a former army hut, and the station took the call sign 2MT, Two Emma Toc, broadcasting a weekly half-hour program of technical information, testing, occasional **music**, and entertaining banter, principally from its main presenter, Captain **Peter Eckersley**. The station closed on 17 January 1923.

Writtle remained a company site for many years thereafter. The historic hut was later removed for use by a local school but was subsequently retrieved and is now housed at the Chelmsford Science and Industry Museum in Sandford Mill. The site of the hut is commemorated by a nearby information board at Melba Court, named after Dame Nellie Melba, who made Britain's first entertainment broadcast from the company's New Street works in Chelmsford (*see* "MELBA" BROADCAST). The board was unveiled in 1997, by Marconi's daughter, Princess Elletra Marconi. The site itself was sold and the land used for a housing development in the 1990s.

In the village of Writtle, the Church of All Saints contains a window commemorating the work of Marconi. It was dedicated by his grandson, Prince Guglielmo Marconi Giovanelli, in 1992. The Writtle station is seen by many as the true birthplace of U.K. radio as a public entertainment form.

WRN BROADCAST. *See* WORLD RADIO NETWORK (WRN).

X

XFM. Xfm refers to a brand of **commercial radio** stations owned by **Global Radio**. The content is characterized by a predominance of alternative **music**, and there are two stations, in London, launched as a **restricted service license** by Sammy Jacob in 1992, and broadcasting full-time since 1997, and Manchester, launched in 2006. The stations had previously been owned by **GCap Media**.

Y

YALDING HOUSE. A building owned by the **British Broadcasting Corporation (BBC)** and situated on Great Portland Street, close to **Broadcasting House**. From 1996–2012, it was the administrative and studio base for **BBC Radio 1** and **BBC Radio 1Xtra**, the former station having previously been based in Egton House. The last broadcast from Yalding House took place on 14 December 2012, after which the two networks were transferred to the **John Peel** Wing of the BBC's refurbished headquarters in Portland Place. Previous usage of the building had been by **BBC Radio 3** and the BBC Central Music Library. Prior to being purchased by the BBC, Yalding House had been a car showroom.

YOU AND YOURS. A daily consumer and social affairs magazine that began its life on **BBC Radio 4** in 1970. Initially in a half-hour slot, its duration was extended to a little less than an hour during the 1990s, by Controller James Boyle.

YOUNG WIDOW JONES. Toward the end of the continent-based commercial revolution of the 1930s, agencies like the **J. Walter Thompson Organization** began developing variations of the **soap operas** then popular on U.S. radio. Among these was *Young Widow Jones*, broadcast on **Radio Luxembourg** beginning in October 1938 and sponsored by Milk of Magnesia. It was billed in *Radio Pictorial* as, "The moving story of a woman's heart and woman's love. Living in the small town of Appleton, Peggy Jones, in her 20s, with two children to support, ponders long on the question of what she owes to her children and what she owes to herself. A story of joy and despair, life and love as we all know it." The **series** was based on the U.S. original *Young Widder Jones*, and this and other such programs introduced British audiences to a genre that, postwar, would become highly significant.

See also DRAMA; SERIALS.

YOUNG, JIMMY (1921–). Jimmy Young was a popular singer for many years, with two chart-topping hits in the mid-1950s; however, it was as a radio presenter that he made his greatest mark. Working as a **disc jockey** for the **Light Programme**, he presented *Flat Spin* in 1949, and later *Housewives' Choice* intermittently from 1955–1960. Thereafter, he worked at **Radio Luxembourg** for a number of years. When **BBC Radio 1** was launched in 1967, Young was a member of the original team, and his mid-morning program was broadcast on both BBC Radio 1 and **BBC Radio 2**. In 1973, he moved to Radio 2 exclusively and remained in the morning slot until being replaced by **Jeremy Vine** in 2003.

Young was known for his interviews with high-ranking world figures, including every British prime minister beginning in 1964. Said to be Margaret Thatcher's favorite interviewer, he was knighted for his services to radio in 2002, the year of his retirement. He was offered a weekend program on the station but declined. Young later criticized the **British Broadcasting Corporation** in his autobiography, implying that the decision to leave the station had not been his. He did return to the Radio 2 airwaves in September 2011, for a special program to mark his 90th birthday, and in March 2012, he took part in a **series** entitled *Icons of the 50s*.

YOUNG, STUART (1934–1986). Stuart Young came from an accounting background and a number of directorships to become a governor of the **British Broadcasting Corporation (BBC)** in 1981. He had originally felt that the corporation should be funded by advertising but changed his thoughts on this to the extent that as chairman (a position to which he was appointed in 1983), he led the BBC's successful argument to the Peacock Committee for a continuation of license funding. It was a time of tension between the BBC and the government regarding editorial matters, particularly in television. When Young died in office in 1986, his place was taken by Vice Chairman Lord Barnett until the appointment of **Marmaduke Hussey**.

YOUR HUNDRED BEST TUNES. A show devised by **Alan Keith** and presented by him on Sunday evenings from 1959 until his death in 2003, when the mantle was assumed by **Richard Baker**. The title was originally *The Hundred Best Tunes in the World*. Originally airing on the **Light Programme**, it moved to the **BBC Home Service** during the 1960s and was subsequently transferred to **BBC Radio 2**. The musical choice was always undemanding, relaxing, and comforting. The last program was broadcast on 21 January 2007, when it was terminated by the controller of BBC Radio 2, **Lesley Douglas**, and replaced by an extended version of *Melodies for You*. In addition to Keith and later Baker, guest presenters during the 47-year history of *Your Hundred Best Tunes* included Lady Evelyn Barbirolli, Rosalind Runcie, Earl Spencer, and Ursula Vaughan Williams (widow of the composer Ralph Vaughan Williams).

See also MUSIC.

YOUR OLD FRIEND DAN. A popular prewar series on **Radio Normandy** that began in September 1936 and featured Canadian broadcaster Lyle Evans. The format was that of songs, instrumental **music**, and homespun philosophy, and it made Evans (as "Dan") a well-known personality during the last years of peace before World War II. The program was sponsored by Johnson's Wax Polish.

See also COMMERCIAL RADIO.

Z

ZOO MAN, THE. A regular **feature** on *Children's Hour* that began in 1924 and was presented by *Daily Mail* journalist Leslie Mainland. In January 1934, it was re-created by David Seth-Smith, curator of birds and mammals at London's Regent's Park Zoo. Seth-Smith maintained regular **talks** in the slot until 1945. **British Broadcasting Corporation** Regions sometimes gave the idea a more local slant by appointing their own "Zoo Man."

See also CHILDREN'S PROGRAMS.

Bibliography

CONTENTS

I. INTRODUCTION

Because radio as a public entertainment is less than 100 years old, the library of works relating to it is both concise and potent. It is interesting to note that it is also growing as the medium approaches its centenary, the inference being that sound not only remains an important part of life, but also that as technologies change, we discover new ways of making sound-based art and communication, as well as new methods of listening to the results of that making. The first decade and a half of the 21st century have produced an impressive number of works that explore radio and audio in a reflective and philosophical sense, as well as within the context of developing technologies and historical perspectives. Thus, we are adding to a body of material that demands more and more to be seen and evaluated as a major aspect of the humanities. This collection of works can be broadly divided into three categories: 1) the writings of its creators, 2) the histories, and 3) growing in size and importance, reflective works of theory and cultural studies.

In the United Kingdom, as elsewhere in the world, radio is increasingly seen as an important subject worthy of academic study, as reflected by the thriving discipline of radio studies, and likewise because of the medium's continuing ability to reinvent itself according to new technologies. Audio documents are finding their "voice" as important and continuing sources of cultural reference. Sound artifacts are also archival objects of great importance, in some cases perhaps even more so than historic written texts or scrolls, an interesting aspect since sound is invisible. It might be said that the increasing number of online journals and texts with which academics, scholars, and students equip themselves provides a metaphor for the new currency of sound in society.

The hearing of sound is the first sense to awaken in us at birth and, some say, the last to desert us at death. British academic and broadcaster David Hendy reflects on the importance of sound in his book *Noise: A Human History of Sound and Listening*. He details how human beings have documented auditory phenomena throughout history in diaries, letters, and numerous other texts, writing that the fact that "so many people [have chosen] to write about sound is a clear measure of how important it was in their lives" (2013, xv).

In the early days of U.K. radio, the wonder—and almost strangeness—of the new medium compelled many of the pioneers to reflect on their first experiences in print. Thus, John Reith's *Broadcast over Britain*, Arthur Burrows's *The Story of Broadcasting*, and Cecil Lewis's *Broadcasting from Within*—works from three of the most important founding fathers of British radio, written within three years of the creation of the British Broadcasting Company in 1922—provide direct and impassioned witness to those first, heady years. These works are invaluable, particularly when read alongside some of the primary material cited in this bibliography, including the official government reports created as radio in the United Kingdom sought to define itself within the model of a public service ethic. For this reason, these commentaries, autobiographies, and personal reflections have been included in the "Direct Sources" section. For the same reason, such journals as *Radio Times*, *Radio Pictorial*, and the *BBC Handbooks* are included in the "Public Journals" section, listing magazines and other regular publications intended by broadcasters for their audiences, offering direct information for those seeking to understand the zeitgeist of the time.

For serious students of U.K. radio—indeed, broadcasting—history, an indispensable source is Asa Briggs's five-volume *History of Broadcasting in the United Kingdom*, located in section III of the bibliography. Told principally from a BBC perspective, it is nonetheless a work to which other scholars of British media history owe a great debt. Likewise, Brigg's *The BBC: The First Fifty Years* provides extremely useful insights. Section III also includes analytical and interpretative writings from the developing academic discipline of radio studies in Great Britain. Readers will find books grouped with journals, papers, pamphlets, and websites.

Section IV, "Making Radio," is a list of sources dealing with the practicalities of creating the medium in its diverse forms; because radio platforms—transmission and receiver technology—are rapidly changing and evolving, it is important to understand the nature and essence of the form itself through a perception of its various facets. Today's instruction manuals will become tomorrow's historical primary source texts, as have those of radio's short past. The section begins with the technical and includes Edward Pawley's seminal *BBC Engineering, 1922–1972*. Production itself is also covered, with sources that offer an understanding of some of the multifarious skills required in the medium. Radio advertising and commercial radio are clearly linked, and radio scholars at any level will find historical and contemporary texts on the genres of music radio, radio drama, and radio journalism.

Because of the nature of the medium, radio is always potentially international. As such, texts on international radio are included; however, most of the works cited here relate to the work of the BBC World Service and the nature of wartime propaganda broadcasting. A number of U.K. radio programs have spawned either spin-off books or specific studies, and both are included here, maintaining the theme of this bibliography's aim, which is to be both reflective and directly engaged with primary sources relating to radio in the United Kingdom. It is pleasing to be able to report the continuing health of radio study, analysis, and interpretation, and anticipate the unwritten works that will further enrich this study as broadcast radio approaches its centenary. Radio/audio—both as a form and subject richly rewarding to the scholar, researcher, and general enthusiast—is alive and well.

II. DIRECT SOURCES

A. Official Sources

Broadcasting Committee Report. Cmnd. 1951. Sykes Committee. London: HMSO, 1923.

Broadcasting in the 1990s: Competition, Choice, and Quality. White Paper. Cmnd. 517. London: HMSO, 1988.

Broadcasting Policy. White Paper. Cmnd. 6852. London: HMSO, 1946.

Broadcasting Policy. White Paper. Cmnd. 9005. London: HMSO, 1953.

The Development of Cable Systems and Services. White Paper. Cmnd. 8866. London: HMSO, 1983.

Report of the Broadcasting Committee. Cmnd. 2599. Crawford Committee. London: HMSO, 1925.

Report of the Broadcasting Committee. Cmnd. 5091. Ullswater Committee. London: HMSO, 1936.

Report of the Broadcasting Committee 1949. Cmnd. 8116. Beveridge Committee. London: HMSO, 1951.

Report of the Committee on Broadcasting. Cmnd. 1753. Pilkington Committee. London: HMSO, 1962.

Report of the Committee on the Financing of the BBC. Cmnd. 9284. Peacock Committee. London: HMSO, 1986.

Report of the Committee on the Future of Broadcasting. Cmnd. 6753. Annan Committee. London: HMSO, 1977.

Report of the Imperial Wireless Committee, 1919–20. Cmnd. 777. Norman Committee. London: HMSO, 1920.

Report of the Television Committee, 1934–5. Cmnd. 4793. Selsdon Committee. London: HMSO, 1935.

B. Public Journals

BBC Handbook. [Sometimes called *BBC Year Book* and *BBC Annual*]. Annually. London: BBC, 1928–1987.

Listener. Weekly. London: BBC, 1929–1991.

Radio Pictorial. Weekly. London: Bernard Jones Publications, 1934–1939.

Radio Times. Weekly. London: Various publishers, 1923–present.

C. Commentaries, Biography, and Autobiography

Adie, Kate. *The Kindness of Strangers.* London: Headline, 2002.

Barker, Eric. *Steady, Barker.* London: Secker and Warburg, 1956.

Boyle, Andrew. *Only the Wind Will Listen: Reith of the BBC.* London: Hutchinson, 1972.

Braden, Bernard. *The Kindness of Strangers.* London: Hodder and Stoughton, 1990.

Bridson, D. G. *Prospero and Ariel: The Rise and Fall of Radio; A Personal Recollection.* London: Gollancz, 1971.

Burrows, Arthur. *The Story of Broadcasting.* London: Cassell, 1924.

Carney, Michael. *Stoker: The Life of Hilda Matheson OBE, 1888–1940.* Llangynog, U.K.: Michael Carney, 1999.

Cleghorn Thomson, David. *Radio Is Changing Us.* London: Watts, 1937.

Conolly, Leonard W. *Bernard Shaw and the BBC.* Toronto: University of Toronto Press, 2009.

Coulton, Barbara. *Louis MacNeice in the BBC.* London: Faber and Faber, 1980.

Cox, Peter. *Set into Song: Ewan MacColl, Charles Parker, Peggy Seeger, and the Radio Ballads.* Cambridge: Labatie, 2008.

Dimbleby, Jonathan. *Richard Dimbleby.* London: Hodder and Stoughton, 1975.

Eckersley, Myles. *Prospero's Wireless.* Romsey: Myles, 1998.

Eckersley, Peter. *The Power behind the Microphone.* London: Scientific Book Club, 1942.

Eckersley, Roger. *The BBC and All That.* London: Sampson Low, Marston, 1946.

Evens, E. *Through the Years with Romany.* London: University of London Press, 1946.

Fielden, Lionel. *The Natural Bent.* London: Andre Deutsch, 1960.

Fletcher, Cyril. *Nice One Cyril.* London: Corgi, 1980.

Gielgud, Val. *Years in a Mirror.* London: Bodley Head, 1964.

Glover, Fi. *Travels with My Radio.* London: Ebury, 2002.

Gorham, Maurice. *Sound and Fury: Twenty-one Years in the BBC.* London: Percival Marshall, 1948.

Green, Hugh. *The Third Floor Front.* London: Bodley Head, 1969.

Grisewood, Freddy. *The World Goes By.* London: Secker and Warburg, 1952.

Grisewood, Harman. *One Thing at a Time: An Autobiography.* London: Hutchinson, 1968.

Guthrie, Tyrone. *Squirrel's Cage.* London: Cobden-Sanderson, 1931.

Hall, Henry. *Here's to the Next Time.* London: Odhams, 1956.

Harding, Gilbert. *Along My Line.* London: Putnam, 1953.

———. *Master of None.* London: Putnam, 1958.

Hawkins, Desmond. *When I Was: A Memoir of the Years between the Wars.* London: Macmillan, 1989.

Heatley, Michael. *John Peel: A Life in Music.* London: Michael O'Mara, 2005.

Heppenstall, Rayner. *Portrait of the Artist as a Professional Man.* London: Owen, 1969.

Hibberd, Stuart. *This—Is London.* London: MacDonald and Evans, 1950.

Hill, Trevor. *Over the Airwaves: My Life in Broadcasting.* Lewes, U.K.: Book Guild, 2005.

Hunter, Fred. "Hilda Matheson and the BBC, 1926–1940." In *Women and Radio: Airing Differences*, ed. Caroline Mitchell, 41–47. London: Routledge, 2000.

Jupitus, Phill. *Good Morning Nantwich: Adventures in Breakfast Radio*. London: HarperCollins, 2010.

Kavanagh, Ted. *Tommy Handley*. London: Hodder and Stoughton, 1949.

Lewis, Cecil. *Broadcasting from Within*. London: Newnes, 1924.

MacPherson, Stewart. *The Mike and I*. London: Home and Van Thal, 1948.

Marconi, Degna. *My Father, Marconi*. London: Frederick Muller, 1962.

Marconi, Maria Cristina. *Marconi, My Beloved*. Boston: Dante University of America Press, 2001.

Martland, Peter. *Lord Haw-Haw: The English Voice of Nazi Germany*. London: National Archives, 2003.

Maschwitz, Eric. *No Chip on My Shoulder*. London: Jenkins, 1957.

McIntyre, Ian. *The Expense of Glory: A Life of John Reith*. London: HarperCollins, 1993.

McWhinnie, Donald. *The Art of Radio*. London: Faber and Faber, 1959.

Messiter, Ian. *My Life and Other Games*. London: Fourth Estate, 1990.

Miall, Leonard. *Inside the BBC: British Broadcasting Characters*. London: Weidenfeld and Nicolson, 1994.

———, ed. *Richard Dimbleby, Broadcaster*. London: BBC, 1966.

Moseley, Sydney. *Broadcasting in My Time*. London: Rich and Cowan, 1935.

———. *The Private Diaries of Sydney Moseley*. London/Bournemouth: Max Parrish/Outspoken Press, 1960

Nicolson, Harold. *Diaries and Letters*. London: Collins, 1967.

Osborne, John. *Radio Head: Up and Down the Dial of British Radio*. London: Simon and Schuster, 2008.

Payne, Jack. *Signature Tune*. London: Paul, 1947.

Peel, John. *Margrave of the Marshes*. London: Bantam, 2005.

Phillips, Justin. *C. S. Lewis at the BBC*. London: HarperCollins, 2002.

Pickles, Wilfred. *Between You and Me*. London: Werner Laurie, 1949.

Plomley, Roy. *Days Seemed Longer: Early Years of a Broadcaster*. London: Eyre Methuen, 1980.

Potter, Julian. *Stephen Potter at the BBC*. Orford, U.K.: Orford, 2004.

Priestland, Gerald. *Something Understood*. London: Andre Deutsch, 1986.

Purves, Libby. *Radio: A True Love Story*. London: Hodder and Stoughton, 2002.

Reith, John. *Broadcast over Britain*. London: Hodder and Stoughton, 1924.

———. *Into the Wind*. London: Hodder and Stoughton, 1949.

———. *Personality and Career*. London: George Newnes, 1925.

Rowntree, Seebohm. *Poverty and Progress*. London: Longman's, 1941.

Shapley, Olive. *Broadcasting a Life*. London: Scarlet Press, 1996.

Sieveking, Lance. *Airborne: Scenes from the Life of Lance Sieveking*. London: Strange Attractor Press, 2013

———. *The Stuff of Radio*. London: Cassell, 1934.

Stone, Christopher. *Christopher Stone Speaking*. London: Elkin Matthews and Marrot, 1933.

Stuart, Charles, ed. *The Reith Diaries*. London: Collins, 1975.

Thomas, Howard. *With an Independent Air: Encounters during a Lifetime of Broadcasting*. London: Weidenfeld and Nicolson, 1977.

Train, Jack. *Up and Down the Line*. London: Odhams, 1956.

Trethowan, Ian. *Split Screen*. London: Hamish Hamilton, 1984.

Wallis, Keith. *And the World Listened: The Biography of Captain Leonard Plugge*. Tiverton, U.K.: Kelly Publications, 2008.

Watt, John, ed. *Radio Variety*. London: Dent and Sons, 1939.

Watts, Agnes. *Cecil E. Watts: Pioneer of Direct Disc Recording*. London: Privately published, 1972.

White, Peter. *See It My Way*. London: Little, Brown and Company, 1999.

Whitney, John. *To Serve the People: My Years at the IBA*. New Barnet: John Libbey, 2013.

III. HISTORICAL, ANALYTICAL, AND INTERPRETATIVE

A. Historical Reference Works

Baker, A. J. *A History of the Marconi Company*. London: Methuen, 1970.

Balk, Alfred. *The Rise of Radio: From Marconi through the Golden Age*. Jefferson, N.C.: McFarland, 2006.

BBC. *Broadcasting House*. London: BBC, 1932.

Beachcroft, T. O. *British Broadcasting*. London: Longman, Green and Co., 1946.

Black, Peter. *The Biggest Aspidistra in the World*. London: BBC, 1972.

Born, Georgina. *Uncertain Vision: Birt, Dyke, and the Reinvention of the BBC*. London: Secker and Warburg, 2004.

Briggs, Asa. *The BBC: The First Fifty Years*. Oxford, U.K.: Oxford University Press, 1985.

———. *Governing the BBC*. London: BBC, 1979.

———. *The History of Broadcasting in the United Kingdom, Vol. 1: The Birth of Broadcasting, 1896–1927*. Oxford, U.K.: Oxford University Press, 1995.

———. *The History of Broadcasting in the United Kingdom, Vol. II: The Golden Age of Wireless, 1927–1939*. Oxford, U.K.: Oxford University Press, 1995.

———. *The History of Broadcasting in the United Kingdom, Vol. III: The War of Words, 1939–1945.* Oxford, U.K.: Oxford University Press, 1995.

———. *The History of Broadcasting in the United Kingdom, Vol. IV: Sound and Vision, 1945–1955.* Oxford, U.K.: Oxford University Press, 1995.

———. *The History of Broadcasting in the United Kingdom, Vol. V: Competition, 1955–1974.* Oxford, U.K.: Oxford University Press, 1995.

Brochand, Christian. *Histoire Générale de la Radio et de la Télévision en France, Tome 1, 1921–1944.* Paris: La Documentation Française, 1994.

Carpenter, Humphrey. *The Envy of the World: Fifty Years of the BBC Third Programme and Radio 3.* London: Weidenfeld and Nicolson, 1996.

Chignell, Hugh. *BBC Handbooks, Accounts, and Annual Reports (1927–2002).* Wakefield, U.K.: Microform Academic Publishers, 2003.

Conboy, Martin, and John Steel, eds. *The Routledge Companion to British Media History.* Abingdon, U.K.: Routledge, 2014.

Cox, Jim. *The Great Radio Soap Operas.* New York: McFarland, 1999.

Crisell, Andrew. *An Introductory History of British Broadcasting.* London: Routledge, 2002.

———. *Understanding Radio.* London: Methuen, 1994.

———, ed. *More Than a Music Box: Radio Cultures and Communities in a Multimedia World.* Oxford, U.K., and New York: Berghahn, 2004.

Currie, Tony. *The Radio Times Story.* Tiverton, U.K.: Kelly Publications, 2001.

Donovan, Paul. *The Radio Companion.* London: Grafton, 1992.

Douglas, George H. *The Early Days of Radio Broadcasting.* Jefferson, N.C.: McFarland, 1987.

Duval, René. *Histoire de la Radio en France.* Paris: Éditions Alain Moreau, 1979.

Elmes, Simon. *And Now on Radio 4: A 40th Birthday Celebration.* London: Random House, 2007.

Fernández, Francisco José Montes. *Los Origenes de la radiodifusión exterior en España.* Madrid: RTVE, 1988.

Foster, Andy, and Steve Furst. *Radio Comedy, 1938–1968.* London: Virgin, 1996.

Gifford, Denis. *The Golden Age of Radio.* London: Batsford, 1985.

Gilliam, Laurence, ed. *BBC Features.* London: Evans Brothers, 1950.

Gorham, Maurice. *Forty Years of Irish Broadcasting.* Dublin: Talbot, 1967.

Hajkowski, Thomas. *The BBC and National Identity in Britain, 1922–53.* Manchester, U.K.: Manchester University Press, 2010.

Hartley, Ian. *2ZY to NBH: An Informal History of the BBC in Manchester and the North West.* Altrincham, U.K.: Willow Publishing, 1987.

Havers, Richard. *Here Is the News: The BBC and the Second World War.* Stroud, U.K.: Sutton Publishing, 2007.

Hawkins, Desmond. *War Report: D-Day to VE-Day*. London: Ariel Books/BBC, 1985.

Hendy, David. *Life on Air: A History of Radio Four*. Oxford, U.K.: Oxford University Press, 2007.

Hennessey, Brian. *Savoy Hill: The Early Years of British Broadcasting*. Romford, U.K.: Ian Henry Publications, 1996.

Hines, Mark. *The Story of Broadcasting House, Home of the BBC*. London: Merrell, 2007.

Kenyon, Nicholas. *The BBC Symphony Orchestra: The First Fifty Years, 1930–1980*. London: BBC, 1981.

Lambert, R. S. *Ariel and All His Quality*. London: Victor Gollancz, 1940.

Méadel, Cécile. *Histoire de la Radio des Années Trente*. Paris: Anthropos/INA, 1994.

Morris, John. *From the Third Programme: A Ten Years' Anthology*. London: Nonesuch, 1956.

Nicholas, Sian. *The Echo of War: Home Front Propaganda and the Wartime BBC, 1939–45*. Manchester, U.K.: Manchester University Press, 1996.

Potter, Simon J. *Broadcasting Empire: The BBC and the British World, 1922–1970*. Oxford, U.K.: Oxford University Press, 2012.

Reid, Colin. *Action Stations: A History of Broadcasting House*. London: Robson, 1987.

Scannell, Paddy, and David Cardiff. *A Social History of British Broadcasting, 1922–1939, Serving the Nation*. Oxford, U.K.: Blackwell, 1991.

Shingler, Martin, and Cindy Wieringa. *On Air: Methods and Meanings of Radio*. London: Arnold, 1998.

Smith, Anthony. *British Broadcasting*. Newton Abbot, U.K.: David and Charles. 1974.

Snagge, John, and Michael Barsley. *Those Vintage Years of Radio*. London: Pitman, 1972.

Sterling, Christopher H., ed. *The Museum of Broadcast Communications Encyclopedia of Radio*. New York: Fitzroy Dearborn, 2004.

Stoller, Tony. *Sounds of Your Life: The History of Independent Radio in the UK*. New Barnet, U.K.: John Libbey, 2010.

Street, Seán. *A Concise History of British Radio, 1922–2002*. Tiverton, U.K.: Kelly Publications, 2005.

———. *Crossing the Ether: British Public Service Radio and Commercial Competition, 1922–1945*. London: John Libbey Media, 2006.

Tomalin, Norman. *Daventry Calling the World*. Whitby, U.K.: Caedmon of Whitby, 1998.

Took, Barry. *Laughter in the Air*. London: Robson, 1976.

Wander, Tim. *2MT Writtle: The Birth of Broadcasting*. Stowmarket, U.K.: Capella Publications, 1988.

Whitehead, Kate. *The Third Programme: A Literary History*. Oxford, U.K.: Clarendon, 1989.

Wood, R. *A World in Your Ear*. London: Macmillan, 1979.

B. Cultural and Theoretical

Anderson, John Nathan. *Radio's Digital Dilemma: Broadcasting in the Twenty First Century*. New York: Routledge, 2013.

Baade, Christina L. *Victory through Harmony: The BBC and Popular Music in World War II*. Oxford, U.K.: Oxford University Press, 2013.

Baily, Leslie. *Leslie Baily's BBC Scrapbooks, Volume 2: 1918–1939*. London: George Allen and Unwin, 1968.

Baldwin, Stanley. *On England, and Other Addresses*. London: Philip Allan, 1936.

Bijsterveld, Karin, and José van Dijck. *Sound Souvenirs: Memory and Cultural Practices*. Amsterdam, Netherlands: Amsterdam University Press, 2009.

Black, Peter. *The Biggest Aspidistra in the World: A Personal Celebration of 50 Years of the BBC*. London: BBC, 1972.

Branigan, Kevin. *Radio Beckett: Musicality in the Plays of Samuel Beckett*. Bern: Peter Lang, 2008.

Briggs, Susan. *Those Radio Times*. London: Weidenfeld and Nicolson, 1981.

Burns, T. *BBC: Public Institution, Private World*. London: Macmillan, 1977.

Cardiff, David. "The Serious and the Popular: Aspects of the Evolution of Style in the Radio Talk, 1928–1939." In *Media, Culture, and Society: A Critical Reader*, ed. Richard Collins, 228–46. London: Sage, 1986.

Carey, John. *The Intellectuals and the Masses: Pride and Prejudice among the Literary Intelligensia, 1880–1939*. London: Faber and Faber, 1992.

Chignell, Hugh. *Key Concepts in Radio*. London: Sage, 2009.

———. *Public Issue Radio: Talks, News, and Current Affairs in the Twentieth Century*. Basingstoke, U.K.: Palgrave Macmillan, 2011.

Clark, J. *Culture and Crisis in Britain in the 1930s*. London: Lawrence and Wishart, 1979.

Coase, R. H. *British Broadcasting: A Study in Monopoly*. London: London School of Economics/Longmans, 1950.

Cooke, Alistair. *The Patient Has the Floor*. London: Bodley Head, 1986.

Crisell, Andrew. *Liveness and Recording in the Media*. Basingstoke, U.K.: Palgrave Macmillan, 2012.

———. "Look with Thine Ears: BBC Radio 4 and Its Significance in a Multi-Media Age." In *More Than a Music Box: Radio Cultures and Communities in a Multimedia World*, ed. Andrew Crisell, 3–19. Oxford, U.K., and New York: Berghahn, 2004.

————, ed. *More Than a Music Box: Radio Cultures and Communities in a Multimedia World*. Oxford, U.K., and New York: Berghahn, 2004.

Curran, Charles. *A Seamless Robe: Broadcasting—Philosophy and Practice*. London: Collins, 1979.

Curran, James, and Jean Seaton. *Power without Responsibility: The Press and Broadcasting in Britain*. London: Routledge, 1997.

Douglas, Susan J. *Listening In: Radio and the American Imagination*. New York: Times, 1999.

Emery, Walter B. *National and International Systems of Broadcasting: Their History, Operation, and Control*. East Lansing: Michigan State University Press, 1969.

Engelman, Ralph. *Public Radio and Television in America: A Political History*. Thousand Oaks, CA: Sage, 1996.

Giddings, Robert. "John Reith and the Rise of Radio." In *Literature and Culture in Modern Britain, Vol. 1, 1900–1929*, ed. Clive Bloom, 146–66. London: Longman, 1993.

Gilder, Eric. *Mass Media Moments in the United Kingdom, the USSR, and the USA*. Sibiu, Romania: Lucian Blaga University of Sibiu Press, 2003.

Goldie, Grace Wyndham. *Facing the Nation: Television and Politics, 1936–1976*. London: Bodley Head, 1977.

Hendy, David. *Noise: A Human History of Sound and Listening*. London: Profile, 2013.

————. *Public Service Broadcasting*. Basingstoke, U.K.: Palgrave Macmillan, 2013.

————. *Radio in the Global Age*. Cambridge, U.K.: Polity, 2000.

————. "Reality Radio: The Documentary." In *More Than a Music Box: Radio Cultures and Communities in a Multimedia World*, ed. Andrew Crisell, 167–88. Oxford, U.K., and New York: Berghahn, 2004.

Hilmes, Michele, and Jason Loviglio, eds. *A Radio Reader: Essays in the Cultural History of Radio*. New York: Routledge, 2002.

Hutchby, Ian. "The Organisation of Talk on Talk Radio." In *Broadcast Talk*, ed. Paddy Scannell, 119–37. London: Sage, 1991.

Jennings, Hilda, and Winifred Gill. *Broadcasting in Everyday Life: A Survey of the Social Effects of the Coming of Broadcasting*. London: BBC, 1939.

Kerwin, Jerome. *The Control of Radio*. Chicago: University of Chicago Press, 1934.

Koshar, Rudy, ed. *Splintered Classes, Politics, and the Lower Middle Classes in Interwar Europe*. New York: Holmes and Meier, 1990.

Lacey, Kate. "Continuities and Change in Women's Radio." In *More Than a Music Box: Radio Cultures and Communities in a Multimedia World*, ed. Andrew Crisell, 145–66. Oxford, U.K., and New York: Berghahn, 2004.

————. *Listening Publics: The Politics and Experience of Listening in the Media Age*. Cambridge, U.K.: Polity, 2013.

Leavis, F. R. *Mass Civilisation and Minority Culture*. London: Minority, 1930.

Lewis, P. M., and J. Booth. *The Invisible Medium: Public, Commercial, and Community Radio*. London: Macmillan, 1989.

Linehan, Andy, ed. *Aural History: Essays on Recorded Sound*. London: British Library, 2001.

Luscombe, Anya. *Sending the Right Message: Forty Years of BBC Radio News*. Utrecht, Netherlands: Joint Books, 2012.

MacDonald, Barrie. *Broadcasting in the United Kingdom: A Guide to Information Sources*. London: Mansell, 1993.

Marwick, Arthur. *Class: Image and Reality*. London: Collins, 1980.

McDonnell, James, ed. *Public Service Broadcasting: A Reader*. London: Routledge, 1991.

Mitchell, Caroline, ed. *Women and Radio: Airing Differences*. London: Routledge, 2000.

Paulu, Burton. *British Broadcasting: Radio and Television in the United Kingdom*. Minneapolis: University of Minnesota Press, 1956.

Pegg, Mark. *Broadcasting and Society, 1918–1939*. Beckenham, U.K.: Croom Helm, 1983.

Rudin, Richard. *Broadcasting in the 21st Century*. Basingstoke, U.K.: Palgrave Macmillan, 2011.

Scannell, Paddy, ed. *Broadcast Talk*. London: Sage, 1991.

———. *Radio, Television, and Modern Life*. Oxford, U.K.: Blackwell, 1996.

———. "The Relevance of Talk." In *Broadcast Talk*, ed. Paddy Scannell, 1–13. London: Sage, 1991.

Siepmann, Charles. *Radio, Television, and Society*. New York: Oxford University Press, 1950.

Silvey, Robert. *Who's Listening? The Story of BBC Audience Research*. London: George Allen and Unwin, 1974.

Starkey, Guy. "BBC Radio 5 Live: Extending Choice through 'Radio Bloke'?" In *More Than a Music Box: Radio Cultures and Communities in a Multimedia World*, ed. Andrew Crisell, 21–38. Oxford, U.K., and New York: Berghahn, 2004.

———. *Local Radio: Going Global*. Basingstoke, U.K.: Palgrave Macmillan, 2011.

Street, Seán. *The Memory of Sound: Preserving the Sonic Past*. New York, Routledge, 2014.

———. *The Poetry of Radio: The Colour of Sound*. Abingdon, U.K.: Routledge, 2013.

———. *Radio Waves: Poems Celebrating the Wireless*. London: Enitharmon, 2004.

Van Leeuwen, Theo. *Speech, Music, Sound*. Basingstoke, U.K.: Palgrave Macmillan, 1999.

Williams, Raymond. *Culture and Society*. Harmondsworth, U.K.: Pelican, 1963.

Williams, Raymond. *Television: Technology and Cultural Form*. London: Fontana, 1974.

Wolfe, Kenneth M. *The Churches and the British Broadcasting Corporation, 1922–1956: The Politics of Broadcast Religion*. London: SCM, 1984.

C. Journals

The Circular Note: Journals of the Vintage Radio Programmes Collectors' Circle. Harrogate.

Historic Record and AV Collector. London.

Journal of Advertising History. Norwich: MCB University Press.

Journal of Media Practice. Bristol, U.K.: Intellect.

Journal of Radio Studies. Washington, D.C.: Broadcast Education Association.

Media Culture and Society. London: Sage.

The Radio Journal: International Studies in Broadcast and Audio Media. Bristol, U.K.: Intellect/Radio Studies Network.

D. Articles and Papers

Lewis, Peter. "Opening and Closing Doors: Radio Drama in the BBC." *Radio Journal* 1, no. 3 (2004): 161–76.

Long, Paul. "British Radio and the Politics of Culture in Postwar Britain: The Work of Charles Parker." *Radio Journal* 2, no. 3 (2005): 131–52.

Luscombe, Anya. "The Future of Radio News: BBC Radio Journalists on the Brave New World in Which They Work." *Radio Journal* 7, no. 2 (2009): 111–22.

Moores, Shaun. "'The Box on the Dresser': Memories of Early Radio in Everyday Life." *Media Culture and Society* 10, no. 1 (1988): 23–40.

Oesterlen, Eve-Marie. "Lend Me Your 84 Million Ears: Exploring a Special Radio Event—*King Lear* on BBC World Service Radio." *Radio Journal* 6, no. 1 (2008): 33–44.

Street, Sean. "BBC Sunday Policy and Audience Response, 1930–45." *Journal of Radio Studies* 7, no. 1 (Spring 2000): 161–79.

———. "Programme-Makers on Parker: Occupational Reflections on the Radio Production Legacy of Charles Parker." *Radio Journal* 2, no. 3 (2005): 187–94.

Thomas, Lyn. "The Archers: An Everyday Story of Old and New Media." *Radio Journal* 7, no. 1 (2009): 49–66.

Wall, Tim. "Policy, Pop, and the Public: The Discourse of Regulation in British Commercial Radio." *Journal of Radio Studies* 7, no. 1 (2000): 180–95.

Williams, Stephen. "Pioneering Commercial Radio the 'D–I–Y' Way." *Journal of Advertising History* 10, no. 2 (1987): 7–14.

Wrigley, Amanda. "A Wartime Radio *Odyssey*: Edward Sackville-West and Benjamin Britten's *The Rescue* (1943)." *Radio Journal* 8, no. 2 (2010): 81–103.

E. Pamphlets

Calling All Nations: BBC Overseas Broadcasting. London: BBC, 1943.

Capital, Local Radio, and Private Profit. London: Commedia Publishing Group/Local Radio Workshop, 1983.

Twenty-five Years of British Broadcasting. London: BBC, 1947.

F. Websites

BBC iPlayer, http://www.bbc.co.uk/radio/

Charles Parker Archive Trust, http://www.cpatrust.org.uk

Chronomedia, www.terramedia.co.uk/Chronomedia/index.htm

Community Media Association, http://www.commedia.org.uk

History of the U.K. Radio License, http://www.radiolicence.org.uk

Listen Live: EU Radio Stations on the Internet, http://www.listenlive.eu/uk.html

Media.Info, http://media.info/uk/radio

Office of Communications, www.ofcom.org.uk

Radio Academy, www.radioacademy.org

RadioCentre, www.radiocentre.org

Radio Days, www.otr.com/index.shtml

RadioDoc Review, http://ro.uow.edu.au/rdr/

Radio Independents Group, www.radioindies.org

Radio Player, www.radioplayer.co.uk

Radio Rewind, www.radiorewind.co.uk

IV. MAKING RADIO

A. Technical

Alkin, G. *Sound Recording and Reproduction*. London: Focal, 1991.

Batten, Joe. *Joe Batten's Book: The Story of Sound Recording*. London: Rockliff, 1956.

Berry, Richard. "Speech Radio in the Digital Age." In *More Than a Music Box: Radio Cultures and Communities in a Multimedia World*, ed. Andrew Crisell, 283–96. Oxford, U.K., and New York: Berghahn, 2004.

Biel, Michael J. *The Making and Use of Recordings in Broadcasting before 1936*. Evanston IL: UMI Dissertation Service, 1996.

Bussey, Gordon. *Marconi's Atlantic Leap*. Coventry, U.K.: Marconi Communications, 2000.

Hill, Jonathan. *The Cat's Whisker: Fifty Years of Wireless Design*. London: Oresko, 1978.

———. *Radio! Radio!* Bampton, U.K.: Sunrise, 1986.

Pawley, Edward. *BBC Engineering, 1922–1972*. London: BBC, 1972.

Reade, Leslie. *Marconi and the Discovery of Wireless*. London: Faber and Faber, 1962.

Reddin, Harry. *Wires, Wheels, and Wings: A Wireless Mechanic's Diary*. Durham, U.K.: Pentland, 1994.

Tarrant, D. R. *Marconi's Miracle: The Wireless Bridging of the Atlantic*. St. John's, Newfoundland: Flanker, 2001.

B. Production

Barnard, Stephen. *Studying Radio*. London: Arnold, 2000.

Beaman, Jim. *Programme Making for Radio*. Abingdon, U.K.: Routledge, 2006.

Crook, Tim. *Radio Presentation: Theory and Practice*. London: Focal, 2002.

———. *The Sound Handbook*. Abingdon, U.K.: Routledge, 2011.

Geller, Valerie. *Beyond Powerful Radio: A Communicator's Guide to the Internet Age*. Oxford, U.K.: Focal, 2011.

Gordon, Janey. *The RSL: Ultra Local Radio*. Luton, U.K.: University of Luton Press, 2000.

Holsopple, C. *Skills for Radio Broadcasters*. London: TAB, 1988.

Horstmann, Rosemary. *Writing for Radio*. London: A and C Black, 1997.

Kaye, Michael, and Andrew Popperwell. *Making Radio: A Guide to Basic Radio Techniques*. London: Broadside, 1992.

Macloughlin, Shaun. *Writing for Radio*. Oxford, U.K.: How-To Books, 2001.

McInerney, Vincent. *Writing for Radio*. Manchester, U.K.: Manchester University Press, 2001.

McLeish, Robert. *Radio Production*. London: Focal, 1994.

McWhinnie, Donald. *The Art of Radio*. London: Faber and Faber, 1959.

Mills, Jenni. *The Broadcast Voice*. Oxford, U.K.: Focal, 2004.

Nisbett, Alec. *The Technique of the Sound Studio*. London: Focal, 1994.

Priestman, Chris. *Web Radio*. London: Focal, 2001.

Starkey, Guy. *Radio in Context*. Basingstoke, U.K.: Palgrave Macmillan, 2004.

C. Radio Advertising

Arnold, Frank A. *Broadcast Advertising: The Fourth Dimension*. New York: John Wiley, 1931.

Butler, George. *Berlin, Bush House, and Berkeley Square: George Butler Remembers JWT, 1952–1962*. London: Privately published, 1985.

Crawford, Sir William, and H. Broadley. *The People's Food*. London: William Heinemann, 1938.

Dyer, Gillian. *Advertising as Communication*. London: Routledge, 1982.

Dygert, Warren B. *Radio as an Advertising Medium*. New York: McGraw-Hill, 1939.

International Broadcasting Company. *This Is the I.B.C.* London: International Broadcasting Company, 1939.

Kaldor, Nicholas, and Rodney Silverman. *A Statistical Analysis of Advertising Expenditure and the Revenue of the Press*. Cambridge, U.K.: Cambridge University Press, 1948.

Montague, Ron. *When the Ovaltineys Sang*. Southend-on-Sea, U.K.: Privately published, 1993.

Nevett, T. R. *Advertising in Britain: A History*. London: Heinemann/History of Advertising Trust, 1982.

Radio Advertising Bureau. *Commercial Radio Revenues*. London: Radio Advertising Bureau, 2002.

Sturmey, S. G. *The Economic Development of Radio*. London: Duckworth, 1958.

Turner, E. S. *The Shocking History of Advertising*. London: Michael Joseph, 1952.

D. Commercial Radio

Baron, Mike. *Independent Radio*. Lavenham, U.K.: Terence Dalton, 1975.

Carter, Meg. *Independent Radio: The First 25 Years*. London: Radio Authority, 1998.

Henry, Stuart, and Mike von Joel. *Pirate Radio: Then and Now*. Poole, U.K.: Blandford, 1984.

Nichol, Richard. *Radio Luxembourg, the Station of the Stars: An Affectionate History of 50 years of Broadcasting*. London: Comet, 1983.

Skues, Keith. *Pop Went the Pirates*. Sheffield, U.K.: Lambs Meadow Publications, 1994.

E. Music Radio

Barnard, Stephen. *On the Radio: Music Radio in Britain*. Milton Keynes, U.K.: Open University Press, 1989.

Chapman, Robert. *Selling the Sixties: The Pirates and Pop Music Radio*. London: Routledge, 1992.

Fairchild, Charles. *Music, Radio, and the Public Sphere*. Basingstoke, U.K.: Palgrave Macmillan, 2012.

Garfield, Simon. *The Nation's Favourite: The True Adventures of Radio 1*. London: Faber and Faber, 1998.

Wall, Tim. *Studying Popular Music Culture*. London: Hodder Arnold, 2003.

F. Radio Drama

Beck, Alan. *The Invisible Play: BBC Radio Drama, 1922–1928*. Canterbury, U.K.: Sound Journal Publications, 2000.

Crook, Tim. *Radio Drama: Theory and Practice*. London: Routledge, 1999.

Drakakis, J., ed. *British Radio Drama*. Cambridge, U.K.: Cambridge University Press, 1981.

Felton, F. *The Radio Play: Its Techniques and Possibilities*. London: Sylvan, 1949.

Gielgud, Val. *British Radio Drama, 1922–1956*. London: Harrap, 1957.

Hughes, Richard. *Plays*. London: Chatto and Windus, 1924.

Lea, Gordon. *Radio Drama and How to Write It*. London: George Allen and Unwin, 1926.

Rodger, Ian. *Radio Drama*. London: Macmillan, 1982.

G. Radio Journalism

Alexander, Ray. *Broadcast Journalism*. Abingdon, U.K.: Focal, 2008.

Beaman, Jim. *Interviewing for Radio*. London: Routledge, 2000.

Chantler, Paul, and Peter Stewart. *Essential Radio Journalism*. London: A and C Black, 2009.

Crisell, Andrew, and Guy Starkey. *Radio Journalism*. London: Sage, 2009.

Crook, Tim. *International Radio Journalism*. London: Routledge, 1998.

Gage, Linda. *A Guide to Commercial Radio Journalism*. London: Focal, 1999.

H. International Radio

Browne, Donald. *International Radio Broadcasting*. New York: Praeger, 1982.

Camporesi, Valeria. *Mass Culture and National Traditions: The BBC and American Broadcasting, 1922–1954*. Fucecchio, Italy: European Press Academic Publishing, 2000.

Kuhn, Raymond. *The Media in France*. London: Routledge, 1995.

Lean, E. Tangye. *Voices in the Darkness: The Story of the European Radio War*. London: Secker and Warburg, 1943.

Lemaitre, Jean. *Allo! Allo! Ici Radio Normandie*. Fécamp, France: L. Durand et Fils, 1984.

Mansell, Gerard. *Let the Truth Be Told: 50 Years of BBC External Broadcasting*. London: Weidenfeld and Nicolson, 1982.

Pedrick, Gale, ed. *The World Radio and Television Annual: Jubilee Edition*. London: Sampson Low, Marston and Co., 1947.

Rolo, C. J. *Radio Goes to War*. London: Faber and Faber, 1943.

Smulyan, Susan. *Selling Radio: The Commercialization of American Broadcasting, 1920–1934*. Washington, D.C.: Smithsonian Institution Press, 1994.

Tomlinson, J. D. *The International Control of Radiocommunications*. Ann Arbor: University of Michigan Press, 1945.

Walker, Andrew. *A Skyful of Freedom: 60 Years of the BBC World Service*. London: Broadside, 1992.

Wood, James. *The History of International Broadcasting*. London: Peregrinus/Science Museum, 1994.

I. Radio Texts

Baseley, Godfrey. *The Archers: A Slice of My Life*. London: Sidgewick and Jackson, 1971.

Brough, Peter. *Educating Archie*. London: Paul, 1955.

Cannell, J. C. *In Town Tonight*. London: George G. Harrap, 1935.

Chilton, Charles. *Journey into Space*. London: Herbert Jenkins, 1954.

Cooke, Alistair. *Letter from America, 1946–2004*. London: Penguin/Allen Lane, 2004.

Donovan, Paul. *All Our Todays*. London: Cape, 1997.

Duncan, Peter. *In Town Tonight*. London: Werner Laurie, 1951.

Edwards, Rex. *The Dales*. London: BBC, 1969.

Garner, Ken. *In Session Tonight: The Complete Radio 1 Sessions*. London: BBC, 1993.

Grevatt, Wallace. *BBC Children's Hour: A Celebration of Those Magical Years*. Lewes, U.K.: Book Guild, 1988.

Hulme Beaman, S. G. *Tales of Toytown*. Oxford, U.K.: Oxford University Press, 1928.

May, Derwent. *Good Talk: An Anthology from BBC Radio*. London: Victor Gollancz, 1968.

———. *Good Talk 2: An Anthology from BBC Radio*. London: Victor Gollancz, 1969.

Murrow, Edward R. *In Search of Light: The Broadcasts of Ed Murrow, 1938–61*. London: Macmillan, 1968.

Priestley, J. B. *Postscripts*. London: Heinemann, 1962.

Thomas, Howard. *Britain's Brains Trust*. London: Chapman and Hall, 1944.

Webb, Geoffrey. *The Inside Story of Dick Barton*. London: Convoy Publications, 1950.

Worsley, Francis. *Anatomy of ITMA*. London: Pilot, 1946.

About the Author

Seán Street (L.R.A.M. drama, Royal Academy of Music; Ph.D., Bournemouth University, F.R.S.A.) is a writer, an academic, a poet, and a broadcaster. His doctoral dissertation is on commercial radio history in the United Kingdom, and he is emeritus professor of radio at Bournemouth University. Steet has worked as a radio practitioner since 1970, in both the public service and commercial sectors, and can frequently be heard as writer/presenter in his own features on BBC Radio 3 and BBC Radio 4, as well as on international broadcasters. Since leaving full-time academic life in 2011, he has continued to make programs and research, write, and lecture on a freelance basis.

Street's anthology, *Radio Waves: Poems Celebrating the Wireless* (2004), has drawn international praise, as have a number of key texts on radio and sound, notably *The Poetry of Radio: The Colour of Sound* (2013) and *The Memory of Sound: Preserving the Sonic Past* (2014). His study of pre–World War II radio in the United Kingdom, *Crossing the Ether* (2006), examines the previously little-explored subject of attacks on the BBC monopoly by commercial radio in Britain during the 1930s. Also in this field is *A Concise History of British Radio* (2005). Other prose includes *The Wreck of the Deutschland* (1992), *A Remembered Land* (1993), and *The Dymock Poets* (1994/2014).

His plays have been widely performed, including *Honest John* (1993), commissioned by the Royal Theatre, Northampton, which won the Central Television Award for new drama, and *Beyond Paradise: The Wildlife of a Gentle Man* (1998), his one-man play about Charles Darwin, which continues to tour, with former Royal Shakespeare Company actor Christopher Robbie as Darwin. Other stage and multimedia work includes the Royal National Theatre–commissioned "Urban Sonnets" for *Metropolis Kabarett* (2001), directed by Henry Goodman. Street has also worked with composer Cecilia McDowall on a number of musical works, including a cantata to mark the centenary of Scott of the Antarctic in 2012.

Street has published nine collections of his own poems, *Radio and Other Poems* (1999), *Time between Tides: New and Selected Poems* (2009), *Cello* (2013), and *Jazz Time* (2014), to name a few. He has been a trustee of the Radio Academy, chair of the Radio Academy (South) branch, and director of the Centre for Broadcasting History Research at Bournemouth University. Street also holds a lifetime fellowship with the Royal Society of Arts.

Lightning Source UK Ltd.
Milton Keynes UK
UKOW04n1328120515

251361UK00001B/21/P